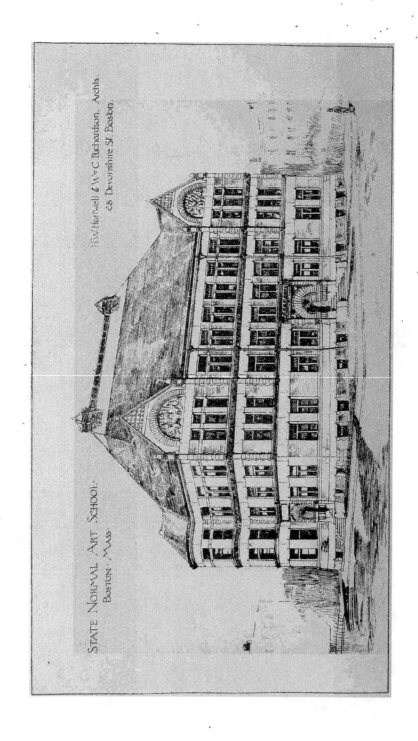

STATE NORMAL ART SCHOOL.
BOSTON · MASS·

H.W.Hartwell & W. C. Richardson. Archts.
68 Devonshire St. Boston.

FIFTIETH ANNUAL REPORT

OF THE

BOARD OF EDUCATION;

TOGETHER WITH THE

FIFTIETH ANNUAL REPORT

OF THE

SECRETARY OF THE BOARD

1885-86.

JANUARY, 1887.

BOSTON:
WRIGHT & POTTER PRINTING CO., STATE PRINTERS,
18 POST OFFICE SQUARE.
1887.

CONTENTS.

	PAGE
I. — REPORT OF BOARD OF EDUCATION,	9
II. — REPORTS OF VISITORS TO THE NORMAL SCHOOLS,	19
Bridgewater,	21
Framingham,	27
Salem,	33
Westfield,	35
Worcester,	41
Massachusetts Normal Art,	46
III. — SECRETARY'S REPORT,	59
Summary of Statistics,	61
Analysis of Returns,	63
Defective Classes,	66
American Asylum for Deaf-Mutes,	67
Clarke Institution for Deaf-Mutes,	68
Horace Mann School for Deaf-Mutes,	69
Statistics of Beneficiaries,	71
Perkins Institution for the Blind,	72
Massachusetts School for Feeble-Minded,	75
Account of the Work of the Board,	76
School Legislation from 1837 to 1886,	88
Members of the Board from 1837 to 1886,	89
School Fund,	91
Normal Schools,	96
Teachers' Institutes and Associations,	99
Schools to be kept,	101
Evening Schools,	101
Private Schools,	102
Institutions for Defective Classes,	102
Teachers,	103
Scholarships,	103
Studies to be pursued,	104
Text Books,	105
Bible in School,	106
Libraries,	106

CONTENTS.

SECRETARY'S REPORT — *Continued.*

	PAGE
School Attendance,	106
Conveyance of Children to Schools,	107
Truant Children and Absentees,	107
Employment of Children,	108
Care and Education of Neglected Children,	109
School Committees,	109
Contagious Diseases,	113
Superintendents,	114
Disturbing Schools and Injuring Schoolhouses,	114
District System,	114
Province of the Public Schools,	117
Organization,	129
Principles of Teaching,	133
Supervision,	137
Duties of Superintendents,	139
School Committees,	140
Normal Schools,	142
Agents of the Board,	145
Teachers' Institutes,	147
School Legislation,	149
Temperance,	150
FINANCIAL STATEMENT,	154
REPORT OF GEORGE A. WALTON, AGENT OF THE BOARD,	163
REPORT OF GEORGE H. MARTIN, AGENT OF THE BOARD,	187
REPORT OF JOHN T. PRINCE, AGENT OF THE BOARD,	211
ABSTRACT OF SCHOOL STATISTICS,	i–cxxxiv
INDEX,	1–67

STATE BOARD OF EDUCATION, 1887.

EX OFFICIO.

His Excellency OLIVER AMES, *Governor.*

His Honor JOHN Q. A. BRACKETT, *Lieutenant-Governor.*

BY APPOINTMENT.

ADMIRAL P. STONE,	*Springfield,*	May 25, 1887.
ABBY W. MAY,	*Boston,*	May 25, 1888.
MILTON B. WHITNEY,	*Westfield,*	May 25, 1889.
FRANCIS A. WALKER,	*Boston,*	May 25, 1890.
EDWARD C. CARRIGAN,	*Boston,*	May 25, 1891.
ELIJAH B. STODDARD,	*Worcester,*	May 25, 1892.
ALONZO A. MINER,	*Boston,*	May 25, 1893.
HORACE E. SCUDDER,	*Cambridge,*	May 25, 1894.

SECRETARY.

JOHN W. DICKINSON, ... *Newton.*

ASSISTANT SECRETARY AND TREASURER.

C. B. TILLINGHAST, ... *Boston.*

AGENTS.

GEORGE A. WALTON,	*West Newton.*
GEORGE H. MARTIN,	*Bridgewater.*
JOHN T. PRINCE,	*Waltham.*

ANNUAL REPORT

OF THE

BOARD OF EDUCATION.

ANNUAL REPORT.

In compliance with the statutes of the Commonwealth, the Board of Education herewith respectfully submits to the Legislature its Fiftieth Annual Report.

In the discharge of its duties during the year, the Board has given careful attention to the various interests and subjects intrusted to its care, and has endeavored to realize that the general supervision of the educational affairs of the State is a responsibility of no ordinary character. While the powers of the Board, as such, are comparatively limited, except in the care and conduct of the Normal Schools, and in the choice of its own secretary and the State agents, its duties, as defined by the statutes, are really comprehensive and of vital importance; it being required to lay before the Legislature, annually, " such observations upon the condition and efficiency of the system of popular education, and such suggestions in regard to the most practicable means of improving and extending it, as the experience and reflection of the Board may dictate."

To this obligation of the Board may be added the general expectation on the part of the public, and more especially of those directly engaged in educational work, that the State Board, in the discharge of its official duties, will present the latest aspect of public school interests and progress, as well as the most approved views upon practical educational work, with its underlying principles and its methods. For the performance of these and other similar duties, the Board, as a whole, holds regular meetings once a month, and oftener if the exigencies of business require; and the several Boards of Visitors of the State Normal Schools, and such special committees as

may be appointed for any purpose, hold frequent sessions for
the consideration of matters intrusted to them for investigation
or action.

A HALF-MILL SCHOOL TAX.

The Legislature of 1886 instructed this Board, by a resolve,
to investigate the subject of a proposed half-mill tax to be
raised and distributed for the support of the public schools,
and to report upon the same, in print, to the next Legislature.
The Board has given careful attention to this subject, and will
present a special report upon the same in accordance with the
instructions above mentioned.

DISTRIBUTION OF THE SCHOOL FUND.

By another resolve of the same Legislature, this Board was
" requested to consider whether a more equitable distribution
can be made of the Massachusetts School Fund, and report its
conclusions to the next General Court."

This subject also, has, been carefully investigated and considered by the Board, whose conclusions thereon will be duly
communicated to the Legislature.

THE NORMAL SCHOOLS.

These highly useful institutions for the improvement of the
instruction and management of the public schools have done a
good work during the year, and appear to be generally in a
flourishing condition.

Normal Schools had their origin in one of the first acts of
this Board ; and, indeed, the creation of the Board itself grew
directly out of a public demand that teachers should have
better qualifications for their work. On the 14th of January,
1837, an order was introduced and passed in the House of
Representatives of this State, directing the Committee on Education to consider the expediency of providing, by law, for
the better education of teachers of the public schools of the
Commonwealth. Two months afterwards a bill passed establishing the Board of Education and defining its duties.

The object of Normal Schools is to give teachers special
training for the responsible work of instructing and managing
their schools, and, more especially, to aid them in directing the
children and youth committed to their care, in securing a cor-

rect and natural development of their powers and in the formation of a well-rounded character. The Board believes that the Massachusetts Normal Schools are doing this work well; that those teachers who go forth from them into our schools are, in good measure, improving the character of those schools, and are giving a higher and a more wholesome tone to the intelligence and morality of the rising generation of this Commonwealth.

But excellent as these schools are, they have not yet reached the highest ideal of a Normal School; and although they are surely improving from year to year, they should be carried forward to a higher degree of excellence. As the common schools improve in their preparation of candidates for the Normal Schools, less academic work will be required of them there, and those schools will then be enabled to confine themselves to their true office, — professional training.

The particulars in regard to the present condition and the work during the year, of the several Normal Schools, will be learned from the reports of the Board of Visitors of those schools, which accompany this report.

THE NEW NORMAL ART SCHOOL BUILDING.

It is a source of congratulation to the friends of the Normal Art School, as well as to the public, that that institution is soon to be located in quarters of its own for its greater accommodation and convenience. This school is furnishing skilled teachers of drawing for the common schools, and is also a recognized promoter of industrial art. Its new building is approaching completion, a description of which will doubtless be given in the accompanying report of the Board of Visitors of that school.

TEACHERS' INSTITUTES.

It has for several years been the policy of the Secretary of the Board and of the State agents, to hold Teachers' Institutes principally, or wholly, in the smaller towns of the Commonwealth. The limited means of these towns oftentimes does not allow them to employ teachers of high qualifications, or of successful experiences. Educational meetings and gatherings are seldom held in them, and there is, consequently, to the schools and the people, an almost entire absence of that stimulus and interest so often experienced for good in larger communities, where the schools occupy a more prominent position before the public, and where the frequent discussion of educational topics serves to enlighten the teachers and the people, and to incite them both to a higher appreciation of educational privileges and to increased efforts for the improvement of their schools. When an Institute is held in one of these small communities the few teachers come together eager for instruction and enlightenment. The School Committee are also in attendance and more or less of the citizens and the older pupils of the schools. . The novelty of the occasion, and the personal interest felt in it by all, serve to make a deep impression upon the minds of all present, and to increase the usefulness of the exercises. The teachers receive new ideas and are stimulated to aim at better work. In the family circles of the town, school matters are discussed, and oftentimes the conclusion is reached that better things are desired and ought to be attained. Thus it happens that in many of these small towns a single Institute of a day or two gives an impetus to the schools that continues to be felt for good long afterwards. The cost of Teachers' Institutes is money well spent, and the children of the Commonwealth receive a lasting benefit therefrom.

During the past year eleven of these Institutes have been held, conducted by the Secretary, the agents and others, and attended by more than 700 teachers.

But few Institutes have been held during the year, and only such as have been invited by local school authorities. The Secretary and agents have, during the time heretofore given to Institute work, been engaged in visiting the schools of the towns, in holding meetings of the teachers and committees, and in addressing the people on the educational needs of the several localities. Though in many respects the nature of the work is the same, it is more personal and direct and applies more emphatically to the actual wants of the schools.

Supervision of Schools.

Among the prime needs of the schools often emphasized in the reports of this Board, are better supervision and better teachers in the towns outside of the considerable centres of population. Good supervision will secure good teachers, but how to obtain the former in these localities is the problem of the day. In the cities and large towns the concentration of wealth and population affords an easy solution to this question by the employment of a paid superintendent who devotes all his time to the care and improvement of the schools. But the expense of such an agency is beyond the means of the sparsely settled towns; and it is every year becoming more and more difficult to find persons in such localities competent for the work, or who are willing to perform it gratuitously, or for the meagre pittance only which the towns can pay. The Secretary of the Board, in his accompanying report, will discuss this subject.

TENURE OF OFFICE.

To secure the best results, every good teacher should be encouraged to make teaching a life-work. By the provisions of the recent Act of the Legislature, School Committees are empowered to contract with teachers during efficiency and good behavior. This is an important advance, and it is hoped that the principle of employing teachers during faithful and efficient service will be generally adopted.

THE STATE AGENTS.

The more immediate points of contact between the Board and the schools and the people, are the secretary and the agents, who visit schools, counsel with teachers and School Committees, and make addresses before them and the people in public meetings called for the purpose. In this way, improvements are suggested and secured, and much valuable information is obtained, which is essential to the Board in its deliberations and actions concerning the schools. The agents have spent another busy year in their field of work, and their views upon the condition and present needs of the schools may be learned, to some extent at least, from their reports herewith presented.

THE STUDY OF PHYSIOLOGY AND HYGIENE.

Until recently, the Public Statutes made the teaching of physiology and hygiene in the public schools a matter of option with the School Committees of the several towns and cities of the Commonwealth. But by the Act of 1885 (chapter

332), "Physiology and hygiene, which, in both divisions of the subject, shall include special instruction as to the effects of alcoholic drinks, stimulants and narcotics on the human system, shall be taught as a regular branch of study to all pupils in all schools supported wholly or in part by public money, except special schools maintained solely for instruction in special branches, such as drawing, mechanics, art and like studies." This law has now had a practical trial of a year and a half. The law was very generally welcomed by the teachers, for many of them had long felt the need of it; and in their attempts to train their pupils to secure for themselves healthy bodies, personal cleanliness and good morals, they have often been embarrassed, and sometimes thwarted, by the ignorance of pupils and parents, with reference to subjects so important to their comfort and well being. So far as information has come to the Board, there has been a very general disposition on the part of School Committees and teachers to carry out the provisions of the law, according to its original purpose and intent. If, as is alleged, and probably with much truth, ignorance is the source of so much misery and vice, the faithful execution of this law will send needed light into dark places, confer a priceless boon upon children and youth, and round out an education that otherwise might be incomplete and one-sided.

EVENING SCHOOLS.

A very considerable improvement has taken place within a few years in many of the evening schools of the State. The law of 1883, requiring all places of ten thousand population, or more, to support such schools, served to call the attention of the public to the subject, and has resulted in a more judicious expenditure of the money appropriated for such schools. It is now found that good organization can be effected, regular studies pursued and discipline maintained in evening schools,— a state of things which a few years since it was not supposed possible to secure to any considerable extent. The schools were not required by law, but their support was voluntary, and too often it seemed to be voluntary on the part of the pupils, also, whether they should betake themselves to study and good behavior, or otherwise. The managers of these schools now recognize the fact that it is the part of economy and wisdom to employ good teachers only, and not to intrust the instruction of persons of defective education to those whose only claim for the position is, that they have no other employment. In cities and large towns, especially, evening schools exert an influence in favor of good order and good morals by bringing into the school those who are destitute of pleasant surroundings and restraining influences at home, and who, in the streets and in places of public resort, are likely to be allured to practices of rowdyism and immorality.

There are in most communities persons who, unfortunately, have been deprived, wholly or in part, of early opportunities to acquire a common education; and some, also, who, having enjoyed such opportunities, neglected them. To give to such persons an opportunity to add to their scanty measure of knowledge and training, especially when they are willing to give their evening hours for that purpose, after laboring during the day, is an object which the tax-payer of the Commonwealth may well recognize as worthy in the highest degree.

THE EMPLOYMENT OF CHILDREN.

The statute regulating the employment of children of certain ages in manufacturing, mechanical and mercantile establishments is wisely intended to secure for all such children a fair amount of schooling; for it is plainly the policy of the Commonwealth to see that no child is deprived of an education. That statute prohibits the employment of children between the ages of ten and fourteen years, in the kind of establishments above named, unless they have attended school twenty weeks during the twelve months preceding such employment. In another chapter of the statutes, there is a requirement that all children between the ages of eight and fourteen years, without regard to employment, shall attend school twenty weeks each year. It is furthermore provided, that such attendance shall be in some public or private day school, under teachers approved by the School Committee of the place where such school is kept, and that "School Committees shall approve a private school only when the teaching therein is in the English language, and when they are satisfied that such teaching equals, in thoroughness and efficiency, the teaching in the public schools in the same locality, and that equal progress is made by the pupils therein, in the studies required by law, with that made during the same time in the public schools."

Now as certificates authorizing the employment of children under this statute are given only by School Committees, or under their direction, it is plain that a grave responsibility rests upon the School Committees of the Commonwealth. They cannot rightfully approve a private school unless they visit it and become familiar with the kind and amount of work done there, and unless they satisfy themselves in regard to the qualifications of the teachers therein. The question may well be raised, whether in all localities School Committees are discharging their duties, in this respect, according to the plain intent of the law; and also whether the duty assumed and exercised by the Commonwealth in regard to the education of her children, does not suggest a relation between school authorities and private schools, not yet fully provided for by law.

THE SECRETARY.

The Secretary of the Board is the working agent of the school department, and the most responsible person concerned in the examination, supervision and direction of the public school interests of the Commonwealth. He is selected for his wisdom and experience. To him the teachers look for inspiration and direction; the School Committees, for counsel; and the Board, for that information concerning the schools which they need, and which he, as does no other one, possesses in large degree.

The Board desires to commend the present incumbent for the candor, good judgment and fidelity he exhibits in the successful discharge of his responsible and delicate duties. His reports, from year to year, have contained much valuable information, sound views of school policy, and suggestions of the highest importance for educational work.

FIFTY YEARS OF HISTORY.

It is now a half century, wanting only a few months, since the State Board of Education was established and organized, and the reconstruction of the common school system of Massachusetts was undertaken by its first Secretary, Horace Mann. Great changes have taken place during this period in all the various interests of the Commonwealth. The population of the State has doubled; and its valuation has increased more than six-fold. In 1837 the public schools cost about $465,000; in 1886 the expense will exceed seven millions of dollars. Then, male teachers received, exclusive of board, an average salary of $15.44 per month. Now, they receive $120.72 per month. Then female teachers were paid an average monthly salary of $5.38; while they are now receiving $43.85 per month. The average length of the schools has also increased more than fifty per cent. The "dormancy and apathy," on the part of the people, in regard to education, of which Mr. Mann so bitterly complained in 1837, has, in large measure, given place to a wholesome and cheering interest, as is everywhere seen by the prominent position occupied by the school in the public mind, and in the generous support accorded to them by the people; and by the pride felt by the citizens of Massachusetts, in the ample provision generally made for the free education of their children. But the schools are susceptible of still greater improvement. Let that improvement be secured. Their highest purpose is to train the children to become well informed and useful men and women, good citizens of a good Commonwealth. For the accomplishment of this object, the Board asks the cooperation of the Legislature, and of all well wishers of the public good.

GEORGE D. ROBINSON, *ex officio.*
OLIVER AMES, *ex officio.*
ADMIRAL P. STONE.
ABBY W. MAY.
MILTON B. WHITNEY.
FRANCIS A. WALKER.
EDWARD C. CARRIGAN.
ELIJAH B. STODDARD.
ALONZO A. MINER.
HORACE E. SCUDDER.

BOSTON, Dec. 1, 1886.

REPORTS OF VISITORS

OF THE

NORMAL SCHOOLS.

STATE NORMAL SCHOOL, BRIDGEWATER.

ALBERT G. BOYDEN, A.M., *Principal.*

The geographical position of Bridgewater has had its influence upon the development of the school. It is a natural scientific and educational station for south-eastern Massachusetts, and the facilities for reaching it, as well as the economy of living which is possible in an agricultural community, conveniently near to a thriving manufacturing centre, have conspired to make it a favorite resort for young men and women of the section, who desire, not only to qualify themselves for teaching, but to enlarge their mental powers beyond the scope given by the high school. The fact, also, that the school has been under few principals in its forty-six years has served to give integrity and continuity to its development. The visitors watch with interest a growth in the work of the school, which is inevitable under the earnest activity of the corps of teachers that is shaping the course of study, and their only desire is to aid the school in a substantial realization of its ideal.

. Of late years, increased attention has been paid to the study of natural and physical science as related to school work. The limitations of this study are apparent. When one considers the tendency of scientific work to minute specialization, one sees how impossible it is that teachers in a Normal School, dealing with pupils who are to make science one only of many subjects in their work as common-school teachers, should be able to carry these pupils through any extensive scientific course. It is not desirable that they should attempt it. For one who purposes to make a profession of science, the higher institutions in our State afford opportunities which are and must be out of the question for the Normal Schools. But this does not mean that the Normal Schools can only give their graduates a smattering of science. It means that they should distinctly avoid such a result, and should indoctrinate the pupils in those methods of scientific study which may be exemplified in the most elementary work.

It is, therefore, praiseworthy that the teachers of science in this school have sought to familiarize their pupils with those fundamental principles which cultivate the scientific habit, and have used that material which is commonest. They have sought for types near at hand, and have accustomed those who are to be teachers to deal directly with objects and to avoid merely written formulas. They have, moreover, used ingenuity in the construction of apparatus for physical experiments out of the simplest and most accessible material, and have taught their scholars to make this apparatus. By this means a graduate going into one of the schools of the Commonwealth is largely independent in resources. With a few bits of wire, pieces of wood and scraps of tin, the teacher can construct apparatus which will demonstrate elementary laws of physics quite as well for the purpose of the school as the most delicate and costly instruments.

The steady cultivation of manipulation, and of what may in general be called laboratory work at Bridgewater, has entailed a great deal of labor on the teachers, and has compelled them to give much time which they would gladly have spent on the higher part of their studies. The result is worth all it has cost, but now that the system has been well established and its usefulness demonstrated, it is proper that the teachers should be relieved of much of this detail, and the system continued by means quite as useful to the school at large, and capable, indeed, of producing specific results of considerable value. The visitors, therefore, recommend that each year one pupil of the graduating class, who has shown fitness for the work, should be retained as an assistant, to serve two years at a moderate salary, in the laboratories; the two assistants thus always on hand, one with increased experience, would not only greatly facilitate the work of the regular teachers by preparing the material for each lesson, but would keep the cabinets in order, assist in keeping up the stock of teaching material, and in many ways be the hands of the teachers. The additional experience which they would thus secure would be of great value to them, and many opportunities would occur both for extending the scope of their studies and for taking some share in the teaching; by all which means they would be especially qualified for their work as teachers in advanced positions when they had completed the two years' work as laboratory assistants.

In proposing this strengthening of the force at Bridgewater, the visitors can scarcely be considered as experimenting. For some time past the policy outlined above has been pursued in a limited way. Mr. Frank W. Kendall, a graduate from the four years' course, has been employed as instructor in the workshop and assistant in the laboratories. His services it is proposed to continue for another term, and to associate with him a more recent graduate at the beginning of the next term. In other respects the teaching force of the school has been subject to little variation. At the beginning of the year, in September, 1885, Miss Elizabeth H. Hutchinson, a graduate from the four years' course, and for four years an assistant in the State Normal School at Nashville, Tennessee, was appointed a teacher, in the place of Miss Mary H. Leonard, whose health did not permit her fully to resume her work. The marriage of Miss Clara T. Wing, principal of the School of Observation, deprived the school of a valuable and important officer. Her sister, a graduate of the Normal School, and principal of one of the primary schools of New Bedford, was appointed her successor at the beginning of the year. It is of great importance that a healthy and cordial relation should exist between the Normal School and the School of Observation, in order that each may serve the other. Even under the limitations which exist in a country town, there is excellent opportunity for the pupils of the Normal School to obtain practical insight into the every-day work of teaching, and thus to supplement their more theoretical studies.

The statistics for the year ending August 31, 1886, are as follows :—

TERMS BEGAN SEPT. 2, 1885, AND FEB. 11, 1886.	FIRST TERM.			SECOND TERM.			FOR THE YEAR.		
	Men.	Women.	Total.	Men.	Wom'n.	Total.	Men.	Women.	Total.
Members, ...	45	138	183	45	141	186	52	162	214
Entering classes, . . .	21	45	66	7	23	30	28	68	96
Graduates, ...	4	9	13	4	30	34	8	39	47
Received State aid, ...	12	13	25	15	18	33	17	23	40

The whole number of students who have been members of the school is 3,169 ; 1,007 men, 2,162 women.

. The number who have received certificates or diplomas is 1,926 ; 628 men, 1,298 women; 87 of whom have graduated from the four years' course, — 52 men and 35 women. Sixty-one per cent. of all admitted have graduated.

Of the 214 members of the school for this year, Plymouth County sent 70 ; Norfolk, 37 ; Middlesex, 29 ; Bristol, 23 ; Barnstable, 10 ; Suffolk, 6 ; Essex, 4 ; Worcester, 3 ; Dukes, 2 ; Nantucket, 2 ; Hampshire, 1 ; the State of New Hampshire, 15 ; Maine, 3 ; District of Columbia. 3 ; Connecticut and South Carolina, each 1 ; Nova Scotia and Province of Quebec, each 1 ; Chili, S. A., 2.

Totals from Massachusetts, eleven counties and seventy-six towns represented, 187 ; other States and countries, 27.

The number of Post Graduates in attendance during the year has been 2 ; of College graduates on the Special Course, 4 ; of under-graduates pursuing the Four Years' Course, 59, — 30 men and 29 women ; of students pursuing the Intermediate Course, 14 ; of those pursuing the Two Years' Course, 135.

The distribution of the pupils the first term was as follows : — Post Graduates, 1 ; Special Course, 3 ; Four Years' Course, 59 ; Interme-diate Course, 12 ; Two Years' Course, senior class, 12 ; sub-senior class, 35 ; ex-junior class, 19 ; junior class, 42.

The distribution during the second term : — Post Graduates, 2 ; Special Course, 2 ; Four Years' Course, 50 ; Intermediate Course, 13 ; Two Years' Course, senior class, 30 ; sub-senior class, 19 ; ex-junior class, 41 ; junior class, 29.

The average age of those admitted during the year was 19 years, four months ; of the men, 19 years, 8 months, — of the women, 19 years, 2 months.

Of the 96 admitted, 1 came from the United States Naval Academy, 4 from colleges, 3 from Normal Schools, 12 from acad-emies and private schools, 66 from high schools (36 graduates,

30 undergraduates), 9 from grammar schools, 1 from a district school.

The occupations of the fathers of those admitted were given as follows: Farmers, 25; mechanics, 25; merchants and traders, 11; seamen, 5; physicians, 4; manufacturers, 4; clergymen, 2; in United States Service, 2; teacher, 1; miscellaneous, 17; total, 96.

Of the 96 pupils admitted during the year, Bridgewater and Brockton sent 6 each; Quincy, Hingham, 5 each; Dedham, 4; Abington, Middleborough, New Bedford, West Bridgewater, Weymouth, 3 each; Braintree, Chatham, Fall River, Marshfield, Nantucket, Reading, Waltham, 2 each; Bedford, Boston, Bellingham, Brewster, Carver, Chelsea, Cohasset, Dennis, Duxbury, Eastham, Hanover, Harwich, Lowell, Marion, Natick, Orleans, Peabody, Phillipston, Randolph, Rockland, Somerville, Somerset, Stoughton, Taunton, Townsend, Wakefield, Whitman, Worcester, 1 each; the State of New Hampshire sent 5; Maine, 1; Connecticut, 1; Washington, D. C., 1; South Carolina, 1; and Windsor, N. S., 1.

Forty-five of the graduates of this year are engaged in teaching, one has entered Amherst College, and one is not teaching. The number of applications for teachers has greatly exceeded the number of graduates.

The boarding-hall has been fully occupied and in successful operation. It does more than furnish convenient shelter and an inexpensive table to the students of the school; it gives an opportunity for the cultivation of studious habits, regularity of life, self-control, the amenities of social life, and above all for that *esprit de corps* which is so marked at this school and so valuable in preserving the high character of the institution. The individual and the common life of the school has also received an important aid in the purchase by the Commonwealth of six acres of land adjoining the school premises. The visitors have suggested that this common should bear the name of Boyden Park, and the title has at once passed into familiar use. The whole area, aside from the pond, is occupied by tennis courts, croquet grounds, and grounds for ball and other athletic sports, and the heartiness with which the students enter into these healthful, out-door sports augurs well for the intellectual work of the school. The whole school community finds a tonic in this natural reaction. In the depth of a New-England winter the Park will still afford an opportunity for skating, but the school will miss that freedom of out-door occupation which the spring and fall seasons permit. We are obliged to guard against the inclemency of our winters by special attention to tightness of building and the requisite heating apparatus; but in a Normal School, where over two hundred young men and women are studying with the zeal, which characterizes those who are qualifying themselves for the profession 'of teaching, it is very important that provision should be made for maintaining and re-enforcing sound physical conditions. It is greatly to be hoped that the mild-weather advantages of Boyden Park may be supplemented, before long, by a convenient gymnasium with simple apparatus, where the students can secure regular exercise during the winter months, thereby adding to their mental and moral vigor, and at the same time acquiring that substantial acquaintance with the laws of healthy action which will serve them in such good stead when they come to have charge of the boys and girls of our common schools.

The appropriation of seven hundred dollars made by the last Legislature was expended, and the bills properly accounted for, in procuring new hard pine floors for four recitation rooms and the lower hall, with new tables, chairs and gas fixtures for these rooms. This improvement has greatly facilitated the class-work, and its need was especially manifested when the new term opened with a substantial increase of membership in the school.

H. E. SCUDDER,
FRANCIS A. WALKER,
Visitors.

STATE NORMAL SCHOOL, FRAMINGHAM.

Miss ELLEN HYDE, *Principal.*

The school opened in September, 1885, with a slight increase in members, there being forty-seven in the entering class.

In October, Miss Hyde went to Baltimore, on leave of absence for a few months. She had brought the school into excellent order before leaving; once in the winter she came back to look after some of its interests; and at the beginning of June, she took up her work again. During her absence, Miss Amelia Davis, for many years a teacher in the school, acted as principal. Having made herself thoroughly familiar with Miss Hyde's purposes and plans for the winter, she sought to carry them out both to the letter and in the spirit; and her success was complete. It is due to her to say that none of the interests of the school suffered while it was in her hands. The best spirit prevailed; each teacher assumed a share of the responsibility of making good the place of the principal, and all the pupils seemed moved by the same good intention. The result was a busy and a successful year. The school was not only somewhat larger than before, but was also improved in quality; in this important respect, the gain has for some years been steady, though gradual. We trust this improvement will continue. Of 71 pupils admitted, 38 were graduates of high schools, and 16 others had taken a partial high-school course. We hope that the day will soon come when all students, entering the Normal Schools of Massachusetts, will have taken a full high-school course or its equivalent. Of the 26 graduates, 23 are teaching, and 2 are in the advanced class.

The year was marked by a most unusual and sad event. One of the pupils went back sick after the winter vacation. She was soon obliged to give up her work, and in May died at her own home. It is many years since there has been a death among those connected with the school, until this one.

Miss Mary L. Bridgman was appointed, at the beginning of the year, to fill a vacancy in the departments of French, Latin and United States History. Miss Mary L. P. Shattuck took Miss Hyde's classes during her absence. One of the teachers was called away by sickness in her own home; Miss Emily M. Bullard, a former teacher in the school, filled the vacant place with great acceptance. There were no other changes among the teachers during the year.

The school was favored with ten lectures in the course of the year. Dr. Z. B. Adams, of Framingham, gave two very interesting and valuable Emergency lectures. Our steadfast friend, Professor W. P. Atkinson also gave two; one on History and one on Political Economy. Mrs. Mary A. Livermore stirred the hearts of all who heard her, with her story of the Sanitary Commission, and the work of the women in the war. Mrs. E. N. L. Walton described the Luray Caves of Virginia. Miss S. P. Hatch, a graduate of the school, gave an account of her work in South Africa. Mr. B. T. Washington told of the Tuskegee Normal School, a young and vigorous school for training colored teachers. Miss Olivia Davidson the first assistant principal of that school was a graduate of the Framingham Normal School. Mr. T. F. Seward explained the Tonic Sol Fa system, and Mr. Dickinson read a paper on Manual Training. Miss Lucia M. Peabody delivered a very interesting address to the mid-year class, on the day of their graduation. An event full of interest was a visit from Miss Laura Bridgman.

Mr. Dickinson visited the school several times; Mr. Prince paid us two visits, and Mr. Walton one. All of these gentlemen made helpful addresses to the pupils. These visits of the secretary and agents serve to give the pupils some insight into the work doing in the schools of the State, the work that they are fitting themselves to do. This is a most valuable result.

The Alumni Association of the school held its biennial meeting on July 1st. A large company of graduates assembled,

representing sixty-five classes; among them was a member of
the first class. The exercises were full of interest. They
included the gift to the school, from his pupils, of a bust of
Rev. S. J. May, an early principal of the school. Several of
his pupils and other friends bore most grateful testimony to
Mr. May's character, and his influence in the school.

We spoke in our last report of the Spencer fire-escapes,
which had been provided in the summer of 1885. Since that
time, the pupils have used them often enough to become
familiar with their management. Our experience satisfies us
that they are well adapted to the use of the school. With
them and the Harden hand-grenades, we feel as secure as is
possible from danger in case of fire.

The statistics for the year are as follows : —

Number admitted : —

September, 1885,	47
February, 1886,	24
Total for the year,	71

Number of these who were graduates of high schools : —

September,	29
February,	9
Total,	38

Average age : —

September,	19 years, 2 months
February,	18 years, 8 months

Whole number in school during the year 1885-86, ... 140

Number of graduates : —

January, 1886,	6
June, 1886,	20
Total,	26

Residence of pupils : —

New Hampshire,	9
Connecticut,	3
New York,	2
Maine,	1
New Jersey,	1
Pennsylvania,	1
Vermont,	1

Residence of pupils (continued),—

South Carolina,	1
Missouri,	1
District of Columbia,	1
Total from other States,	21
Middlesex County,	76
Worcester County,	18
Norfolk County,	14
Essex County,	6
Suffolk County,	2
Plymouth County,	2
Bristol County,	1
Total from Massachusetts,	119
Total,	140

Occupations of parents : —

Farmers,	35
Mechanics,	33
Merchants,	21
Shoemakers,	12
Clerks,	8
Insurance agents,	4
Express agents,	3
Clergymen,	2
Manufacturers,	2
Teachers,	2
Lawyers,	4
Postmasters,	2
Physicians,	2
Unclassified,	10
Total,	140

The practice-school, with ninety scholars, is as usual more than full and is doing an admirable work, both for the children and for the Normal pupils. We have good reason to be proud of its management and its results; to it is largely owing the success of our graduates, when they assume the responsibility of their first school. Their inevitable, early mistakes being made in the practice-school, under the eyes of thoroughly competent and critical teachers, do no harm to the children; and originality in teaching is encouraged and developed. Actual practice with children is obviously essential in the training of teachers; and no money spent on our Normal schools yields a better return, it seems to us, than that expended on a good practice-school. It is not a very costly appendage compared with its great importance.

The two boarding-houses are full and doing their good work. The resident pupils get much more from the school than is possible to the day-scholars, and through them the tone of the school is raised.

In March, the legislative Committee on Education visited the school twice and inspected it carefully. We submitted to them a plan and specifications for an additional boarding-house. Subsequently the Legislature made an appropriation for building in accordance with the plan. On July 24, ground was broken and the work has gone steadily forward since that time. There seems no reason to doubt that the house will be ready for occupation when the next class shall enter, in February. The house which has been hired for the last three and a half years will then be given up. This increase of boarding-accommodations has long been needed and will add much to the efficiency of the school.

The present great need is of proper accommodation for the practice-school. This is overcrowded, and is using rooms not fit for continuous use. They have but little sunshine, and are very low and difficult to ventilate; besides this, they are needed by the Normal classes for recitation rooms. For that purpose they are fairly well-adapted. We ask for an appropriation to meet this need, confident that an inspection of the building will show its importance.

As the school grows in numbers, the need becomes more apparent of having a man on the premises by night as well as by day. In our judgment, it would be wise to add to the present buildings a small house for the janitor. The first cost would not be large and the use of the house would be equivalent to a part of the janitor's salary.

The present boarding-house needs the outlay of a moderate amount of money, for enlarging the dining-room, and giving some additional accommodation needed for the health of the well, and the proper care of those who may be overtaken by sickness. We have had estimates made of the cost of these improvements and are ready to submit them, at the proper time.

The school is now full to overflowing; its teachers and pupils alike deserve and receive our hearty commendation, and we can hardly wish anything better for it in the future than that it may continue to be faithful, as now, to its opportunities, and as earnest in the endeavor to keep in the line of progress.

ABBY W. MAY, }
A. A. MINER,
Visitors.

SALEM NORMAL SCHOOL.

D. B. HAGAR, *Principal.*

The visitors with great satisfaction recognize the continually increasing usefulness of this truly available school.

No changes have occurred during ten years within the corps of teachers. No important changes have been made in the course of instruction, — the usual work of the school has been well done in peace and quietness, without any incidents which call for mention here.

The statistics of the school are as follows : —

1. The whole number of pupils belonging to the school during the year was 280.

Of this number, Essex County sent 151; Middlesex, 73; Suffolk, 10; Plymouth, 5; Bristol, 2; Barnstable, Hampden and Worcester, 1 each. The State of Maine sent 9; New Hampshire, 19; Vermont, 4; Florida, 1; Illinois, 1; Nevada, 1; and the West Indies, 1.

The number present during the term which closed Jan. 19, 1886, was 229; the number present during the term which closed June 29, 1886, was 232.

The whole number of pupils that have been members of the school since its opening in September, 1854, is 3,111.

2. The number graduated from the regular course, Jan. 19, 1886, was 26; the number graduated from the same course, June 29, 1886, was 44; and from the advanced course, 6.

The whole number of graduates of the school (62 classes), is 1,505.

3. The number that entered the school, Sept. 1, 1885, was 89; the number that entered, Feb. 9, 1886, was 49.

4. The average age of the class admitted Sept. 1, 1885, was 18.14 years; of the class admitted Feb. 9, 1886, 18.35 years.

Of the 89 pupils admitted to the school in September, 1885, 2 came from Normal schools; 75 from high schools (57 graduates, 18 undergraduates); 2 from grammar schools; 3 from district schools; 3 from academies; 3 from private schools; and 1 from a sisters' school.

Of the 49 pupils admitted in February, 1886, 2 came from Normal schools; 27 from high schools (16 graduates, 11 under-graduates); 6 from grammar schools; 5 from district schools; 4 from academies; 2 from seminaries; 1 from a private school; and 2 from sisters' schools.

5. The fathers of the pupils admitted during the year are by occupations as follows: Mechanics, 40; manufacturers, 21; farmers, 20; traders, 19; agents, 14; professional men, 4; miscellaneous, 20.

6. Of the class admitted in September, 1885, 10 had taught school; of the class admitted in February, 1886, 12 had taught.

7. The number of pupils connected with each of the classes during the first term of the year was as follows: Special students, 3; advanced class 11; class A (senior), 34; class B, 54; class C, 33; class D, 94.

The number during the second term: Special student, 1; advanced class, 9; class A, 53; class B, 31; class C, 73; class D, 65.

8. Of the 138 pupils admitted during the year, Salem sent 15; Lynn, 8; Gloucester, 7; Danvers and Peabody, 6 each; Andover, Beverly and Lowell, 5 each; Wakefield, 4; Cambridgeport, East Cambridge, North Reading and Somerville, 3 each; Amesbury, East Boston, Hamilton, Lexington, Manchester, Middleton, Topsfield, Waltham, West Peabody, Winchester, Winthrop and Woburn, 2 each; Brockton, Chelsea, East Somerville, Groveland, Halifax, Hingham Centre, Lincoln, Medford, Nahant, Newburyport, North Andover, North Billerica, Reading, Rowley, Saugus, Saxonville, South Groveland, Stoneham, Taunton, Watertown, West Newbury, and West Somerville, 1 each. The State of Maine sent 3; New Hampshire, 12; Vermont, 1; Florida, 1; Nevada, 1; and the West Indies, 1.

All of which is respectfully submitted,

E. C. CARRIGAN,
FRANCIS A. WALKER,
Visitors.

STATE NORMAL SCHOOL, WESTFIELD.

JOSEPH G. SCOTT, *Principal.*

The past year of this school has been one of uninterrupted prosperity. The corps of teachers has remained unchanged, and there has been, so far as we can judge, great sympathy and unbroken harmony between teachers and pupils during the entire year.

With added experience the teachers have had better knowledge of the needs of the public schools, better judgment in the application of methods of teaching and training, better facilities for doing their work, and " less friction of machinery." As a result, the work accomplished has been highly satisfactory.

The membership of the school has been only slightly larger than during the previous year, but the number of graduates has been more than doubled. It has been the policy to advance the standard of graduation from year to year; but although highly desirable to raise the standard of admission, it would not be possible to do so, to any considerable extent, without rejecting a very large proportion of the applicants from the country towns, — a class, perhaps more than any other, needing the benefits of the school. A majority of the pupils come from country schools many of whose teachers possess limited qualifications, and from families which find it difficult and sometimes impossible to pay for a long course of schooling for their children, some of whom are compelled by reason thereof to leave the school before graduation. These conditions interfere with the highest usefulness of the school; but it has done in the past, and is still doing, a grand work in the elevation of the common schools, especially in the western counties of the Commonwealth.

The entering class of the present term is larger than usual, and probably the membership of the school for the current year will be larger than during the last. Any considerable increase in members would call for increased accommodations and additional teachers. There are now two divisions of the lowest class in each subject, and each division crowds the ordinary recitation rooms.

The past school year has been an unusually prosperous one at the boarding-hall, especially in a financial way; the causes of which were two, — an increase of boarders and a decrease in prices of supplies. We have thus been enabled, while maintaining the excellence of the table, to expend a large sum for much-needed repairs, and to add somewhat to the reserve fund, which now amounts to more than three thousand dollars.

The most pressing need of the school is a practice or training department. This department should be made up of two or more grades of pupils like those in the average common school; it should be under the control of the principal of the Normal School, that there may be no divided responsibility for failure, or divided credit for success, and it should be under the immediate charge of an experienced and accomplished teacher.

The advantages of a training school are too numerous to be here enumerated; perhaps too obvious to need even partial enumeration. It would furnish such facilities for the illustration and practical application of the principles inculcated in the Normal School, that they would be much more readily and completely understood; it would enable the pupils to see, as they could in no other way, what a well-taught and well-trained school is, how the mind of the child develops, what are the difficulties of teaching and governing, how to meet and overcome these difficulties; in short, to acquire experience under the most favorable conditions, with the least possible loss to the Commonwealth. It would enable us better to sift out the unpromising or the unworthy among our pupils, to recommend teachers with more discrimination, putting more certainly the right teacher in the right place, and to remove the doubts of sceptical committees as to the feasibility and excellence of Normal methods.

During the past year the needs of the school in this direction have been partially met by frequent visits of the members of the senior class to one of the best of the public schools in the town, and by bringing small detachments of children from the same school into the Normal School building, to be there taught by the Normal School pupils. But such provisions are very inadequate. The great need is a training school; if a building was furnished, the pupils would be found at once. We recommend a legislative appropriation sufficient to purchase a lot and erect a suitable building.

Another pressing need is a gymnasium, or at least a play-ground. If the place was a suitable one, there is no room for a gymnasium either in the Normal or Boarding Hall. The life of the pupils in the boarding-house has been made as free as possible, but they must of necessity be under restraint there at all times, and the house must always be quiet. At the boarding-house there is absolutely no yard — only a narrow strip of ground a few feet in width, open to the public streets. The schoolhouse yard is bounded on three sides by public streets, and is too small to furnish suitable or sufficient space for the proper exercise of any considerable part of the pupils. The young women of the school are obliged in the main to get their exercise by walking through the streets of the village. The disadvantages of this mode of obtaining exercise can be readily seen.

We recommend the purchase of a lot large enough for a play-ground, and the erection of a small gymnasium thereon as soon as the necessary appropriation can be had.

Cases for specimens have long been needed. A small appropriation will be sufficient for the purpose.

So far as we have been able to learn, the graduates of the past year are nearly all engaged in teaching in the public schools, and are doing very satisfactory work.

Addresses have been made to the school during the year by the Legislative Committee upon Education, and by the Secretary of the Board, upon various educational topics; by George H. Martin, agent of the board, upon "Lessons from my Note-book"; by Rev. A. D. Mayo upon "Country Schools"; by Rev. Frederick Woods, D. D., upon "Human Nature"; by Rev. Joseph Scott upon "Lessons from a Night with Peter";

by Mrs. Mary A. Livermore upon "A Dream of To-morrow"; by Prof. George L. Weed upon " Education of the Deaf and Dumb." Prof. H. A. Williams gave an hour of miscellaneous readings.

Mr. Scott resigned the position of principal of the school more than two years ago, on account of failing health and the onerous duties of the position ; but at the urgent solicitation of the visitors consented to remain temporarily at the head of the school until a suitable successor could be found.

He will retire from the principalship at the end of the present term ; but we are happy to state that, after an absence of one term for much-needed rest, he will return and give the school the benefit of his valuable experience as an associate teacher in some department of the school.

Mr. Scott has held the position of principal of the school for nearly ten years, and his administration has been a highly successful one. He has exercised a wise and economical supervision over the affairs of the boarding-house, has been an able, earnest and painstaking teacher, a firm but kind disciplinarian, and, in short, has devoted his entire energies to the performance of his various duties with conscientious fidelity and singleness of purpose. He has been a faithful servant of the Commonwealth, and has earned the gratitude of all well-wishers of the school.

Mr. James C. Greenough, Ex-President of the Massachusetts Agricultural College, who has had a large and successful experience in Normal School work, as a teacher in the school at Westfield, and afterwards as principal of the State Normal School at Providence, R. I., has been elected as Mr. Scott's successor, and will assume the duties of the position at the commencement of the next term. We confidently expect that the school, under his direction, will not only maintain its present high standard of excellence, but advance to a still higher standard.

The tables appended present the usual statistics and some items not heretofore reported.

Statistics of Westfield State Normal School — 1885-86.

	Winter Term.			Summer Term.			For the Year.		
	Young Men.	Young Women.	Totals.	Young Men.	Young Women.	Totals.	Young Men.	Young Women.	Totals.
Number of pupils in school,	7	125	132	8	106	114	8	148	156
Number of pupils in entering classes,	3	43	46	1	16	17	4	59	63
Number of pupils in graduate classes,	—	17	17	2	25	27	2	42	44
Average age of enterers,	Yrs. 18 Mos. 2.1	Yrs. 18 Mos. 4.6	Yrs. 18 Mos. 4.5	Yrs. 33 Mos. 6.9	Yrs. 19 Mos. 5.8	Yrs. 20 Mos. 3.7	Yrs. 22 Mos. 0.3	Yrs. 18 Mos. 8.2	Yrs. 18 Mos. 10.7
Average age of graduates,	—	Yrs. 21 Mos. 11	Yrs. 21 Mos. 11	Yrs. 20 Mos. 1.6	Yrs. 20 Mos. 5.9	Yrs. 20 Mos. 5.6	Yrs. 20 Mos. 1.6	Yrs. 21 Mos. 0.8	Yrs. 21 Mos. 0.3
Number of enterers who had taught,	—	11	11	1	4	5	1	15	16
Number of pupils who received State aid,	3	30	33	5	20	25	5	36	41

Statistics of Westfield State Normal School — 1885-86 — Concluded.

Number of States, Towns, etc., represented by pupils.		Number of pupils from each State represented.		Number of pupils from each county of Mass. repres'd.		Occupations of fathers of enterers.		Number of enterers from High Schools, etc.	
States,	8	Connecticut,	8	Berkshire,	16	Engineers,	1	District,	4
Towns and cities,	64	Michigan,	1	Bristol,	1	Farmers,	25	Grammar,	9
Counties in Massachusetts,	7	New Hampshire,	1	Essex,	1	Laborers,	2	High,	39
Families,	154	New Jersey,	1	Franklin,	9	Lawyers,	1	Normal,	2
		New York,	2	Hampden,	88	Machinists,	1	Private,	9
		Pennsylvania,	1	Hampshire,	15	Manufacturers,	1		
		Vermont,	4	Worcester,	6	Mechanics,	14		
		Virginia,	2			Merchants,	8		
						Mill officers,	3		
						Miscellaneous,	7		

M. B. WHITNEY, } *Visitors.*
A. P. STONE, }

STATE NORMAL SCHOOL AT WORCESTER.

E. HARLOW RUSSELL, *Principal.*

STUDENTS.

The visitors find a larger attendance of students this year than ever before in the history of the school. The conditions of admission have been in no way relaxed, but if anything, rather more strictly maintained, with the gratifying result that the newly admitted pupils stand, on the whole, above the average in attainments and maturity.

The publication in the annual catalogue of the entrance examination questions, from year to year, seems to have had a beneficial effect in securing a better preparation on the part of those having the Normal School course in view. Candidates have more generally come to recognize the necessity of regularly fitting themselves beforehand for the Normal School, instead of trying to squeeze through the entrance examination with all their imperfections on their heads, trusting to the school itself to make good afterwards, in some miraculous way, all deficiencies of elementary knowledge.

But while there is this improvement to be noticed, the impression still lingers in the minds of many that the Normal School is the be-all and the end-all of preparation for teaching, an impression to be removed only by insisting more and more upon such preparatory study, in high schools or elsewhere, as may enable the student to enter with advantage upon something like professional training.

The visitors believe that this school is behind no other in the State in doing its share towards this very desirable end.

It is, therefore, earnestly hoped that the present Legislature will promptly make an appropriation needed to finish this wall and put the whole enclosure into proper condition.

ADDRESSES.

The school is much indebted to Mr. Charles Dudley Warner, who gave the anniversary address in June, a most able and interesting essay on "Practical Education."

Our thanks are also due to Professor G. Stanley Hall, of Johns Hopkins University, and to Principal E. A. Sheldon, of the Oswego Normal School, for informal addresses to the school, of much interest and value.

STATISTICS.

1. Numbers: —

Enrolled Nov. 1, 1885,	129
Enrolled Nov. 1, 1886,	164
Temporarily absent by permission,	15

Whole number of different pupils enrolled during the year:

Young men,	4
Young women,	227
Total,	231

2. Number in entering classes: —

In February,	18
September,	54
Total,	72

3. Average age of pupils admitted: —

In February,	18 years, 9 months.
September,	18 years, 7 months.

4. Of the pupils admitted, there were: —

From Worcester County,	59
Middlesex County,	2
Norfolk County,	2
Suffolk County,	1
Connecticut,	3
Nebraska,	2
New Hampshire,	1
Vermont,	2
Total,	72

5. Occupations of pupils' parents: —

Professional,	2
Mercantile,	11
Skilled labor,	38
Unskilled labor,	16
Unknown,	5
Total,	72

6. Number in graduating classes: —

In January,	10
June,	16
Total,	26

7. Average age of graduates: —

In January,	22 years, 1 month.
June,	21 years, 11 months.

8. Number of the above graduates now teaching (November 1, 1886): —

January class (all),	10
June class (all but two),	14

9. Increase of numbers: —

Number enrolled in 1885,	198
enrolled in 1886,	231
Increase,	33

10. Additions to the library: —

Text-books,	469 volumes.
Reference-books,	185 volumes.
Total,	654 volumes.

11. Number of volumes now in the library: —

Text-books,	4,207 volumes.
Reference-books,	2,122 volumes.
Total,	6,329 volumes.

E. B. STODDARD,
A. P. STONE,
Visitors.

Of these, the number who had received certificates, or one or another of the diplomas, is as follows : —

Certificate A, ... 5
Certificates A and B, ... 6
Diploma A and C, ... 8
Diploma A, B and D, ... 2
Diploma, four-years course, ... 8
Still in Class A, ... 1
                                              ——
Total, ... 20

The annual graduating exercises of the school took place June 25, 1886. Besides the usual devotional services and music, various papers and illustrative exercises were given in the presence of a large and deeply-interested audience, — an audience which would have been much larger had it been possible to admit greater numbers. First were given illustrative teaching exercises for grammar-school children. Then followed "Construction of a Scholar's Companion," by Miss Sarah E. Jewett, Class A; "A Design for Application to Needle-work," by Miss Amy Swain, Class A; a "Portraiture in Clay," by Mr. Herman A. MacNeil; a paper entitled "Principles of Design," by Miss Florence Cleaves, Class D, illustrated by Mr. Skinner, Class C, and Misses Sanborn and Harding, Class D; "The Science of Perspective, with its Principles Pictorially Applied," by Miss Gertrude Roberts, Class B, and Mr. Milton H. Bancroft, Class D; and a paper on "Harmony of Color," by Miss Alice Austin, illustrated by Mr. Noyes, Misses Blake, Ellinwood and MacLauthlin, Class B.

These exercises were followed by several brief addresses. The Principal, Mr. George H. Bartlett, made some very appropriate explanatory remarks, commending the ability and fidelity of his associate teachers, and the industry and success of the pupils. The Chairman of the Board of Visitors gladly bore his testimony to the general satisfactoriness of the work of the school, and to the excellence of its administration and its increasing efficiency.

The Secretary of the Board of Education, Mr. John W. Dickinson, to whom the school is greatly indebted for a course

of lectures during the year on psychology, expressed his warm commendation of the school and its work.

The Rev. C. B. Rice, a former member of the Board of Visitors, said he had witnessed the exercises with great satisfaction, and bore cordial testimony to the marked advance of the school.

The wisdom of the changes in both work and discipline introduced in the last two or three years is vindicating itself, and the school is thus adapting itself more and more to the public needs. The organization of a preparatory class for such as are conditioned in drawing on admission to the school is enabling class A to attain much greater success, and is fulfilling the expectations of both teachers and visitors. The method of Normal instruction adopted in all of the more advanced classes, by which pupils are frequently brought before the whole school and required to present teaching exercises in the work of those classes, has won universal favor.

It is believed by the principal and teachers that the time has come for another forward step. The intention and scope of the school are broad. It aims to fit pupils for two very different kinds of work, viz.: 1. To train students to teach and supervise drawing in the public schools. Candidates for this work need greater maturity and broader qualifications than can be expected at sixteen years of age, the age at which pupils are admitted to this and other Normal Schools. They should not only be qualified to take the platform and present accurately the facts and principles of the several branches taught, but also to address intelligently and persuasively the teachers whose work they are to supervise. Such work requires general and literary attainments equivalent, at least, to those of high-school graduates, as well as thorough Normal training. 2. The second kind of work is to fit pupils to give instruction in the various branches of study in the evening and other industrial drawing schools. The members of such schools are mostly adults. The improvement of the industries being the more direct aim, mastery of the principles to be taught and of the manipulation of the mediums in which those principles are to be embodied, with the ability to present them in an orderly way, is all that need be insisted on. The general scholarship hitherto required, especially during the last two taken into the account. The janitor's labors will be increased. Two or three subordinate teachers, in justice, require each a slight increase of salary. The advance step in respect to the public-school section of class A, if the recommendation shall be acted upon, will necessitate an increased expenditure in that direction. The principal of the school, who has been obliged to give his whole time in instruction and oversight, though not hitherto paid for all, should receive the same salary as other Normal School principals. The total amount required for salaries will thus become $12,350. The amount expended for fuel, gas, water, advertising and printing during the present year has been $1,027. Rent of building, at present occupied by the school, for six months (all of which it is hoped will not be needed), $2,200. As the school is about to take possession of the new building, involving possible exigencies that cannot be foreseen, we deem it wise to add $423 for incidentals, making the total sum $16,000. The visitors will be glad to save as much of this as shall be practicable, consulting the best interests of the school.

We subjoin a description of the new building, with an indication of the uses to which the various rooms are to be appropriated. For the Newbury and Exeter Street elevations, see frontispiece to this volume.

> A. A. MINER,
> HORACE E. SCUDDER,
> ABBY W. MAY,
> FRANCIS A. WALKER,
> *Visitors.*

Boston, Dec. 3, 1886.

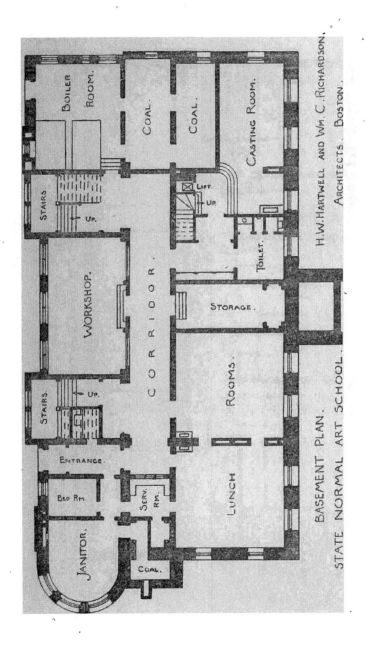

BASEMENT PLAN.
STATE NORMAL ART SCHOOL.
H.W. Hartwell and Wm. C. Richardson, Architects. Boston.

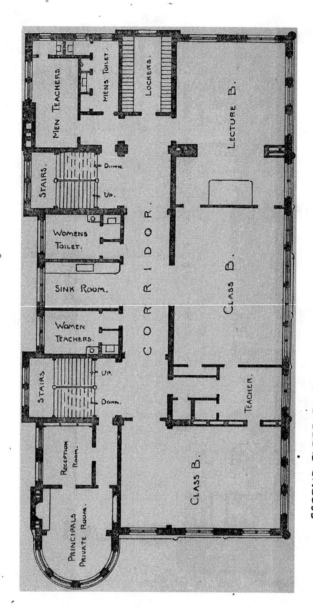

SECOND FLOOR PLAN.

STATE NORMAL ART SCHOOL.

H.W. HARTWELL AND WM. C. RICHARDSON.

ARCHITECTS. BOSTON.

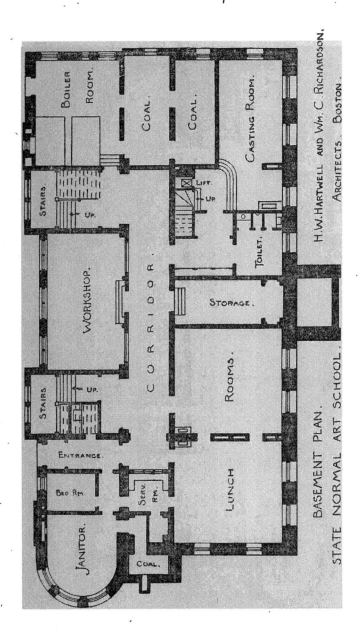

BASEMENT PLAN.

STATE NORMAL ART SCHOOL.

H. W. HARTWELL AND WM. C. RICHARDSON, ARCHITECTS. BOSTON.

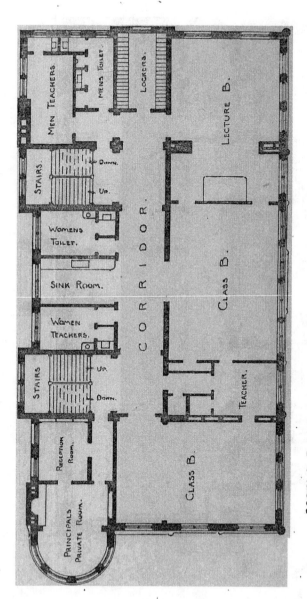

SECOND FLOOR PLAN.

STATE NORMAL ART SCHOOL.

H.W. HARTWELL AND WM. C. RICHARDSON.

ARCHITECTS. BOSTON.

THE NEW BUILDING.

The new building for the Massachusetts Normal Art School is located at the south-westerly corner of Newbury and Exeter Streets, with a frontage upon the former of 126 feet and upon the latter of 58 feet, 10 inches. The building is three full stories high above the basement, which is also finished throughout and set well above the street grades.

The materials used in the exterior of the building are the best hard bricks of good color, and Longmeadow freestone.

The treatment of the building, architecturally, is simple; the windows being square and kept close to the ceilings of the various rooms in order to afford the best light for working purposes. The exterior effect is chiefly obtained from a quiet grouping of the windows and other openings and by the use of the stone in simple masses, certain lines being obtained by broad bands of the stone running entirely around the building. The general surface of the freestone is rough, precisely as it came from the quarry, with a few mouldings and dressed surfaces so disposed as to give a quiet and dignified effect, consistent with the purpose of the building and with the fact that the appropriation for the erection of the same was limited.

The arrangement of the different floors will be understood by reference to the accompanying plans. It will be noticed that a portion of the basement is used in connection with the large room devoted to sculpture, in the first story; it being intended that the casting of plaster and work involving much use of water shall be done in this basement room, which is especially constructed for that purpose, having an asphalt floor laid upon a honeycomb construction of brickwork placed upon the top of a bed of concrete, in order that it shall be water-tight and, at the same time, not too cold for the comfort of the pupils whose work obliges them to occupy it.

In addition to the foregoing, the basement contains the heating apparatus, accommodations for the janitor, a large room to be used as a workshop, and two rooms taking their light from the front of the building which will be occupied by teachers and pupils at recess and luncheon times.

The principal entrance is in the centre of the Newbury Street front, from which we pass between class rooms upon the right and left, to a large gallery located upon the southerly side of the building, between the two principal staircases. This gallery is intended, as time goes on, to be occupied with sculpture and pictures; having a southern light it is not serviceable as a working-room. This consideration also governed the location of the stairs which are placed against the southern wall. The arrangement of the stairs, corridors, toilet and coat rooms, and teachers' waiting rooms, — of all of which there are a sufficient number throughout the building, — is such that the north and east light is left free for the use of the work of the school, and it is wholly appropriated by the rooms devoted to the work of the several classes.

The entrance for use of students is upon Exeter Street, opening upon a corridor which traverses the length of the building, crossing the gallery before mentioned and giving access to the staircases.

A similar corridor connects the staircases and opens upon rooms in each of the stories above.

The arrangement of the apartments has been carefully adapted to the various demands of the school, including complete control of the light required for working purposes. One room — the largest, that of Class A — has been provided with ceiling light and otherwise arranged to serve for the proper exhibition of the drawings and other works of the students.

A thorough system of warming, fresh-air supply and ventilation has been provided.

Wherever possible, brick walls have been used for the interior partitions. The floors under partitions and furred walls are thoroughly fire-stopped. The stairs are wire-lathed and fire-stopped, and every precaution has been taken to render the spread of fire throughout the building impossible.

The limited appropriation for the building, together with the demands of the problem, made necessary a more than usually careful study of the scheme from an economical standpoint.

No waste of material, seen or unseen, has been allowed, but a firm and substantial building has resulted, containing the full value of the money provided for its erection.

The contracts which have been made cover the entire completion of the work within the limits of the appropriation.

FIFTIETH ANNUAL REPORT

SECRETARY OF THE BOARD.

SECRETARY'S REPORT.

To the Board of Education.

I respectfully present herewith the Fiftieth Annual Report of the Secretary.

SUMMARY OF STATISTICS FOR 1885–86.

Number of cities and towns: Cities, 23; towns, 325.
All have made the annual returns required by law.

Number of public schools, ...	6,717
Increase for the year, ... 270	
Number of persons in the State between the ages of 5 and 15, May 1, 1885, ...	348,903
Increase for the year, ... 5,093	
Number of pupils of all ages in all the public schools during the year, ...	349,617
Increase for the year, ... 9,903	
Average membership of pupils in all the public schools during the year, ...	288,610
Increase for the year, ... 6,486	
Average attendance in all the public schools during the year,	260,088
Increase for the year, ... 6,133	
Per cent. of attendance based upon the average membership,	.90
Number of children under 5 years of age attending the public schools, ...	1,433
Decrease, ... ,32	
Number of persons over 15 years of age attending the public schools, ...	27,972
Increase for the year, ... 2,474	
Number of persons employed as teachers in the public schools during the year: men, 1,060; women, 8,610; total, . .	9,670
Number of teachers required by the public schools, . .	8,275
Number of teachers who have attended Normal Schools, .	3,003
Increase for the year, ... 137	
Number of teachers who have graduated from Normal Schools,	2,420
Increase for the year, ... 28	
Average wages of male teachers per month in public schools,	$111 23
Decrease, ... $9.49	

Average wages of female teachers per month in public schools, $43.97
    Increase, ... $0.12
Aggregate of months all the public schools have been kept
    during the school year, ... 59,729–15
Average number of months the public schools have been kept
    for the entire year, ... 8–12
Number of high schools, ... 224
Number of teachers in high schools, ... 677
Number of pupils in high schools, ... 21,370
Amount of salaries paid to principals of high schools, . . . $283,948 56
Evening schools: Number, 138; kept in 40 cities and towns.
Number of teachers, 667; whole number of pupils, 15,594;
    men, 12,106; women, 3,488; average, 8,254; number of
    evenings, 4,165; expense, ... $94,906 14
Amount raised by taxation for support of public schools, in-
    cluding only wages of teachers, fuel, care of fires and school-
    rooms, ... $4,817,429 01
        Increase for the year, ... $141,556 57
Expense of supervision of the public schools, ... 202,230 36
Salaries of superintendents, included in the above, . . . 87,918 59
Expense of preparing and printing school report, . . . 12,552 23
Expense of sundries, — books, stationery, globes, maps, etc., . 488,210 44
Amount expended in 1885–86 for new school-houses, . . 864,122 05
Amount expended for alterations and permanent improve-
    ments in school-houses, ... 182,153 31
Amount expended for ordinary repairs, ... 427,830 94
Amount of voluntary contributions to public schools, . . 1,933 75
Amount of local school funds, the income of which can be
    appropriated only for the support of schools and academies, 1,882,813 67
Income of local funds appropriated to schools and academies, 102,837 08
Income of funds appropriated for public schools at the option
    of the town, as surplus revenue, tax on dogs, etc., . . 87,551 83
Income of State school fund paid to cities and towns in aid of
    public schools for the school year 1885–86, ... 67,061 46
Of this amount, there was appropriated for apparatus and
    books of reference, ... 4,126 30
Aggregate returned as expended upon public schools alone,
    exclusive of repairing and erecting school-houses, . . 5,676,969 08
Of the above, to each child in the State between 5 and 15
    years of age, ... 16 27
Including in the aggregate above the expense of repairing and
    erecting school-houses, the sum is 7,151,075 38
To each child in the State between the ages of 5 and 15 years, 20 44
Percentage of valuation of 1885 appropriated for public schools,
    including only wages of teachers, fuel, care of fires and
    school-rooms, ... $.002\frac{75}{100}$
Percentage of valuation of 1885 appropriated for public
    schools, including all the items in the last aggregate above, $.004\frac{1}{100}$

Number of academies, ... 74
Whole number of students for the year in academies, . . 9,279
Amount of tuition paid, ... $476,106 38
Number of private schools, ... 348
Whole number attending for the year, ... 28,114
Estimated amount of tuition, ... $393,136 45

ANALYSIS OF THE RETURNS.

An analysis of the returns of the schools from the 348 towns
and cities of the State for 1885–86 shows an increase in the
number of children between the ages of five and fifteen years,
of 5,093, with an increase in the whole number of pupils of all
ages in attendance upon the schools, of 9,903, in the average
membership, of 6,486, in the average attendance, of 6,133, in
attendance upon the high schools, of 881, and an average
attendance, based upon the membership in all the schools, of
ninety per cent.

The whole number of pupils attending the schools, the number in high schools, the average membership, average attendance, and the number attending over fifteen years of age, all
show an absolute increase for the year considerably above the
average increase for a series of years previous. And when compared with the increase in the number of children between five
and fifteen years, which is less than for several years, the increase in the above particulars is very gratifying. The increase
in the number of pupils of all ages in all the schools, 9,903,
is somewhat remarkable. This increase, with the increase in
the number over fifteen years of age, and in the number in
high schools, may be attributed, we think, to the operation of
the free text-book law, which has lightened the burden of expense for books, especially of the more costly sort. The number
of graduates from Normal Schools employed as teachers, the
number of high schools in the · State, the number of evening
schools and the number of pupils attending them, remain about
as last year. The number of high schools as reported is 224.
They continue to have the confidence and support of the
people.

The aggregate returned as expended upon the public schools
exclusive of erecting and repairing buildings was $5,676,969.08.
This was an average to each child in the State between the ages
of five and fifteen, of $16.27, a decrease for the year of $0.11.

Including the expense of erecting and repairing school buildings, the aggregate expenditure was $7,151,075.38; an average to each child of $20.44, an increase for the year of $0.02.

The whole amount expended upon the public schools during the year 1885–86 was over four mills upon each dollar of taxable property in the Commonwealth.

The returns show a decrease in the average wages of male teachers of $9.49 per month, and an increase in the average wages of female teachers of $0.12 per month.

ACCURACY OF RETURNS.

Under this head a few suggestions were made in the last annual report. While it would seem that the directions given in the blanks forwarded for making the school returns are sufficiently specific, over two hundred letters have been written by this department during the year directing attention to errors more or less important which were manifest upon the face of the returns. In any case of doubt or misunderstanding of the intent of the directions given upon the blanks, committees are invited to confer freely with the Secretary of the Board of Education. That the returns may be of value, it is essential that they should have a uniform basis, and be correct.

In the graduated tables, page cxxiv, the ratio of attendance to the number between five and fifteen years of age, in a few towns, is above one hundred per cent., in several others the ratio is as high as one hundred. If every pupil in town May 1, between five and fifteen years of age, was in constant attendance for the whole time the schools keep, the attendance would be one hundred per cent. If some children under five years, May 1, attain to that age and enter the schools during the year, the per cent. would then exceed one hundred; and if children should move into the town after May 1, or come from neighboring towns and attend the schools, the per cent. would be still further increased. Moreover, the returns call for a report of the numbers under five and over fifteen as a separate item, so that those who reach these ages while attending school may be twice reported,—once when under five and fifteen and again when over these ages. Reporting twice should be guarded against in making out the ratio of attendance by counting such persons but once. All pupils under five and over fifteen years of age tend, of course, still further to increase this ratio. So it is not impossible that, taking for the basis the number in town between five and fifteen May 1, the attendance in some towns may exceed one hundred per cent. Presumably, however, the cases are rare, and the excess is slight in any case. And if we take into account the number of children who do not enter the schools at the early age of five years, the number of those who leave before they are fifteen, of those who attend private schools, and the number of absences from providential and other reasons, it is extremely improbable that any town can have an attendance above one hundred per cent.

It is far more likely, on the other hand, that those towns at the other end of the series, that report a ratio of forty to sixty per cent. of attendance, are more nearly exact; for among these are manufacturing towns with large parochial schools and large numbers of half-time pupils. At both extremes, and all through the series, the returns, before they are forwarded, cannot be too carefully scrutinized by the committees. Even then an understanding of all the modifying circumstances above referred to, is necessary to an intelligent interpretation by the reader of the report.

The ratio of attendance based upon the average membership shows a wide range, extending from fifty-eight to ninety-eight per cent. These per cents. indicate the degree of regularity with which the pupils registered attend the schools. All the children who are enrolled for any part of a year or term form the basis of the average membership, and from this average the ratio of attendance is calculated.

It is almost incredible that such disparity can really exist. But the rules laid down in the school registers are so explicit, that errors in the method of calculating seem impossible. It must be accounted for on other grounds. It is well known that in some places great vigilance is exercised to secure good attendance, while in others there is extreme laxity in this regard. Regularity of attendance is so important for the individual and for the success of the school as to justify the most persistent efforts to secure it.

There may be occasion for definite instructions in reference to membership and absence.   Formerly a pupil who
attended less than two weeks was not considered a member
at all.   The present rule considers the child a member from
the day he enters.   Some teachers still work by the old rule.
Most, doubtless, observe the new.   Usage differs again in case
of a pupil's leaving school.   Some record absences as beginning at the time the pupil leaves the school and as continuing to
the end of the term, whether he gives notice of leaving or not;
others record them till the fact of the leaving becomes known;
others cancel all absences that have been recorded as soon as
the fact becomes known.

If the pupil gives notice on leaving that he is not to return
for the term, no absences should be recorded against him
thereafter: he ceased to be a member the day he left.
If he re-enters, he should not be considered a member for
the time he was in non-attendance.   If no notice is given,
however, the case is different.   If he does not return at all,
it would seem to be right and proper to consider that his
membership ceased on his leaving school as truly as if he
had given notice.   But if he returns, the case is not so clear.
We would suggest that, for the sake of uniformity, the membership should be considered to have ceased at the end of one
week of absence; that this absence be counted in the total
of absences, and that the pupil's membership be renewed when
he returns.

A matter which presents much difficulty in many schools is the
dismissing of pupils during the school session.   If the pupil learns
and recites none of his lessons, but is absent during the whole
session except at devotions or at roll-call, it would appear that
such pupil should be counted absent; yet here again usage
differs.   It is difficult to make a satisfactory rule which is
founded on a compromise.   Returns made in accordance with
the facts must report the pupil to be present during the time he
is in school attending to his school duties, and to be absent at
all other times.

THE DEFECTIVE CLASSES.

Brief reports are given below of the asylum at Hartford, the
Clarke Institution at Northampton, and the Horace Mann School,

in which are trained the deaf-mutes of the State; the Perkins Institution at South Boston, in which are taught the blind, and the Massachusetts School for Feeble-Minded Youth.

The following amounts have been expended by the State for the support of her wards in these institutions during the year:—

For the Deaf-mutes, ...	$27,511 44
Blind, ...	30,000 00

These amounts but partly meet the expenses of those received into the institutions from the State, the balance being provided for by endowments.

AMERICAN ASYLUM FOR DEAF-MUTES.

The principal medium of instruction in the Asylum School is the sign language. Fifty-four pupils, however, are at present receiving instruction in articulation and lip-reading, and the results are declared to be quite satisfactory. One instance is recorded of a student that left the school nine years ago, who has a well-stocked shoe-store and transacts business with a great variety of customers, relying almost entirely upon speech and lip-reading. Others are reported as having facility, some in articulate speech, some in lip-reading, others in both, and all as having enough to be useful to them in the family and among their friends.

Almost from the foundation of this institution industrial training has formed an important part of the education of every able-bodied pupil. The pupils receive instruction in three trades, viz., cabinet-making, shoe-making and tailoring. Most of the girls learn to sew and do the lighter kinds of housework.

Drawing is carefully taught as a training for the mind through the hand and eye, as a preparation for understanding working-plans in the mechanical arts, and to lay the foundation for designing and other art work.

Each student in the Institution is furnished with a good elementary education in the branches ordinarily taught to hearing pupils; a portion are trained to recognize what others utter with their lips and to communicate their own thoughts in audible speech; all to use the language of form in drawing and the hands in those constructive arts through which a living may be earned.

CLARKE INSTITUTION FOR DEAF-MUTES.

Quiet progress has characterized the work of this institution during the year. It began the year with ninety-one pupils, and ended with ninety; boys forty-five, girls forty-six. Of these eighty-seven are boarding, and four are day pupils. Seventy-two are from Massachusetts, the remaining nineteen from ten different States.

The instruction given the pupils of this school is wholly through spoken language, and corresponds to that of first-class primary and grammar schools; and going beyond these, includes the branches taught in high schools,—algebra, geometry, physiology, zoölogy, botany, astronomy, history, rhetoric, English literature, political economy, psychology, etc.

The pupils having graduated from this course, or having partially completed it, are found in schools and academies of hearing pupils, and in not a few instances honorably complete the course of studies in still higher institutions.

An event of the year, which in common with all friends of the deaf-mutes the trustees of this institution deeply lament, is the constrained resignation of the principal, Miss Harriet B. Rogers, under whose able management, for seventeen years, the institution had grown from a small beginning to its present prominence and prosperity. A worthy successor to Miss Rogers is found in Miss Caroline A. Yale, whose ability has been demonstrated by her long experience in the school, as acting-principal for the last two years.

The following extract is from the report of Miss Yale for the current year : —

From the opening of the institution until failing health forced her to resign her work this has been pre-eminently "Miss Rogers' School," and abroad is usually so designated. To no other single person does the cause of oral teaching for the deaf of America owe so much. Steadfastly refusing to engage in controversy, she has left it to results to prove the value of her methods. . . . Her name will never cease to be a treasured household word in the school and family where for so many years she has been indeed, as in name, "The Principal."

The reports of this institution have sought with great earnestness for the past two years to obliterate some impressions existing in the public mind which are prejudicial to the deaf-mutes. It is claimed that all laws which discriminate against this class of persons, treating them as if they were objects of charity, should be abolished; that institutions in which they are instructed should not be called asylums, or be especially dependent upon endowments; that the education of the deaf-mutes should be considered a State obligation or State policy. Instead of " institutions aided by the State," in reality aiding the State, these institutions should cease altogether to be eleemosynary, and come at once to be supported, wholly if need be, at State expense. The poor man whose child is deaf should claim the child's education, and not be compelled to sue for it as a mendicant.

Nothing seems to be wanting to perfect the intellectual and moral culture of the deaf, to elevate them in the social scale, to increase their self-respect and self-reliance, to open to them manifold avenues to self-support, but the discontinuance of all treatment which implies incapacity. The low estimate of the deaf is seen in the reluctance of most business men to give them employment; in the surprise often evinced by casual school visitors at their demonstrated intellectual capacity; and especially in the laws of a few of the States, our own included, which make invidious distinctions between the hearing and the deaf.

HORACE MANN SCHOOL.

The last school year — 1885–86 — opened on Monday, Sept. 7, with seventy-three pupils, — thirty-seven boys and thirty-six girls. During the year eight pupils were admitted, two former pupils were readmitted and five were discharged. Of the latter number three went to work, one removed from the State and one was transferred to an institution.

Eighty-three different pupils were enrolled as members during the year, — fifty-four from Boston, twenty-seven from surrounding towns and two from other States. At the close of the year in June, 1886, there were seventy-eight pupils belonging to the school, — fifty from Boston, twenty-six from towns in the vicinity, one from New Hampshire and one from Pennsylvania.

The following statements are quoted from the last report of the committee on this school : —

This school differs from other schools, as is well known, not only in the condition of its pupils, but in the methods of instructing them. Those who enter as deaf-mutes are taught at first in a very elementary way. They learn through sight and touch the elements of speech, then the combination of these elements in words, then the written and printed forms of the words thus acquired. Reading words from the lips of teacher or fellow-pupil begins as soon as articulation becomes sufficiently distinct. Simple sentences are formed, orally and in writing, to describe familiar actions and objects. Lessons from objects and pictures develop ideas of number, size, form, color and quality. Then simple reading-books and arithmetics are brought into use, rudimentary exercises in geography, letter and journal writing, and other suitable means lead on to a course of study, corresponding in most respects to that prescribed for children who can hear. Such pupils as have once heard and gained the knowledge of spoken language before becoming deaf, can be trained, of course, without resorting to the initiatory steps here described. Instruction is given to all our children from the lips, from objects and from blackboards, as well as from books.

Industrial training is regarded as particularly desirable for these children. Eight boys attended the Manual Training School of the city. Eight girls were received into the private cooking school on Tennyson Street. Several boys were trained in the North Bennet Street Industrial School as carpenters, shoemakers and printers. Clay modelling was taught to some of our pupils in the same school.

The Horace Mann School offers instruction, not merely to the deaf, but to those of defective hearing. It is possible that some children now in our grammar or primary schools, and laboring under imperfect hearing, would be better off if transferred to our care. It is very much to the benefit of children who do not hear well to learn to read the speech of those about them from the lips, and this they can learn most readily in a school where it is specially taught. Doubtless the senses which the deaf retain are quickened, and their capacity of acquiring and using knowledge is far greater than would be imagined by those who never see them in school.

MASSACHUSETTS BENEFICIARIES.

Clarke Institution.

Number of Massachusetts beneficiaries Jan. 1, 1886, ...	71
" admitted during the year, ...	15
" discharged during the year, ...	9
" in the institution Jan. 1, 1887, ...	77

Horace Mann School.

Number of Massachusetts beneficiaries Jan. 1, 1886, ...	72
" admitted during the year, ...	5
" discharged during the year, ...	11
" in the institution Jan. 1, 1887, ...	66

American Asylum.

Number of Massachusetts beneficiaries Jan. 1, 1886, ...	57
" admitted during the year, ...	6
" discharged during the year, ...	11
" in the institution Jan. 1, 1887, ...	52

Whole number of beneficiaries in all the institutions Jan. 1, 1887, . 195

AMOUNT EXPENDED FOR THEIR INSTRUCTION DURING THE YEAR.

Paid Clarke Institution.

71 beneficiaries for quarter commencing Jan. 1, 1886,	$3,400 50	
71 beneficiaries for quarter commencing April 1, 1886,	3,043 75	
71 beneficiaries for quarter commencing July 1, 1886,	3,043 75	
77 beneficiaries for quarter commencing Oct. 1, 1886,	3,337 50	
		$12,825 50

Paid Horace Mann School.

75 beneficiaries from Feb. 1, 1886, to July 1, 1886, .	$3,679 12	
66 beneficiaries from July 1, 1886, to Feb. 1, 1887, .	3,220 50	
		6,899 62

Paid American Asylum.

57 beneficiaries for quarter commencing Dec. 1, 1885,	$2,493 75	
57 beneficiaries for quarter commencing March 1, 1886,	2,493 75	
57 beneficiaries for quarter commencing June 1, 1886,	2,493 75	
Clothing furnished beneficiaries for the year ending July 1, 1886, ...	304 07	
		7,785 32

Aggregate amount expended during the year, . . . $27,510 44

PERKINS INSTITUTION AND MASSACHUSETTS SCHOOL FOR THE BLIND.

Organized fifty-four years ago, with six pupils, in the house of Dr. Samuel G. Howe's father, this institution has grown with great rapidity, and has led the way in this country in all improvements for the education of the blind and the amelioration of their condition. It has sent forth hundreds of youth of both sexes, well trained and fitted to rank with other members of the community in intelligence, industry and attainments.

The annual reports of the trustees and of the director show that hardly any mental, moral, physical or industrial interest of the blind has been overlooked, either in the organization or the administration of the establishment.

The movement for the establishment of a kindergarten and primary school for little sightless children has been carried on during the past year with unremitting energy. A commodious brick building has been erected on the new estate in Roxbury, and arrangements have been made for the immediate opening of the infant institution with twelve or fifteen pupils.

In addition to this project, the trustees of the institution have taken the preliminary steps to establish a *post-graduate course* for the benefit of those of the graduates of the school " who show a marked talent and a capacity for higher attainments in some important branch of study or music."

According to a report presented to this Board, the financial status of the institution may be summarized as follows : —

Receipts.

Cash in the treasury Oct. 1, 1885, ...	$2,011 02
Annual appropriation from the State of Massachusetts, ...	30,000 00
Income from all other sources, . . .	52,228 53
Legacies and donations, ...	5,907 30
Donations and contributions to the kindergarten fund, ...	16,126 39
Collections of mortgage notes that fell due, . .	13,000 00
	$119,273 24

Disbursements.

Maintenance, superintendence and instruction,	.	$13,813 23
Kindergarten, grading and building, . .	.	21,903, 15
All other expenses, ...	.	11,566 66
Investments, ...	.	5,662 75
Cash in the hands of the treasurer, . .	.	36,327 45
		$119,273 24

The total number of blind persons connected with the institution in all its departments on the 1st of January, 1887, was 179. Of these, 161 are in the school proper and 18 in the workshop for adults.

The first class includes 149 boys and girls enrolled as pupils, 10 teachers and employés, and 2 domestics.

The second class comprises 13 men and 5 women employed in the industrial department for adults.

Number of Massachusetts beneficiaries Jan. 1, 1887, ...	80
" adults belonging to Massachusetts, ...	26
" blind persons belonging to other States, ...	73
Total, ...	179

The following extracts, taken from the fifty-fifth annual report of the director to the trustees, give an idea of the variety and character of the work of the institution and of the system of instruction and training therein pursued : —

During the past year a high degree of success has been attained in every department of the institution.

The usual course of physical training, of literary studies, of music, and of handicrafts, has been pursued uninterruptedly, and has borne good fruit.

The school has been preparing the youth of both sexes to free themselves from the incubus of dependence, which weighs so heavily upon them, and to vindicate that capacity for perfect development, which is their birthright, in common with all other classes of children.

The number of pupils in actual attendance has been greater than ever before ; it is indeed larger than would be desirable in institutions organized upon the usual plan. In ours the evil effects of the congregation of so many defectives are less perceptible, because they are divided into five distinct families, live in separate dwellings, and come together in classes only for purposes of instruction, as ordinary children go to day-school.

The course of bodily training pursued in the gymnasium has been prosecuted with uncommon energy, and no pains have been spared on the part of those in charge to improve and systematize a regular,. intelligent, and, to some degree, scientific series of exercises, consisting of free gymnastics, calisthenics and military drill. These exercises are calculated to enlarge and strengthen the various muscles of the trunk, neck, arms and legs; to expand the chest so as to facilitate the play of the lungs; to render the joints supple, and to impart to the pupils grace, ease and steadiness of carriage, combined with vigor, elasticity and quickness of movement.

The school proper is a sort of intellectual gymnasium, where the muscles of the mind and the tissues of the brain are thoroughly and systematically exercised and developed.

The various studies included in our curriculum have been selected with much care and due deliberation, and are pursued not as ends but as means of mental discipline.

All methods which tend to inflate the pupils' vanity, and to give them an over-estimate of their attainments, have been studiously avoided as injurious.

As often as occasion has seemed to require it, the subsoil plough of reform has been pushed so deep as to turn up the weeds of empiricism by the roots. But no changes of any kind have ever been effected for the sake of novelty or from a flippant pride in being in the van of progress.

Efficiency and thoroughness have been held to be of paramount importance, and they have not been allowed to suffer from any consideration. The pupils have not been taught in great masses by machine methods. They have been divided into small classes and have received a certain amount of individual instruction in a simple and natural way. The fossilized spelling-books, the antiquated geographies, the obsolete grammars, and all that endless hash of à priori deductions and of confused statements and misty definitions, with which the minds of children are invariably nauseated, have been gradually discarded and supplanted by the methods of Pestalozzi and Froebel. The change has proved to be very wholesome, and the influence of a diet of *things* prescribed by the former in the place of words, and a little vigorous practice of *doing* in lieu of empty talking, induced by the system of the latter, have been truly magical.

The number of pupils who received instruction in music during the past year was 113. Of these, 88 studied the pianoforte; 10, the cabinet and church organs; 6, the violin; 7, the clarinet; 1, the flute; 19, brass instruments; 81 practised singing in classes, of which we have five; 25 received private lessons in vocal training; and 38, divided into seven separate classes, averaging five members, studied harmony. The means and facilities afforded by the institution for the best musical instruction, and the ample opportunities it offers for practice, can hardly be surpassed anywhere. Yet, cognizant of the fact that the standard of music is advancing very rapidly throughout the country, and that the success of those of our students who intend making it their profession for life depends in no small measure upon the thoroughness of their equipment, we strive to improve the department dedicated to this art in every possible way, and to keep it in the line of progress.

The importance of handicraft is fully recognized in this institution; and the employment of the body as well as of the mind is a very essential part of the education of our pupils. The experiment has been faithfully tried for more than fifty years, and the result has been uniformly favorable. We find that intellectual improvement, instead of being retarded, is decidedly aided by manual training. Resolution and all the preparatives for vigorous and successful application to study are gained. Habits of industry and thrift are formed. Cheerfulness and health are promoted. The tedium of the schoolroom is relieved. Manual dexterity and bodily elasticity are secured. Valuable mechanical knowledge is attained; and in many cases a trade has been acquired, whereby a livelihood might be obtained.

The work in both branches of this department has been conducted with marked earnestness and fidelity, and with equally satisfactory results in each case.

The cottage plan, which is in full operation in the girls' department of our school, affords excellent opportunities for the thorough mastery of manual and domestic occupations. Here fifteen or sixteen pupils sit at the same table and form one circle in family affairs with their teachers and other officers, who are four in number. The close and beautiful relationship that is thus brought about by the tie of domestic and social duties performed in common, and by enjoyments shared with one another, has a most powerful influence.

THE MASSACHUSETTS SCHOOL FOR THE FEEBLE-MINDED.

By statute of 1886, it was made the duty of the Trustees of the Massachusetts School for the Feeble-minded to annually prepare and send to the Board of Education a written or printed report of its proceedings, income and expenditures, also to give the whole number and the average number of inmates, and such other information as the Board may require. This institution reports the whole number of inmates during the year 181, — boys 108, girls 73. The average number during the year, 148.

Section 1 of the statute above referred to requires the establishment and maintenance of two departments: "one for the instruction and education of feeble-minded persons who are within the school age, or who, in the judgment of the trustees thereof, are capable of being benefited by school instruction, to be known as the School Department; and one for the care and custody of those feeble-minded persons who are beyond the school age, or are not capable of being benefited by school instruction, to be known as the Custodial Department."

Adopting the classification of the statute, the institution had inmates as follows : —

Beneficiaries of Commonwealth in school department,	62
Custodial cases supported by Commonwealth,	18
Custodial cases supported by cities and towns,	39
Beneficiaries of other New England States,	17
Private pupils,	15
Total,	151

A Brief Account of the Work of the Board of Education since its Establishment in 1837.

The Massachusetts Board of Education was established by an act of the Legislature passed on the twentieth day of April, 1837. By this act it was provided that the "Board shall consist of the Governor and eight persons appointed by the Governor with the advice and consent of the Council, each to hold office eight years from the time of his appointment, and one to retire each year in the order of appointment; and the Governor with the advice and consent of the Council shall fill all vacancies in the board."

On the 27th of May, an official communication of the appointment of the following persons to constitute the Board of Education was made : —

Original Members of the Board.

James G. Carter.	Edward A. Newton.
Emerson Davis.	Thomas Robbins.
Edmund Dwight.	Jared Sparks.
Horace Mann.	George Hill.

Ex-Officiis.

Edward Everett.	George Hall.

Of the establishment of the Board of Education, Mr. Mann, in his diary of May 27, writes: "It is the first great movement towards an organized system of common schools which shall at once be thorough and universal."

On the twenty-ninth day of June, 1837, in the council chamber at the State House in Boston, the Board held its first meeting.

The act creating the Board made provision for the appointment of a secretary, who should spend his whole time in its service. It also defined the duties which both the Board and Secretary were expected to perform.

Fifty years have passed away since the Board was created. It may be interesting to make a brief historical review of the changes that have taken place in the administration of our public educational institutions during the last half-century.

At the first meeting of the Board, the Honorable Horace Mann, then president of the Massachusetts Senate, was elected secretary.

The act of the Legislature that authorized his appointment defined his duties as follows: —

The Secretary shall, under the direction of the Board, collect information of the actual condition and efficiency of the common schools and other means of popular education, and diffuse as widely as possible throughout every part of the Commonwealth, information of the most approved and successful methods of arranging the studies and conducting the education of the young to the end that all children in this Commonwealth, who depend upon the common schools for instruction, may have the best education which those schools can be made to impart.

The acts of the Board and Secretary are advisory rather than authoritative. They may discover defects in school work and suggest the remedies, but they have no authority by any direct exercise of power to restrain or compel. The duties relate principally to a general supervision of those educational institutions that are supported by the State, to an observation of the working of the public-school system, and to making an annual report to the Legislature which shall present such facts and statistics as may form the basis of all school legislation.

Mr. Mann entered upon the duties of his office about the 28th of August. At a meeting of the Board held at the council chamber June 30, 1837, it was *voted*, That the Secretary be directed to prepare and lay before the Board, at their next meeting, an abstract of the school returns received by the Secretary of the Commonwealth.

In compliance with this vote, the abstracts were submitted to the Board Jan. 1, 1838. The following represents the form of the first abstracts and the particulars to which they refer:—

NAME OF COUNTY.

NAME OF TOWN.	BOOKS USED IN THE SCHOOLS.
Number of public schools:—	
In winter,	
In summer,	
Average attendance in the schools:—	
In winter,	
In summer,	
Number of persons between 4 and 16 years of age in the town,	
Aggregate length of the schools:— Mos. days.	REMARKS.
In winter,	
In summer,	
Number of teachers in summer:—	
Males,	
Females,	
Number of teachers in winter:—	
Males,	
Females,	
Average wages paid per month, including board:—	
To males,	
To females,	
Amount of money raised by taxes for the support of schools,	
Amount raised by taxes for teachers' wages, including board, if paid from the public money,	
Amount raised voluntarily to prolong com. schools, including fuel and board, if contributed,	
Number of academies or private schools,	
Aggregate of months kept,	
Aggregate of scholars,	
Aggregate paid for tuition,	
Amount of local funds,	
Income from same,	

Following the abstracts of the individual towns was a recapitulation for the counties and for the State.

By comparing the returns of 1837 with those of 1886 a good view may be obtained of the changes which fifty years have produced in whatever pertains to the growth and character of our system of public schools.

Number of towns in the State in 1837, ... 305
Number of towns that made returns, ... 294
Number of towns in 1886, ... 348
    All made returns required by law.
Population (May 1) 1837, ... 691,222
Population (May 1) 1886, ... 1,942,141
Valuation of 1830, ... $206,457,662 58
Valuation of 1886, ... $1,847,531,422 00
Number of public schools in 1837, ... 2,918
Number of public schools in 1886, ... 6,717
Number of scholars of all ages in the public schools, 1837 : —
    In winter, ... 141,837
    In summer, ... 122,889
Number of scholars of all ages in the public schools in 1885, . 349,617
Average attendance in public schools in 1837 : —
    In winter, ... 111,520
    In summer, ... 94,956
Average attendance in the public schools in 1885, . ＝ . 260,088
Number of persons between 4 and 16 in 1837, . . . 177,053
Number of persons between 5 and 15 in 1885, ... 348,903
Average length of schools in months and days in 1837, . 6 mos., 25 dys.
Average length of schools in months and days in 1885, . 8 mos., 12 dys.
Number of teachers in the public schools (including summer and
    winter terms), 1837 : —*
    Males, ... 2,370
    Females, ... 3,591
Number of teachers in public schools in 1885 : —
    Men, ... 1,060
    Women, ... 8,610
Average wages per month of teachers, including board, in 1837 : —
    Males, ... $25 44
    Females, ... $11 38
Average wages per month of teachers, including board, in 1885 : —
    Men, ... $111 23
    Women, ... $13 97
Amount of money raised by taxation for all the children in the
    State between 4 and 16 in 1837, ... $165,228 04
For each child between 4 and 16 years of age, ... $2 63

* The number of different teachers for the year cannot be ascertained.

Amount raised by taxation for the support of schools, including only wages of teachers, board, fuel and care of fires and school-houses in 1885, ... $4,817,429 01
For each child between 5 and 15, ... $16 27
Amount raised by taxation for all school purposes in 1885, $7,838,226 57
For each child of school age, ... $22 46
Number of academies and private schools in the State in 1837, . . 854
Whole number of pupils attending, ... 27,266
Amount of tuition paid academies and private schools, . . . $328,026 75
Number of academies in 1885, ... 74
Number of private schools, ... 348
Whole number attending academies, ... 9,279
Whole number attending private schools, ... 28,114
Amount of tuition paid academies, ... $476,106 38
Amount paid private schools, ... $393,136 45

Comparing the returns of 1837 with those of 1886, it appears that the population of the Commonwealth has increased in fifty years from 691,222 to 1,942,141; and the value of taxable property from $206,457,662 to $1,847,531,422. There are now three times as many schools as existed fifty years ago, and three times as many pupils to attend them.

In 1837 the average attendance of children of all ages in the public schools was in winter 53,533 less than the whole number of school children in the State, and in summer it was over 70,000 less.

In 1886 the average attendance of children of all ages in the public schools was only 54,195 less than the whole number of school children in the State, although the school population had nearly tripled since 1837.

It should not be forgotten in making these comparisons that our compulsory laws apply only to children between the ages of eight and fourteen, and that the parochial schools have taken large numbers from the public schools.

The average length of the schools in 1837 was six months and twenty-five days; in 1886, eight months and twelve days. The early schools in some of the large towns were kept nearly through the year. The average length of the Boston schools in 1837 was reported to be twelve months; and of the schools of Suffolk County, eleven months and twenty-six days. It appears that in the report no account is taken of the several short vacations.

Formerly a school month was a calendar month. At the present time twenty school days constitute a school month.

Long vacations in the school year are a modern invention. They now continue in summer from about June 25 to September 1, with various shorter vacations for Thanksgiving, Christmas and other legal holiday periods.

In modern times male teachers seem to be disappearing from the public schools. Out of a total of 9,670 teachers, reported as employed last year in the public schools, 1,060 were men, 8,610 were women. In 1837 about two-fifths of the public-school teachers were men. The winter schools were quite generally taught by men, and the summer schools quite as generally by women.

Many of the country school teachers had little or no special preparation for the skilful performance of their duties. Their education was such as could be obtained in the district school. They had little or no educational literature at their command, nor were there any associations of teachers for them to attend.

The Normal Schools had not yet opened their doors for the free instruction of those who desired to pursue a course of pedagogical study.

Teachers did over again for their pupils what had been done for themselves. They spent their time in keeping order, and hearing recitations of lessons committed to memory from the books.

Since the establishment of the Board of Education six State Normal Schools have been organized for the training of teachers; training schools in many of the cities and large towns have been added to their system of public schools, and county associations of teachers have been formed in nearly every one of the fourteen counties of the State, for the discussion of those problems which present themselves in the every-day work of the public school.

About one-fourth of our public teachers are Normal graduates, and nearly one-third have attended a Normal School. Many more have had the advantages of such instruction as the training schools can give, and all others have had their ideas and practices modified by the example of those who have been trained in the theory and practice of the best methods.

The male teachers of fifty years ago received for their services an average of $25.44 per month, and the female $11.38.

By the last returns it appears that male teachers are receiving an average of $111.23, female $43.97, — a fourfold increase over former times. This increase of compensation is significant, indicating a higher and more intelligent appreciation of the importance of popular education, and a higher standard by which ability to teach is measured.

It was the custom in the early days of the Commonwealth for school teachers to board around in the families of the parents sending children to school. The time passed in each family depended upon the number of children sent to school and the length of the school term.

This custom of boarding round produced some good results. It brought the teacher in contact with the parents of the pupils, and furnished the occasion for an acquaintance which sometimes resulted in an awakened interest in the well-being of the school.

It also furnished the teacher an opportunity to learn something of the home life of the children, from which could be derived a knowledge of their peculiar wants and of the method of training to which they should be subjected. On the other hand, the custom prevented the teacher from enjoying the pleasures of a permanent home, and it deprived him of the opportunity of systematic study in preparing his daily tasks.

The aggregate amount returned, as expended upon public schools in 1886, was $7,838,226.57, — a sum equal to $22.46 for every child between the ages of five and fifteen years, or to four mills on every dollar of the taxable property of the State. In 1837 the whole amount expended on public schools was $465,228.04, — a sum equal to $2.63 for each child of school age, or to 2.2 mills on the dollar of taxable property for that year.

The establishment of the University at Cambridge and of the colleges in Massachusetts created the necessity for preparatory schools. These at first were called grammar schools. The grammar schools were established in 1647 after the plan of the cathedral schools of England. They were designed especially to fit boys for the university.

Every town of one hundred families or householders was required to maintain a grammar school. In 1683 all towns containing five hundred families were required to maintain two grammar schools. The early grammar schools have gradually passed into the modern high schools. The grammar schools of 1647 furnished secondary instruction to the people living in the larger and more populous towns, but the wants of the smaller towns led to the establishment of institutions of the same grade, called academies. The academies, although supported in part by public funds, were essentially private institutions, managed by authorities not subject to State control. In 1837 there were eight hundred and fifty-four academies and private schools, with 27,266 pupils paying a yearly tuition of $328,026.75. The income of local funds for the same year was $9,571.79, which added to the sum paid for tuition amounts to $337,598.54, — paid for the support of academies and private schools in 1837. The sum raised the same year by taxation for all the children of the State was $465,228.04.

By the returns of 1886 there were seventy-four academies and three hundred and forty-eight private schools, with an aggregate of 37,393 pupils in attendance and paying a tuition of $869,242.83 for their support. As already stated, the amount raised this year by taxation for all the children of the State was $7,838,226.57. In this connection it must not be forgotten that in 1837 there were no parochial schools, while at the present time there are, in many of the cities and large towns, such schools returned as private institutions, and which are maintained for other reasons than because the public schools are not successful in accomplishing the ends for which they were established. Thus it appears from the returns of 1837 that about one-sixth of the school children were in private schools, while in 1886 there were only one-tenth of the whole number. In 1837 the amount of money paid for the support of private schools and academies was equal to three-fourths of the amount raised for the public schools. In 1886 the amount paid for the support of private schools and academies was one-sixth the amount raised for the public schools.

The statutes require every town containing five hundred families and more to maintain a secondary or high school for the benefit of all the inhabitants of the town. In 1837 there were forty-three towns, exclusive of the city of Boston, containing the required number of families for a high school, and yet there were only fourteen such schools in the State. Many of the delinquent towns were among the most populous and wealthy. In one of them, with a population of over three thousand persons, so little interest was taken in popular education, that in the most important district no public school was maintained for more than two years.

In 1886 there were one hundred and fifty high-school towns and two hundred and twenty-four high schools. Every town in the Commonwealth required to maintain a high school is obeying the law, and about fifty other towns, taking advantage of the permissive provisions of the law, are maintaining high schools by a voluntary support.

From these comparisons it appears that the public schools are now in great favor with the people, and that public sentiment in regard to their necessity and value has greatly changed within the last fifty years.

In 1837 the supervision of the schools was wholly by school committees. From returns to interrogatories sent out this year by the Board, it was found that no more than fifty or sixty towns made any effort to obey the law relating to visiting the schools for inspection and supervision. In one town containing forty school districts it was discovered that for eight successive years the school committee had never examined a teacher nor visited a school. The services of school committees rendered as superintendents of the schools do not appear to have been appreciated at this time. In only one-fifth of the towns did they receive any compensation for their labor, either in money or in gratitude; and if they were so presuming as to present a bill of expenses even, they were reminded of the impropriety of their act by being excused at the next election from further service.

The school committees of the State made their first annual returns to the Board of Education in 1838. In these returns there is a general complaint of the condition of the school-houses provided for the children, of the literary and professional qualifications of the teachers employed, of the irregularity of attendance upon the public schools, of the preference given to private over public schools, and of the general apathy manifested by all towards popular education.

This condition of things had arrested the attention of thoughtful men, and led them to see the necessity of creating

a public-school system that would offer to every child of the
State the advantages of good common-school instruction. The
first steps taken to secure a revival of interest in the welfare of
the schools, and to provide efficient means for improving their
condition, were the creation of the school fund and the establishment of the State Board of Education. The first work of
the Board was to obtain accurate information of the condition
of the public schools of the State. This information was obtained from answers to inquiries sent by the Secretary of the
Board to the school committees of the towns, and from a personal observation commenced during his first year of service.

The first report of the Board and its Secretary, based on the
information thus obtained, and to which reference has been
made, directed the attention of the friends of the public schools
to their defects, to the want of public interest in them, and to
the necessity of an immediate and thorough reformation in
their management.

As a result, the public teachers throughout the State began
to assemble in county associations to consider the changes
demanded in methods of teaching; the school authorities began
to inspect their school buildings and to improve them; to exercise more care in the selection of teachers, and more justice in
paying them for their services; to make better courses of
studies; to introduce a greater uniformity in the text-books
used; to employ better methods of teaching; to grade the
schools in accordance with the age, ability and acquisitions of
the pupils; to adopt means for increasing the school attendance;
to provide for increasing the length of the school terms, and
for better school supervision.

Governor Lincoln said in an annual message, delivered in
1827, "The cause of learning languishes, both from the
paucity and incompetence of instructors;" and he recommended
the adoption of measures for the preparation and better quali-
fication of teachers of youth.

In the following winter the Committee on Education presented a bill for the establishment of what was called the
Massachusetts Literary Fund. The bill provided for the
endowment of an institution for the instruction of school
teachers in each county of the State, and also for the aid and
encouragement of the common schools. This bill did not

become a law. In 1833, a bill to establish a School Fund was introduced, and referred to the next General Court. In 1834, an act was passed to establish the Massachusetts School Fund, the income of which should be appropriated for the aid and encouragement of common schools. No provision was made in this act for the better education of teachers. The Board of Education, immediately after its establishment, in 1837, recommended the appropriation of a portion of the school fund for the support of Normal Schools. In 1838, a member of the Board of Education and an earnest friend of the public schools, the Hon. Edmund Dwight of Boston, offered the gift of ten thousand dollars, to be expended, under the direction of the Board, for the training of public-school teachers, provided the State would furnish an equal amount for the acomplishment of the same end. The Legislature accepted the offer and appropriated the money.

On the third day of July, 1839, the first State Normal School ever established on this continent was opened at Lexington, Massachusetts. Since that time five other State Normal Schools have been organized in the State. For more than forty years these training seminaries have been sending out their graduates into the public schools. By the last returns it appears that there are now more than three thousand of them in actual service in the Commonwealth.

Normal teachers are distinguished for their superior methods of teaching, for their more rational forms of government, and for their intelligent enthusiasm. The results of their work are not confined to the schools which they are appointed to teach, but may be observed in the improved methods introduced into all other schools in the surrounding communities.

As soon as the Normal Schools directed the attention of teachers to a study of the principles upon which correct teaching is founded, they began to discover that much of the work done in the common schools was unphilosophical and not adapted to accomplish the ends for which these schools were established. They found also that the forms of school government too generally adopted had a tendency to corrupt the minds of the children and to lead them into a strong dislike for their school duties, rather than to train them to obedience and to fill them with a love of learning.

The reform in methods of teaching and discipline introduced into the schools half a century ago, seems, to those who have observed it along through the years, to have made slow progress; and yet if we compare the present with the past, we can easily see that great improvements have been made. Fifty years ago, as a rule, the schools did not pretend to teach in the true sense of that term. Lessons were assigned to be memorized, and recited as they were learned. The attention of the teacher was quite fully directed to the text-book, and the pupil did not have frequent occasions to look to other sources for either knowledge or information.

There were some skilled teachers in the schools of that day. They were persons of distinguished natural ability, who had received their training through experience. They belonged to that small class of teachers who are endowed with the educational instinct which seems to force its possessor through an irresistible impulse to teach in accordance with the natural method, and to keep in mind the ends of education.

But the great mass of public-school teachers had no such preparation for their work. They were for the most part graduates of the grade of schools they were called to teach. Their knowledge both of things and books was limited to a small amount. The formalities of the school day occupied their attention, but they did not think it to be any part of their duty to develope the intellectual and moral faculties of the children. Then memorizing was substituted for study, hearing recitations for teaching and keeping order for government. The higher principles of action were not always used as the basis of either intellectual or moral effort. Simple conformity to rules was accepted too frequently for obedience,— a kind of activity that generally fails of producing a symmetrical development of the faculties. Fifty years of experience in conducting the public schools of the Commonwealth, together with a careful study by the best educators, has produced a science of education and an art founded upon its principles. It may be interesting to take note of the school legislation of the State during the last half-century, and compare the school laws of the present with those of the past.

School Legislation from 1837 to 1886.

BOARD OF EDUCATION.

Board of Education established.
1837, 241, § 1.
1838, 55.

April 20, 1837, the act establishing the Board of Education and prescribing its duties was approved by the Governor. Incidental expenses were provided for by Act of 1838.

To prepare an abstract of school returns.
1826, 143, § 8.
1837, 241, § 2.

By an act of 1837 it was provided that the Board of Education shall prepare and lay before the Legislature in a printed form an abstract of the school returns received by the Secretary of the Commonwealth.

Returns made up in office of Secretary of Commonwealth.
1838, 107, § 7.

In 1838 it was provided that the school returns shall be made up, under the direction of the Board of Education, in the office of the Secretary of the Commonwealth.

Made up in office of Board of Education.
1847, 183.

In 1847 it was first enacted that the returns shall be made up in the office of the Board of Education.

Board of Education may appoint secretary, who shall make abstracts, etc.
1837, 241, § 2.
1847, 183, § 1.
1849, 215, § 1.
G. S., 34, § 4.

The act which established the Board of Education authorized it to appoint its own secretary, who, under its direction, was required to make the abstract of school returns, collect information respecting the condition and efficiency of the public schools and other means of popular education, and diffuse as widely as possible throughout the Commonwealth information of the best system of studies and method of instruction for the young, that the best education which public schools can be made to impart may be secured to all children who depend upon them for instruction.

Secretaries of the Board.

Under the authority to appoint its secretary, the Board of Education elected Horace Mann, who continued in office twelve years. His successor was Barnas Sears, who held office seven years. The third secretary of the Board was George S. Boutwell, who was secretary for five years. Joseph White, the successor to Mr. Boutwell, served sixteen years. He was succeeded by John W. Dickinson, the present secretary, who entered upon the duties of the office in May, 1877.

MEMBERS OF THE BOARD OF EDUCATION FROM 1837 TO 1886, INCLUSIVE.

The following list of the members of the Board, named in the order of their appointment or connection with it, is complete to the present time : —

James G. Carter.
Emerson Davis.
Edmund Dwight.
Horace Mann.
Edward A. Newton.
Robert Rantoul, Jr.
Thomas Robbins.
Jared Sparks.
George Putnam.
Charles Hudson.
George N Briggs.
William G. Bates.
John W. James.
Elisha Bartlett.
Heman Humphrey.
Stephen C. Phillips.
Barnas Sears.
Edwin H. Chapin.
Henry B. Hooker.
Stephen P. Webb.
Thomas Kinnicutt.
Joseph W. Ingraham.

John A. Bolles.
George B. Emerson.
Charles K. True.
Mark Hopkins.
Edward Otheman.
Isaac Davis.
Alexander H. Vinton.
George S Boutwell.
Henry Wheatland.
Hosea Ballou.
Ariel Parish.
Cornelius C. Felton.
Alonzo H. Quint.
William A. Stearns.
Russell Tomlinson.
Erastus O. Haven.
David H. Mason.
John P. Marshall.
Emory Washburn.
Abner J. Phipps.
James Freeman Clarke.
William Rice.

John D. Philbrick.
Samuel T. Seelye.
George T. Wilde.
Gardiner G. Hubbard.
Alonzo A. Miner.
Henry Chapin.
Constantine C. Esty.
Edward B. Gillett.
Phillips Brooks.
Chri-topher C Hussey.
Charles B Rice.
Elijah B Stoddard.
Horatio G. Knight.
Miss Abby W. May.
Charles Francis Adams, Jr.
Milton B. Whitney.
Thomas W. Higginson.
Admiral P. Stone.
Francis A. Walker.
Edward C. Carrigan.
Horace E. Scudder.

MEMBERS EX-OFFICIIS.

Governors.

Edward Everett.
Marcus Morton.
John Davis.
George N. Briggs.
George S. Boutwell.
John H. Clifford.
Emory Washburn.

Henry J. Gardner.
Nathaniel P. Banks.
John A. Andrew.
Alexander H. Bullock.
William Claflin.
William B. Washburn.
William Gaston.

Alexander H. Rice.
Thomas Talbot.
John D. Long.
Benjamin F. Butler.
George D. Robinson.
Oliver Ames.

Lieutenant-Governors.

George Hull.
Henry H Childs.
John Reed.
Henry W. Cushman.
Elisha Huntington.
William C. Plunkett.

Simon Brown.
Henry W. Benchley.
Eliphalet Trask.
John Z. Goodrich.
John Nesmith.
Joel Hayden.
J. Q. A. Brackett.

William Claflin.
Joseph Tucker.
Thomas Talbot.
Horatio G. Knight.
Byron Weston.
Oliver Ames.

An act of 1849 required the Secretary to make
suggestions to his Board and to the Legislature concerning improvements in the present system of public
schools; to visit, as often as other duties permit,
different parts of the Commonwealth for the purpose
of arousing and guiding public sentiment in relation
to the practical interests of education; to collect and
keep in his office school-books and apparatus; to
receive and arrange in his office the reports and
returns of school committees; and receive, preserve
or distribute the State documents in relation to the
public-school system.

Resolves of 1850, 1851, etc., authorized the Board
of Education to appoint agents to visit the several
towns and cities for the purpose of inquiring into
the condition of the schools, conferring with teachers and committees, lecturing upon subjects connected with education, and in general of giving and
receiving information upon such subjects in the
same manner as the Secretary might do if he were
present.

Authority to appoint agents was given to the
Board from year to year until 1860, when the authority was made perpetual.

Under this provision the following persons have
been employed for longer or shorter periods of
time: Nathaniel P. Banks, Charles W. Upham, S. S.
Greene, R. B. Hubbard, J. T. Burrill, Charles
Northend, Horace James, Henry K. Oliver, Daniel
Leach, Richard Edwards, Alpheus Crosby, A. R.
Pope, Cornelius Walker, B. G. Northrop, A. J.
Phipps, George A. Walton, E. A. Hubbard, John
Kneeland, George H. Martin and John T. Prince.

By a law of 1850 the Board of Education was empowered to hold in trust for the Commonwealth any
grant or devise of land, and any donation or bequest
of money or other personal property, made to it for
educational purposes, and was forthwith to pay over
to the treasurer of the Commonwealth for safe keeping and investment all property so received. Such

income as accrues is payable to the Board on the warrant of the Governor.

SCHOOL FUND.

Before referring to the different acts passed since 1837 regulating the distribution of the income of the school fund, it may be well to give a brief statement of the legislation relating to the subject prior to that period.

Reference to school fund prior to 1837.

The Massachusetts school fund was established in 1834. It was created from moneys already in the treasury derived from the sale of lands in the State of Maine, and from the claim of the State on the government of the United States for military services, togther with fifty per centum of all moneys thereafter to be received from the sale of lands in Maine.

School fund created from moneys in the treasury on account of sales of lands in the State of Maine, etc. 1834, 149, § 1.

The act creating the fund restricted its amount to one million dollars, to be invested by the treasurer and receiver-general with the approval of the Governor and Council. The mode of distribution was left to the action of the next Legislature.

Amount of fund restricted to $1,000,000. 1834, 149, § 1.

In the year 1835 a law was passed authorizing the secretary and the treasurer of the Commonwealth to divide the income of the school fund into two parts: to apportion one moiety to the city of Boston and to the towns and districts on the ratio of population; and to apportion the other moiety on the ratio of the amount of money raised by taxation in each town, city and district, for the support of common schools in the next preceding year.

Manner of distributing the income of the school fund, the distribution to be based, one-half upon the population, the other half upon amount of money raised by town. 1835, 149, § 1.

In the year 1839 the mode of distributing the income of the fund was changed by paying to the cities and towns according to the number of persons in such cities and towns between the ages of four and sixteen years, on condition that the school returns and reports be made according to law, and that the towns shall have raised by taxation for the support of schools for the current year at least one dollar and twenty-five cents for each person between the

The distribution based upon number of persons between four and sixteen years of age. 1839, 56, § 3.

ages of four and sixteen years belonging to said town on the first of the preceding May.

In the year 1840 an act was passed distributing the income of the school fund according to the number of persons in the cities and towns.

In 1841 the law was re-enacted distributing the income according to the number of children between four and sixteen years of age.

By an act of 1849 the income was apportioned to the several cities and towns according to the number of persons between the ages of five and fifteen.

In the same year, 1849, the towns and cities were required to raise one dollar and fifty cents for the schooling of each child between five and fifteen years of age, as a condition of receiving a share of the income of the school fund.

In 1851 the act limiting the fund to one million dollars was repealed, and an act was passed allowing it to accumulate until it amounted to one million five hundred thousand dollars.

In 1854 provision was made for the increase of the fund, as follows : —

The Treasurer of the Commonwealth was authorized to transfer to the fund such a number of shares held by the Commonwealth in the Western Railroad Corporation as at one hundred dollars a share shall increase the school fund to one million five hundred thousand dollars.

This year, 1854, it was provided that the annual income of the fund should be distributed, one half to towns, as heretofore provided, and that all appropriations for general educational purposes should be made chargeable to the other half, unless otherwise specially provided for. No sums of money thereafter drawn from the treasury were to be chargeable to the principal of the fund.

In 1859 an act was passed to increase the school fund, and to grant aid to the Museum of Comparative Zoölogy, to Tufts, Williams and Amherst Colleges, and to Wesleyan Academy at Wilbraham, out of proceeds of the sales of the Back Bay lands. Zoölogy and other institutions.

Williams, Amherst and Tufts Colleges were to support each three free scholarships, to be under the control of the Board of Education. 1859, 154, §§ 1-5.

General Statutes, 1860, ch. 36, § 3. The income of the fund applied to the support of public schools shall be apportioned by the Secretary and Treasurer, and paid over by the Treasurer to the treasurers of the several cities and towns. Income to be apportioned by the Secretary of the Board and State Treasurer. G. S., 36, § 3.

General Statutes, ch. 36, § 4. The income of the school fund received by the several cities and towns shall be applied by the school committees thereof to the support of public schools therein; but said committees may, if they see fit, appropriate therefrom any sum not exceeding twenty-five per cent of the same to the purchase of books of reference, maps and apparatus, for the use of said schools. Income to be applied by school committee. May appropriate twenty-five per cent. for apparatus, etc. G. S., 36, § 4. P. S., 46, § 6.

Under this section it becomes the duty of each town treasurer to open an account with the school committee, and to hold the fund received from the State subject to their order.

In 1865 an act concerning the distribution of the income of the school fund provided that the towns may be entitled to a share of it if they have complied with all statutes before existing relating to the distribution, and have raised at least three dollars per capita for all children between five and fifteen years of age. Towns or cities to be entitled must have complied with statutes and have raised $3 per capita between five and fifteen years. 1865, 142, § 1.

1866. Every city and town shall receive seventy-five dollars, and the residue of the moiety of the income of the school fund shall be apportioned among the several cities and towns in proportion to the number of children between five and fifteen years of age, in which towns the district system does not exist. Every city and town to first receive $75. 1866, 208, § 1.

Every town maintaining a high school was exempted from the forfeiture. Exemption from forfeiture. 1866, 208, § 2.

An act of 1867 fixed the time of paying the income of the school fund at the 25th of January. 1867, 98.

1874. Every town whose valuation does not exceed one million dollars shall annually receive two hundred dollars; every town whose valuation is more than one million and does not exceed three million, shall receive one hundred and fifty dollars; and every town whose valuation is more than three million and does not exceed five million, shall receive one hundred dollars. The remainder of said half shall be distributed to all the towns and cities whose valuation does not exceed ten million dollars, in proportion to the number of children between five and fifteen years of age belonging to each city or town.

By an act of 1878 it was provided that their share of the income of the school fund shall be withheld from towns not complying with the laws relating to truancy.

1884. Every town whose valuation does not exceed one-half million dollars shall annually receive three hundred dollars; every town whose valuation is more than one-half million and does not exceed one million, shall receive two hundred dollars; and every town whose valuation is more than one million and does not exceed three million, shall receive one hundred and fifty dollars. The remainder of said half shall be distributed to all the towns and cities whose valuation does not exceed ten million dollars, in proportion to the number of children between five and fifteen years of age belonging to each.

The school fund was established to give aid and encouragement to the common schools. Several methods have been devised for making a just and equal distribution of it, according to the intent of those by whose acts the fund was established.

At the time of the establishment of the school fund, and for some years before, the public schools of the Commonwealth were in a low condition, and were held in low estimation by the people. These facts are made evident by the small amount of money expended for the public education of each child of school age, and by the relatively large number of the children of the State in private schools.

In 1826 the returns from 214 towns show that the children of the public schools were educated at an expense of $1.93 each for the year, while each child attending a private school was supported at an expense amounting to four times that sum. These same towns sent in the same year 117,186 pupils to the public schools, and over 25,000 to the private schools and academies, and there were 3,000 children that did not attend either the public or private schools.

The distribution of the income of the school fund encouraged and enabled the towns to give to their schools a better support than they had before received, and it prepared the way for the appointment of the Board of Education. The reports of the Board and of its Secretary called the attention of the people and the government to the sad condition of public instruction in the State, and the establishment of training schools for teachers was the result. The graduates of these schools introduced improved methods of teaching, and the public-school system began to grow in favor with the people and to enlist their earnest efforts in its administration.

PRESENT CONDITION OF THE SCHOOL FUND.

Cash on hand Jan. 1, 1886,		$72,897 53
Net income for 1886,		137,037 11
		$209,934 64
Paid cities and towns in 1886,	$67,061 46	
Paid educational expenses in 1886,	68,411 78	
Paid to the fund, balance of income, 1885,	5,836 07	
		141,309 31
Cash on hand Dec 31, 1886,		$68,625 33
From which there is to be paid to cities and towns one-half of income for 1886,	$68,518 50	
For expenses of Normal Art School in 1886,	106 83	
		$68,625 33
The Massachusetts School Fund amounted, Jan. 1, 1886, to		$2,710,241 30
Amount of fund, Dec. 31, 1886,		2,715,944 00

NORMAL SCHOOLS.

Various attempts were made prior to the establishment of the Board of Education to secure legislation in favor of normal schools. Reference is made to these attempts in the Fortieth Annual Report of the Board.

Incorporation of Plymouth County Normal School. 1839, 72.

An act to incorporate the Plymouth County Normal School passed the Legislature in 1839. Artemus Hale, Seth Sprague, Jr., Ichabod Morton and others were made the corporation.

Gift of $10,000 for qualifying teachers.

In March, 1838, Hon. Edmund Dwight of Boston, then a member of the Board of Education, offered, through the Secretary of the Board, to give $10,000, "to be expended under the direction of the Board for qualifying teachers for our common schools, on condition that the Legislature would appropriate for the same purpose an equal amount."

Resolve appriated $10,000 for Normal School. 1838, 70.

On the 19th of April, 1838, the Legislature passed resolves accepting Mr. Dwight's proposition, and appropriated $10,000 to be placed at the disposal of the Board of Education, to aid in qualifying teachers for the common schools.

First normal school at Lexington July 3, 1839; West Newton 1844; Framingham, 1852.

A school was opened July 3, 1839, at Lexington. This school was removed to West Newton in 1844, and thence to Framingham in 1852. The removal in each instance took place on account of the increased demand for accommodations.

Second normal school at Barre, 1839.

A second school was opened at Barre, Sept. 14, 1839. The removal of this school to Westfield was

Removed to Westfield; re-opened 1844.

directed May 13, 1843. After a brief suspension, it was re-opened at Westfield, Sept. 4, 1844.

Bridgewater, Normal School opened

A third school was opened at Bridgewater, Sept. 9, 1840.

Salem Normal School. 1854.

A fourth school was opened at Salem, Sept. 14, 1854.

Normal Art School, Boston. 1873.

A school for training in art was opened at Boston Nov. 6, 1873. This school is called the Normal Art School.

The sixth normal school was opened at Worcester, Worcester Normal School. 1874.
Sept. 15, 1874.

The early normal schools were all provided at
first with such buildings as were available. None of
them were built for the schools, nor were they
adapted to their needs.

The Lexington School occupied a small academy
building in that town. On the removal of the school
to West Newton, it was kept in a building purchased
by Josiah Quincy, and known as the Fuller Academy. When at last the school reached Framingham, it found rest in a home of its own.

The Barre School occupied rooms fitted up in the
town hall. On the removal of the school to Westfield, it occupied rooms in the old academy building.
Later it was provided with rooms in the town hall,
and still later it was moved into its own house.

The Bridgewater School was kept for a time in the
town hall. From that place it was moved into a
building of its own, standing on the site of the
present schoolhouse, forming the germ from which
that structure has been developed.

The normal schools were established partly through
the pecuniary aid furnished by the towns in which
they are located. They are maintained entirely by
the State. The money appropriated for their support is derived from the income of the moiety of the
school fund set apart for general educational purposes.

In 1842 a resolve passed the Legislature appro- 1842.
priating $6,000 per year for three years to the sup-
port of the normal schools.

A resolve of 1852 appropriated $6,000, from the Appropria- tion for site and building for normal school at W. Newton. 1852, 63.
proceeds of public lands or school fund, to provide
a more commodious site and building, furniture and
apparatus, for the accommodation of the State Normal School at West Newton.

The appropriations for the normal schools are
increasing year by year, owing to the increased

attendance upon them and the better appliances for teaching furnished.

Boarding-house for Bridgewater Normal School. 1869.

The Legislature of 1869 authorized a loan of $25,000 from the school fund to the Board of Education, to be spent in erecting and furnishing a boarding-hall at Bridgewater for the use of the students.

Boarding-house for Westfield Normal School. 1872.

An appropriation of $75,000 was made in 1872 for the erection and furnishing of a boarding-house for the normal students at Westfield.

Boarding-halls for Framingham Normal School. 1869.

A boarding-hall for the students of the Framingham Normal School was provided in 1869 by a resolve which appropriated for the purpose a sum not exceeding $15,000.

A resolve of 1870 made a further appropriation of $6,500 for furnishing the boarding-hall at Framingham.

1886.

A second boarding-hall was erected at Framingham in 1886, an appropriation of $20,000 being made by the Legislature for the same.

The six normal schools all now have well-constructed buildings conveniently located, and well supplied with the means for teaching.

Three of the schools are provided with commodious and convenient boarding-halls, in which the students find good homes furnished for them at simple cost.

Todd fund applied to normal schools. 1850, 88.

The Todd Normal School fund, the gift of Henry Todd, Esq., of Boston, is used to aid normal pupils. The income is applied by the faculty of the respective normal schools, with the advice and consent of the Board of Education.

Resolve appropriating $1,000 annually to aid normal pupils. 1853, 62.

A resolve of 1853 appropriated $1,000 to each of the four normal schools, to aid those pupils who find it difficult to meet their expenses.

The State has thus shown her faith in the common schools by making liberal appropriations for the training of her teachers. The appropriations for normal schools have been intrusted to the Board of Education. The expenditure has been made with a wise economy and strict regard to the sacred trust imposed. The entire charge of the schools has devolved upon the Board. The service has been all the more grateful for being a labor of love.

TEACHERS' INSTITUTES AND ASSOCIATIONS.

TEACHERS' INSTITUTES.

In 1846 provision was made for teachers' institutes, to be held under direction of the Secretary of the Board. Under this statute an institute could be organized when a reasonable assurance should be given that not less than seventy teachers of common schools shall desire it. The institute, if appointed, was to continue in session for not less than ten days. Expenses were to be paid from the capital of the school fund. *(Meeting of not less than 70 teachers for not less than 10 days. 1846, 99.)*

By an act of 1848 the number of teachers designated as the minimum for holding an institute was fifty. *(Meeting for 50 teachers. 1848, 10. G. S., 35, § 1. P. S., 42, § 1.)*

By act of 1849 the length of time for holding institutes was left to the Board of Education. *(1849, 62. G. S., 35, § 3.)*

COUNTY TEACHERS' ASSOCIATIONS.

In the year 1837 the Essex County Teachers' Association was incorporated; Nehemiah Cleveland, Benjamin Greenleaf, George Titcomb, their associates and successors, being the corporation. *(Essex County Teachers' Association incorporated. 1837, 197.)*

For about eight years this county association had been in active operation. Other county associations have been formed, some of them by direct efforts of the Board of Education, till at present they are found established in every county of the State except Suffolk.

In 1848 county associations of teachers and others holding semi-annual meetings of not less than two days each were allowed fifty dollars a year from the State. *(County associations holding semi-annual meetings to receive $50. 1848, 301. G. S., 36, § 4.)*

By act of 1864 associations were to receive twenty-five dollars, and meetings of not less than two days were to be held annually. *(Annual meetings of two days required. $25 paid. 1864, 58.)*

Meetings of
one day.
P. S., 42, § 4.

It was provided in 1880 that meetings of not less than one day might be held annually, with appropriation from the State, as before.

MASSACHUSETTS TEACHERS' ASSOCIATION.

Convention of
Massachusetts
teachers
called.

A call for a convention of practical teachers to meet at Worcester was issued by the Essex County Teachers' Association, Nov. 3, 1845. The convention met under this call, Nov. 25, 1845, and formed the Massachusetts Teachers' Association.

Massachusetts
Teachers'
Association
incorporated.
1846, 213.

In 1846 the Massachusetts Teachers' Association was incorporated, the incorporators being Oliver Carlton, Samuel Swan and associates.

State appro-
priates $300
annually for 5
years.
1853, 9.

In 1853 aid to the amount of $300 annually for five years was granted by the State to the Massachusetts Teachers' Association.

Appropria-
tion of $900 in
three annual
payments for
sending
"Massachu-
setts Teacher"
to school
boards.
1857, 35.

In 1857 the sum of $900 in three annual payments was granted, on condition that the Association shall furnish a copy of the "Massachusetts Teacher" to each board of school committee in the several cities and towns of the Commonwealth. An appropriation of $600 a year was thus made; and this amount was

Total amount
increased to
$800.
1865, 41.

continued till 1865, from which time the sum of $800, with conditions as above, was appropriated each year till 1875.

Return to ap-
propriation of
$300.
1875, 114.
Res., 1880, 30.
P. S., 42, § 5.

In 1875 the "Massachusetts Teacher" was merged in the "New England Journal of Education." From and after this year an appropriation of $300 was made year by year till 1880, when a

Approval of
Board of Edu-
cation.
Res., 1880, 30.
P. S., 42, § 5.

resolve was passed providing that the sum of $300 shall be paid to the Association annually, subject to the approval of the Board of Education.

AMERICAN INSTITUTE OF INSTRUCTION.

American
Institute of
Instruction.
Appropria-
tion of $300
annually.
Res., 1835, 54.
Res., 1840, 44.

Resolves of 1835 and 1840 respectively appropriated annually for five successive years to the directors of the American Institute of Instruction the sum of $300.

Appropria-
tion discon-
tinued in 1873.

This amount was continued for successive years till 1873, from which time the Institute was made self supporting.

The American Institute of Instruction was incorporated by an act of the Legislature of Massachusetts in 1830. Nominally national, the Institute was virtually limited in scope to New England. That Massachusetts alone for thirty-eight years appropriated even the small sum of $300 a year towards the maintenance of the Institute is one of many illustrations of her abiding faith in institutions for promoting education, and of her great liberality towards them.

American Institute incorporated. See Special Laws, 1830, 67.

SCHOOLS TO BE KEPT.

In 1839 schools were required to be kept at least six months in each year.

Schools required. 1839, 56, § 1. See page 103 of this report.

By an act of the year 1839 provision was made for the employment of female assistants in schools containing fifty scholars as the average attendance, unless the town votes to the contrary.

An act passed in 1882 forbade the granting of licenses for the sale of intoxicating liquors in any place or building within four hundred feet of a building occupied in whole or part by a public school and situated on the same street.

Intoxicating liquors not to be sold within 400 feet of a public school. 1882, 220.

EVENING SCHOOLS.

Provision was made in 1857 for maintaining day or evening schools for persons over fifteen years of age.

Evening schools for persons over 15 yrs. of age. P. S., 44, 7, 12.

A law was passed in 1883 requiring evening schools to be maintained in all towns and cities having ten thousand or more inhabitants.

Cities and towns of 10,000 inhabitants or over to maintain evening schools. G. S., 38, § 7.

Chapter 236 of the Acts of 1886, authorizes the establishment and maintenance of evening high schools in certain cities.

Evening high schools may be established on petition in cities having over 50,000 population.

SECTION 1. Every city of fifty thousand or more inhabitants shall establish and thereafter annually maintain an evening high school, in which shall be taught such branches of learning as the school committee thereof may deem expedient, whenever fifty or more residents, fourteen years of age or over, who desire, and in the opinion of the school committee are competent, to pursue high-school studies, shall petition in writing for a high school, and certify that they desire to attend such school.

School committees to superintend evening high schools.
1886, 236.

SECT. 2. The school committee shall have the same superintendence over such school as they have over day schools; may determine the term or terms in each year and the hours of the evening during which such school shall be kept, and may make such regulations as to the attendance thereat as they may deem proper.

The following cities have a population of more than fifty thousand : Boston, Cambridge, Fall River, Lowell, New Bedford, Worcester.

PRIVATE SCHOOLS.

Private-school teachers to be approved by school committee.
1855, 379.
P. S., 47, § 2.

In 1855, in order that children attending private schools may receive certificates to work in mills, the teachers of such schools must be approved by the school committee.

Private schools to be approved by committee.

Private schools, by a law of 1878, were made subject to the approval of school committees. The teaching must be in the English language, and the committee must be satisfied that the efficiency of these schools is equal to that of the public schools.

1878, 171.
P. S., 47, § 2.

This provision was made for the purpose of complying with the law requiring attendance upon the schools for a certain time.

INSTITUTIONS FOR THE DEFECTIVE CLASSES.

Special institutions to report to Board of Education.
1867, 123.
P. S., 41, 13.

Officers of all literary, scientific or professional institutions of learning, incorporated, supported or aided by the Commonwealth, shall, on or before the first day of June in each year, make a report in writing to the Board of Education of such statistics as the Board shall prescribe. This provision was made in 1867.

Reports of the institutions for deaf, dumb and blind to be made to the board.
1875, 118.
P. S , 41, § 15.

In 1875 it was enacted that such duties with reference to institutions for the instruction of the deaf and the dumb and of the blind as are now vested by law in the Board of State Charities are hereby transferred to and vested in the Board of Education.

The above-named institutions were transferred from the directing care of the Board of State Charities to the superintendence of the Board of Education, that they might be treated as educational rather than as charitable institutions.

TEACHERS.

In 1838 provision was made by statute that the teachers shall be selected by prudential committees, if the town so vote; otherwise, the selection shall be made and the qualifications determined by school committees.

Teachers may be selected by prudential committees by vote of town. 1838, 105.

In 1844 committees were empowered to dismiss teachers at any time.

Teachers may be dismissed by school committees. 1844, 32.

By an act of 1859 school committees alone were authorized to select teachers.

G. S., 38, § 24. P. S., 44, § 30. Teachers to be selected by school committee. 1859, 60.

By Revised Statutes, 1836, a duplicate certificate of his qualifications must be filed with the town treasurer before the teacher can claim his pay. In 1850 the duplicate was required to be filed with the selectmen.

Pay of teachers depends upon certificate. R. S., 23, 14. 1850, 115.

In 1855 the law authorized the teacher to claim his pay at the close of a term.

1855, 126.

An act of 1886 provided that the school committee of any city or town may elect any duly qualified person to serve as a teacher of the public schools during the pleasure of such committee, *provided* such person has served in the public schools of such city or town for a period of not less than one year.

Teachers may be elected during the pleasure of school committee. 1886, 313.

SCHOLARSHIPS.

An act of 1853 established State scholarships for the purpose of educating young men to become principals of high schools.

State scholarships established. 1853, 193.

The act of 1853 establishing scholarships was repealed by an act of 1866, it having been virtually inoperative so far as its beneficent purpose is concerned.

Repeal of act establishing State scholarships. 1866, 3.

STUDIES TO BE PURSUED.

What schools shall be provided by towns of 50 families. By act of 1826, approved March 10, 1827, it was required that each town or district containing fifty families or householders shall be provided with a teacher, of good morals, to instruct children in orthography, reading, writing, English grammar, geography, arithmetic and good behavior, for such term of time as shall be equivalent to one school of six months in each year. As the number of families increased, the length of time increased for which the schools must be kept.

What schools provided by towns of 500 families. If the town had five hundred families, one school additional for all the inhabitants must be kept for ten months each year. In this school, besides the branches aforesaid, the history of the United States, book-keeping by single entry, geometry, surveying and algebra were to be taught. Towns of four thousand inhabitants were to provide instruction also in Latin and Greek, in history, rhetoric and logic.

By towns of 4,000 inhabitants. 1827, 143, § 1. R. S., 23, §§ 1-6.

Instruction in physiology provided for. 1850, 229, §§ 1, 2. Act of 1850 provided for instruction in physiology and hygiene in all cases in which the school committee deem it expedient. It provided that teachers shall be examined in this study.

An act was passed in 1857 prescribing the studies to be taught in the several kinds of schools.

Studies prescribed to be taught in elementary schools. 1839, 56, § 1. 1857, 206, §§ 1-3. R. S., 23, § 1. The branches to be taught in elementary schools: Orthography, reading, writing, English grammar, geography, arithmetic, algebra, history of the United States, good behavior; physiology and hygiene at the option of the school committee.

Studies in lowest class high schools. The branches to be taught in high schools of the lower class: The branches above enumerated; also general history, book-keeping, surveying, geometry, natural philosophy, chemistry, botany, the civil polity of Massachusetts and Latin.

Studies in highest class high schools. G. S., 38, §§ 1, 2. The branches to be taught in high schools of the higher class: The above branches; also Greek and French, astronomy, geology, rhetoric, logic, intellectual and moral philosophy and political economy.

The teaching of drawing and music was made permissible by General Statutes in 1860 ; the teaching of agriculture by act of 1862. Agriculture, drawing and music may be taught. P. S., 44, § 1.

By an act of 1870 the General Statutes were amended so as to include drawing among the branches of learning required to be taught in public schools. Drawing must be taught. 1870, 263, § 1.

It was also provided that every city and town may, and that every one having more than ten thousand inhabitants must make provision for giving free instruction in industrial and mechanical drawing to persons over fifteen years of age, either in day or evening schools, to be under the direction of the school committee. All towns may provide for teaching persons over 15 years old. Towns of over 10,000 inhabitants must. 1870, 263, § 2. P. S., 44, § 1.

By an act of 1871 the Board of Education was directed to report a plan for technical instruction in public schools. Technical instruction in public schools. P. S., 44, §§ 7, 8, 9.

In 1884 training in the use of hand tools was authorized by public statute. Training in use of hand tools. 1884, 69.

Sewing in public schools was permitted by act of 1876. Sewing permitted to be taught. 1876. P. S., 44, § 1.

Physiology and hygiene, with special reference to the effects of alcohol, stimulants and narcotics upon the human system, was, by a law of 1885, made a required study in all public schools. Study of physiology and hygiene made compulsory. 1885. P. S., 44, §§ 1, 2.

TEXT BOOKS.

As early as 1826 the school committee were required to direct what books shall be used in the schools. They could direct what books should be used in particular classes. Text books to be prescribed by school committee. 1826, 143, § 7.

Parents were required to supply the books for their children.

A copy of the Webster's Unabridged or of the Worcester's Quarto Dictionary was furnished to each school in the State by a resolve of 1850. Dictionary furnished to each school. 1850, 99.

By act of 1855 towns were authorized to purchase and loan to the pupils the books used in the schools, also to supply the stationery. The school committee were to take charge of the same. Text books loaned. 1855, 436. P. S., 44, § 40.

Free text
books.
1884, 103.

In the year 1884 towns were required to purchase the books to be used in the schools, and to loan them to the pupils without charge.

BIBLE IN SCHOOLS.

Bible to be
read in public
schools.
1855, 410.
R. S., 23, 23.
G. S., 38, 27.
P. S., 44, 32.

The reading of the Bible in the public schools, in the common English version, was made obligatory by an act of 1855.

No books to
be introduced
favoring any
religious sect.
1862, 57.

In 1862 an act provided that no book favoring any particular religious sect should be introduced into the public schools.

Pupils of pa-
rents having
conscientious
scruples, etc.
1880, 176.

The reading of the Bible without note or comment was required by act of 1880; but such reading was not to be required of any child whose parent or guardian informs the teacher in writing that he has conscientious scruples against it.

LIBRARIES.

District school
libraries.
1837, 147.

In 1837 districts were authorized to raise money to establish and maintain school libraries. Not more than thirty dollars could be assessed in any one year.

Libraries and
apparatus
may be pur-
chased by dis-
trict or town.
1849, 81.

It was enacted in 1849 that any school district or any city or town may raise money for the purchase of libraries and necessary school apparatus.

Statute ap-
propriating
from the
school fund
$15 for dis-
trict libraries.
1842, 74, § 2.

A resolve of 1842 appropriated fifteen dollars to be taken from the school fund for every school district to establish libraries for the use of the public schools.

The Board, in its early years, took an active interest in the establishment and maintenance of libraries in the school districts. Most of these libraries have ceased to exist; town libraries have been substituted.

SCHOOL ATTENDANCE.

Act imposing
fine upon pa-
rent for non-
attendance of
child at
school.

1852. By an act of this year every child between the ages of eight and fourteen years was required to attend school for twelve weeks each year. Six weeks of the twelve must be consecutive.

1852, 240, § 1.
G. S., 41, § 1.
P. S., 47, § 1.

For a violation of this act a fine of twenty dollars was imposed upon the parent or guardian. It was made the duty of the school committee to report violations of the act to the city or town in their annual report. The treasurer of the city or town was to prosecute for violations of the act.

By an act of 1873 the time of attendance was increased from twelve to twenty weeks, and the limit of the age of attendance was changed to be from eight to twelve years. *Time of attendance extended to twenty weeks. Age made eight to twelve. 1873, 279.*

The acts of 1874 changed the age again to be from eight to fourteen years, and divided the twenty weeks of attendance into two terms of ten consecutive weeks. *Age made eight to fourteen. 1874, 233. P.S., 47, §§ 1, 2.*

Provision was made by an act of 1859 for the attendance of children at schools in adjoining towns, under regulations of school committees of said towns. *Pupils may attend schools in adjoining towns. 1859, 89.*

CONVEYANCE OF CHILDREN TO SCHOOL.

In the year 1869 an act was passed permitting towns to raise money to convey children to and from school. *Towns may furnish conveyance to school. 1869, 132. P. S., 27, § 10.*

TRUANT CHILDREN AND ABSENTEES FROM SCHOOL.

An act was passed in 1850 requiring towns to make all needful provisions for the instruction, confinement and discipline of truant children and absentees from school. *Act concerning truants and absentees from school. G. S , 42, §§ 4, 5, 6.*

Under this act towns were required to adopt by-laws, and to provide places for the restraint, discipline and instruction of truants, and the committees were required to appoint truant officers under the by-laws. *P. S., 48, §§ 10, 11, 12, 13, 14, 15, 16.*

Towns and cities were required by act of 1862 to make all needful provisions for truant children who are between seven and sixteen years of age. *Fine of $20 for breach of by-laws.*

A fine of not less than twenty dollars was to be imposed for a breach of the by-laws. Instead of this fine, the person convicted could be sent to an institution provided by the town for the restraint of truant children. *Truant may be committed instead. 1862, 207, § 2. 1873, 279, § 1. 1874, 233, § 1. G. S., 41, § 1. P. S., 47, § 1.*

By subsequent legislation (1873) the period of time was changed to be from five to fifteen years.

An act of 1873 provided that, on petition of three or more cities or towns in any county, the county commissioners shall establish a truant school for the county.

By an act of 1881 it was provided that certain counties, and by act of 1884 that two, three or four contiguous counties, may establish a union truant school, on petition of three or more cities in each of said counties.

The act of 1884 reads as follows : —

SECTION 1. Three or more cities or towns in each of two, three or four contiguous counties may require the county commissioners of such counties to establish union truant schools, as provided by section fourteen of chapter forty-eight of the Public Statutes.

EMPLOYMENT OF CHILDREN.

An act passed in 1842, in addition to an act of 1836, provided that no child shall be employed in any manufacturing establishment more than ten hours a day, if said child be under twelve years of age.

An act was passed in 1876 concerning the employment of children in manufacturing establishments.

No child under ten years of age was thereafter to be employed in any such establishment.

No child under twelve was to be employed while the public schools are in session.

No child under fourteen years was to be employed unless he had attended school twenty weeks during the year next preceding.

By an act of 1883, section one of chapter forty-eight of the Public Statutes was amended so as to read : —

SECTION 1. No child under ten years of age shall be employed in any manufacturing, mechanical or mercantile establishment in this Commonwealth; and no child under twelve years of age shall be so employed during the hours in which the public schools are in session in the city or town in which he resides. Any parent or guardian who permits such employment shall for such offence forfeit not less than twenty nor more than fifty dollars, for the use of the public schools of the city or town. factuiing and other estab-
lishments.
1883, 224.

The above section was amended in 1885, by striking out "during the hours" and inserting "at any time during the days." Amended.
1885, 67.

Care and Education of Neglected Children.

Public Statutes, chap. 48, sects. 18–21, make provision for the care of neglected children under sixteen years of age. If such persons are suffered to be growing up without salutary parental control and education, or in circumstances exposing them to lead idle and dissolute lives, any town may, and all towns and cities of five thousand or more inhabitants shall, make all such by-laws respecting such children as shall be deemed most conducive to their welfare and to the good order of the town or city. Towns to make provi-
sion for care,
etc , of neg-
lected chil-
dren under
sixteen years.
1866, 283, § 1.
1867, 2, § 1.
1878, 217, § 1.
P. S , 48, § 18.

Suitable persons must be appointed to make complaints of violations of by-laws adopted for the care of such neglected children. The persons so appointed shall be authorized to make complaints and carry into execution the judgments thereon. Suitable per-
sons to be ap-
pointed to
make com-
plaints, etc.
1883, 245.
P. S., 48, 19.

School Committees.

The custom of electing special officers to take charge of the schools can be traced to the first half of the seventeenth century. Until the year 1826 the election of these officials by the towns was optional. In this year every town was required by statute to elect three, five, or seven school committee-men, and towns containing four thousand inhabitants were empowered to choose an additional number not to exceed five. Towns re-
quired to
elect school
committees.
1826, 170, § 1,
1827, 143, § 5.

Change in
number of
committee.
R. S. 23,
§ 10, 12.
In 1836, by the Revised Statutes, the duty of electing school committees was reaffirmed, and the authority was given to choose six additional members instead of five.

Committee to
make annual
report to
town.
1838, 105.
Contract with
teachers.
1838, 105.
G. S., 38, § 23.
P. S., 44, § 28.
Keep perma-
nent record-
book.
1838, 105.
G. S., 38, § 22.
P. S., 44, § 27.
In 1838 it was made the duty of school committees to present annual reports to their towns, to contract with the teachers of the public schools, and to keep a permanent record-book of their proceedings. They were allowed one dollar a day for their services.

Committees
required to
ascertain the
number of
children in
town.
1839, 56, § 3.
1849, § 117.
1874, 303, § 1.
P. S., 46, § 3.
In 1839 it was provided that the school committee shall annually, in the month of May, ascertain, from actual examination or otherwise, the number of persons between the ages of four and sixteen years belonging to such town on the first day of May. The ages were subsequently changed, by act of 1849, to " five and fifteen."

Towns losing
their income
from school
fund, may
withhold com-
pensation
from school
committee.
1847, 183.
G. S., 40, § 12.
P. S, 46, § 11.
By act of 1847 any city or town may withhold from the school committee compensation for services, if, through failure of the school committee to comply with the provisions of the law relating to school returns, the town shall forfeit its share of the income of the school fund.

Vacancies in
board of
school com-
mittee how
filled.
G. S, 38, § 18.
P. S., 44, §§
22, 23.
An act passed in 1851 provided that vacancies in school committees shall be filled by the remaining members of the Board with the selectmen of the town, or, in case of cities, with the mayor and aldermen.

Private-school
teachers sub-
ject to ap-
proval by
school com-
mittee.
1855, 379.
See also
1873, 279, § 1.
1878, 171, § 1.
P. S., 47, § 2.
In 1855 it was made the duty of school committees to ascertain the qualifications of teachers of private schools before permitting children from these schools to be employed in manufacturing establishments.

Children to be
vaccinated.
1855, 414.
G. S., 41, § 8.
P. S., 48, § 9.
In 1855 it was provided by statute that the school committee shall not allow any child to be admitted to or connected with the public schools who has not been duly vaccinated.

Board to con-
sist of three
or a multiple
of three.
1857, 270,
The act of 1857 fixed the number of members of the Board at three or some multiple of three; it provided that after the first election one-third of the

members should be elected annually, each for a term
of three years.

An act of 1860 made provision for increasing and
diminishing the number of the school committee.

To change
number.
G. S., 38, 21.
P. S., 44, 26.

In 1859 it was enacted that school committees of
the towns shall print their annual reports in octavo
form, the page to be of the size of that in the report
of the Board of Education, and send two copies to
Secretary.

Form of
school re-
ports; two
copies to sec-
retary.
1859, 57.
G. S., 40, § 6.
P. S., 46, § 8.

The school committees were required by act of the
same year, 1859, to select and contract with teachers, to obtain full and satisfactory evidence of their
good moral character, and by personal examination
to ascertain their qualifications for teaching and governing.

School com-
mittee to have
satisfactory
evidence of
good charac-
ter and ability
of teachers.
1859, 60.
G. S., 38, § 23.
P. S., 44, § 28.

Another act of this year, 1859, provided for the
attendance of children living in an adjoining town
remote from any public school, under such regulations as the school committee may agree upon and
prescribe ; and the school committee of the town in
which such children reside is authorized and required
to pay out of the appropriations of said town for
the support of schools such sum as may have been
agreed upon.

Children liv-
ing remote
from schools
in one town
may attend in
adjoining
town.
1859, 89.
G. S., 41, § 5.
P. S , 47, § 6.

Under an act of this year, 1859, abolishing the
district system, it was provided that the school committees shall have and exercise the control and
supervision of all the public schools and schoolhouses
within their respective towns.

Abolition of
district sys-
tem.
Towns to
take property
and dispose of
same.
1859, 252.

Another act of the year 1859 provided that if the
school committee of any city or town shall neglect
to make the report and returns required by law, and
transmit the same on or before the last day of April
in each year, said city or town shall forfeit ten per
cent. of its share of the school fund ; and if they
shall fail to make and transmit the same before the
first day of June in each year, said city or town shall
forfeit its whole share of the income of the school
fund, and in addition thereto a sum not less than one
hundred nor more than two hundred dollars.

Penalty for
neglect of
town or city
to make re-
port.
1859, 238.
G. S., 40, § 9.

Income of
school fund to
be applied by
school com-
mittees.
Twenty-five
per cent. for
maps and ap-
paratus.
G. S., 36, § 4.
P. S., 43, § 6.

See Gen. Stat., chap. 36, sect. 4. The income of the school fund shall be applied by school committees for the support of the public schools. The committees may, if they see fit, appropriate twenty-five per cent of the income to the purchase of books of reference, maps and apparatus, for use in the schools.

Agriculture
taught at op-
tion of school
committee.
1862, 9.
P. S., 44, § 1.

In 1862 provision was made for teaching agriculture, by lectures or otherwise, in all the public schools in which the school committee deem it expedient.

Office of
school com-
mittee in cit-
ies to com-
mence at
same time
with that of
city council.
1865, 134.

An act of 1865 provided that the term of office of school committees in cities, where no different provision had been before made, should commence at the same time from year to year as is provided in regard to members of the several city councils.

Women may
serve on
school com-
mittee.
1874, 389.
P. S., 44, § 21.

An act of 1874 provided that women may serve upon school committees, it being declared that no person is ineligible on account of sex.

Committee to
direct what
books to be
used and pre-
scribe course
of studies.
1876, 47.
P. S., 44, § 33.

An act of 1876. The school committee shall direct what books shall be used in the public schools, and shall prescribe, as far as is practicable, a course of studies and exercises to be used in the schools.

Change of
text books.
P. S., 44, § 33.

Provisions of this act fixed the conditions upon which a change of text books may be made.

School com-
mittee to visit
schools at
stated times;
purpose of
visits.
1876, 186.
G. S., 38, § 26.
P. S., 44, § 31.

A further provision was made by an act of this year, 1876, that in towns having no school superintendent the committee — some one or more of them — shall visit all the public schools of the town on some day during the first week after the opening of such schools, and also on some day during the two weeks preceding the close of the same; and shall also visit, without giving previous notice to the instructors, all the public schools in the town once a month, the purpose being to examine the schools for their efficiency.

Private
schools to be
approved by
school com-
mittees.
Thorough-
ness and prog-
ress to equal

An act of 1878 provided that, for the purpose of compliance with the law requiring attendance upon school for a certain time each year, if such attendance be at a private school, the school committee shall have satisfactory evidence that the teaching in such the same in public schools. 1878, 171. P. S., 47, § 2. See also, 1855, 379. 1873, 279. 1876, 52. schools corresponds in thoroughness and efficiency with the teaching in the public schools, and that the progress made by the pupils in studies required by law is equal to the progress made during the same time in the public schools; and such teaching shall be in the English language.

School committees of towns and cities were re- Committees to report concerning provisions for truants. 1878, 234, § 2. quired by act of 1878 to report to the Secretary of the Board whether their respective towns and cities have made necessary provisions relating to truancy.

In 1881 the right to vote for school committees School committee suffrage granted to women. 1881, 191. P. S., § 3. was granted to women.

In 1884 it was enacted that the school committee of every city and town shall purchase at the expense Text books and school supplies to be loaned to all pupils free of charge. 1884, 103. of such city or town text books and other school supplies used in the schools; and said text books and supplies shall be loaned to the pupils of said public schools free of charge, subject to such rules and regulations as to care and custody as the school committee may prescribe.

The third section of this act provided that the act shall take effect on the first day of August, 1884.

By an act of 1886 the school committee of any Teachers' tenure of office to be at pleasure of committee. 1886, 313. city or town may elect any duly qualified person to serve as a teacher in the public schools of such city or town during the pleasure of such committee: *provided* such person has served as a teacher in the public schools of such city or town for a period of not less than one year.

CONTAGIOUS DISEASES AND VENTILATION.

By a law enacted in 1855 school committees were Children to be duly vaccinated on entering school. 1855, 414, § 2. G. S., 41, § 8. P. S., 47, § 9. not to allow to be admitted to or connected with the public schools any child who has not been duly vaccinated.

An act passed in 1884 provided that school com- Duties of committee in reference to children exposed to contagious diseases. 1884, 64. mittees shall not allow any child to attend the public schools while any member of the household to which such pupil belongs is sick of small-pox, diphtheria or scarlet fever, or during two weeks after the death, recovery or removal of such sick person.

Certificate of physician or board of health required in case of exposure to contagious diseases. 1885, 198.

In 1885 it was provided that in case of a pupil's returning to school after exposure to contagious diseases, as in preceding act of 1884, he shall be required to present a certificate from the attending physician or board of health of the facts necessary to entitle him to admission.

Ventilation of schoolhouses. Agents to report upon. 1853, 27.

A resolve passed in 1853 required the secretary of the Board of Education to instruct the agents to examine the schoolhouses in reference to their ventilation, and report to the board.

SUPERINTENDENTS.

At the time of the establishment of the Board of Education, the schools had no other supervision than that provided for by school committees.

Superintendents of schools may be employed by towns. 1854, 314.

In 1854 towns and cities were empowered to appoint superintendents of schools, and fix their salaries.

School committees to fix salaries. 1870, 117.

A law of 1870 authorized school committees to fix the salary of the superintendents.

Towns may unite to choose a superintendent. 1870, 183, § 2. P. S., 44, 45.

An act of the same year, 1870, provided that two or more towns may unite to appoint the same person as superintendent of schools.

DISTURBING SCHOOLS AND INJURING SCHOOLHOUSES.

Disturbance of schools punished. 1849, 59. G. S., 165, § 23. P. S., 207, § 23.

In 1849 an act was passed which imposed a heavy penalty for disturbing schools and public meetings.

Of injury to school buildings. 1857, 222. G. S., 161, § 67. P. S., 203, § 78.

1857. An act of this year imposed a fine not exceeding $500, or imprisonment not more than one year, for defacing, marring or injuring schoolhouses, churches or other public buildings, used for purposes of education or religious instruction. The law applies also to out-buildings, fences, wells or other appurtenances to said buildings.

DISTRICT SYSTEM.

On account of the dispersed situation of the inhabitants of the towns in the last century, it was found inconvenient to collect the children and youth into one place for their instruction. Accordingly, it was enacted in 1789 that a division may be made of the towns into school districts. The districts were not made corporations in fact until 1799, and not in name until 1817; and not till 1827 were they authorized to elect prudential committees. The act of 1789, "so innocent in language and name," to use the words of Secretary Boutwell, from subsequent legislation became the source of much evil. Mr. Mann said, "I consider the law of 1789, authorizing towns to divide themselves into districts, the most unfortunate law, on the subject of common schools, ever enacted in the State."

Establishment of school districts.

Reference to, by Secretaries Boutwell and Mann.

By act of 1850 towns were directed how to proceed in disposing of the schoolhouses, in case it was deemed expedient to abolish the districts.

Disposition of school property if districts are abolished. 1850, 286. G. S., 39, § 3.

An act of 1853 provided for the discontinuance of districts at the discretion of the school committee, unless the town, as often as once in three years, votes to retain them. In case of their abolition, the management of the schools shall devolve upon the school committee of the town.

School committees may discontinue school districts, unless town votes to retain. 1853, 153. G. S., 39, § 4.

In 1859 the district system was abolished.

Abolition of district system. 1859, 252.

The above act was repealed at the autumn session of the same legislature by which it was enacted.

Repeal of above act. G. S., ch. 182.

In 1869 the district system was again abolished.

Abolition of. 1869, 110, 423.

By act of 1870 any town whose districts had been abolished by the above act, or under the act of a previous date, might, at a meeting called for the purpose within two years from the passage of the act of 1869, by a vote of two-thirds of its legal voters, present and voting thereon, re-establish such school districts.

Re-establishment of districts. 1870, 196.

The final act abolishing the district system was passed in 1882. The act took effect Jan. 1, 1883.

Final act abolishing the district system. 1882, 218.

Thus finally disappeared from the statutes of the Commonwealth all provisions concerning a system of school administration which every secretary and agent of the Board had found to be the greatest obstacle to any intelligent progress in the schools.

General Remarks.

The foregoing abstract of the school laws, passed during the last fifty years, shows that careful attention has been given to every phase of our common-school interests.

These laws relate to the support of schools by the towns from the income of a public tax; to the aid and encouragement offered in their support by the distribution of the annual income of the school fund; to the duties of school committees in establishing schools, in supplying them with competent teachers, with suitable means of teaching, with comfortable and convenient schoolhouses and with proper courses of study; to the compulsory attendance of all the children of school age; to the establishment of normal schools for the training of teachers; to the support of schools for the deaf and blind and feeble-minded; to the introduction of the industrial element into public-school exercises; to teaching temperance as a cardinal virtue, to be practised as well as understood; to the tenure of office of teachers who behave well in the discharge of their responsible duties, and to the appointment of school superintendents.

Most of the school laws now on the statute book are the results of experience, and need only to be faithfully executed to prove the wisdom of their enactment.

A careful study of the school legislation of the State for the past fifty years reveals the facts that progress towards better things has always been very slow, but at the same time very constant. Some changes may be made at once; but those that depend on a growth, and are in human beings, require time and persistent effort for their accomplishment.

The schools are State institutions, and are controlled by the laws of the State; therefore, the progress made in the administration of their affairs must depend on the progress effected in public opinion. This progress, if healthy and wise, must of necessity be slow. It was a long time after the normal schools were established before their graduates were allowed full liberty to practise their improved methods of teaching. The objective method has pushed its way into the schools only by slow advances. The old school-district system contended many years for its continued existence, and came back to life several times after it was supposed to be completely dead. It is still maintaining a sort of spiritual existence in some of the small towns. The permissive law, authorizing the towns to form themselves into districts for superintendents, has been in force for nearly twenty years, and yet the towns have not to a very great extent availed themselves of the advantages of efficient supervision.

But notwithstanding all that may be said of our tardiness, the progress we are making towards a higher life in our means and methods of public instruction is important and encouraging. There is no longer any opposition to the practice of the best methods of teaching. Trained teachers are everywhere in demand for the public schools. The normal schools are cheerfully sustained as a necessary part of our system of public schools. All believe that the children should be educated together, that they may become homogeneous members of a society whose free institutions they are to perpetuate; and no necessary expenditure of money and labor is considered too great for the promotion of popular education.

The Province of the Public School.

There is doubtless a wide difference of opinion among educators concerning the ends which the public schools should labor to attain.

Some affirm that the public schools have failed to accomplish their purpose unless they have prepared the children for their special places in life, or have trained them in some of the special applications of their active power.

Others believing that in the general education of every child he should be considered an end unto himself, rather than an instrument for the production of some end outside himself, would direct him to those exercises which have a tendency to produce a symmetrical development of all his faculties. This, they think, is the legitimate work of the public schools, and the direct end to be sought in all disciplinary study.

In the first case the educator would direct his attention to the communication of knowledge and to training his pupil in some of the occupations of life. In the second case his mind is fixed on what he can lead his pupil to become.

On account of the existence of these two opinions, and of the two plans of instruction that grow out of them, we hear much on the one hand of the advantages of practical knowledge, and on the other of the value of a symmetrical development of the mind.

It seems necessary, therefore, for those who have anything to do in forming public opinion on educational methods, to determine what the public schools of the country should attempt to accomplish for their pupils.

This appears the more necessary when we become aware that a choice of ends to be secured by school-life will determine what subjects of study or occupations shall become the occasions of public-school exercises.

If it is the function of the public school to prepare the children for some special mode of gaining a living, those exercises may be introduced which will train them to some special employment. This would graft upon our common-school work the professional and industrial elements, and the schools would be no longer common schools. The next generation of citizens would be composed of men who might practice and pursue the trades with skill, but all would be done with special reference to supplying the wants of life. That intelligent desire for a higher life of the individual and a higher civilization of the State, which is strong in every rightly trained mind, would be obscured, and men would be moved chiefly by the mechanical and animal principles of action. But no system of public schools can be maintained for private utility alone. All social institutions must be founded on the idea of promoting public utility also, and in the administration of the system the public good must not be sacrificed for private ends.

It is because there is a human education which should precede the acquisition of special professional or industrial skill, and which will have a tendency to elevate the individual above the narrowing effects of any profession, or trade, or occupation, and bring him to his special work with a trained mind, a strong will and a manly spirit, that we may establish public educational institutions, to be supported by a general tax, and may gather all the children into them for a common course of study. This sort of human training is what John Stuart Mill says every generation owes to the next, as that on which its civilization and worth will principally depend. It should be the ultimate end of public instruction to so direct the attention of the learners to themselves as individuals, and to their relations to one another as social beings and members of the State, that they will become true men, intelligent, loyal, and virtuous in all the relations of private and public life. If this solid foundation can be established, men will turn to their trades as branches of intelligence and not as mere trades, and they will pursue them with a conscientious regard not only for their own highest good, but also for the highest good of all with whom they hold any relations.

Theodore Parker once said to a convention of teachers in his own State, that " to the instructed man his trade is a study, — the tools of his craft are books, his farm a gospel, eloquent in its sublime silence; his cattle and his corn his teachers, the stars his guides to virtue and to God; and every mute and every living thing by shore or sea, a heaven-sent prophet to refine his mind and his heart."

The spirit which the individual brings from the public school to his special work is of more importance, as far as either public or private utility is concerned, than that sort of special skill which public schools will ever be able to communicate. For this spirit will determine the use he will make of his skill after it is acquired.

Mill says that if we can succeed in the disciplinary schools in making sensible men, they will be sure to make of themselves sensible laborers in the pursuit of whatever occupation they may choose.

After the disciplinary studies have been taken, then the industrial, technical and professional schools should open their doors and offer to all who desire to enter, the advantages of a special education.

We now have in the Commonwealth such schools, — the best that human ingenuity and generosity have thus far been able to establish; and the way should be made easy to their instruction for all who desire a technical training. But these institutions have a right to demand that those who apply for admission to their classes shall already know the elementary facts of science, — the processes by which the mind passes from particular to general knowledge, and the principles and rules which govern the use and construction of the language we speak. They have also a right to require, of those who apply for technical instruction, that training of the faculties which enables them to think accurately and to behave with all the proprieties of a well-ordered public and private life.

It has been found that those who take up the work of preparing for their special places in life with minds trained to observe, to analyze and to reason, joined with that self-control which enables one to turn his full attention to whatever he desires to do, soon outstrip all others by what they are able to accomplish.

Boys have been known to pass through the preparatory schools and the university with credit to themselves as scholars in the branches of learning pursued in those institutions. In their courses of study they were trained to use their active power in gaining a personal knowledge of the real objects and subjects of their thoughts. In this way they formed the habit of accurate observation for facts, and of performing with skill all those acts by which the mind passes from individual experiences to a knowledge of general truth. They left the university with that enthusiasm for practical life which a consciousness of the power of self-activity and a love for excellence always produce. Their collegiate education had not made them shiftless or indolent, or despisers of hard, honest labor. Their acquired knowledge had excited in them a love for more knowledge. The development of their faculties and their modes of thinking had created within them the power of an intelligent and indefinite progress. With this general preparation for any application of their active power they entered the mills in a manufacturing town, to learn all the mechanical processes that work up the raw material into the finished product, and with the idea of some time becoming the directing agents.

The most menial service known to the business was performed with the skill which intelligence communicates to the eye and hand, and with the pleasure which a foresight of good results adds to even manual employment.

They were in actual contact with that which they were to understand. No manual exercises disconnected from any real material products were perverting their practice. With minds trained to observe and to generalize, by the exercises of the schools, now directed to the particular operations of their business, they at once became conscious of what must be generally true.

This power of generalization, the product of right training in the elementary and scientific schools, enabled them to pass easily by all those who see only what is actually before their eyes.

The experiences and testimony of these young persons and of their overseers prove that general intelligence and the power of self-control form the true basis of all high success in the practical applications of active power.

With this basis a course in the technical schools would have given them a more direct and easy way to experience and skill.

The term "practical" is sometimes applied to knowledge. This use of language often leads us into error, for by it we are in danger of attributing to knowledge that which belongs to power only. The most practical men in the world are those who have the largest and most symmetrical development of their active power. A philosophical system of education, then, should provide for a general cultivation of the individual, as a human being, before his activities are turned into an unnatural channel by the pursuit of any trade or profession.

But the idea of introducing into the public school any exercises that have for their immediate end to train the children for special places in life, has been quite generally abandoned, and for two reasons : —

1st. It has been discovered that a citizen of a free State has no special place for which he is to be prepared, and to which he is to be assigned. The place that he is to fill is to be determined not by the accidents of birth, of race, or of wealth, but by the qualities of his mind and the use he makes of his power. The children as they enter the public schools do not bring with them the facts from which the teachers may infer what special instruction the future of each one will require.

2d. There is a growing sentiment in favor of directing public instruction towards that general development of the individual which will make a man of him, and in accomplishing this end fit him to enter with intelligence upon any service to which his capacities and his inclinations may finally lead him.

It seems now to be generally admitted that any system of public instruction that does not make human development, with all that is implied in it, an end, is false in theory and a failure in practice. To justify the support of a system of public schools by a general tax, there must be some common end which they are adapted to accomplish, and which is necessary to the well-being of the people considered to be citizens of the State. This is the only solid ground upon which the public school may rest and expect public support.

Suppose, then, it be the concurrent opinion of those best able to judge, that the proper function of the public school is to furnish the occasions of a symmetrical human development, it still remains to be determined what are these occasions.

Human development is produced by the right exercise of power. In school the occasions of this exercise are objects and subjects of thought. These collected and rightly arranged constitute our public-school courses of study.

The schools are criticised for the poor quality of their products. Their graduates, it is said, pass out of their classes into active life with grave defects in their education. They know something of books, but they neither have the ability nor the inclination to produce anything. They can understand what is explained to them, but cannot invent for themselves. They may have some power of thinking, but they cannot realize their thoughts in any product outside their own minds. Their capacities have been trained, but their faculties have been neglected. The criticism, while it is largely the product of an active imagination, has some foundation in fact, and directs our attention especially to one defect, charged against the work of the schools. This defect consists of a failure to train the children to an independent use of their powers. It is proposed to remedy this defect by adding to our public-school exercises a manual element, in the form of training in the use of mechanical tools.

The most enlightened advocates of the new education, as it is sometimes called, would not occupy the attention of the public school with manual exercises for the sake of the manual skill which would result from them, but for the sake of that general development of active power, which an orderly use of tools is said to be adapted to produce. For no other reason than this could the practice with mechanical tools find a legitimate place in the public schools.

Admitting that the defects supposed actually exist, it does not follow that they are due to defective courses of study, nor that they may be removed by adding the operations of the workshop to the list. Both of these things are assumed, but neither of them has yet been proved to be true.

Mere manual dexterity without reference to invention or construction is the product of imitation; to produce it requires simply a long practice in imitating a few mechanical movements that are first made by a master, for examples to be followed. After a time the states of mind that give origin to the skilful movements of the body are hardly objects of consciousness at all, and the individual moves on under the influence of the mechanical principle of action.

Great manual skill is not unfrequently found with those whose general intelligence is not of the highest order. In our experience we find instances of the existence of the one without the other.

Some minds are conscious of that knowledge only which they have obtained by experience, and of that power only which they have acquired by repetition. They may become skilled in imitating, but they will be wanting in independent and progressive power. They will also be wanting in that general intelligence which is necessary for the regulation of their private conduct as Christians, or of their public acts as members of a free state. It was a significant remark made by one who had devoted his life to the promotion of technical and industrial education, that we send missionaries to countries the skill of whose artisans is the admiration and envy of the missionaries themselves.

The public schools of Massachusetts were established that the learning necessary to the successful practice of self-government might not be buried in the graves of the fathers; that the learning necessary to set the people free from the bonds of those prejudices that enthrall the reason and the liberty of man might not be lost.

It appears from what has been said that in every complete system of public instruction ample provision should be made for the cultivation of general intelligence before the attention is directed to any special mode of life. This is because the individual is of more consequence to himself as a well-developed man than he is as a mechanical instrument, and because he is more valuable to the State as an intelligent and virtuous citizen than he can be as a skilful artisan. It does not appear that the cultivation of mere mechanical dexterity holds any necessary relation to general intelligence or to virtue. It may exist apart from all those states of mind and body which fall within the legitimate province of the public school to produce. It does not appear to be necessary to prepare the individual to pursue his disciplinary studies with greater facility, or to enter upon the race of life with the ability to acquire for himself the highest order of either professional or industrial skill.

A distinguished president of an industrial institution recently read a paper before a large convention of public-school teachers upon the topic entitled " The Workshop in the Public School." He says that " For many years I have worked to develop the material and technical relation of education. I have sought so to direct both my own work and that of my pupils that there might ever be an open bridge between the theories of science and the familiar facts of every-day life, that each might be better developed by constant contact with the other. It may be that I have not worked as earnestly as I might have done; but I have not been able to discern such valuable results from hand culture as my friends seem to find. I do not find that the exact construction of a box leads to the exact construction of an English sentence, but that mechanical students need as much drill in writing as any other. I have not found that students in mechanical courses were especially good in their mathematical work. On the contrary, I do find that the best workers in wood and metal are they who have proved that they have clear thoughts, and can express them clearly, and they who have shown large mathematical ability. Is it not possible, in these materialistic days, we push the methods of the laboratory too far? May not the gross and material concepts gathered in the shop so stand as to obscure the clearer and exacter intellectual concepts?"

Says another most distinguished authority: " The fundamental idea of our theory of mental education is, as I think, that of the superiority of man to his uses." " Our primal thought has been to develop the individual man roundly and fully in himself." " The service which he does for the world is the natural outgrowth of what he is." This is the language of experience and philosophy. It directs our attention to the use of other means than the workshop for a proper modification of the work now done in the public schools. What changes, then, do we need in the conduct of the public schools, that they may do their own work in the most productive manner? If the defect consists in a failure to cultivate practical power in the minds of the children, then the reform we need is not so much in courses of studies as in the method employed in presenting these courses to the learner's mind.

If it is true, as affirmed, that the children are not able to do any independent work when they leave the schools, it is because they were not permitted to work independently in their class exercises. A skilful analysis of the mind of a school graduate will expose the processes to which it has been subjected during the periods of its tuition. In the examination we should inquire for the nature of the knowledge acquired, and for the kind of training the faculties have received. Pupils who have been brought up on books alone, will show when they take their places in the world that the world is a new object of thought.

The words of a book, if understood, direct attention to the ideas which they name, and not necessarily to anything beyond them; one may use a book and understand it, and still be ignorant of the objects it describes.

From these statements it appears that in the acquisition of knowledge, words were never intended to take the place of things. When used exclusively in the schools, they seem to close the senses and the understanding against the true objects of knowledge, and the individual passes through the world without seeing it. Again, if we turn our attention to the effect on the mind produced by the abstract use of language in study, we shall find that such a use is adapted to cultivate the passive powers only. The mind is active in receiving effects whenever it uses language as a substitute for objects as occasions for ideas. In such a case its labor is simply to discover the ideas invented by other minds. The result of such an exercise of the faculties is to prepare them to obtain information rather than knowledge; to feel impressions, but not to produce them; to be controlled, but not to govern; to imitate the acts of others, but not to invent an independent course of conduct.

All this is changed when things take the place of words. Then the mind becomes conscious of knowledge, and of obtaining it by its own efforts. Under a system of objective teaching the learner is brought in direct contact with whatever he is to know, — with natural objects, language, abstract truth and states of mind. These are all made objects of consciousness as a condition of knowledge. The pupil in this way becomes an original investigator. He is trained to handle the objects of his investigation. He learns the true method of thinking by using it, and in time he will 'find the source of his activity within himself. An individual trained in this way will acquire a knowledge of the facts of science by the use of his own observing powers; he will become skilled in analyzing the objects of his study by practice in analyzing them, and so will furnish his mind with that elementary knowledge which will form the basis of scientific classifications and of reasoning for general truth. This training leads to self-control and to a preparation for taking up the work of life with a good prospect of success. In addition to the objective study of things, of which I have spoken, we have two exercises in the schools that are especially adapted to train the mind to a skilful use of the eye and the hand. I refer to drawing, and to the practice by the pupils of constructing their own simple illustrative apparatus. Drawing is the language of form, and may take the place of written speech as a mode of expression. It implies a careful and prolonged observation of things to be described. It presents occasions for a free exercise of judgment, imagination and invention. It is one of the best means of cultivating the taste by requiring that exercise of the faculties upon which the activity of taste depends, and by directing attention to the beautiful in the works of nature and art.

In constructing the means of reproducing physical phenomena to be observed, the mind is most thoroughly exercised in the study of the phenomena themselves. The exercise of making the apparatus is not now a simple imitation of a few mechanical motions; it is an invention of the means of illustrating ideas, and of presenting the phenomena of nature in a convenient form for a prolonged and systematic observation.

Our schools are overcrowded with work already. In the elementary grades there seems to be no time for the systematic study of the qualities of objects, nor for the application of the knowledge thus gained to a systematic observation of natural objects, nor for such an exercise of the faculties as will add to their original state a facility in acting.

In most schools there is no opportunity given for acquiring, in a philosophical way, an orderly knowledge of the facts of any of the sciences. Even language itself is learned as a collection of words, rather than as a means of expressing ideas.

As a result of these omissions there is a failure to train the powers of observation and analysis, upon whose culture and products all future scientific study, all true exercise of the reflective powers, and all high success in the operations of practical life will depend.

It is a common criticism that pupils pass from the elementary to the scientific schools with little or no preparation for the pursuit of scientific knowledge, — that the high schools, the technical schools and the colleges are compelled to stop in their courses and teach the facts of science before scientific study is possible.

It is urged that sewing and cooking should take their places among the branches of learning and practice pursued in the public schools, as a matter of plain necessity. If our civilization and the conditions of our social life render it necessary, then let these occupations be taken in the public schools as a burden upon them, but not as in harmony with the spirit or work peculiar to these institutions. It should be the aim of every wise educator to so train those under his care that when they come to take direction of home affairs, they will perform with skill and fidelity all the duties of home life; especially the duties of preparing in a proper manner food and clothing for the nourishment and protection of the body.

The object of public-school life, then, is not to teach special professions nor occupations nor trades, nor to practice those exercises which produce mere manual dexterity, but to develop the child and bring him to his special work with trained faculties and an honest purpose.

After the powers are sufficiently unfolded, and good habits are formed, and independent ability to acquire knowledge from the study of things and information from communication with other minds have been acquired; after the foundations for a true manhood have been established by the disciplinary exercises of the public schools, — then let the technical and industrial schools offer to all who desire it, the opportunity of preparing for special places in life.

The cities and large towns may establish industrial schools where the school population, who cannot be trained at home, may have the opportunity offered to them of acquiring manual skill. Technical schools may also be organized for those who, having passed through their disciplinary studies, desire to obtain the advantages of a technical education. But the public common schools of the State must not be confused and burdened with work of the home, or of society, or of the church. These schools will fail of accomplishing their purpose, and will lose their hold on public confidence, if they attempt to teach that knowledge which is not necessary for all to know, or to produce that cultivation which is not necessary for all to acquire. The common schools are necessary for the State, special schools for the individual. The one should be made universal and the attendance upon them compulsory; the other should be offered to all who desire to enjoy their advantages.

Let the work in the public schools, as they are now organized, be done in accordance with the true philosophy of teaching and study, and the children will graduate from them prepared to enter, with every prospect of success, upon the performance of the duties of either private or public life, or if they choose they can enter with disciplined minds into the professional schools for special instruction. In either case they will be likely to become honest and intelligent citizens of a free Commonwealth.

ORGANIZATION.

The mode of employing the teaching power in school will determine its organization. The early schools were not arranged in classes, but the master, seated at his desk, called up the children one at a time to recite the lesson committed to memory, or to receive such aid as the case might seem to require. Each pupil pursued his independent way over the studies assigned, and was treated as though he held no class relations to the other members of the school.

The individual system of organization had its advantages. It enabled the teacher to understand the individual peculiarities of every pupil's mind, to know its strength and its weakness, and to adapt his instruction to individual wants.

The system required the pupil to depend on himself for the accomplishment of his tasks, and was favorable for study at home as well as at school. It permitted the bright boys and girls to go on as fast as their talents and industry would carry them, and prevented the dull from being hurried beyond their capacity to comprehend. It prevented also much of the nervous strain which is produced by class exercises, in which the members are subject to a constant comparison with one another in recitations and examinations, and in the system of ranking sometimes based upon them. Under the individual system the complaint of overwork in school was seldom heard.

The exclusively individual system had its disadvantages. In a large school the teacher had but little time for the instruction of each pupil. The recitation consisted in listening by the teacher to a hurried repetition by the pupil of the lesson as it was taken from the book. There was little time for correcting mistakes or for illustrating difficult topics. There was no time for teaching the advance-lesson by the method which presents the true occasions for knowledge and for that independent exercise of power which is the true cause of mental development.

To remedy some of the defects that inhere in the individual system, in schools taught by one teacher, the mutual or monitorial system of Bell and Lancaster was invented.

In the application of this system the pupils of the school were separated into sections, and each section was taught and controlled by its best scholars. It was the duty of the master, to arrange the studies of the school, to make up the sections, to inspect and examine them, to instruct the pupil-teachers, and to have the general supervision of all that was done.

The mutual system made it possible to keep all the children busily employed, and thus keep them under better control and hasten their progress in learning. It gave the head-master an opportunity to direct more of his attention to the general management of the whole school, and it enabled him to give more time to the older and advanced pupils. It was an economical system, for it permitted the size of the school to be increased indefinitely without materially increasing the expense.

Some claimed that the pupil-teachers could do better service than the master himself, for by directing attention to their own personal experience they could better understand the difficulties with which the children under their instruction had to contend, and they were better able to invent ways of removing them. Their language, too, was more intelligible to young minds, and their relations were more familiar and agreeable. By teaching what they knew to others, the boy-teachers would naturally make clearer to themselves their own knowledge. The necessity of teaching more than they knew stimulated them to increased activity in the pursuit of new knowledge.

A feeling of responsibility, arising from the work committed to their charge, led them to be thoughtful for themselves as well as for others. It brought them into sympathy with the government of the school, and relieved the master of much of the hard labor and anxious care that would otherwise consume his time and strength and diminish his courage.

The mutual system, notwithstanding its advantages, proved to have some grave defects. It ignored the important facts, that the right development of the faculties, rather than the acquisition of a certain amount of information, is the end to be secured by school exercises; that the character and condition of the teacher's mind, his method of teaching and his style of government, have more influence in directing the development than the whole mass of facts which he may lead his pupils to accumulate; that any system which prevents the master from knowing his pupils, through a personal and constant contact with them, and from leading them by a personal direction, is fatal to the accomplishment of the high results which all schools of the young should endeavor to produce.

The monitors were generally boys with characters unformed, with a small amount of information and less knowledge at their command, and with no training in the application of the principles of teaching. They were as poorly equipped for teaching as are many of the young persons put over the schools of more modern times. Indeed, they were not expected to teach, in the true sense of that term: they were to hear the lessons repeated, to correct the mistakes, or report them to the master for his correction and discipline.

The monitors frequently used their authority in an arrogant and tyrannical manner. As is frequently true of young teachers, they were inclined to spend their strength in preserving order rather than in hearing recitations.

The individual system in its early and simple forms was impracticable, and it deprived the children of the stimulus that numbers produce.

The mutual system proved a failure, because the pupil-teachers were not fitted for their work, and the organization of the schools was such as to render the application of the true method of teaching impossible.

To combine the advantages found in the two sytems and escape from their defects, various methods have been devised.

The most satisfactory organization yet tried seems to be found in the graded system, in which children of about the same age, ability and attainments are collected into separate schools or classes and taught by adult and permanent teachers.

In our own complete system of public schools are found four grades, called primary, intermediate, grammar and high school grades. These grades may be distinguished from one another by the nature of the knowledge acquired in each, and by the modes of mental activity occasioned by the pursuit of the knowledge.

The successful application of the objective method of teaching requires a grading of the children to be taught. The different grades should be collected into separate schools, or into different classes in the same school. The courses of studies made out for the different grades should be progressive, so that the primary course may lead in an orderly manner into the in--

termediate, the intermediate into the grammar, and the grammar into the high school course. The person making out these courses should keep constantly in mind the different phases of knowledge to be mastered, the relations that one kind of knowledge holds to another, and the different modes of mental activity to be occasioned in acquiring the knowledge. If these things are observed, the different grades of pupils will be limited to tasks they can comprehend and perform.

The school and classes taught by a single teacher should be so limited in numbers as to allow frequent recitations by every pupil. The daily recitation of every pupil in all his classes will produce two or three important results.

1. It will stimulate the pupil to attend to the instruction by the teacher in presenting the lessons to the class.

2. It will furnish a strong motive for study in preparing the lessons for review.

3. The act of reproducing before the teacher and class what has been taught and learned is one of the best means of mental training.

The recitation hour should be divided into two parts : one to be devoted to a review by the class of the lesson previously taught them ; the other to be occupied by the teacher in teaching the topics of the advance-lesson. The teaching itself should be conducted in accordance with the principles of the objective method.

Although the class is taught as a class, the teaching should be specially directed to one individual member at a time, who is required to observe and consider what is presented. After he comprehends what he is directed to study, he may describe his knowledge to the teacher and to the other members of the class. While this is done by the one standing before the teacher, all others should be performing the same mental processes, each for himself. The lessons should be presented by topics carefully prepared. If the pupils are advanced enough, they should be required to record the topics as they are presented, and to follow them in their future study and recitations. The lesson given by the teacher is to prepare the class for study. It should furnish the pupil with topics, with a guide to the objects of knowledge, with a method of analyzing them, and with the meaning of technical terms used in scientific study, and with definitions. A knowledge of all these things should be occasioned by the true method of teaching.

The recitation also should be conducted by topics. The method employed in teaching is the method for the review. The pupils of the class should be called, each in turn, to unfold the topics assigned, and to do this without questions or aid from the teacher.

This plan of review will allow each pupil to exhibit what he knows of the lesson, from which may be inferred what of it he does not know, and it will require him to use an independent activity in the process. After this has been done the teacher may ask questions for the accomplishment of two ends: 1. To test the pupil's knowledge and lead him to correct any mistakes he may have made. 2. To teach additional truth which the topic may require to be presented.

If questions are put, they should be such as to direct the mind to the true object of thought, and they should not involve the answer. Some teachers, in conducting recitations by questions, continue talking until they answer the question themselves, or enable the learner to guess the answer they desire to obtain; others start off the pupil by supplying him with a few words of the beginning of the answer, and they help him out by repeating for him the closing sentence. These are vicious practices, as they defeat the very ends for which recitations should be conducted. Again, the teacher should have definitely in mind the matter to which he would direct attention by his questions, or he will be likely to confuse his pupil with the introduction of loosely related circumstances.

The time of a recitation is not unfrequently spent in the discussion of subjects foreign to the lesson, and of little value in themselves either as objects of knowledge or as occasions of mental activity. The evil results of such ways are found in the bad mental habits of thinking produced and in the unrelated condition of ideas formed.

In framing questions, both the rules of logic and the laws of association must be observed.

PRINCIPLES OF TEACHING.

An act which consists in presenting objects and subjects of thought to the learner's mind, so as to occasion such mental activity as produces mental development and knowledge, is teaching.

A full understanding of this definition of teaching requires an explanation of its significant terms.

An object of thought is anything of which we may think. The term subject is used to designate those objects of thought that exist only in the mind as mental states.

To present objects and subjects is to bring them into such relations to the learner's mind as to lead it to know them.

Mental development is that change produced in the faculties which adds to their original state a facility in acting.

Knowledge is the consciousness of the agreement or disagreement of ideas and thoughts.

The art of teaching has been defined. If the definition is a true one, the principles or science upon which the art is founded must be derived from a knowledge of the way in which the mind acts in obtaining its knowledge and development.

Through our experiences we learn that knowledge of all kinds is occasioned by the presence to the mind or in it of the objects of knowledge.

One of the principles of teaching, then, is found in that law of the mind which limits its activity in acquiring knowledge to objects in its presence. This principle is fundamental, and no act of the teacher in which it is not employed should be called teaching. It requires that whatever is to be made the object of study shall be brought into the presence of the learner's mind.

One of the conditions of knowledge requires that both objects and subjects shall be presented first as units or wholes. If this is done, the learner is able to use the analytic process in study, — the one process to which the mind is limited in all its independent investigations.

Material things may be thus presented to the observing powers through the senses; mental things may be presented through reflection. The one prepares the mind for the intelligent use of names; the other, for definitions.

Another principle of teaching is found in that law which requires objects of knowledge to be presented first as units or wholes.

The analysis of the whole that may follow will find occasions for a knowledge of parts and qualities. This knowledge should be obtained in an orderly way. The parts of a material thing may be taken up in the order in which they are found distributed in nature, called the natural order. The qualities of things may be presented in the order of their importance in future classifications, or in the order in which they attract attention, directing the mind first to the primary qualities, then to the secondary.

The parts of a subject should be taught in the order of their logical relations, or in such order that the thoughts occasioned by their presence may hold the relation of dependence of one that follows upon one that next precedes, called the logical order.

This order may be illustrated. If rhetoric is a knowledge of the right use of language, the definition would be presented in a logical manner, by, — 1st, Teaching what language is. In this the whole is presented. 2d, By analysis of language the use of language may be shown. 3d, By analysis of the use of language may be found the right use of language.

If we examine the relations which the thoughts occasioned by the employment of the above order in teaching the definition of rhetoric, we shall find that a thought of what is the use of language depends upon a thought of language itself, and that a thought of what is the right use depends upon a thought of its use. In this way the significant ideas expressed in the definition of rhetoric may be made to hold a logical relation in the learner's mind.

Another and most important principle of teaching is found in that law of the mind that requires the parts of objects and subjects to be presented in a natural and logical order. The importance of this principle may be seen if we consider the fact that a complete knowledge of a thing implies a knowledge of it as a unit, of the relations which its parts or attributes hold to one another, and of the parts or attributes themselves. Again, a knowledge of facts relating to individual objects or subjects form the elements of scientific knowledge, which is always general and abstract. Therefore the facts of a science must be known before a knowledge of the science is possible. From this relation of elementary to scientific knowledge appears another principle of teaching, found in a law of the mind, which requires a knowledge of individuals as a condition for a knowledge of classes.

From an analysis of its definition, teaching seems to be founded upon the following principles, in so far as the teaching has reference to acquisition of knowledge : —

1st. The laws of the mind require the objects of knowledge to be brought into its presence.

2d. That they shall be presented first as integral units.

3d. That the parts or qualities of material things shall be taught in their natural order, of mental things in their logical order.

4th. That elementary knowledge must be acquired as a condition for scientific knowledge.

If we turn our attention to the accomplishment of the second and by far the most important end of teaching suggested by the definition, namely, mental development, we shall find that a condition necessary to the right development of the faculties is an opportunity for their right exercise. This condition is observed when the teaching is so conducted as to require the pupil to exert the largest amount of self-activity in acquiring knowledge.

From the necessary conditions of mental development arises another principle of teaching, found in the mental law that requires the learner to exercise his active power in obtaining his knowledge.

From a knowledge of the principle already illustrated, a way or method can be formed in which the principles may find a practical application. The principles, from the nature of the case, must determine and limit the method.

There are those who say that there is no one way of teaching which is absolutely the best; that all ways are good, each in its turn. They affirm that too much attention to the study of methods leads to a mechanical formality which has a tendency to obscure the higher results of teaching. No thorough student of pedagogical science ever feels inclined to treat this subject with indifference, for he knows that a method of teaching founded on true principles must be natural, and that its use must result in the accomplishment of the two ends for which the act of teaching is always supposed to be exercised.

A method should never be confounded with a manner of teaching. The latter arises from the peculiar characteristics of the teacher rather than from the principles of teaching. Manner gives individuality to a teacher's work. It relates to the accidents of time, and place and motion, and devices for illustration, and to forms of speech. Therefore in manner let there be freedom, while the method employed should be as persistent as the principles upon which it should be founded.

An intelligent discussion of a method of teaching renders it necessary to keep in mind what teaching is, what are its ends, and what are the principles upon which it is founded. A clear distinction should also be made between knowledge and information. If these things are observed, no confusion will arise concerning the legitimate use of books and lectures and illustrative apparatus in teaching. The conditions of knowledge and mental development are fixed, and it is the duty of the teacher to understand them, and to have his methods of teaching conform to their requirements.

SUPERVISION.

The public schools of the Commonwealth should be so directed in their work that they will accomplish three ends : —

1. They should teach some accurate knowledge.

2. They should communicate a good way of discovering and using the truth.

3. They should train the children to that self-control which will enable them to perform skilfully and with a good purpose the duties of life.

For the accomplishment of these ends there must be an intelligent people, who, acting together under self-imposed rules, are agreed in supporting the schools by a general tax and in compelling the attendance of all the children of school age upon them. The schools must be taught by teachers who have been made skilful by study and experience. The teachers must teach good courses of studies by the use of proper means and a correct method, and the whole work must be directed by those who understand the theory of popular education and are employed to give their time to its management. The statutes have given this directing power to the school committees of the towns.

From the nature and extent of the duties of school committees it will at once appear that they should be skilled educators, able and willing to devote their time and study to school work. In some cases much time and study are freely given, and with good results. It is generally true, however, that school committeemen are quite fully employed with their individual concerns; that their school supervision is accidental, and not always performed with the skill which knowledge and experience alone can give.

To strengthen and perfect the supervision of the schools, the State has made it lawful for any town to require its school committee to annually appoint a superintendent of schools, who, acting under direction, and as an agent of the committee, shall perform all those acts that are peculiar to school supervision.

About sixty cities and towns have availed themselves of the provisions of the law, by requiring their school committees to elect superintendents and commit to them the general care and supervision of the schools.

The schools in these towns are the best in the State. The reasons for this are obvious. The conditions necessary for the existence of good schools are not likely to be secured, except through the service of those who know what the conditions are, and who have been chosen for the special work of supervision.

The schools in towns employing efficient supervision are supplied with better teachers; the schools are directed in accordance with a plan towards some definite results. All those things that come under the head of *means* of teaching are promptly furnished, and the whole school population is in school. The schools of the small towns are suffering for the want of good management. They are falling behind the schools provided with special supervision, as may be seen by their annual returns, and by the inferior advantages they offer to the children who attend upon their instructions.

Experience and observation both prove that the conditions necessary to good schools cannot exist, unless they are provided with efficient superintendence. There is a common agreement among educators on this subject that the cause of popular education " will ever languish " in towns not provided with an intelligent and special management.

This opinion prevails among the people themselves of such

towns, and they are generally willing to do all in their power to secure, in common with the larger towns, the advantages of special school supervision.

Inability to support such an agency is the obstacle in the way of its general introduction. The large towns are able to provide each its own supervisor. This they have generally done. The smaller towns may unite into districts and support union supervisors. There is already a permissive statute providing for the union of towns into districts, for the support of such officers.

Five districts have taken advantage of the provisions of the law, and have the district system of superintendency in active and most successful operation. The small towns need aid in supporting their educational institutions, and no aid could be given that would produce such radical and needed reforms in our common-school affairs as that given in support of an educated supervision.

DUTIES OF SUPERINTENDENTS.

As the State, by a permissive statute, has signified its approval of special superintendence of schools in the towns, and as the towns are inclined to accept the provision so far as they are able, it follows that wherever superintendents are appointed it is the will, both of the State and of the towns, to commit to the care of these persons the performance of all those duties which properly belong to supervision.

It is expected, therefore, that the school committees will require the superintendents they have appointed to perform all those acts that imply the possession of special educational learning, skill and experience. They should be allowed to nominate the teachers of the schools and to direct them in their methods of teaching; to construct courses of studies; to select the text-books that are to be used; to be the agents in providing the means of teaching; to look after the attendance of the children; to examine candidates for entering the schools, for promotion from one grade of instruction to another, and for graduation. This work of examination should always be done with the advice and assistance of the regular teachers. The superintendent should have the general charge of the school janitors and should be well acquainted with the condition of the schoolhouses.

It should be borne in mind, however, by the superintendents that their authority is delegated to them, and that all their acts should be submitted to the school committees for approval. This may be done by monthly reports, presented at the monthly meetings of the committees, in which a brief statement of what has been done and of what is thought best to be done may be made.

The time has come when the people should insist that the public-school education of the children should be committed to the care of educators. Then the public mind would not be so likely to become confused in regard to the legitimate province of the public common school, nor concerning the methods by which they may be made to produce the truest and largest results.

The questions that are now presenting themselves for an answer are, —

1. What shall the public schools teach?
2. By what method shall the teaching be conducted?
3. What results should the schools attempt to produce?

The first two questions have reference to the means to be employed; the last one, to the ends to be attained.

It would be well for the cause of popular education to have these questions answered by those who have made popular education, in all its phases, a careful study. The State has made provision for the employment of a class of leading educators, who, by their wisdom, may be able to direct the processes of public instruction to the production of the best ends.

These educators should be able to direct public sentiment, to prevent the schools from being burdened with work that does not belong to them, to establish the conditions necessary for the best results, and to offer their advantages to all orders of the people. To accomplish these ends, they must be permitted to exercise their power in proportion to their ability and responsibility.

School Committees.

The organization and management of the public schools of the Commonwealth are intrusted to town Boards of Education called school committees.

As the Public Statutes invest these Boards with almost unlimited power over the schools, the public good requires that the power shall be exercised in good faith and with great wisdom. If experience proves that the power is thus exercised, then the interests of popular education will be promoted, and the wisdom of the school laws will be established.

Discretionary power is always liable to abuse. If abuse exists to any degree, the power should be guarded and limited; if the abuse is common, the power should be withdrawn altogether.

The school committees of the State have large discretionary power granted to them, and, on the whole, they use it with a due appreciation of their responsibilities. Some cases of abuse have been reported and examined during the year; and in one or two instances found to be of sufficient importance to attract attention. It is not to be expected that a school committee, or any member of it, will so far forget the dignity and responsibility of the office as to sacrifice the educational interests of a community to gratify personal prejudices or to promote selfish interests. If this should ever happen, the community should not rest until there has been devised some mode of relief from the disastrous consequences of the mischief that is sure to follow. It is a sad thing for the children to be subjected to the influences of a teacher who is weak in intellectual strength, or deficient in pedagogical knowledge; but they should never be allowed to endure for a day the presence of one who is deficient in any of the moral attributes.

It is a legal as well as moral duty to select for the public schools teachers of competent ability and good morals; and neither the law nor the people will accept as an excuse for disregarding this duty, that the one selected is a native of the district whose school he is to teach, or that he is a near relative of some member of the school committee.

The law, the vital interests of the State and of every citizen require that a sufficient number of schools shall be kept for all the children who may legally attend them. What name shall we apply to that conduct on the part of school officers, resulting either from indifference or from personal considerations, that deprives the children of their school privileges for a year or for a single term?

Extraordinary powers have been granted to school officers,

for wise reasons. The right organization of the schools and their right management require much technical knowledge and a large experience, and they forbid the interference of all partisan influences. The committees must therefore be intelligent persons, and be placed entirely beyond the reach of all partisan considerations.

When the office of school committee was established, and laws were passed granting the authority to exercise absolute control over the schools, it was not expected that the authority would be used in refusing or neglecting to provide a sufficient number of schools for all the children, or to provide the schools with teachers of competent ability and good morals, or to furnish the teachers with the means of teaching, or to supervise them so that they may produce the best possible results.

It was never expected that school committees would use the opportunities of their high office for promoting selfish ends. The only sure way of preventing such results from ever occurring in any community is to select for the members of school boards persons of known ability and virtue.

NORMAL SCHOOLS.

The Normal Schools of the State have had a prosperous year. The entering and graduating classes have been larger than ever before, as will be seen by the accompanying statistics : —

	FOR THE YEAR.	
	No. of Students.	No. of Graduates.
Bridgewater, ...	214	47
Framingham, ...	140	26
Westfield, ...	156	44
Worcester, ...	231	26
Salem, ...	280	76
Normal Art School, ...	143	–
Number receiving certificates, ...	–	64
Number receiving diplomas, ...	–	27

The Normal Schools are improving in the methods of training they practise and in the results they produce. The present entering classes of these schools are better prepared for a professional course of study than were those of former times. This previous preparation will, in time, relieve the Normal Schools of a large amount of academical work which is now required in connection with professional study.

It has been found that theoretical knowledge is not enough to insure success in teaching. No one can be sure that he has a true theory even, if he has obtained it independent of practice. For these reasons every Normal School should include in its organization a training school, in which the Normal pupils may find an opportunity to acquire skill in teaching in accordance with a theory formed by study and experience.

To prevent the pupil teacher from groping for good methods and a profitable experience, he must be prepared for his practice work before he attempts it. What this preparation shall be, is an important question to decide.

When the Normal graduate enters the public school as a teacher, he should be prepared to direct his pupils to the accomplishment of three ends : —

1. To acquiring knowledge.
2. To learning a method of using his faculties.
3. To securing mental development.

If this is true, the work in the Normal Schools should consist of those exercises that will have a tendency to give to their pupils this directing power. That such a result may follow a course of training in the Normal Schools, the pupils who enter the Normal classes must be sound in body, in mind and in heart. They must also be prepared to pass a satisfactory examination in the branches of learning that are required to be taught in the public schools.

The same branches should be included in the Normal course of instruction, and passed over in order, for the purpose of making a list of topics on each that will present the different subjects in a good manner for teaching and study, for determining the best means of illustrating the topics, and for practice in teaching them to others.

The topics thus made out should be objects of study by members of the class. They should be led to see the philosophy of their selection and arrangement.

The recitations in the Normal Schools should be divided into two parts. One part should consist of a review by the class of a previous lesson taught by the regular teacher, and by the same method employed in his teaching. If the Normal pupils recite their topics by teaching them, they will acquire skill in contriving means of illustration, in handling them before the class, and in conducting the minds of others to an independant investigation for knowledge, and to a right activity for mental discipline. This skill is acquired only after much practice under careful supervision. An opportunity for such practice should be given in every Normal School. The other part of the exercise in the recitation hour should be conducted by the regular teacher of the class. His teaching should be in accordance with the objective method, presenting whatever is to be the object of study, and simply directing the pupils in their investigations. All the lessons in the course should be taken up in this way with special reference to teaching the same in the public schools. This method of presenting subjects of study always produces better results than the lecture method, in the use of which the teacher sometimes unfortunately falls into the habit of talking much and teaching little. In the last year of the Normal course, the study of the principles of teaching should be taken up, together with a thorough investigation of the best method of applying them.

The study of psychology should now be introduced, that from a knowledge of the mind the conditions of knowledge and mental development may be derived. By a study of the mind it will be found that the conditions upon which the acquisition of knowledge depends, require that the objects or subjects to be known should be brought before the mind; that these things should be presented first as units or wholes, — the wholes to be analyzed, and their parts or attributes to be so presented as to lead the mind of the learner to consider them in their natural or logical order.

It will now be seen that the conditions which limit the mind in the acquisition of knowledge require the use of the objective-analytical method of teaching. It will also appear that the conditions of mental development require self-activity on appropriate objects presented in accordance with the same objective method.

The next step in the Normal work should direct attention to selecting and arranging a course of studies adapted to the different grades of the public schools. This course should be so selected as to present occasions for useful knowledge and for the right development of the mind. In arranging the course, constant reference should be made to the relation that different branches of knowledge hold to one another and to the order of the development of the faculties. The pupils are supposed to be prepared for this work by their experience and their knowledge of principles.

They may now enter the practice schools for the acquisition of that facility in teaching which practice alone can give. A knowledge of principles and methods founded upon them will guide them in every phase of their work. They will not now teach at random, without knowing beforehand what will come of it; nor will they attempt to control their classes, ignorant of the relations that exist between their methods and the results produced by a practical application of them in actual teaching. Their methods will no longer be derived from the simple observation of the practices of others, but from the principles they have discovered. They will now teach and govern with reference to that self-control which is the great end to be secured by all intellectual and moral activity, and when they go from their training schools to the public schools, they will show that they already have had a successful experience.

Exercises in the practice classes should be under the direction of skilled teachers and subject to their intelligent criticisms. This will be likely to prevent the formation of bad habits, which, when once fully formed, hold one in their relentless grasp forever.

AGENTS OF THE BOARD.

At the beginning of the year, the schools of one hundred and fifteen towns were selected to be visited by the agents of the Board. These schools were arranged in three divisions, one division being assigned to each of the three agents, to be the field of his labor.

In visiting the schools of a town, the agent has been accustomed to invite one or more members of the school committee to accompany him in his visits. It has been found by trial that the committee and agent, by visiting together, may greatly assist each other in seeing what they look upon in the schools.

The observations were directed to the location of the school-houses; to the conditions of the school grounds and out-buildings; to the ventilation, lighting and heating of the school-rooms; to the quality and construction of the furniture; to the means of teaching furnished; to the courses of study taught; to the methods of teaching used; to the forms of school government adopted; to the attendance of the children, and to their progress in study.

After the schools in the towns were all visited, the teachers and committee were invited to come together for a familiar discussion of what had been observed. At this meeting a good opportunity was offered for encouraging the teachers to continue to do what they were already doing well, and to adopt those methods of work which reason and experience have proved to be the best. A good opportunity was also offered for urging upon the committee the necessity of employing skilled teachers, for furnishing them with suitable means of teaching, and for retaining them permanently in their places. The instructions given to the teachers at these meetings were adapted to awaken in their minds, and in the minds of the committee, good ideas concerning their duties as teachers and supervisors.

In the evening, after the personal work with the schools was completed, the people were invited to listen to a familiar address by the secretary or agent on the duties of citizens to give to their public schools a generous and cordial support. They were reminded that the statutes of the Commonwealth require the schools to be supported, and all the children of school age to be collected into them for instruction and discipline; that, as ignorance is the parent of poverty and crime, education is cheaper than ignorance, and that there is no place for ignorance in a free State. They were reminded that the laws of the State require all public instructors to teach, not only the facts and truths of science, but also the principles and practice of every virtue, and that it is the duty of the people to encourage such instruction by cheerfully furnishing every facility for its introduction.

This mode of influencing the teachers, school officers and the people was substituted in part for the State institutes held in former times. Visiting the schools and consulting with those who have. anything to do in managing their affairs seem to be the most effectual ways of preparing the schools for those changes which in many cases the good of the children requires.

Besides this work of the agents, they have assisted in conducting eleven teachers' institutes, in which instruction has been given to about seven hundred teachers, representing fifty-three towns. They have also been present at many of the annual examinations of the public schools, and, on invitation, have given formal addresses to graduating classes.

The influence of the agents is constantly increasing. They supply, to a limited degree, the place of local school superintendents. Their familiarity with all forms of school work and their knowledge of the progress made in methods of instruction in the best schools render their supervision most helpful to all who are ambitious to produce the best results in the public schools.

Mr. Martin, worn down by a long term of hard service as teacher in the Normal School at Bridgewater, and as agent of the Board of Education, has asked for a term of rest. The loss of his skilled labor in the State work is severely felt. Eminently fitted by nature, learning and experience for the peculiar service in which he has been engaged, his enforced absence from it is the cause of deep regret. All sincerely hope that he will soon be able to take his place again, and cause his friends and the State to rejoice over his restored health and renewed strength.

TEACHERS' INSTITUTES.

Eleven institutes have been held the past year, each for one or more days, and in the following towns : —

Attendance of Committees and Teachers.

North Brookfield, ...	84
Brockton, ...	97
Westford, ...	30
Harwich, ...	70
Tyngsborough, ...	45
Shelburne Falls, ...	48

Goshen, ... 33
Cottage City, ... 30
Orange, ... 69
Southborough, ... 154
Winchendon, ... 25

The exercises of the institutes were conducted by the following persons : —

Mr. Dickinson, ...	{ Principles of Teaching. Methods of Teaching.
Mr. Walton, ...	{ Language. Reading. Penmanship. Arithmetic.
Mr. Martin, ...	{ Geography. History. Political Economy. Mineralogy.
Mr. Prince, ...	{ Language. Reading. School Organization.
Mr. A. C. Boyden, ...	{ Physiology and Hygiene. Arithmetic. History.
Mr. Aldrich, ...	{ Geography. Arithmetic. Reading and Language.
Mr. Hubbard, ...	Arithmetic.
Miss Carver, ...	{ Geography. History. Composition.
Mrs. Guild, ...	{ Methods of organization and teaching in primary schools.
Mr. Kimball, ...	{ Alcohol and its effects on the human system.

In addition to the regular exercises of the day sessions, one or more evening lectures have been given in connection with the institutes. The lectures were given by the secretary, Prof. Wm. H. Niles, and the agents of the Board.

The people have manifested great interest in the institutes, both by their hospitality to the members and by their attendance upon the meetings. The members have uniformly given their undivided attention to the exercises, and have expressed their great interest in the improved methods of teaching illustrated by the lessons of the institutes. In most cases school committees have accompanied their teachers and have become learners with them.

The institute at Shelburne Falls was held on invitation of Rev. H. A. Pratt, a member of the school committee and superintendent of the schools of Shelburne. It was organized in March, during the spring vacation of the schools, and was intended to aid the teachers of the hill towns. The institute continued nine days, — a departure from the custom observed for many years. There were about forty-eight members in regular attendance. Eight towns were represented by their teachers. In addition to the regular members, the students of Arms Academy were also in attendance, making the whole number present one hundred.

The Shelburne Institute was a short-term Normal School. Class exercises were conducted in reading, geography, penmanship, history, composition and language. Simple object lessons on form, color, minerals and plants were also given.

There were lectures on principles of teaching and school organization. The exercises were fully appreciated by those who were taught.

A modification of the institute work has been carried on through the year by the agents of the Board.

The schools of one hundred and fifteen towns have been visited by the agents in company with the school committees, and on the last day of the visits, committees and teachers have been called together for suggestions and instruction.

These visits to the schools were generally closed by an evening lecture for the people, given by the secretary or agents.

SCHOOL LEGISLATION.

A good school system will not of itself produce good schools. Laws may be passed requiring the people to maintain schools, to organize them, and to conduct their exercises in accordance with some prescribed plan. But after all, the results produced will correspond to the intelligence and good-will of the people. School legislation should have its origin in a well-considered necessity, and should never be far in advance of public sentiment.

All attempts to promote popular education by legal enactments alone, or by those that do not express the will of the people, will fail. Such enactments will be soon repealed or

practically nullified. " There is a higher law than legal statutes, — it is the popular will overruling them."   It is in vain to
attempt to execute a law against which there is arrayed a general indifference or a general opposition.   Frequent changes in
existing laws should be avoided.   Such changes destroy the
advantages that arise from experience, and they produce confusion and uncertainty in the minds of all affected by them.

All new legislation relating to the public schools and all
proposed changes in the present school laws should be well
considered by those who have made our system of public
education a study, before any final action is taken.   The laws
we have are for the most part the results of experience, and
there should be a combined effort on the part of the whole
people to see that they are thoroughly applied.   " To secure
permanency in any policy, it should take no step which it must
afterward retrace."

TEMPERANCE.

Instruction in physiology and hygiene, with special reference
to the effects of alcohol on the human system, was introduced
into the list of required studies to be pursued in the public
schools, by an act approved June 16, 1885.

This is thought to be an important act, inasmuch as it requires all grades of the public schools to teach, as a regular
branch of learning, to their pupils both the philosophy and the
value of temperance.

When the law requiring physiology and hygiene to be taught
in all the public schools was enacted, the teachers of the Commonwealth were generally unprepared for the work ; but they
began at once to acquire for themselves a knowledge of what
they were directed to teach.

The Normal Schools turned their earnest attention also to
devising the best methods of teaching to the children, in a
simple yet effective manner, the facts of the new subjects.
The committees of the towns entered heartily upon the performance of their duties in relation to the new requirement.
Ignorance of what was required to be taught, and of the best
methods of teaching, has prevented the towns from attaining,
at once, all desirable results.   But the good-will of the people and of the schools gives assurance that they will soon

accomplish the ends for which the friends of the new law secured its enactment.

School committees should provide the best means of teaching, and encourage the best methods. They should also take care that the work is thoroughly done, both by teacher and pupil.

It has long been a maxim with educators that all forms of education should begin with the young. This maxim is founded on a law of the mind that renders the formation of habits the necessary result of mental activity. Hence it is that childhood and youth are the periods of time set apart as most important for systematic study and training.

As habits are the products of activity, the young should be directed to a course of right conduct. This may be accomplished through the influences of a good example and right methods of education.

Temperance, in its unrestricted sense, includes all that is meant by complete self-control. Self-control implies knowledge of the truth, an inclination to do what ought to be done, and a strong will. By a knowledge of these things the teacher may be guided in the performance of his most important duties.

The statutes of the Commonwealth require all instructors of youth to use their best endeavors to impress on the minds of children and youth committed to their care the principles of all the virtues, among which temperance holds an exalted place.

The children of the Commonwealth must be made intelligent and conscientious, with reference to the gratification of their physical desires. They must be led to form such habits as will best promote the health of the body and make it as perfect as possible for the use of the mind.

JOHN W. DICKINSON.

The surface of a cylinder will need to make...
...and and texture, with reference to its gratification of its
physical texture. Often invisible light, to both the colour
of the texture is the beauty of the body and...at on the
of the hand to the more subtle...

FINANCIAL STATEMENT.

FINANCIAL STATEMENT OF THE BOARD OF EDUCATION.

APPROPRIATION FOR SUPPORT OF NORMAL SCHOOLS.

DR. 1886.			CR. 1886.	
Bridgewater Normal School:			Appropriation, chapter 12, Acts of 1886,	$65,350 00
Salary of principal,	$2,800 00			
Salaries of assistants,	9,790 16			
Janitor service,	230 00			
Watchmen,	519 75			
Repairs,	155 26			
School of Observation,	414 17			
Laboratory service,	466 69			
Printing,	88 00			
Advertising,	95 92			
Fuel,	440 05	$14,960 00		
Framingham Normal School:				
Salary of principal,	$2,600 00			
Salaries of assistants,	7,376 48			
Janitor service,	603 70			
Repairs,	507 81			
Rent of Haven House,	385 00			
Printing,	50 87			
Advertising,	93 31			
Fuel,	432 09			
Chemicals,	3 34			
Gas,	14 70	12,067 30		
Salem Normal School:				
Salary of principal,	$3,000 00			
Salaries of assistants,	8,949 00			
Janitor service,	400 00			
Repairs,	479 21			
Fuel,	314 06			
Gas,	41 65			
Advertising,	64 41			
Chemicals,	17 71			
Water,	49 50	13,315 48		

Westfield Normal School:		
Salary of principal,	$2,800 00	
Salaries of assistants,	6,649 97	
Janitor service,	499 92	
Watchmen,	447 86	
Repairs,	441 37	
Fuel,	422 42	
Water,	20 00	
Gas,	33 19	
Stationery,	90 99	
Advertising,	22 00	
Apparatus,	40 43	
Printing,	79 01	
		11,547 16
Worcester Normal School:		
Salary of principal,	$2,800 00	
Salaries of assistants,	6,662 22	
Janitor service,	600 00	
Repairs,	423 42	
Fuel,	573 97	
Water,	12 66	
Ice,	36 27	
Telephone,	37 75	
Apparatus,	17 50	
Stationery,	171 11	
Printing,	258 20	
Advertising,	80 00	
Music,	32 50	
		11,705 60
Balance unexpended Dec. 31, 1886,		63,595 54
		1,754 46
		$65,350 00

$65,350 00

FINANCIAL STATEMENT OF THE BOARD OF EDUCATION — Continued.

APPROPRIATION FOR NORMAL ART SCHOOL.

Dr.		Cr.	
1886.		**1886.**	
Salary of principal,	$2,400 00	Appropriated by chap. 12, Acts of 1886,	$16,210 00
Salaries of assistants,	7,940 07		
Janitor service,	480 00		
Repairs,	268 45		
Fuel,	421 70		
Water,	45 40		
Gas,	76 80		
Printing,	156 95		
Rent,	3,600 00		
Advertising,	139 93	Excess of appropriation,	66 06
Taxes,	746 76		
	$16,276 06		$16,276 06

APPROPRIATION FOR AID TO NORMAL PUPILS.

Dr.		Cr.	
1886.		**1886.**	
Amount paid:		Appropriated by chap. 12, Acts of 1886,	$4,000 00
Bridgewater school,	$590 47		
Framingham school,	114 28		
Salem school,	609 53		
Westfield school,	514 29		
Worcester school,	171 43		
	$2,000 00		
Dec. 31, Balance unexpended,	2,000 00		
	$4,000 00		$4,000 00

APPROPRIATION FOR AGENTS OF THE BOARD.

Dr.			Cr.
1886.			**1886.**
George A. Walton, salary,	$2,250 00		Appropriated by chap. 12, Acts of 1886, $9,390 00
George A. Walton, expenses,	403 70		
George H. Martin, salary,	2,250 00		
George H. Martin, expenses,	325 69		
John T. Prince, salary,	2,250 00		
John T. Prince, expenses,	368 71		
Charles W. Carter, salary,	374 98		
Charles W. Carter, expenses,	84 12		
		$8,257 20	
Dec. 31, Balance unexpended,		1,132 80	
		$9,390 00	$9,390 00

APPROPRIATION FOR TEACHERS' INSTITUTES.

Dr.			Cr.
1886.			**1886.**
Paid for instructors and expenses of institutes at North Brookfield, Brockton, Westford, Harwich, Tyngsborough, Shelburne Falls, Goshen, Cottage City, Orange and Southborough,		$604 13	Appropriated by chap. 12, Acts of 1886, $2,000 00
Dec. 31, Balance unexpended,		1,395 87	
		$2,000 00	$2,000 00

FINANCIAL STATEMENT OF THE BOARD OF EDUCATION — CONCLUDED.

APPROPRIATION FOR INCIDENTAL EXPENSES OF THE BOARD.

Dr.			1886.	Cr.
1886.			Appropriated by chap. 12, Acts of 1886,	$1,200 00
School registers and printing,	$434 20			
Stationery and postage,	254 96			
Messenger and expressage,	263 40			
Tabulating returns,	125 00			
Papers for report and telegrams,	88 72	$1,166 28		
Dec. 31, Balance unexpended,		33 72		
		$1,200 00		$1,200 00

APPROPRIATION FOR TRAVELLING EXPENSES OF MEMBERS OF THE BOARD.

Dr.			1886.	Cr.
1886.			Appropriated by chap. 12, Acts of 1886,	$100 00
Jan. 21, Paid H. E. Scudder,	$9 17			
Mar. 31, " A P. Stone,	49 64			
Oct. 7, " Abby W May,	7 12			
Dec. 7, " A. A. Miner,	15 75			
15, " M. B. Whitney,	97 12			
20, " A. P. Stone,	61 86			
31, " E. B Stoddard,	42 00			
31, " F. A. Walker,	8 22	$290 88		
31, Balance unexpended,		109 12		
		$400 00		$100 00

C. B. TILLINGHAST, *Treasurer.*

APPENDIXES.

A.

REPORT OF GEORGE A. WALTON,

AGENT OF THE BOARD.

SCHOOL ATTENDANCE AND TRUANCY.

REPORT.

To the Board of Education:

The extent of my work during the present year has been as great as in any year since my first appointment as agent of the Board. Its aims are the same from year to year; the general character not essentially different, though sufficiently varied to give it ever fresh interest. The Board has been made acquainted with the details through monthly reports. I need not review these further than to say that I have systematically inspected the schools of thirty-three towns, holding in most of them one afternoon meeting of the teachers and committees, and addressing the people in the evening. In addition to this, I have visited a number of towns to render special services connected with the administration of the schools, given instruction in the teachers' institutes, attended conventions of teachers and superintendents, made visits to all the Normal Schools, and assisted in preparing statistical and other matters in the office of the secretary.

SCHOOL ATTENDANCE.

During the year my attention has been more than usually directed to school attendance, and I propose to make that subject the special topic of this report.

SCHOOL REGISTERS.

In a recent communication the following question was asked : —

Are there two rules in force for finding the average attendance in the schools of the State? Rule No. 3 directs that a pupil shall be considered a member of the school from the first day till the last day of his attendance in any term, unless he leaves with no intention of returning, in which case he may be counted out.

Then is given an illustrative example, as follows : A boy attended school two weeks and was then absent four weeks, after which he returned to school. In the case supposed, the twenty days of non-attendance were included in the average membership and were scored against the pupil as absences ; in another school under similar conditions the twenty days would not have been counted at all. Would this be right?

Rule No. 3 of the school register, to which reference is made, reads as follows : —

Every pupil shall be considered a member of the school from the time of his first entrance to the day of his last attendance for the term. If, however, a pupil withdraws from the school with no purpose of re-entering during the term and gives notice of the same, but subsequently re-enters the school, he shall not be considered a member during such absence.

There is but one rule applicable to the case cited, and that requires that the twenty absences should be charged against the pupil.

That usage varies is well understood. There are schools where the attendance is a matter of seeming indifference to the teacher and pupils. The latter are absent from day to day without signifying what is their intent, — they have no definite intention of leaving school, but the term passes and they do not re-enter; absences are recorded against them during the whole period of non-attendance, and these are counted in making up the record for the month or term. Here the rule is violated; the absent marks should have been cancelled at the close of the term. So far as membership is concerned, the case is the same as if the notice of intention to leave had been given by the pupil the last day of his attendance at school.

If the pupil leaves school with no expectation of returning, he should give notice to that effect on leaving. The teacher must not assume, however, that the pupil's membership has ceased till he has good evidence of the fact. In the above case the membership evidently continued while the pupil was in non-attendance.

The inconvenience of recording absences for long periods of time, with the labor attending the recasting of monthly averages, which is required when absences once recorded have to be cancelled, has led to the practice in.many schools of considering the membership to cease after five days of absence have been recorded. This is sometimes called the "five days' rule." Other considerations may have led to the adoption of this rule. It is necessary to have uniformity throughout the schools. The five days' rule is so well established in many localities, that, for the sake of this uniformity, it may be found wise to make the rule general.

In one town visited, I found it was the practice of some of the teachers to excuse pupils for an entire session upon the written request of the parent, and yet to record no absences against them; I do not know how common this practice is. In a former report allusion was made to the custom in a certain locality of excusing pupils after some brief exercise, even after roll-call or devotions. Dismission is provided for in the register, but to make it stretch through the whole session, one who reflects upon the subject cannot but see is an immoral act, and one which in every way is bad for the school. All the time lost by the pupil should be recorded against him, whether it be for non-attendance during the whole session or for tardiness and dismission. It is recommended that in making up the average attendance such lost time be counted as absence. If the time were to be counted, the record could be so kept as not greatly to burden the teacher. The requests for dismission would certainly be fewer, and the exact truth would be given in the report of attendance.

TRUANCY AND ABSENCE FROM SCHOOL.

Among the earliest enactments of the New England colonies were laws requiring towns to maintain schools for the various grades of instruction. Passing over a period of two hundred years, we find laws requiring every town or district of fifty families or householders to keep a school for the instruction of children in orthography, reading, writing, English grammar, geography, arithmetic and good behavior; one such school must be kept for six months, or two or more for a term which in all would equal six months. A longer and longer term of schooling was required as the number of families in the towns increased.

Towns of five hundred families were required to maintain

during ten months in each year for all the inhabitants of the town an additional school, in which should be employed a master of good morals and of competent ability to give instruction in the branches above named, also in the history of the United States, book-keeping, surveying, geometry and algebra. And towns of four thousand or more inhabitants were required to maintain one such school, in which should be employed a master competent to give instruction in the Latin and Greek languages, general history, rhetoric and logic, as well as in the aforesaid branches. These were the studies of 1826.

From time to time the curriculum has been extended, till at present every study deemed of practical value is provided for in the public school.

It has been the aim of the State to make the instruction free to all. The increase in the number of studies required to be taught created a demand for additional means of teaching; this demand met a ready response in legislative enactments. In 1826 towns were required to furnish school books free of charge to the children of indigent parents. By a law of 1850, unabridged and quarto Dictionaries were provided for all schools at public expense. Later a law was passed giving to the school committees the entire control of the town's share of the income of the school fund to be expended for school purposes, it being left to the option of the committees to expend one-fourth of the same for books of reference, apparatus and means of instruction. The free text-book law at first permitted the towns to furnish school books and supplies free of charge to all pupils; an act of 1884 required this of all towns.

Legislation has aimed to make the education universal. In the early history of the colonies all parents and guardians were to cause their children and wards to be instructed. In 1642 the *selectmen* of the town were required to "have a vigilant eye over their brethren and neighbors, to see that none of them shall suffer so much barbarism in any of their families, as not to endeavor to teach, by themselves and others, their children and apprentices so much learning as may enable them perfectly to read the English tongue, and a knowledge of the capital, laws."

Later it was made the duty of resident ministers of the gospel, the selectmen and the school committees to exert their best endeavors that the youth of their towns should regularly attend the schools established for their instruction.

In 1852 the laws required every person having under his control a child between eight and fourteen years of age to cause such child to attend school at least twelve weeks each year, six of which must be consecutive. Afterwards the term of attendance was changed to twenty weeks, ten of which were to he consecutive. This is the requirement of our present compulsory law.

To remove as far as possible the temptation to deprive the children of their schooling for the sake of their earnings, a law was passed in 1836 which provided that no child under ten years of age should be employed to work in any manufacturing establishment; that children from twelve to fifteen years of age should not be so employed unless they had attended school one term of eleven weeks during the preceding year; and that no child under twelve years should be so employed unless he had attended school eighteen weeks. Laws of a more recent date provide that no child between eight and fourteen years of age shall be so employed except in vacations, unless he has attended school during the preceding twelve months at least twenty weeks, of which ten shall be consecutive; that no child under twelve years, and no child under fourteen who cannot read and write, shall be so employed any part of the year during the days the schools keep. Since this law was enacted its provisions have been extended to mechanical and mercantile establishments.

Laws are in force imposing fines upon persons and corporations giving employment contrary to these enactments. The establishments referred to are visited by officials whose duty it is to enforce the observance of the laws relating to the employment of children.

The Acts of 1850 required the towns to make all needful provisions concerning truants and absentees from school, between the ages of five and sixteen years. The penalties imposed were either fines or imprisonment. The present law requires towns to make provisions concerning this class of persons between seven and fifteen years of age.

These provisions compel the towns to adopt by-laws relating to truants, to provide a suitable place for the restraint, discipline and instruction of persons committed under the by-laws. School committees are required to appoint two or more truant officers whose duty it shall be to make complaints and execute the judgments of the courts under the by-laws.

Formerly any person between seven and sixteen years of age found wandering about the streets, not subject to parental control and growing up in ignorance, was subject to fine or imprisonment; now a fine is imposed upon the parent or guardian who neglects the schooling of his child. In case the parent is unable to keep his child in school from want of power to control him, the child may be sent to a truant school for a term of two years.

The statutes require school committees, in their annual returns to the Board of Education, to state whether the towns have made the needful provisions required by law relating to truants and absentees from school.

The laws compelling attendance and fixing penalties for violations are a logical sequence of the law which puts a tax upon the property of the citizen for the support of the schools. The tax-payer has the right to demand that the children whose schooling he pays for shall be kept in school and not be allowed to grow up in ignorance, or wander about the streets and pastures to prey upon his property.

Following out to its logical conclusion the principle upon which laws for compulsory attendance are based, they might fairly compel attendance for the entire period for which taxes are levied to support the schools. The laws are presumed to express the maximum of compulsion for which the average mind of the people is prepared; they certainly express the minimum of instruction the State can afford to have the children receive. To raise the minimum of instruction, it is necessary to elevate the average mind to a fuller appreciation of the needs and duties of the State in the matter of educating the children.

ENFORCEMENT OF THE LAWS RELATING TO TRUANTS.

Is the average mind ready for this elevation? Can better laws be enacted? Can the present laws be more fully enforced? And, first, how far are the laws enforced which are already enacted?

From forty-five cities and towns in Massachusetts, all having superintendents, responses were received to the following inquiry recently made : —

" Are the laws relating to truant children complied with in your city or town ? "

Twenty-seven replied unconditionally, " yes," " strictly," or " vigorously ; " one finds " little occasion for the laws." The remaining answers are : two, " tolerably ; " two, " as far as possible ; " four, " partially," or something to this effect ; one each, " not fully," " not," " no," " not well," " truants are followed but not reformed ; " four others appear to have no place provided for their truants.

This testimony may be taken as a fair statement of the facts concerning the enforcement of the laws in towns and cities having professional superintendents. There is here much effective work done to suppress truancy and to restrain and discipline truant children. Yet there is considerable truancy that for various causes goes uncontrolled and unchecked.

Where there are no superintendents whose whole business it is to look after the schools, the enforcement of the laws is dependent upon school committees. The danger to some towns of losing their share of the income of the school fund induces a formal compliance with the laws ; so that now, with a few exceptions, the committees declare in their annual returns that the statutes concerning truancy are complied with. But the agents of the board find radical defects in the provisions made, and often extreme laxity in the enforcement of the statutes applicable to truants and absentees from school. Sometimes we learn incidentally of cases of truancy, and not infrequently, either in this way or through the committee, we hear of whole families of children whose schooling is being neglected.

Many committees are alert in securing constant and punctual attendance of all the children in town. From the answers of some we are led to more than half suspect that an acknowledgment of existing truancy is felt by the committees to be criminating themselves. Sometimes when we ask if the town has adopted by-laws relating to truancy, and if these make all needful provisions for the restraint and instruction of truant children, we are met with the response, " We have no truants, so no provisions are needful."

There is much absenteeism for trifling causes, which is by the consent or requirement of the parents. In many towns there are districts in which are known to exist neglected children who are growing up in ignorance and without parental control. The truant officer is a harmless body in some of these districts; he does not want to make enemies among his neighbors, and therefore does nothing. The arm of the school committee is paralyzed by the same prudent regard for comfort. Committees in some towns of considerable population, on applying for permission to assign a certain truant school as the place to which their truant children may be committed, have given assurance that there will be no truants sent. This shows either insensibility to the beneficent provisions of the law, or a foreknowledge which is somewhat remarkable.

For the purpose of forming some estimate of the average number of inhabitants to one truant, I have selected the following cities and towns, the number of whose convicted truants I know: Boston, Brockton, Cambridge, Chelsea, Chicopee, Clinton, Fall River, Fitchburg, Lynn, Lawrence, Marlborough, Medford, New Bedford, Newton, Salem, Somerville, Springfield, Wakefield, Woburn, Worcester.

A majority of these towns and cities keep one truant officer or more constantly employed; all have provided a place for their truants.

The aggregate population of these places is 831,782; the number of truants at present in truant schools and sent from these is 230, which is one for every 3,616 inhabitants. It is thus possible to estimate approximately the ratio of the number of truants to the population throughout the State; and allowing for the differences in the character of the population, an estimate can be made for any locality.

With all the obstacles to a strict enforcement of the laws, it is safe to assume that their provisions are not properly enforced if fewer than one arrest a year is made to every 4,000 inhabitants; and probably were the laws more strictly enforced, there would be one to every 3,000 or even 2,000.

The one county in the State which has a truant school has received all her truants convicted within the county from five municipalities, not one from the remaining seventeen; yet these contain one-fifth of the school population. Is it probable that with a proper enforcement of the laws not one truant child could be found in these seventeen towns? No one can doubt that diligent search would discover many.

These towns are not peculiar. The returns from all sections of the State show a large percentage of absence from school. Inquiry and observation teach that much of it is without reasonable excuse, that it is largely confined to the class which most needs to form those habits of order which punctual attendance at school and attention to its duties tend to promote.

There is one provision in our compulsory laws which is almost entirely inoperative; it is the section which imposes a fine upon the parent for neglecting to send his child to school for twenty weeks each year. Instances of such neglect are common. We often hear of them, but seldom of the parent's paying the penalty.

In general the manufacturing, mechanical and mercantile establishments are in hearty sympathy and readily co-operate with the officers appointed to enforce the laws relating to the employment of children. We are fortunate in the officers whose duty it is to inspect these establishments, and to make complaints and prosecute violations of the laws.

DIFFICULTIES ATTENDING THE ENFORCEMENT OF THE LAWS.

The enforcement of the laws relating to attendance requires vigilance, and is sometimes attended with difficulties. Pittsfield, for example, adopts by-laws which designate as habitual truants "for the purpose of these by-laws" any pupil who absents himself for three or more days without excuse. Being submitted to the judge of the superior court, for his approval, the by-laws are rejected on the ground that it is not competent for the town to state what constitutes a truant. So Pittsfield waits till another town meeting. Some informality discovered in the by-laws of North Adams leaves her in the same predicament. Instances have occurred in which the school committee have secured the adoption by the town of a code of by-laws; the State Primary School, the State Reform School, the house of a citizen of the town, a certain school therein, the almshouse or the lock-up is named as the place for the discipline and instruction of truants. These by-laws must have the approval of the judge of the proper court, or arrests cannot be made under them. With such places of assignment as some of those named, no judge can deliberately approve them. Here the matter rests till another annual town meeting, or perhaps altogether, till the town is awakened by finding that through neglect she has forfeited her share of the school fund.

The town of Brookline assigns the "Home of the Angel Guardian" as the place for the confinement and instruction of her truants ; but her by-laws leave it to the option of the parent to allow the child to be committed,— a proper provision, since the institution is managed and controlled by a particular religious denomination, but a provision which leaves the town with no absolute control of her truants. She cannot be said to have made all "needful provisions" concerning this class of persons.

In the town of ———, the ruling of the judge is that no truant can be committed to the place named in the by-laws of the town, the truant school at Lowell, except by the consent of the parent. Here the intent of the law and the purpose of the town are impeded by a judicial opinion. Irregular attendance, which leads to truancy, results from the neglect or over-indulgence of parents ; too many of these will be in desperate straits before they will choose for their children wholesome restraint rather than the liberty of the street.

A superintendent of one of our cities writes : "If you could send us a judge who would be a little firmer in dealing with the few who need severer treatment than we find necessary in most cases, you would make us entirely happy."

Fall River, with her ample means for following up truants, would gladly include in her supervision the parochial schools ; but their teachers fail to report to the officers, and the truants from these schools are reached only as they are found on the streets.

The superintendent of Northampton says : "The means employed for enforcing the laws are the appointment of two truant officers, who look up all cases of truancy reported to them, and return the truants to the schools as far as they are able without entering a formal complaint against them to the district court. Complaints have been entered in some instances ; but we find such a course worse than useless, as the magistrate refuses to commit truants to our lock-up, which is the only place provided by our city for their restraint, discipline and instruction."

The enforcement of the laws depends largely upon the judge having jurisdiction. If he deems the by-laws to be inadequate in any respect, he may refuse to convict. Right and justice are served by having it so. But every facility should be given for the execution of the laws, so far as their fundamental purpose, the moral reform of the children, is concerned.

To illustrate the effect of improving the provisions for the discipline and instruction of this unfortunate class of children, take an instance which came under my observation. The city of ——— passed by-laws assigning the almshouse as the place of commitment. Truant officers were appointed year after year; complaints were entered, but no commitments were made. Finally arrests ceased; no more complaints came from the teachers, and the law was a dead letter, the three truant officers meantime regularly drawing for their services twenty-five dollars each per annum. The presumption was that this was an exceptional city : it had no truants. Every year, under a solemn oath, the school committee returned "yes" to the interrogatory of the Board of Education, "Are the Statutes relating to truant children and absentees complied with ?"

At length a proposition was made in the same committee to appoint, with an annual salary, one truant officer who should devote his whole time, if need be, in looking after truants. "We have none," was the whispered reply. Inquiry among the principals and janitors of the several schools had already secured the names of sixty-one persons, between eight and fourteen years of age, who were not attending any public school; and thirty-four of these were not attending any school whatever, and were wholly without excuse for non-attendance.

Two truant officers, as required by law, were appointed, one to give his whole time to the prescribed duties of his office. Patient and persistent following of the city government, after much delay, secured an ordinance assigning the Lawrence Industrial School as the place for the commitment of truants. The truant officer was vigilant; he monthly reported twenty-five to thirty cases of absentees investigated; the children were brought to school; if their offence was truancy, a repetition rendered them liable to arrest. The first year, three or four incorrigible truants were complained of to the police judge; he approved of the place of assignment and promptly committed the children, feeling that he was performing a benignant act.. The moral effect upon the schools of the city was immediately felt; truancy was controlled; the attendance and discipline at once improved. No investment made by this city will yield a larger dividend than that made for the confinement, discipline and instruction of these children at this excellent industrial school.

Holyoke has in the last year met with a serious obstacle to the hitherto efficient work of her truant officers; this is in the decision of the judge to the effect that the truant cannot be arrested without a warrant, and not until the individual case has been passed upon by the school committee and the arrest ordered. The opinion of the judge is sustained by that of the city solicitor.

No such conclusion has been reached elsewhere, and it is a common if not universal practice in other places for the officer finding upon the street a boy unable to give a satisfactory excuse for being out of school and presumably a truant, to take him to his home or to the school; and only good is known to have resulted from the practice. The consciousness that he is liable to be promptly arrested while in the act, blunts the appetite of the truant for the indulgence.

The absence of suitable places for their confinement is a great hindrance to successfully dealing with idle and vicious boys.

There has been a popular distrust—not always well founded, I am happy to say—of our State Reform School. A boy expelled from the public school is kept from the Reform School for fear, bad as he is, to send him would make him worse. The same feeling is entertained regarding the almshouse and the "lock-up."

By statute all cities and towns are required to provide themselves with suitable places for the restraint, discipline and instruction of truant children.

Lawrence early established for herself an industrial school to which are committed this class of persons. She seems to be the only city or town in the State that has literally complied with the statutes. Others have virtually met the required conditions by assigning this or some other suitable institution as the place for committing their truants.

The committee on truant officers of the Board of School Committee of Boston for 1883, in their report earnestly directed the attention of the Board to the necessity of providing some other place than Deer Island for the detention of truants and absentees from school. "The unwisdom and injustice," they say, "in compelling the truants from school to be associated in any way with the criminals sent to Deer Island is a physical and moral injury to such children, and should at once be corrected."

In March, 1884, the city council were requested to take some action upon this important matter, and again, in December of the same year, the subject was brought to their notice. In 1885 the Superintendent, in his report upon school attendance, spoke of the benefits that would result from a change in the locality of the truant school. The committee again urged that action be taken. So far as the School Board is concerned, the system in force for controlling truants in Boston receives the most earnest and enlightened consideration. A law was passed by the Legislature of 1886 authorizing the establishment of another truant school in Boston, and the mayor of the city made the subject a special topic of his recent inaugural address.

The superintendent of schools of Fall River says: "Our ordinance designates our almshouse as the place of confinement, etc., for truants. We have a good school-room on the premises, and the teacher teaches both the truants and the pauper children together. The school is a good one of its kind, but the surroundings are not what they should be."

The superintendent at Brockton says: "Three [truants] have been sent to the almshouse, and several more would have been sentenced if we had had a proper place."

The truant school of New Bedford is attached to the almshouse. "The institution," says the superintendent, "is by no means what it ought to be, but the fear of it stops truancy among the boys. We have no place to which to send truant girls, or with the fear of which to frighten mothers into keeping their daughters steadily at school."

Many of the towns have assigned the almshouse as the place for the commitment of their truants; none, I believe, without a shadowy sense of the inadequacy of the provision; indeed, in most towns, I suspect the provision is only in name. One such school for reform which I have seen, if I may judge from a single visit, itself stands much in need of reforming.

Sometimes the by-laws adopted by the towns name places for the confinement of their truants without asking consent of the proper authorities. One set recently brought to my notice named the State Primary School at Monson; the authorities of this school do not grant the privilege. Hampden County has a truant school. A charge of ten dollars is made to every town outside of the county for the privilege of assigning this truant school as the place for the discipline of the truants from such town. Several towns have been granted the privilege; but as I learned at a recent visit to the school, only three have ever paid the charge. The towns which have not paid are not entitled to send, and so have not provided a place for their truants.

A law passed in 1873 provided that, on petition of three or more cities or towns in any county, the county commissioners shall establish a truant school for the county. An act of 1881 provided that the commissioners of certain counties, and an act of 1884, that the commissioners of two, three or four contiguous counties, shall, on petition as before, establish a union truant school. Though in several counties petitions have been presented from a sufficient number of towns to meet the conditions of the law, these have not been so numerous as to compel the commissioners to obey the law, except in one county. Compliance was prompt in Hampden; this county has had a well-ordered county truant school for six years in the city of Springfield.

Some expense attends the arrest and conviction of truants. If committed to a truant school the town is chargeable with their support. By statute the maximum charge against any municipality for the support of its truants in a county truant school is two dollars for each per week. In some towns, it is said, the expense is a drawback to the enforcement of the law. Can it be that the means which might transform many a prospective criminal into a self-respecting and respectable member of society, placed in one scale of the balance, does not outweigh a few dollars placed in the other?

Thus, from imperfections, real or imagined, in the laws, from wrong interpretations of them, from the inefficiency in their administration by reason of poorly paid and incompetent officers, and the indifference, ignorance and cupidity of parents and people, and especially from the want of suitable places for the instruction of this class of our children, there exists a large amount of truancy and unnecessary absence from school throughout the State.

How can the Laws be made more Effective?

What can be done to secure a better enforcement of existing laws?

The laws look primarily for their enforcement to the school committees. No more important duty is imposed upon the committees than that of securing regular school attendance. They are required to have made, once each year, a list of all the children of school age in town. with the age of each; in large towns and cities, the name of the street where the child lives should be recorded. This list should be compared with the names in the teachers' registers. The whereabouts of the absentees should be discovered, and personal effort should be made by the committee to secure punctual and constant attendance of all who are absent without excuse on account of age, occupation or previous attendance for the required time.

Parents often need a personal appeal from the school committee. One of my correspondents, in reply to the question, What better means can be provided for controlling truancy? replied, "A new set of parents." Some parents wink at, excuse and assume the responsibility for their children's unnecessary absence: this should be met by kindly but emphatic rebuke. They should be made to see that direct practical results follow to themselves and their children from the discipline and instruction of the schools. If a child is incorrigible and refuses to accept school privileges at his own door, the parent should be led willingly to intrust to the proper authorities the training of the child for a brief time in a good school away. In some of our cities parents have learned that the officers of the law are acting the part of true friends to their children when they secure their committal to a good truant school.

A most important duty of the committee is to present to the towns for their adoption a code of by-laws, fully complying with the statutes concerning truants, including all necessary provisions for their full and prompt enforcement. Having secured their adoption, it is the duty of the committee to see that the provisions are enforced, regardless of all else but the interest of the children and the community. There are intimations in the earlier part of this report that these duties are not uniformly so discharged. Laboring in this spirit, committees will not connive at the fraudulent statements of parents regarding their children's age, their own or the children's condition; nor will they blindly make such statements to excuse their own or the town's neglect.

All necessary provisions relating to truant children include, first, a suitable place for their confinement, discipline and instruction. It should not be a house of correction or reformatory, or any place with which is associated the idea of criminality. It should not be a poor-house, suggestive of insanity, infirmity, shiftlessness and imbecility. Truant children are unfortunate in their constitution or in their surroundings; they are often bright, and almost always sensitive; they are wayward, but not criminal; they are sometimes more "sinned against than sinning;" they are to be reclaimed by being trained to habits of cleanliness, regularity and self-respect. After their brief absence from society, they must not be restored to it with a stigma upon them. They have too often come from poor, bad, wicked homes. What they need is the influences which pervade the well-ordered, Christian family. The institution, whatever it is, to which they are sent should be small, — not containing much over thirty, including the inmates, a teacher, a skilled mechanic, and the superintendent and his wife or a matron, who should be virtually father and mother to the children.

Connected with the institution should be a few acres of land easy of cultivation, — no walls need surround it. There should be also a workshop and a school. The truant can often work easier than he can study. Here, under competent directors, work and study will alternate. The children will learn to use tools, they will read good books and be taught the elements of a good education. At the table, in the sitting or reading room, and in their plays, under the eye of a sympathizing friend and guardian, they will practise the amenities

of social life. . The school should be furnished with a teacher
who can and will find in every child some good motive to which
to appeal; a teacher who can eliminate the bad by augmenting
the good; a teacher who by tack and sympathy, and a sincere
desire for his welfare, will become an object of personal interest to the child.

While I write I have in mind an institution where these
ideal relations actually exist. It is the duty of school committees to secure similar institutions in sufficient numbers to
give every truant child the experience of a home upon which
he can model his own, should he ever have one. Let the petitions from the towns be so multiplied that the county commissioners, whose duty it is to provide them, will yield from
importunity if they do not from the sense of obligation. These
truant schools are the crying need of the time, and will go far
towards settling the truant problem.

NUMBER OF TRUANT SCHOOLS NEEDED.

A rough estimate, based upon the fact that about one commitment may be anticipated for a population of 4,000 people,
shows that the several counties should make provision for
truants as follows : —

County.	Truants.	County.	Truants.
Berkshire,	17	Suffolk,	97
Franklin,	9	Norfolk,	24
Hampshire,	12	Bristol,	35
Hampden,	26	Plymouth,	19
Worcester,	57	Barnstable,	7
Middlesex,	80	Dukes,	1
Essex,	61	Nantucket,	1

If 3,000 should be taken as the average population for one
truant, the number of truants to be provided for would be
proportionately increased. If proper provisions were made,
and due vigilance were exercised in enforcing the laws for
compulsory attendance, probably the number of arrests would
considerably exceed the above estimates. It can be seen from
this what the number of truant schools for the whole State
should be, what counties could unite to maintain one, and what
counties would require one or more.

It is well known that in every town there are children attend-

ing school who are disobedient and difficult to control. Such
non-conforming pupils, while they annoy the teacher and inter-
rupt the good order of the school, do not profit by their
attendance. Whipping, if it were effective, is too unpopular
to be a common resort for discipline; such pupils have sometimes to be dismissed from the school and turned into the
street. It has been proposed to so amend our truant laws,
that on complaint of the school committee such pupils shall be
sent for short periods of time to truant schools; the fear of
being sent would have a restraining influence. The class of
children for which such an amendment would provide, though
very small, is one that causes a great deal of trouble. If such
amendment should be made, it would necessitate still larger
accommodations in the truant schools.

Another duty which the town by-laws devolve upon the
school committees is to appoint truant officers and fix their
salaries. These officers should be discreet persons having ex-
ecutive ability combined with a kindly spirit and an elevated
character. They must know how to manage truants, and their
parents also.

"The importance of the services of these officers," says
Superintendent Cogswell, "is not to be judged by the number
of truants brought before the court, or even by the number
of cases of truancy which have occurred during the year; but
rather by the number of children now in our schools, who, but
for the watchful care and personal influence of these faithful
officers, would be wandering about the streets, exposed to the
dangers and temptations of a vagrant life. They are helpful
to parents as well as to teachers, and have gained the respect
and confidence of both."

Superintendent Edgerly of Fitchburg says: "Their work does
not consist in arresting boys and endeavoring to send them to reform schools. People are beginning to realize this. Parents and
pupils, oftentimes, need advice more than censure. Children
are kept from school because they have not sufficient clothing.
There is work at home to be done, and the child must do it.
The interposition of a benevolent society is needed more than
that of the officer of the law. Occasionally there will be found
a family careless or stubborn in regard to this subject, the
parents refusing to allow the attendance of the children when

there is no good reason for non-attendance. The strong arm of the law must deal with these exceptional cases."

Where no attempt is made to enforce the laws, the schools become demoralized by irregular attendance, illiteracy increases, vagrants abound, the vicious and criminal classes are augmented. Any feeble or partial enforcement of the laws may serve only to show the extent of the absenteeism, without holding it in check. The number of convictions for truancy might increase even, and yet the evil might not be controlled. It is only when the right kind of men are employed as officers that truancy is kept within narrow limits. The experience of one city is like that of many. In one, under a defective system for executing the laws from 1865 to 1873, truancy was rife; thirty-five truants were committed in one year. In 1874 a proper truant school was established. One efficient officer was employed. Idle boys were no longer found in the streets, absenteeism was sensibly diminished, and the commitments for truancy were reduced to less than one-half their former number.

In the smaller towns few requisitions will be made upon the truant officer; he will attend to special cases brought to his knowledge by the teacher or school committee. Cities and towns of ten thousand inhabitants or more should have at least one officer who is subject to immediate call; his compensation should be such as to enable him to give all his time to the service. In the smaller of these cities and towns he may have some other duties, such as taking the school census and distributing school supplies. He should become acquainted with the people, know of all new families moving into town, and see that their children are placed in school. In larger cities he will not neglect these duties, but he will be mainly employed, especially during school hours, in looking after truants and absentees. He will secure the co-operation of the employers of children who work in manufacturing and other establishments. This will involve his seeing that children discharged from work shall at once return to school. Especially should it be his duty to arrange with overseers of mills a system by which, without break between school and work, the classes of pupils who are required to attend school can pass from one to the other.

The duties of these officers are greater in number and variety than the name *Truant Officer* would imply. A vigilant officer with a co-operating police-force will make the streets and by-ways of a large city as lonesome to a boy as the tombs of the dead, and the school-room, in comparison, a delight.

Where the time of one well-paid officer — or more than one, if the service demands it — is exclusively devoted to the work, the results reached are the most satisfactory. The most effective work is done in the cities. Here, officers give their entire time to it. At the commencement of each school session they are notified of all suspected cases of truancy. For this purpose the teacher fills out and furnishes to the officer blank forms giving the circumstances of each case, including the name and residence of the absentee. The officer at once attends to looking up the absent pupil; dependent upon what the facts are, the absentee is excused, placed in the school, or under arrest to be brought to trial. A return of the case is made to the teacher or committee.

SALARIES AND PAY OF TRUANT OFFICERS.

The following table shows what compensation is paid truant officers for their services in certain Massachusetts cities and towns : —

	No. of Paid Officers.	Pay of Each.		No. of Paid Officers.	Pay of Each.
Adams,	–	$30 00	Lowell,	3	$817 00
Attleborough,	3	25 00	Lynn,	1	900 00
Boston,	Chief,	1,500 00	Marlborough,	1	100 00
	14	1,200 00	Milton,	3	30 cts. pr hour.
Brookline,	1	400 00			
Cambridge,	3	900 00	Milford,	1	100 00
Chicopee,	1	250 00	New Bedford,	1	800 00
Clinton,	1	700 00	Newton,	1	600 00
Dedham,	3	$1 per head	North Adams,	1	100 00
			Northampton,	2	50 00
Fall River,	3	600 00	Quincy,	–	30 cts. pr hour.
Fitchburg,	1	300 00			
Gloucester,	1	750 00	Salem,	1	800 00
Haverhill,	1	600 00	Somerville,	1	325 00
Holyoke,	2	800 00	Springfield,	1	900 00
		825 00	Taunton,	1	375 00
Hyde Park,	1	25 cts. pr hour.	Waltham,	1	300 00
			Watertown,	2	20 00
Lawrence,	1	900 00	Winchester,	2	15 00
Leominster,	1	$1.50 pr head.	Woburn,	1	360 00
			Worcester,	2	900 00

There is a great disparity in the amount paid for this service. Some of the towns employ the police officers, whose fees are additional to a stated salary; but to a considerable extent the sum paid indicates the kind and amount of service demanded and rendered.

The surest means for reducing truancy and absenteeism to their smallest terms is to improve the schools. "Make the schools so good," says one of my correspondents, "that the people will want the children to attend;" says another, "We rely largely upon the personal efforts of teachers and superintendent, — upon the officers last; we make but few arrests." And still another says, "Put more emphasis upon moral means, less upon the merely restrictive. To this end have better teaching, more personal work by teachers and school officials, more attractive school-rooms." "The best means to reduce truancy," says a fourth, "is to place a good teacher in every school-room. As long as inferior teachers are employed and parents are ignorant and debased, so long shall we have a certain amount of truancy."

A few suggestions looking to modifications in the laws and to additional means for their enforcement, will conclude what I have to say upon this subject.

1. The laws relating to the employment of children in manufacturing and other establishments should be extended to all kinds of wage labor.

2. The attendance of every well child should be required from the age of seven to twelve, during the whole time the schools keep; from twelve to fifteen for two terms a year, and for the whole time, unless the child is at work.

The reasons for this are: First, if under twelve years of age, children cannot be employed to work in manufacturing or other establishments during the days the schools keep. Second, the children of well-to-do people attend school the whole time. Third, by being allowed to stay out of the school half the time, as they may where the schools keep forty weeks, those least disposed to attend school can waste half their time in contracting the itinerant habits of the truant, and, by associating with others, help to swell the vagrant class.

3. In case the children are in need of clothing suitable for attending school, and parents are unable to provide it, or are in

circumstances to need help, it should be furnished by the town, and not at the expense of the child's schooling.

4. So far as possible, the parents should be held responsible for the children's absence from school, whether it be caused by truancy or otherwise. This is the design of a law passed by the State of Connecticut in 1885. After specifying the time during which parents must cause children of certain ages to attend school, the law provides for a fine to be imposed upon the parent, as follows: " Each week's failure on the part of any person to comply with the provisions of the preceding sections, shall be a distinct offence, punishable with a fine. not exceeding five dollars." Under this law a judge may impose for six weeks' absence a fine of thirty dollars; he may collect five of it, and leave the other twenty-five hanging over the parent to induce him to keep his child in school for the coming weeks. In case he succeeds, the balance can be remitted. A motive is thus brought to bear upon parent and pupil which secures, it is said, constant attendance; the pecuniary burden is not greater than almost any parent can bear.

5. In case of absence from school the burden of proof should be thrown upon the parent; he should be required to show that his child's absence is necessary, or that his education is otherwise properly provided for. At present the school official is obliged to prove that the education is being neglected.

6. By imposing the penalties, and making them greater if need be, towns should be encouraged to more fully comply with the laws relating to truancy and absenteeism.

7. Provision should be made for enforcing the laws relating to truancy by a State official. The principal reliance in the State of Connecticut, outside of four cities, for executing the laws is one State agent. Under his administration sixty-five fines have been imposed for non-compliance with the laws requiring parents to send their children to school within a period of nine years, while under our system, with local officers to enforce the law, not one-tenth as many are known to have been imposed, in the period of thirty-five years that our law has been in force, and this with our larger population.

8. Truant officers should be empowered to make arrests for the purpose of placing in school, or for temporary detention, under the general instruction of school committees.

9. If the law under which county commissioners are required to provide truant schools is inadequate, amend it. Then let towns petition for and insist upon their establishment.

10. Let the law requiring county truant schools to be established be so amended that, instead of two dollars a week being charged to the town for the support of her children committed, the whole expense shall be borne by the county or State.

11. Let the time for which the truants may be sent to these schools be changed to four years; also provide a board of visitors for every such school.

12. So amend the truant law that those pupils who persistently violate the reasonable rules and regulations of the common schools may be sent, upon complaint of school committees, for brief periods of time to the truant school.

13. Make more ample provisions for the care of girls in truant schools.

The grounds for many of these suggestions are shown in the illustrations already given. I need not state the reasons for others: these will at once occur to the reader; they are all occasioned by something observed or brought to my notice during the year. Though they may seem to reflect discredit upon our truant laws and upon their enforcement, it is doubtless true that the provisions of these laws as a whole are wiser and better than those of any other State, and that where they are faithfully enforced they are as effective as any laws upon the statute book.

Respectfully submitted,

GEORGE A. WALTON.

West Newton, Dec. 31, 1886.

B.

REPORT OF GEORGE H. MARTIN,

AGENT OF THE BOARD.

REPORT.

To the Board of Education:

I have spent the school year of 1885–86 in inspecting the schools of the following towns : —

BERKSHIRE Co. — Great Barrington, Monterey, New Marlborough, Mt. Washington, Sandisfield, Sheffield.

HAMPDEN Co. — Agawam, Hampden, Holland, Montgomery, Southwick, Wales, Springfield.

WORCESTER Co. — Auburn, Dudley, Oxford, Southbridge, Sturbridge, Webster, Worcester.

NORFOLK Co. — Randolph, Stoughton, Weymouth, Wrentham.

BRISTOL Co. — Berkley, Freetown, Fall River, New Bedford.

PLYMOUTH Co. — Hanover, Kingston, Marshfield, Pembroke, Plympton, South Scituate.

In the cities but few of the schools were visited. In the towns, with one or two exceptions, all the schools were seen, usually in company with one or more members of the school committee. I have made few formal examinations and have tabulated no percentages.

Meetings of teachers and committees were held in all but two of the towns, and evening lectures were given in about half of the towns.

The afternoon conferences have been spent in criticism upon the schools, based upon notes taken during the visits, and suggestions of possible improvements in means and methods. The subjects treated and the amount of time given to each have varied with the need of the town. Sometimes the most prominent topic was the school buildings and their care ; sometimes the spirit and discipline of the school, and the relation of teachers and pupils ; more often the methods of teaching the common branches.

At the evening meetings I have spoken on one of the following topics: A Practical Education, A Good School and How to Secure It, Some Popular Errors concerning Education.

These lectures are designed to deepen the public interest in the schools, to call the attention of the citizens to the local needs, to impress upon parents their responsibility for the success of the schools, to advocate the cause of higher education as embodied in the high schools.

Concerning this agency work a superintendent writes: "Your visit has done our schools more good than any institute we have attended. The teachers seem to feel a personal responsibility for their work and a deeper interest in it than ever before." Concerning the evening talks the committees say: "This is just what our people need to hear."

Invitations to take part in the graduating exercises of several high schools have given an opportunity to speak in favor of high-school instruction to larger audiences than usually gather at educational meetings. It might be to the advantage of these schools if the services of the Board of Education were more generally called into requisition upon such occasions.

A School Standard.

Before passing any judgment upon the schools, we should settle upon some standard which, though ideal, shall be reasonable and uniform. Such a standard may be found by considering the statutory requirements of the Commonwealth as found in chap. 44 of the Public Statutes, with the additions made by subsequent legislation.

Reasoning from these laws we should say that every child in the State should, on reaching the age of fifteen, be able to read at sight, so as to get the sense, good English as found in standard and current literature, and to express his thoughts in writing, legibly, grammatically and with correct spelling; that he should be able with promptness and accuracy to perform the ordinary operations with numbers, and to apply these in the every-day transactions of common business life; that he should know something of the earth on which he lives, its products, its peoples and their relation to each other; especially of his own country, its position and extent, its natural

advantages and resources, its industries, its productions and
their distribution, its political and business centres; that besides the geography of his country he should know its history,
the story of its development from the feeble germ in the early
colonies to its present greatness, including in this a knowledge
of the government under which he lives and of the steps by
which and the cost at which his civil freedom has been obtained; that he should have a general knowledge of the structure of his own body, the various systems and their functions
and how to care for them, and should be especially impressed
with a sense of the dangers to health in the use of alcoholic
drinks, stimulants and narcotics; that he should have learned
some principles of drawing which would be useful in the mechanic arts, and should have acquired some skill in applying
them.

That besides this knowledge he should cherish a regard for
those virtues which adorn and conserve society, and an abhor-
rence of vice.

So much as this is expressly called for by the laws regulating
the common schools. By implication the State would seem to
expect that in the process of obtaining this knowledge the
child should have acquired some control over his mental and
moral powers; that he should be able to form judgments
based upon his observations; that he should be able to discover
the more obvious relations between things that differ, upon
which memory depends; that he should be able to come to
some general knowledge through analysis and comparison;
that he should be able to perform some of the simple processes of reasoning logically; that he should be able to concen-
trate his powers upon an object of thought and hold them for
a reasonable time; that he should be able to create by the use
of his imagination such ideals of things as master-workmen in
every business require, and such an ideal of character as he
would wish to realize in himself; and that he should be able to
control his appetites and desires so as to practise the virtues
which he has learned to admire.

By its compulsory laws the State virtually says that so much
education as this is necessary to make intelligent, self-supporting, law-abiding citizens. Official examiners and the public
who are interested in youth have a right to test up to these

limits all who have passed through the common schools, always remembering that at fifteen boys are still boys and girls
girls, and that all the mental and moral powers are still in the
gristle.

The casual observer of children discovers the fact that a
large number who have come to the end of their common-school
life fall short of this ideal standard which the State has set up
both in knowledge and power. Any extended inspection of
the schools discloses the same fact more fully.

LIMITATIONS ON PUBLIC-SCHOOL WORK.

Such inspection, however, reveals what the casual observer
often fails to see, — certain limitations upon public-school work
which must be considered in forming a just judgment. From
failing to take these into account many well-meaning critics
have reached unfounded conclusions.

These limitations are primarily four : —

1. In the quality of the material which the schools have to
work upon.

2. In the physical conditions under which the work is done.

3. In the quality of the teaching force in the schools.

4. In the quality of the directing force in the charge of the
schools.

THE MATERIAL.

The standard which the State has fixed presupposes children
with sound bodies, in possession of all the faculties, in regular
attendance through the school period, and coming from decent
homes where they are under some moral restraints.

Where all these conditions are found to exist, investigation
shows that the State's standard is a reasonable one, and that
children can and do attain to it, and having so attained go out
into life and enter at once upon successful careers.

But some of these conditions are often wanting. Sometimes
all are wanting in individuals, occasionally in whole schools.

Attendance. — In the schools which I have visited during the
year, one-fifth of the pupils registered were absent at the time
of my visit. This probably represents very nearly the yearly
average throughout the State, as my visits covered all seasons
of the year, all grades of schools in manufacturing and farming
communities, and this in six counties. Whether we consider

that one-fifth of the pupils are absent all the time, or that all the pupils are absent one-fifth of the time, it is evident that from this cause alone the outcome of school life is materially reduced both as to knowledge and power.

Health. — The registers show only a small part of the actual interruption. Children in school are not always in condition to do the work of the school. That work demands continuous attention. Whatever the powers called into exercise at any time, whether perceptive or reflective, they must be held steadily to the object of thought until the truth is apprehended. Such continuous attention is only possible when the body is in good condition. The child has not power to control the mind when experiencing physical pain or discomfort.

There are many hours, often days, sometimes weeks when children are not sick enough to be kept at home, but are not well enough to do the regular school work. Colds, toothache, wounds, the lassitude and uneasiness which indicate approaching disease, the weakness which follows such disease, — these, or some of these, have their victims in every school.

The power of attention thus being intermittent, the whole work is intermittent in its character, and while the school as a whole seems to be moving along the course of study prescribed, much of the individual work is fragmentary and disjointed.

All this is true of children called healthy. But the schools contain children who are not healthy; how many, we have no means of knowing, but probably more than we have suspected, and enough to interfere seriously with the successful progress of school work.

The report of Dr. Hertel, Municipal Medical Officer of Copenhagen, who instituted careful inquiries into the health of the school children of that city, is most suggestive. In fourteen schools, preparatory and secondary, containing 3,141 boys from the higher classes of Danish society, 1,900 are reported healthy, 978 sickly, while reports are wanting from 263. In percentages, — healthy, 60.5; sickly, 31.1; non-returned, 8.4.

In ten schools containing 1,211 girls between the ages of five and sixteen, 644 are reported healthy; 477 sickly; non-returned 90. In percentages, — healthy, 53.1; sickly, 39.4; non-returned, 7.5.

The term " sickly " in this report means " unsound children who suffer from chronic complaints, but who are nevertheless able to attend school regularly." It does not include such children as those to whom I have before referred as suffering from acute and temporary illness.

I have no data upon which to base a judgment concerning the proportion of sickly children in our own schools, but from some casual inquiries along the line of Dr. Hertel's investigations which I have made during my visits I believe that there is enough of chronic weakness to affect materially the total results of school work.

Mental Ability. — All these limitations may exist in the case of children having average mental ability. There are many children below this average. Some are weak along single lines of mental efforts, dull of perception, or slow to see relations, or with little power to imagine, or weak in reasoning power. There are children who are deficient in all of these, known as "stupid" children. There are others who are only slow.

Some of these defects are inherited, some are produced by disease, some by unfortunate conditions of living; but whether congenital or acquired, they constitute an ever-existing limitation upon educational processes.

Homes. — Again, large allowances must be made both as to intellectual and moral progress, in view of the homes from which many of the children come. I have recently visited a school composed almost wholly of Polish children. In the manufacturing cities and villages French children are numerous, and there are many Portuguese.

Many of these children cannot speak English when they come to school. They do not hear it at home. An extra burden is thus imposed upon the schools. From homes of poverty and vice, homes of ignorance and brutality, in city and country, children come to the schools bringing those mental and physical weaknesses of which we have spoken.

I have found whole neighborhoods from which the typical New England character has disappeared. The families which remain are idle, shiftless, poor, without hope for themselves or ambition for their children; the children are scantily clothed, poorly fed, feeble alike in body and mind, and subject to no moral restraints at home, and a perpetual source of trouble to teachers and school officers.

An old farmer who as committee-man accompanied me to a school said, on leaving : " This is a bad lot. They are all block-heads- and their parents before them. They are as vicious as they are ignorant." While it is not common to find whole schools composed of such material, individuals are frequently met with.

It is impossible for children from such homes to accomplish the full measure of work which the school laws contemplate. Their experience has furnished them with such a narrow range of ideas that the language of books is to them practically a foreign language, and as I see them, they go stumbling along bewil-dered by the obscurity which envelopes them, and reaping scanty advantages from the means of education at their hands. Such is the first general limitation upon public-school work, — in the material which the schools have to work upon.

SANITARY CONDITIONS.

A second limitation is in the physical conditions under which the work is done. There is a sufficient amount of physical discomfort to interfere seriously with that continuous thinking upon which successful school work depends.

Heating. — One cause of this discomfort is defective heating. There is often too little heat; more often too much. I have frequently found children with outer garments on huddled about the stove. In one primary-school room heated by a fur-nace, I have been told that at the opening of school during cold weather the thermometer rarely stands higher than 50° F. Children cannot study well and shiver at the same time.

On the other hand, I have found in a grammar-school room hot-air pouring through two large registers near the front of the room, while the thermometer on the rear wall registered 84° F. The teacher was unconscious that the room was too warm, though the faces of the pupils plainly showed it. The janitor had left the draft on the furnace and gone home, taking the key of the cellar.

In another primary room heated by an enormous cast-iron stove, I found the thermometer in the back of the room at 80°. Placing it on the desk nearest the stove, the direct radiation sent the mercury up to 110°. A boy five or six years old sat blistering at the same desk.

Unequal distribution of heat is another prevalent source of discomfort. A valuable series of experiments was conducted in 1885 by Mr. Nathaniel Morton of Plymouth, Mass., the results of which were published in the "Old Colony Memorial" of April 16, 1885, and in the "American Architect and Building News" of April 17, 1886.

By the courtesy of Mr. Morton I am permitted to copy from his report : —

Surprise at the great difference in the temperature of the room at five feet above the floor, and at the floor, led to making tests of the temperature of the air of fourteen school-rooms, three times a day for the three weeks, from January 26 to February 13, 1885. Three thermometers were hung in each room, on light tripods, the bulbs of the thermometers being at a height of five feet, three feet, and two inches from the floor, and so placed in each room as to be out of the direct influence of the sun and heating apparatus, and not near to any window or other opening, nor near the outside wall. The thermometers for each room were selected to read alike at the same height from the floor. The readings of the thermometers in each room were taken soon after opening, and just before recess in the morning, and before recess in the afternoon. The temperature of the outside air was recorded at the same time each day. All apparent errors in the records have been omitted.

TABLE I.

Room, 12′ x 28′ x 38′, heated by a furnace, ventilated by two chimney exhaust-flues with openings near the floor and fresh cold-air supply at the ceiling, after the plan of Durant's patent, as applied by A. B. Brown, Architect, Worcester.

Time of Observation.	DEGREES.				DEGREES.	
	Outside Temperature.	Room Temperatures at			Differences of Temperature at	
		5 feet.	3 feet.	2 inches.	5 feet and 2 inches.	3 feet and 2 inches.
9	33	73	69	62	11	7
10½	34	72	70	68	4	2
3	32	72	70	67	5	3
9	10	61	59	55	6	4
10½	12	65	63	57	8	6
3	16	72	68	66	6	2
9	35	73	70	67	6	3
10½	35	72	68	65	7	3
3	22	72	68	65	7	3
9	6	69	67	65	4	2
10½	9	72	70	68	4	2
3	12	80	75	70	10	5
9	15	58	56	52	6	4
10½	21	69	66	58	11	8
3	29	75	70	69	6	1
9	10	71	69	65	6	4
10½	11	70	68	65	5	3
3	10	80	75	71	9	4
9	8	69	65	60	9	5
10½	15	78	70	65	13	5
3	17	74	70	70	4	–
9	27	71	69	66	5	3
10½	29	78	72	70	8	2
3	33	72	70	69	3	1
9	30	70	68	64	6	4
10½	34	78	72	68	10	4
3	32	72	70	68	4	2
9	23	60	56	50	10	6
10½	25	66	60	56	10	4
3	26	68	62	60	8	2
9	28	66	60	56	10	4
10½	30	70	64	60	10	4
3	35	72	68	66	6	2
9	48	60	58	54	6	4
10½	50	70	64	60	10	4
3	45	72	68	66	6	2
9	6	62	58	52	10	6
10½	7	70	66	60	10	6
3	9	74	70	66	8	4
9	8	68	62	56	12	6
10½	12	68	64	60	8	4
3	20	70	66	60	10	6
9	22	68	66	60	8	6
10½	24	70	66	62	8	4
Average of 44 tests..	22½	70	66	63	7.6	3.8

TABLE II.

Room, 9' x 19' x 38', heated by a cast-iron stove with a smoke-pipe nearly the whole length of the room to the chimney.

Time of Observation.	Outside Temperature.	DEGREES. Room Temperatures at			DEGREES. Differences in Temperature between	
		5 feet.	3 feet.	2 inches.	5 feet and 2 inches.	3 feet and 2 inches.
9	33	68	66	58	10	8
10½	34	72	68	60	12	8
3	32	74	72	66	8	6
9	10	60	56	44	16	12
10½	12	66	64	54	12	10
3	16	80	76	66	14	10
9	35	68	62	58	10	4
10½	35	80	76	62	18	14
3	22	72	70	62	10	8
9						
10½	9	76	72	52	24	20
3	12	78	76	64	14	12
10½	21	74	70	56	18	14
3	29	74	72	62	12	10
10½	11	70	62	52	18	14
3	10	72	70	60	12	10
9						
10½	15	68	66	50	18	16
3	17	68	66	56	12	10
9	27	66	60	42	24	18
10½	29	76	72	52	24	20
3	33	71	68	61	10	7
9	30	70	65	50	20	5
10½	34	79	77	61	18	16
3	32	78	73	66	12	7
9	23	67	61	56	11	5
10½	25	78	72	60	18	2
9	28	62	58	44	18	14
10½	30	74	70	56	18	14
3	35	80	76	66	14	10
9	48	70	66	52	18	14
10½	50	74	70	58	16	12
3	45	80	76	66	14	10
10½	7	68	66	52	16	14
3	9	74	71	62	12	9
9	8	65	63	41	24	22
10½	12	71	70	54	17	16
3	20	74	70	62	12	8
9	22	64	61	42	22	19
10½	24	78	72	58	20	14
Average of 34 tests.	24	72	69	56	15.6	12.1

TABLE III.

RECORDS AT OTHER SCHOOL-ROOMS.

ROOMS.	Tests.	DEGREES.		
		Average Outside Temperature.	Difference in Temperature at 5 ft. and 2 in.	Difference in Temperature at 5 ft. and 2 in.
Heated by furnace, Durant's Ventilation, ...	41	22	6½	4
" " "	39	22	10	5.9
Heated by coal and wood stoves (fires all night), . . .	42	22	10.3	8.3
Heated by open ventilating stove, made by N. Y. Open Stove Ventilating Co., ...	36	22	12	8
Heated by Michigan Ventilating Stove, some exhaust from the floor, ...	40	22	13.1	9.1
Heated by coal stove (fire all night) ventilated by exhaust from floor, and supply of fresh air at the ceiling, . .	40	22	13.6	12.4*
Same as room above, ...	40	22	13.7	9.3
Heated by Ventilating Stove of John Grossius, Cincinnati, ventilated by air-supply through the stove and also at the ceiling, exhausts at the floor, ...	40	22	13.9	9.3
Heated by N. Y. Open Ventilating Stove, ...	33	22	14.2	10.1
Heated by Grossius's Ventilating Stove, exhaust at the floor, ...	41	22	14.9	7.9
Heated by coal stove, no ventilation, ...	12	21	12.5	8.1
Heated by coal stove (continuous fire), no ventilation, .	12	17	19	15.6
Heated by wood stove, low ceiling, ...	16	24	22	18

* This bad result was due to having the openings for supply of air too small compared with the exhaust.

Mr. Morton says : —

The rooms found to be heated the best (which are supposed also to be ventilated the best, although no tests were made of the purity of the air) are the three rooms which are heated by furnaces, ventilated by chimney exhaust flues with openings near the floor and fresh air supplied automatically at the ceiling when the air from the furnace is not sufficient to supply the place of the air taken from the room by the exhaust flues. In these three rooms an average of forty-one tests to each room shows an average difference in temperature between the air at the floor and at five feet above the floor, of less than eight degrees, the average outside temperature being twenty-two degrees.

The rooms found to be the most unevenly heated are those with low (nine feet) ceilings, heated by stoves with long pipes, in which the fire is not kept over night, and not made until one or two hours before opening school in the morning. Such rooms may be very warm at the height of the head of the teacher and be near freezing point at

the feet of the scholars. In such rooms, when the outside temperature is near zero, over thirty degrees difference in temperature has
been found between the air at the floor and the air at the height of
five feet. It is near noon before such rooms get properly warmed.
A remedy would be to keep the fires through the night, or make the
fires much earlier in the morning, to get all of the air in the room
thoroughly warmed before beginning school.

One thermometer placed anywhere in a school-room is not a sufficient guide for regulating the temperature of the room.

If a school-room has but one thermometer, it should be placed
much nearer the floor than is customary.

The colder the weather the more difference there is in the temperature of a room at different heights from the floor.

A warm room may be considered to be evenly heated when there
is less than ten degrees difference in temperature between the floor
and a point five feet above the floor, in weather colder than twenty
degrees Fahrenheit.

One moral of all this is suggested by Mr. Morton: "When
children are confined for hours where their feet are in a temperature but little above freezing, there is small chance for mental
improvement, and far greater chance for contracting colds or
other forms of disease."

I would add to this that "there is small chance for mental
improvement" where, as these tables show, for days in succes-
sion the temperature of the room at the middle of the session
ranges from 74° to 80°.

My observation leads me to believe that these tables are rep-
resentative not only of Plymouth, but of the school-rooms of the
State, except those in the new buildings in the cities. Most of
the rural schools are in buildings similar to the one described
in Table II., which gave the worst results.

Ventilation. — Added to the discomfort arising from defective heating is that from defective ventilation. This evil is most
marked in the older buildings in the cities and manufacturing
villages, where the rooms are filled with children to the full
seating capacity, often beyond it, and where the provisions for
ventilation are of the scantiest and most unscientific kind.

Few scientific tests have been made of the air in school-
rooms, but its state is revealed to the visitor by the odor which
greets his entrance and by the lethargy which marks the ap-
pearance of the school. The few tests which have been made

serve to show what some of the children are breathing, and how little can fairly be expected of them in the way of mental or moral progress.

In 1883 a most valuable report was made by a special committee appointed to investigate the sanitary condition of the school buildings of the city of Lynn, Mass. Before giving the results of the analyses the report says: "Dr. Parker, one of the highest authorities on sanitary subjects, says that air which contains more than 6 parts of carbonic acid per 10,000 volumes is unfit to breathe; that with a ratio of 8, 9, or 10 parts per 10,000, the air smells stuffy and close, and beyond this becomes foul and offensive."

"Dr. Angus, Smith says: 'When people speak of good ventilation they mean, without knowing it, air with less than .07 per cent. of carbonic acid.'"

Then follows the tabulated results of the analysis of the air from different rooms as made by Professor Hills of the Harvard Medical School, and pronounced "strictly correct."

HOUR.	Temperature of Room.	Outside Temperature.	Carbonic Acid per 10,000 vols.
11.25 a. m., ...	72° F.	40° F.	18.15
11.35 a. m., ...	70° F.	40° F.	17.05
11.50 a. m., ...	72° F.	40° F.	12.65
3.45 p. m., ...	68° F.	25° F.	29.10
4.00 p. m., ...	70° F.	25° F.	17.95
10.28 a m., ...	68° F.	41.5° F.	17.21
11.35 a. m., ...	68° F.	41° F.	15.17
11.30 a. m., ...	76° F.	41° F.	12.82
11.55 a. m., ...	–	41° F.	3.69

The last describes the air as found out of doors on the same day.

The committee say of this table: "The results speak for themselves. If air containing more than 6 parts of carbonic acid per 10,000 volumes is unfit to breathe, what shall be said of air which contains from 12 to 29 parts, but that it is very bad."

They say also : " If we had tested the air in every school-room of the city, there is no good reason to suppose that our general conclusion would have been different." I believe that " State " might be substituted for " city " in the above sentence without doing any violence to facts.

School-room air may be vitiated in a more dangerous way than by the presence of a large proportion of carbonic acid. Vaults and cesspools are frequently found in close proximity to school-houses, and urinals and water-closets in the basements are not uncommon. It is perhaps enough for the present purpose to say that these may become nuisances, without affirming that they are always such.

In a city grammar-school building containing several hundred children, on one of the coldest days of last winter, when all doors and windows were closed to preserve the heat, I found in the corridors a perceptible smell from the urinals in the basement, and in the basement itself the odor was almost nauseating. I was glad to learn that this was an exceptional occurrence, and was due partly to the extreme weather and partly to some neglect by the janitor. But so long as extremes of weather are likely to occur and janitors to forget, the possibility of a recurrence would be a perpetual menace to the health of the children. With less watchful teachers the danger from defective closets and drainage is evidently great.

Owing to these two causes, — defective heating and defective ventilation, — it is plain that there must be many hours during the school life of children when they are unfitted by the existing physical conditions to do the amount and kind of work which the State standard requires. Herein lies the second general limitation upon public school work.

THE TEACHING FORCE.

Another limitation is in the quality of the teaching force. The standard for the pupils expressed or implied in the school laws presupposes certain qualities in the teachers.

First, they should have an acquaintance with the subjects required to be taught amounting to familiarity, — the whole subject and the parts being held in the mind clearly and not 'obscurely, distinctly and not in confusion, so that the teacher can handle them with confidence and not timidly.

Since learning implies a mind to learn as well as truth to be learned, the teacher should, secondly, know something of the minds to be taught, — their powers, what each has to do, and how it does it, and how it can be made to do it better, — the motives to conduct, and how to influence the will through them.

Added to this learning is needed what is called natural aptitude for teaching. The elements of this are clear thinking, analytic power, seeing the general and the particular at the same glance so that the illustration is ready as soon as the need of it appears ; perception quick, acute, and delicate, enabling the teacher to see, almost to divine, the exact mental state of the learner ; mind alert, facile, prompt to adapt means to ends ; and patience.

Superadded to these are needed force of character, power of continuance, moral integrity and moral earnestness.

Such qualifications can only be attained through the combined influence of nature, studies and experience. "Studies perfect nature, and are perfected by experience."

But it is scarcely possible that all of the teachers employed in the public schools of Massachusetts should possess all of these qualifications. In every other occupation in life men and women get into the wrong places. No other occupation in society is subject to general official inspection and criticism. There is no one authorized to determine and report upon the character and work of the lawyers, doctors, ministers, editors, mechanics, merchants, farmers, cooks, housekeepers, dressmakers, as upon teachers. But no one doubts that people are engaged in all these pursuits who have no natural fitness for them, and who are consequently making miserable failures in them. It would be strange if the same were not true of teachers, and if some children were not, throughout a part at least of their school course, in the hands of teachers who do not know what to do with them or for them. Large losses due to this cause seem almost inevitable.

Again, many teachers have never studied the principles or methods of their work. Of the 9,670 teachers employed last year 3,003 have graduated from Normal Schools. Besides these, several hundred, perhaps, have attended city training schools. All these are supposed to have studied psychology, the science and art of teaching, the principles of school organization and government, and something of the history of education.

Of the remaining number a large proportion have spent no time in such study. Of the last 125 teachers in country and village schools in different parts of the State whom I asked to name some educational books they had read, 73 had read none, 25 had read one, 12 had read some but could not remember the names, and 15 had read two or more. Of the same 125, sixty reported themselves as taking an educational paper. Forty-five teachers, or 36 per cent., had read no educational book and took no educational paper. In some towns every teacher reported himself as belonging to this illiterate class.

Three causes explain this neglect of professional study, — ignorance, indifference and conceit. Some have never seen or heard of a book on education ; some feel too little responsibility in their work and have too little ambition for professional success to induce them to spend the money and time required to read ; some feel that nature and experience have done so much for them that study is superfluous.

Not only are there teachers at work who have neither natural aptitude nor the benefit of study, but the third condition of successful work, experience, is often wanting. Of the teachers whose schools I have inspected this year, 10 per cent. had taught less than one term, 18 per cent. had taught less than one year and 42 per cent. less than three years. Twenty-six per cent. were new to the schools in which I found them. In estimating the result of the school work in these thirty towns we must consider that all the time one-tenth of the children are in the care of persons who are just beginning to learn what school-keeping means, — for whom the lamp of experience has just been lighted. We must consider further that more than one-quarter of the children are in the hands of teachers who have known them but a few weeks, — who are practically strangers to them. That the progress of the pupils in learning and discipline cannot be continuous, and that large discount must be made from the standard requirements, goes without saying.

How large this discount must be when all the conditions on which good teaching depends are wanting, as is sometimes the case; when the education of the children is entrusted to persons without natural endowments, without experience of their own and ignorant of the experience of others, can be suggested more easily than estimated.

I have frequently left a school with an admiration almost amounting to awe for the human mind that can continue its activities, and gain some knowledge and some increase of power, under conditions so adverse.

THE DIRECTING FORCE.

A fourth limitation is in the quality of the directing force in charge of the schools. By giving to the school committees "the general charge and superintendence" of the schools, the State has made these bodies responsible for bringing the children to the educational standard it has set up.

The authority entrusted to the committees is supposed to be ample for this purpose. They may establish the schools, organize them, make rules for conducting them, plan courses of study, select and furnish text books and supplies, and choose and appoint the teachers. More than this, if the details of administration are too burdensome, they may appoint a superintendent as their agent.

The wise exercise of these powers is one of the conditions of public-school work. But we find much of this work imperfectly done. To do it well requires not only general intelligence and practical judgment, but special intelligence growing out of familiarity with schools. While the first is usually found in the governing boards, the second is often wanting. There are good ministers and doctors and farmers and mechanics serving on the school committees, but few of them are school men. A young physician who took me to some schools said : "I find myself in a school-room much in the same condition that you would be in a sick-room. I may see that something is the matter, but I have no means of finding out just what the matter is, nor should I know what to do if I found out." His case is a typical one.

Indeed, I find that professional men have few advantages over others as school committee-men. In a town whose committee consisted of two young farmers and an old clergyman, the schools cared for by the farmers were in every particular superior to those in charge of the clergyman. The most judicious and efficient committee man whom I met this year was a carpenter. Women on the school boards are, with few exceptions, among the most useful members.

Imperfect supervision works both negatively and positively to defeat the end for which the school laws are made. Often through ignorance of the proper standard the supervision fails entirely to direct the schools.

Through neglect, absenteeism and truancy are allowed to exist. Many schools are badly organized, and much unnecessary friction results, with consequent loss of power. Unscientific courses of study are laid down, false standards are erected, — together working toward cram rather than development. Text books without merit are selected by persons who have never taught the subject. These are a perpetual hindrance to the work. The teachers are required to use artificial stimuli, and are worn and worried by elaborate marking systems with endless percentage. Some teachers are thwarted in their endeavor to introduce improved methods of teaching, and others are forced to spend their energies upon trivialities. Want of harmony in the local boards often produces temporary disaster. Recently in five of the towns coming under my inspection open quarrels between members of the school committee have seriously injured the schools.

Owing to these four causes, — the quality of the material, the physical conditions, the quality of the teachers and the quality of the supervision, — large numbers of boys and girls come to the end of the school period with less of learning and less of mental and moral power than they need to meet successfully the responsibilities of life.

Critics, friendly and unfriendly, overlooking these limitations, have hastened to pronounce the public-school system radically defective, to affirm that it is out of gear with the requirements of every-day life, and to demand large modifications in its principles and methods, in order, as they say, to make it *practical*.

I have dwelt at length upon the limitations which my work everywhere forces upon my notice, in order to furnish a basis for judgments more just, and for demands less revolutionary. I am persuaded that the requirements of our statutes afford theoretically, and when complied with in letter and spirit, furnish actually adequate preparation for the duties of life. The evidence of this is everywhere apparent. From the best schools of the State boys and girls are issuing continually and taking their places among the self-supporting members of the community. Public and private interests, political, financial, social, charitable, are daily devolving upon them, and find in them reliable conservators. Never more so. The wonder is, not that the children are so poorly prepared for life, but that they are so well prepared.

So far as the limitations which I have described lie in the infirmities of human nature, they will always exist, and will necessarily keep the actual results below the theoretical. The appropriate work of legislation is to reduce their effects to a minimum.

The losses resulting from non-attendance may be largely reduced by the establishment of truant schools, and a faithful enforcement of the truant laws.

Thorough sanitary inspection of school buildings by competent persons would tend to improve the physical conditions for school work, and so increase its outcome.

Measures to secure higher qualifications in the teaching force of the State are greatly needed. Among these are the establishment of fully graded schools for observation and practice, wholly under State control, as an essential part of each Normal School; model primary schools equipped and maintained by the State at various points accessible to country teachers; institutes of several weeks' duration for the aid of teachers who have not received the advantages of Normal Schools, and some system of examining and certificating teachers which shall exclude the most ignorant and incompetent.

In addition to these, there is extreme need of placing all the schools under the immediate superintendence of men qualified by education and training to direct them toward the ends contemplated by the statutory requirements.

Most of the limitations of which I have spoken have their maximum effect in the small towns; and it is just these towns which are the least able to resist their influence.

Since the State imposes school duties on the poor towns equally with the rich ones, justice to the towns, as well as the good of the children in them, requires that the State should furnish some aid in meeting the obligations. With such aid, judiciously distributed and expended, the children in the rural schools would be free from many of the disadvantages which they now labor under, and might hope to contend for the prizes of life on more equal terms.

To secure such equality I conceive to be one of the chief ends for which the agents of the Board of Education are appointed.

GEO. H. MARTIN.

C.

REPORT ON SCHOOL ORGANIZATION.

BY

JOHN T. PRINCE, AGENT OF THE BOARD.

REPORT.

To the Board of Education:

In past reports, both monthly and annual, I have given the results of my observation, mainly in respect to the actual condition of the schools and to methods of teaching. In this report I desire to call attention to some features of school organization which I have observed, with the double object of making known to you the means employed in the schools to carry on the work, and also of giving assistance to some committees and teachers who are working at a disadvantage with a poor or imperfect organization.

FURNITURE.

I have found comparatively few school-rooms not provided with suitable desks for the pupils. Even in the poorer houses of the country the rude and uncomfortable benches, marred "with the jack-knife's carved initial," have quite generally been replaced by convenient desks and comfortable seats. In a few cases I have found the desks and seats quite unsuitable in size, — some of them being so small as to force the pupils to take a cramped position, and some so large as not to allow the pupils to rest the feet upon the floor or to take a good position in writing.

The size and height of desks and seats found in the best furnished rooms are indicated in the following table. The measurements here given are of single desks, which are much to be preferred to double ones.

GRADE.	Height of seat.	Distance from floor to top of desk next to pupil.	Distance from front to back of top of desk.	Distance from side to side of top of desk.	Depth of shelf holding books, etc.
	Inches.	Inches.	Inches.	Inches.	Inches.
Primary, . . .	10-12	20-23	10-12	18	5
Intermediate, . .	12-13¼	23-24½	14-16	24	6
Grammar, . . .	13½-16	24½-28	14-16	24	6
High, . . .	15-17	27-29	18-22	26	8

The figures of the above table are of course only a general guide. In all schools there are likely to be a few pupils who will require larger or smaller seats than the rest. To accommodate such pupils it will be necessary to provide three or four seats of a larger and of a smaller size in every graded school. In ungraded schools there should be a few desks and seats of each size. Care should be taken to place the seat at a proper distance from the desk. For most pupils of all grades, the front of the seat may extend one inch beyond a vertical line let fall from the front edge of the desk. If there is sufficient room the rows should be placed from twenty-four to thirty inches apart. Ink-wells with covers should be placed in all desks designed for pupils who write with pen and ink.

Other necessary furniture for the school-room is comprised in the following list: Desk for teacher, chairs for teacher and visitors, crayons, erasers, pointers, clock, bell, thermometer, broom, ink-filler, dust-pan, dusters, closet, or book-case and table for number work.

In addition to the above-named articles many school-rooms have toilet appliances, sponge-pail, waste-basket, moulding table and piano or organ.

APPARATUS.

From a careful estimate made from my notes, I judge that not twenty-five per cent. of the school-rooms of the Commonwealth outside of the large cities are even fairly supplied with proper means of teaching, and that perhaps one-third of this number would embrace all schools which are fully supplied.

All of the apparatus included in the following list I have not found in any one room; yet there is no article in the list which may not be put to good use. For the convenience of committees proposing to furnish a full supply for the schools, separate lists are given for primary, grammar and high schools. For ungraded or partially graded schools a careful selection from all the lists should be made. It will be seen that the lists do not comprise many useful means of illustration and teaching which may be gathered from day to day from the fields, shops and homes.. Apparatus for the observation lessons of the primary and grammar grades may be thus supplied, including plants, leaves, animals, rocks, and parts of animals obtained from the butcher's.

Primary Grade. — Toys and other objects for reading; blocks, splints and shoe-pegs for number and "busy-work;" foot rule; yardstick; pint, quart and gallon measures; quart and peck measures; pictures for language; cardboard for number and language work; colored cardboard for form and color lessons; colored worsted; box of toy-money; blacked globe; reading chart; number chart; slates and pencils; pen-holders and pens; sponges; lead-pencils; ruled paper; ruler; coarse files for sharpening pencils (when pencil-sharpeners are not provided); minerals; mounted plants and insects; models for form lessons and drawing; clay for modelling; box of letters for making words; box of words for making sentences; dissected pictures; cardboard in different shapes for tracing.

Grammar Grade. — Measures (dry, liquid, linear and metric); balance; globe; wall-maps; music chart; writing chart; anatomical charts; arithmetical drill chart; pictures for language, geography and history; minerals; mounted plants and insects; vegetable products; models for drawing; pen-holders and pens; slates and pencils; sponges or slate-cloths; lead-pencils; paper; blank-books; ruler; pencil-sharpener.

High School. — Laboratories for teaching chemistry, physics and mineralogy should be furnished in every high school where these subjects are taught. Tables for individual observation and experiment should have an asphalt covering and be provided with proper burners at convenient distances. If there are no gas-burners kerosene lamps may be used for all common heating, and alcohol lamps for blow-pipe work. Bowls, slop-jars, drawers and closets should be within convenient distance of each pupil. In the drawers and closets there should be placed such articles as are likely to be used in the experiments, such as, for the physical laboratory, fruit cans, ale glasses, bottles, corks, plates, files, funnel, tuning-fork, shot, glass-tubing, rubber-tubing, alcohol lamp, flask, test-tubes, convex lens, violin string, glass tube for frictional electricity, sealing-wax; and for the chemical laboratory, saucer, glass plates, funnel, tweezers, blow-pipe, glass tube, candle, charcoal, spoon, test tubes, corks, iron wires, rubbers, iron stand and sand bath, Bunsen burner, test-tube racks, files, bottles, tin can. Other apparatus for teaching physics and chemistry should be kept constantly at hand. What cannot be provided or made by the pupils themselves should be bought. The extent of the supply will depend upon the extent to which the studies are pursued. Recently published books of physics and chemistry indicate the kind and amount of apparatus which is needed to teach the various subjects.

For teaching mineralogy it will be necessary to have a collection of rocks of the vicinity and, so far as possible, of the State. Specimens may be obtained at the Natural History rooms in Boston at a nominal price.

For zoölogy a set of *typical* animals should be mounted or preserved in alcohol. Other animals for dissection, such as the bird and frog, will be procured as they are needed.

For botany mounted specimens illustrating the flora of the country should be provided; also microscopes for plant analysis.

A celestial sphere, sticks, balls, hoops, globes and disks will be useful in teaching astronomy.

Good maps and photographs will be found of great assistance in the study of history.

REFERENCE BOOKS.

Few of the schools that have come under my observation outside of the cities have anything like a good supply of reference books. In many schools a single dictionary constitutes the only book of reference beyond the regular text books, and in some schools not even a dictionary is provided.

Since the passage of the free text-book law there has been a marked increase of supplementary reading matter, the use of which has tended to lessen the close adherence to text books, especially of geography and history. In language, also, less reliance than formerly is placed upon the text book, and there is consequently a greater demand for suggestions that can be found in books of reference.

It would be manifestly out of place in this report to give the titles of books which should be used by teachers and pupils in addition to the regular text books. It may, however, be said that there should be in every school of the higher grades dictionaries, — one unabridged and several smaller ones, — an encyclopedia and three or four books of each of the studies pursued. Some of these books should be for the exclusive use of the teacher, and some for both teacher and pupils.

CLASSIFICATION.

Some of the defects of the public schools to which attention has been called from time to time by agents of the Board can doubtless be directly traced to unwise classification. There is frequently seen in graded schools a want of adaptation of work to the needs and capacity of some pupils, due in a measure, at least, to arbitrary methods of promotion. When the attainments only of pupils are considered in promoting from class to class, and especially when the attainments are determined by a single examination in which memory has a large share, there are likely to exist faults of a very serious nature which even the most skilful teaching cannot remove. Where the method of promotion is such as I have mentioned, dull pupils are likely to be " kept back" to their injury, and pupils bright only in a single direction are pushed forward too rapidly. In some places the questions which test the pupils' ability to go into a higher class are prepared by the school committee or superintendent. It may be well to have such examinations; but when they alone determine the pupils' promotion right teaching is discouraged, for the teacher is likely to be influenced by the demands which are made upon him, and give an undue amount of memory work which will give certain required results when the test for promotion comes. The consideration of classification or promotion should be solely that of the good of the pupil.

In what class or place can he do most for himself?   To decide
this question wisely, it may be necessary sometimes to call into
exercise the combined wisdom of the teacher, supervisor and
parent, as the age, natural propensities, health, habits and
purposes of the pupil are to be considered as well as his intellectual acquirements.

Graded Schools.

A close classification would make all the pupils of a class
recite together in the same studies.   There are certainly advantages in this plan; but it is a question whether it may not
be well sometimes to allow pupils to recite in a higher or lower
class in one or two studies.   For example, a boy is by nature
or by extra study farther advanced in arithmetic than in reading
and geography.   If he has but a limited time to attend school,
it would seem to be right to have him recite with one class in
reading and geography and with another class in arithmetic.

Again, there are occasionally pupils who, by reason of weakness or ill health, cannot take all the studies taught in the
school.   Such pupils should be allowed to omit one or more
of the regular studies, and even be excused from school attendance except when their classes are reciting.

There is of course danger in such irregularities, and the
number of exceptional cases should be limited; but there are
instances where it is not only justifiable, but necessary to the
best interests of the pupils for exceptions to be made.

Basis of Classification. — The rights of active and bright-
minded pupils should be protected no less than those of the
weak and dull.   Inequalities both in the abilities of pupils
and in the amount accomplished should be recognized in classifying as well as in arranging the course of studies and conducting the recitation.   The average abilities and attainments,
therefore, should be the guide in classification, so far as the
amount of work required is concerned.   Where close classification is required, as it generally should be required in graded
schools, it is customary to take reading as the basis in the
primary schools and arithmetic in the higher grades.

Size of Classes. — The mistake should not be made of making the classes too large.   The number should be sufficiently
small for the teacher to reach every individual member, at least
to the extent of knowing the peculiarities of each pupil and

of adapting the teaching and instruction to the needs of each. Thirty pupils in primary grades and forty in grammar grades are quite as many as one teacher should be expected to teach. A less number would doubtless be better for individual pupils, while more would tend to force the teacher into mechanical ways of teaching, making one pupil do the same work as every other one, and precisely in the same way.

Divisions. — In some of the larger towns and cities the practice is quite general of having pupils of the same grade in one room, and of hearing them recite together. The practical result of such an arrangement is, that the pupils get no time for independent study and reflection. There may be times set apart for study, but those times are so interrupted by questions and explanations, that the pupils come to depend wholly upon others in doing their work. An additional disadvantage of large classes reciting together is the danger of neglecting the needs of individual pupils and of resorting to questionable methods of teaching. The remedy lies in a division of the class into two sections for recitation in some of the studies, — one section studying while the other is reciting.

Intervals between Classes. — In most graded schools at the present time the classes are one year apart; that is, the graduation is so made as to render a readjustment or promotion necessary only once a year. This plan of grading may be necessary in some places and under some circumstances; but where there is a sufficient number of pupils, the interval should be shorter and the promotions more frequent. The aim should be to have the work adjusted as nearly as possible to the wants and capacity of each pupil. If this aim is a true one, it is manifest that the shorter the interval between the classes the better, provided, of course, the transfer of pupils from one grade to another does not necessitate a too frequent change of teachers. An interval of only ten weeks, or one-fourth of a year, has been tried with success in some places. In other places the interval is twenty weeks. This plan is entirely feasible in most of our cities and large towns, and its adoption would do much to overcome the faults of the system of yearly promotions. The advantages of semi-annual promotions are seen in classifying new pupils, or those who have been absent a part of the year, and in adapting the work of pupils to their capacity and strength.

Partially Graded Schools.

In some places the conditions require all the pupils of a neighborhood to be placed in two or three rooms. When this is the case it is advisable to make the intervals between the classes one year or more, and to have three or four classes in each room.' Under such circumstances a close classification should not be insisted upon, especially in the higher grades; but pupils should be allowed to join any class in which they can work most advantageously.

Ungraded Schools.

In some of the ungraded schools of the State the classification is so minute in all subjects as to permit but five or eight minutes to each recitation. Others have so few classes, as to oblige the pupils to do too difficult or too easy work. Both of these dangers should be avoided so far as possible. Much, of course, will depend upon circumstances. If there are two teachers (as there should be if there are more than twenty-five pupils), more minute classification may be made than if there is only one. In some ungraded schools the older pupils predominate; in others, the younger. In some places the older pupils are taken from the ungraded schools and placed in a central grammar or high school; in other places no higher school of any kind supplements the work of the ungraded school. No exact rule, therefore, for classifying ungraded schools can be laid down. But in general it may be said that no close classification should be attempted in ungraded schools, but that every pupil should recite in the class for which he is best fitted, whatever the subject may be. For instance, a pupil may be in the first class in arithmetic and the second in' reading; while another pupil may be in the second class in arithmetic and the first in reading.

Again, great care should be taken in determining the number of classes. The number of classes in any subject should not be so small as to prevent all pupils from deriving some advantage of the study; nor should there be so many classes as to give too small amount of time for each recitation. Time may

be gained by having some studies of the older pupils alternate
with each other; as, for example, history and geography, drawing and writing, grammar and physiology, — giving two or three
recitations a week in each branch.

It is understood, of course, that there may be a less minute
classification in some studies than in others. In geography, for
example, the number of classes may be much less than in reading or arithmetic.

The following classification may be made in many ungraded
schools, consisting of pupils from five to fifteen years of age :
Four or five classes in reading, including one class in the reading of history; five classes in arithmetic; two classes in geography, besides the class of younger pupils who recite orally
lessons in home geography; three classes in spelling; one or
two classes in physiology, alternating with the same number of
classes in history; one class in English grammar and one in
language. The singing, drawing and observation lessons may
be taught as general exercises.

DAILY PROGRAMME OF RECITATION AND STUDY.

The good teacher always has, either in mind or on paper, a
carefully prepared programme in which the times and subjects
of recitation and study are well defined. Without a definite
plan of work there is danger of unequal attention being given
to the subjects and of disturbance in the preparation of lessons. To make a programme in which a proper share of time
is given to recitation and to study, and in which the time al-
lotted to each subject is commensurate with the importance of
that subject, is no easy task. It is obvious that no one programme would be suited to all schools, or even to all schools
of the same kind and grade, so widely dissimilar are the conditions in different schools, and even in the same school at
different times. The following programmes which were found
in actual operation may be suggestive to teachers : —

PRIMARY SCHOOL. — Four Grades.

Thirty-nine pupils from six to twelve years of age.

TIME.		RECITATION.	BUSY-WORK AND STUDY.			
Begin.	Length.		Grade I. (Lowest.)	Grade II.	Grade III.	Grade IV.
A.M.	MIN.					
9.00	5	Devotional Exercise	–	–	–	–
9 05	5	Mem. Gems (all)	–	–	–	–
9.10	5	Music (all)	–	–	–	–
9.15	15	Writing (all)	–	–	–	–
9.30	30	I. and II. Reading	....	....	Number	Number
10.00	15	III. Number	Slate and Splints	Number	....	Number
10.15	15	I. Number	....	Number	Writing	Number
10.30	15	Recess.	–	–	–	–
10.45	5	General Exercise	–	–	–	–
10.50	20	IV. Number	Slate-work	Number	Reading	....
11.10	10	II. Number	Slate-work	....	Reading	Language
11.20	15	III. Reading	Copying	Language	....	–
11.35	15	IV. Geography	Designs	Language	Language	....
11.50	10	IV. Sp. and Lang.	Splints	Language	Language	....
12 00	–	Intermission.	–	–	–	–
P.M.						
1.30	15	Music (all)	–	–	–	–
1.45	15	I. Reading	....	Reading	Reading	Reading
2.00	10	II. Reading	Busy-work	....	Reading	Reading
2.10	15	III. Sp. and Lang.	Busy-work	Busy-work	....	Geography
2.25	5	Recess.	–	–	–	–
2.30	15	IV. Reading	Busy-work	Busy-work	Language	....
2.45	15	IV. Drawing	Busy-work	Busy-work	Language	....
3.00	30	Obs. L. and L'g (all)	–	–	–	–
3.30	–	Dismission.	–	–	–	–

Tuesday A. M. 11–12. Sewing Teacher.
Monday. Once in two weeks. 9.30–10. Music Teacher.
Friday P. M. 3–3.30. Good time.

PRIMARY AND INTERMEDIATE SCHOOL.

Twenty-five pupils, ranging from six to twelve years of age. The youngest pupils are beginners, and the most advanced pupils are studying Fractions and reading in the Fourth Reader. There are four classes in most subjects.

TIME.		RECITATION.	BUSY-WORK AND STUDY.			
Begin.	Length.		Grade I. (Lowest.)	Grade II.	Grade III.	Grade IV.
A.M.	MIN.					
9.00	15	Dev. Ex.and Singing	....	....	....	....
9.15	20	Writing (all)	....	....	....	....
9.35	10	I. Reading	....	Arithmetic	Arithmetic	Language
9.45	15	II. Read. and Spell.	Copying	....	Arithmetic	Arithmetic
10.00	20	III. Arithmetic	Splints and Pegs	Arithmetic	....	Arithmetic
10.20	15	*Recess.*	–	–	–	–
10.35	20	IV. Arithmetic	Cop'g, etc.	Language	Geography	....
10.55	15	I. and II. Arithmetic	....	....	Geography	Geography
11.10	10	Gymnastics	*Dismissed.*	....	....	....
10.20	20	III. Geography	–	Language	....	Geography
10.40	20	IV. Geography	–	R'g & Sp'g	Language	....
12.00	60	*Intermission.*	–	–	–	–
P.M.						
1.00	20	I. Read. and Numb.	....	R'g & Lan.	Language	Language
1.20	20	II. Read. and Lang.	Busy-work	....	R'g & Sp'g	Language
1.40	25	III. and IV. Lang.	Busy-work	Copying	....	....
2.05	5	Gymnastics	–	–	–	–
2.10	10	Ment. Arith. (all)	....	....	....	....
2.20	15	I. and II. Obs. Less.	....	....	R'g & Sp'g	R'g & Sp'g
2.35	10	*Recess.*	*Dismissed.*	–	–	–
2.45	25	III. Read. and Spell.	–	Language	....	R'g & Sp'g
3.10	25	IV. Read. and Spell.	–	Reading	Arithmetic	....
3.35	15	Obs. Lesson (all)	–	....	....	....
3.50	10	Gen. Exercise (all)	–	....	....	....

SIXTH GRAMMAR GRADE.—Two Divisions.

| TIME. | | RECITATION. | STUDY. | |
Begin.	Length.		A Division.	B Division.
A.M. 9.00	MIN. 5	Devotional Exercise	. . . .	. . . .
9.05	15	Singing	. . . .	. . . .
.20	20	General Exercise	. . . .	. . . .
9.40	20	Arithmetic. A.	. . . .	Arithmetic
10.00	10	Arithmetic. A. & B.	. . . .	. . . .
10.10	20	" B.	Reading	. . . .
10.30	15	Recess.	–	–
10.45	20	Reading. A.	. . . .	Reading
11.05	20	Reading. B.	Geography	. . . .
11.25	35	Language. A. & B.	–	–
12.00	–	Intermission.	–	–
P.M. 1.30	30	Writing or Drawing. A. & B.	–	–
2.00	30	Geography & Sight-Reading. A.	. . . .	Geography
2.30	30	Geography & Sight-Reading. B.	Spelling	. . . .
3.00	15	Recess.	–	–
3.15	15	Spelling. A. & B.	. . . .	. . . .
3.30	30	General Exercise and Study	–	–
4.00	–	Dismission.	–	–

FRIDAY.

A.M.
Observation Lesson.
Physiology.
Compositions.

P.M.
History.
Reading and Recitations.

UNGRADED SCHOOL.

Thirty-five pupils from five to sixteen years of age.

[One afternoon each week given to general exercises.]

A.M.	P.M.
Min.	Min.
5. Devotional Exercise.	15. Grammar.
10. Singing.	15. First Reader and Number.
15. First Reader and Number.	15. Second Reader.
15. Second Reader.	20. Third Reader.
20. I. Arithmetic.	25. Writing or Drawing.
15. IV. Arithmetic.	15. Recess or Gymnastics.
15. Recess or Gymnastics.	15. I. Geography or History.
15. III. Arithmetic.	15. II. Geography.
15. II. Arithmetic.	20. Fourth Reader.
15. I. and II. Spelling.	25. General Exercise.
20. Primary and Intermediate Language.	
20. General Exercise (Observation Lesson).	

UNGRADED HIGH AND GRAMMAR SCHOOL.

A.M.	P.M.
Min.	Min.
5. Devotional Exercise.	20. Geometry.
10. Singing.	15. Latin.
20. I. Arithmetic.	20. II. Geography.
20. II. Arithmetic.	20. I. Geography.
25. I. Reading or Rhetoric.	25. History or Physiology.
15. Recess or Gymnastics.	15. Recess or Gymnastics.
25. II. Reading or Grammar.	25. Writing and Book-keeping or Drawing.
15. Algebra.	
25. Spelling and Language (all).	20. III. Reading.
15. General Exercise.	20. General Exercise.

RECORDS AND REPORTS.

From my observation I judge that less time than formerly is given to making and tabulating unnecessary statistics. Yet there are seen occasionally teachers who, either by direction of superior officers or by their own choice, are giving time and strength to work which does not, directly or indirectly, conduce to the welfare of the school.

No records for mere show should be kept, nor reports and averages be made out which appeal to the pride of any one, or which serve as an artificial stimulant to study.

In addition to such statistics as the State requires, there should be kept such records as will enable the teacher to note the progress of his pupils and to aid him in placing them where they will do most for themselves.

For the purpose of informing the parents of the character of their childrens' work and of securing their co-operation, blanks should be filled out, either periodically or when occasion requires. It is well for parents to receive a report as often as once a month. This report should indicate in a general way how the pupil is doing in each branch of study and what his conduct is. It should not contain the standing of the pupil with reference to others in his class, nor is it necessary to indicate fine distinctions such as would be made by per cent. marks. All that it is necessary to give in the report is what the teacher would give in reply to the parent's questions : How is my child doing in each branch of study? What is his behavior? What is his attendance? The following report (A) for grammar-school pupils is suggested. It should be upon a card six or seven inches long and four or five inches wide. The months can be indicated to suit the circumstances. The blanks which follow will be found useful in securing the co-operation of parents : —

(A)

PUBLIC SCHOOLS.

Report of

School,   Class.

For the Month of	Reading.	Spelling.	Arithmetic.	Language.	Writing.	Drawing.	Geography.	History.	Conduct.	Days absent.	Times tardy.	Signature of Parent or Guardian.
SEPT.												
OCT.												
NOV.												
DEC.												
JAN.												

To the Parent or Guardian : —

A means Excellent; B, Good; C, Fair; D, Poor; E, Very Poor.

If the Scholarship or Deportment continues to be poor, will you please call' at the school-room for further particulars, especially if poor health or any other circumstance prevents h   from doing more work. Irregularity of attendance greatly interferes with the progress of the pupil, and may oblige h   to repeat the work of a term or year. You are cordially invited to visit the school at any time.

Please sign and return as soon as possible.

, *Teacher.*

(B)

SCHOOL.

188 .

M

You will see by   Monthly Report that is not doing thoroughly the work of the School. Thus far this term neither the written examination nor daily work indicate that it will be best for   to go into a higher division next   , but that it may be necessary to review the present studies another term. If, however, you think it possible or best for   to do more work, will you please call here at the School-room, or drop me a note, so that we can have a better understanding of   needs and capacity, and arrange the work with eference to them.

Respectfully,

, *Teacher.*

Please sign and return this.

[Place for signing.]

(C)

SCHOOL.,

188 .

M

deportment at school is not satisfactory.

I think it best to inform you of the fact, that all influences may be brought to bear upon   before any serious form of punishment is resorted to.

Respectfully,

, *Teacher.*

To aid in maintaining good order, please sign and return this.

[Place for signing.]

The registers provided by the State are quite faithfully and accurately kept; but, unfortunately, in some places the method of ascertaining the average membership and attendance of pupils differs quite essentially from the method as laid down in the registers. By counting all pupils members of the school until they leave town or give notice of their intention to leave school, the average percentage of attendance is much smaller than it would be if pupils were dropped from the roll of membership at the end of five consecutive days' absence from any cause, — a practice which is followed in several cities and towns. I would recommend that means be taken to secure uniformity in the method of making statistics of attendance, that they may be of some value for purposes of comparison.

Respectfully submitted,

JOHN T. PRINCE.

Jan. 1, 1887.

D.

SPECIAL REPORT ON HALF–MILL TAX AND SCHOOL FUND.

REPORT.

To the Honorable Senate and House of Representatives.

Chapter 37 of the Resolves of 1886 requested the Board of Education to consider whether a more equitable distribution can be made of the income of the Massachusetts School Fund, and report its conclusions to the General Court; and by chapter 76 of the Resolves of 1886 the Board was requested to investigate the entire subject and method of the proposed " bill to establish a half-mill fund for the public schools, and to distribute the same for their support," — printed as House document number four hundred and forty, — the necessity for and effect of the same, with such statistics as shall illustrate the operation and effect of the law, if adopted, upon each city and town in the Commonwealth, provided they recommend its adoption, and report in print separate from their general report to the next General Court at the beginning of the session, with such recommendations concerning this phase of our public-school system as they may deem wise.

The Board has given the matter of both resolves careful attention. With the aid of statistics it has considered the effect of all the propositions for legislation that have been suggested, and respectfully submits its conclusions upon both resolves to the consideration of the Legislature.

DISTRIBUTION OF THE INCOME OF THE SCHOOL FUND.

Two or three different plans of redistributing the moiety of the income of the school fund apportioned to the towns have been carefully considered.

One is based on the amount of taxable property represented by each child of school age in towns having a certain specified valuation, such towns being arranged in classes according to their valuation, the class having the smallest valuation receiving the largest sum, this sum being increased or diminished to each town from year to year inversely as the valuation of such town increases or diminishes. This plan also includes the allowance of a certain sum for each school in towns so aided.

Another plan considers the valuation of the taxable property of the towns, and the number of schools required to be maintained, as the principal factors in the problem of distribution.

Both of these plans fail to make a just and equal distribution of the public-school fund, and the Board is by no means satisfied that as great inequalities would not exist under either one of them as exist under the present law.

If a new plan of distribution is to be enacted, it should be so constructed as to aid those towns least able to help themselves, and produce as few inequalities as possible, and encourage the towns to improve their schools, rather than to relieve themselves from taxation.

In view of the fact that the present law has been in operation but little over two years, and that no new plan free from serious objections has yet been found, the Board recommends only such a departure from it as shall give to the towns that most need help the small portion of the fund that is now given pro rata to the towns above three millions valuation. To accomplish this result it recommends the passage of the bill appended to this report.

THE PROPOSED HALF-MILL TAX.

A State school tax can be levied for the accomplishment of two ends : —

1st. To equalize the burden of taxation in the towns.

2d. To increase the efficiency of the schools, and to render their advantages more equal throughout the Commonwealth.

In attempting to equalize the burden of taxation in so far as the support of schools is concerned, we must determine the causes of expense and the ability to pay.

In levying a tax for promoting the efficiency of the schools, we must determine what relations pecuniary aid holds to that end.

The cost of schools, in any community, will depend on the standard of excellence which the people may choose to attain, on the number of children to be educated and on the number of schools that must be maintained.

From these statements it will appear that the burden of supporting the schools of a town may be largely voluntary, and with which the State is not called upon to interfere.

The ability to pay the cost of the schools will depend on the amount of taxable property which each child of school age will represent, and on the general rate of taxation levied on the taxable property.

The efficiency of the public schools will depend on the ability of the people to support them, and on the intelligence and goodwill of the people in organizing them and in administering their affairs.

From this it may be seen that there are many elements which must be considered in levying a general tax for the schools, and in distributing its proceeds among the towns, so that justice, equality and the best educational results may be secured.

By the statistics that have been prepared, it may be shown that the proposed bill for levying a general school tax does not make provision for equalizing the burden of taxation in the State.

By the provisions of the bill eleven cities and towns, whose present rate of taxation is $12.80 or over on a thousand dollars, would be required to raise $181,264.85 more than would be returned to them, while one hundred and twenty-five cities and towns whose present tax rate is the same or under, would receive more than they would raise.

Thus it appears from these statistics that one group of towns with a certain rate of taxation would raise much more money than they would receive, while another group, with the same rate or under, would raise much less than they would receive.

The same result appears in a still more marked degree, if we compare the amounts raised and received in some individual towns.

New Bedford with a tax rate of $16.30 would be required to raise $2,567.26 more than would be returned, while Attleborough with a tax rate of only $10.00 per thousand would raise $2,869.53 less than they would receive.

Beverly with a tax rate of $15.80 would lose $1,056.85; Marblehead with a rate of $12.20 would gain $1,325.68.

Arlington with a tax rate of $18.40 on a thousand dollars would lose, while Stow, raising only $3.60 on a thousand, would gain.

Besides results such as these, some towns would receive aid that do not need it, and would not even be willing to receive it. Experience has proved that the efficiency of the schools is never secured by the use of pecuniary means alone. If the means are obtained without some sacrifice and to such an amount as to allow a community to relax its efforts in supporting its schools, that community is quite likely to take advantage of the opportunity, and with the diminished efforts the school spirit and interest in the welfare of the schools is generally diminished in proportion.

It has been the policy of the State in the distribution of the income of the State school fund to gradually withdraw it from the towns that have become able to support their schools without its aid, and to distribute it among those towns only that actually need its help.

The wealthier towns have not only given up their share of the public money without objection, but have recommended the redistribution. The school fund was established not for the purpose of supporting the schools, but to aid and encourage the towns in promoting the efficiency of these institutions.

As good teachers are necessary to the existence of good schools, it was thought from the first that the best and most legitimate use that could be made of a portion of the income of the school fund was to expend it in maintaining normal schools and in encouraging the establishment of teachers' associations, for the better preparation of teachers for their responsible work.

In this no mistake has been made. Our present improved methods of teaching owe their origin largely to the influence of these schools and these associations, and to that system of supervision with which the cities and wealthier towns have generally supplied themselves.

From the earliest period of our history the burden of supporting the public schools has fallen upon the local municipalities; and, on the whole, they have been generous in the discharge of their duty. They have enlarged and improved our school system to meet the growing needs of the population. In this work they have ever shown an intelligent self-reliance, and a general disposition to exceed the requirements of the law.

The statutes require the schools to be kept for at least six months in the year. The towns of small valuation are unable to continue their schools longer than the law requires, and still the average time in the year for the State is nearly nine months.

The law requires the towns to raise at least three dollars for every child between five and fifteen years of age. By the returns of last year it appears that almost every town raised more than that sum, and that the average for the State was nearly twenty dollars for every such child.

It is most important for the State and for the public schools that this habit of self-reliance on the part of the towns, and the intelligent, earnest school spirit that always grows out of it, should be everywhere encouraged.

There are, however, about one hundred towns in the Commonwealth, mainly on Cape Cod and among the hills of Western Massachusetts, that each recurring census finds with a depleted population and a diminished valuation of taxable property, which stand in need of immediate aid.

The Board of Education is of the opinion that this aid can best be rendered by an increase of the State school fund, which shall insure a larger permanent income, to be distributed to those towns which imperatively need help.

In view of these considerations the Board recommends that a half-mill tax be levied with the next State tax, the proceeds to be known as the " Half-Mill Public School Fund "; the income arising from it to be distributed in the same manner as the moiety of the income of the school fund is distributed to the towns. The Board, therefore, recommends the passage of the appended bill : —

AN ACT RELATING TO THE DISTRIBUTION OF THE SCHOOL FUND.

Be it enacted, etc., as follows:

Section 1. One-half of the annual income of the Massachusetts school fund of the Commonwealth shall be apportioned and distributed, without a specific appropriation, for the support of public schools, and in the manner following, to wit: The said one-half of the said annual income shall be distributed to towns complying with all laws in force relating to the distribution of said income, and the valuation of the real and personal estate of each of which, as shown by the last returns thereof, does not exceed three million dollars. Said towns shall be annually classified upon the basis of the last valuation; the first class shall include all such towns the valuation of the real and personal estate of each of which does not exceed one-half million dollars; the second class shall include all such towns the valuation of each of which is more than one-half million dollars and does not exceed one million dollars; the third class shall include all such towns the valuation of which is more than one million dollars and does not exceed three million dollars. Each town in these several classes, in the order named, shall respectively share in the proportion of six, four and three in the distribution of said one-half of said annual income. All money appropriated for other educational purposes, unless otherwise specially provided, shall be paid from the other half of said income.

SECT. 2. Chapter twenty-two of the acts of the year eighteen hundred and eighty-four is hereby repealed.

SECT. 3. This act shall take effect upon its passage.

AN ACT TO ESTABLISH A HALF-MILL FUND FOR THE SUPPORT OF PUBLIC SCHOOLS, AND TO PROVIDE FOR THE DISTRIBUTION THEREOF.

Be it enacted, etc., as follows:

SECTION 1. A tax of one-half of one mill on the dollar shall be assessed and collected upon all the taxable property of the Commonwealth according to the valuation thereof, and shall be known as the one-half mill tax for the support of schools.

SECT. 2. Said tax shall be assessed, collected and paid into the treasury in the same manner as other State taxes, and the product of said tax, together with such additions as may be made thereto, shall constitute a permanent fund, to be called the "Half-Mill Public School Fund," the principal of which shall not be diminished, and which shall be invested and managed in the same manner as the "Massachusetts School Fund," as provided in section two of chapter forty-three of the Public Statutes.

SECT. 3. The annual income of said "Half-Mill Public School Fund," shall be appropriated and distributed without a specific appropriation for the support of public schools, and paid over and expended in the same manner as the one-half of the annual income of the "Massachusetts School Fund" is now or shall be hereafter appropriated, distributed, paid and expended for the support of public schools.

SECT. 4. Any portion of said fund not expended as herein provided shall be added to the principal of said fund.

SECT. 5. This act shall take effect upon its passage.

AN ABSTRACT

OF THE SCHOOL RETURNS MADE BY THE SCHOOL COM-
MITTEES OF THE SEVERAL TOWNS AND CITIES
IN THE COMMONWEALTH, FOR THE
SCHOOL-YEAR 1885-86.

BARNSTABLE COUNTY.

TOWNS.	Population—State Census, 1885.	Valuation—1885.	No. of Public Schools.	No. of persons in town between May 1, 1885, 5 and 15 years of age.	No. of persons in town between May 1, 1885, 8 and 14 years of age.	No. of different pupils of all ages in the Public Schools during the school-year.	No. attending within the year under 5 years of age.	No. attending within the year over 15 years of age.	No. attending within the year between 8 and 14 years of age.	Average membership of all the Schools.	Average attendance in all the Public Schools during the school year.	The per cent. of attendance based upon the average membership.	No. of teachers required by the Public Schools.
Barnstable,	4,050	$2,722,030	24	656	367	825	—	123	473	640	595	.93	24
Bourne,	1,363	940,350	11	260	185	277	—	25	185	213	195	.92	11
Brewster,	934	447,791	7	172	102	182	—	18	102	153	137	.90	7
Chatham,	2,028	622,957	11	352	234	382	4	53	220	315	265	.84	11
Dennis,	2,923	1,146,077	13	512	326	626	—	81	315	494	453	.92	13
Eastham,	638	211,451	3	90	90	124	—	36	70	91	73	.80	3
Falmouth,	2,520	3,597,761	16	383	302	475	—	72	270	360	310	.86	17
Harwich,	2,783	989,390	16	490	325	585	—	109	313	512	467	.91	16
Mashpee,	311	135,440	2	30	17	56	1	9	18	48	47	.98	2
Orleans,	1,176	443,814	6	165	106	176	—	13	106	133	115	.86	6
Provincetown,	4,480	2,019,592	16	810	520	950	—	125	530	827	748	.90	19
Sandwich,	2,124	933,850	12	393	245	434	—	43	245	366	333	.91	13
Truro,	972	260,641	6	165	95	178	—	34	95	144	130	.90	6
Wellfleet,	1,687	852,098	9	284	198	320	—	45	204	280	259	.93	10
Yarmouth,	1,856	1,445,606	10	300	250	346	—	45	243	252	224	.89	10
Totals,	29,845	$16,768,848	162	5,062	3,342	5,936	5	881	3,389	4,828	4,851	.90	168

BERKSHIRE COUNTY.

TOWNS.	Population—State Census, 1885.	Valuation—1885.	No. of Public Schools.	No. of persons in town between May 1, 1885, 5 and 15 years of age.	No. of persons in town between May 1, 1885, 8 and 14 years of age.	No. of different pupils of all ages in the Public Schools during the school-year.	No. attending within the year under 5 years of age.	No. attending within the year over 15 years of age.	No. attending within the year between 8 and 14 years of age.	Average membership of all the Schools.	Average attendance in all the Public Schools during the school year.	The per cent. of attendance based upon the average membership.	No. of teachers required by the Public Schools.
Adams,	8,283	$3,155,470	31	1,738	1,098	1,750	10	81	1,102	1,304	1,232	.95	35
Alford,	341	231,003	3	63	45	62	1	9	45	57	48	.84	3

Becket,	938	357,536	8	162	92	177	2	23	90	148	119	.80	8
Cheshire,	1,448	701,802	9	370	236	390	–	32	248	298	259	.87	9
Clarksburg,	708	191,072	3	131	79	145	4	3	98	92	79	.85	3
Dalton,	2,113	1,617,093	12	423	256	465	9	42	256	352	324	.92	12
Egremont,	826	417,300	3	87	73	139	1	7	77	98	78	.80	3
Florida,	487	160,245	6	135	123	129	5	5	67	105	94	.90	6
Gt. Barrington,	4,471	2,845,517	22	837	520	940	4	81	447	775	666	.86	24
Hancock,	613	370,493	6	120	74	136	3	10	80	97	79	.81	6
Hinsdale,	1,656	720,138	12	397	248	438	3	12	254	359	296	.82	12
Lanesborough,	1,212	557,643	9	265	180	303	3	35	180	233	193	.83	9
Lee,	4,274	1,955,868	18	796	478	906	14	121	486	712	654	.92	20
Lenox,	2,154	1,537,814	13	433	271	458	11	62	262	349	309	.89	13
Monterey,	571	227,156	6	115	68	122	3	24	53	95	84	.88	7
Mt. Washington,	160	106,878	2	27	18	27	1	5	18	20	16	.80	2
New Ashford,	163	82,770	2	27	15	29	–	7	15	25	21	.84	2
New Marlboro',	1,661	632,057	13	318	221	324	7	52	221	283	243	.86	13
North Adams,	12,540	4,986,894	44	2,705	1,864	2,590	–	133	1,289	1,923	1,766	.92	55
Otis,	703	211,080	8	136	64	193	2	16	103	135	121	.90	8
Peru,	368	120,524	5	50	34	61	–	9	34	47	38	.81	5
Pittsfield,	14,466	8,588,437	50	2,547	1,753	3,050	27	221	1,720	2,695	2,453	.91	71
Richmond,	854	509,654	7	219	157	207	–	17	114	151	127	.84	7
Sandisfield,	1,019	392,206	12	202	136	221	5	33	135	187	157	.84	12
Savoy,	691	185,589	8	116	68	135	5	8	67	197	152	.77	8
Sheffield,	2,033	902,155	14	411	293	500	10	57	293	334	273	.82	14
Stockbridge,	2,114	2,422,319	9	393	240	363	–	33	227	299	273	.91	10
Tyringham,	457	232,392	5	114	78	116	4	5	72	101	82	.81	5
Washington,	470	203,604	6	101	64	111	2	8	64	81	66	.81	6
West Stockbridge,	1,648	697,732	11	311	202	433	3	34	251	361	310	.86	11
Williamstown,	3,729	1,707,250	16	639	493	712	4	58	491	424	355	.84	17
Windsor,	657	211,260	8	110	74	141	3	18	74	105	91	.87	8
Totals,	73,828	$37,238,951	381	14,498	9,615	15,773	146	1,261	8,933	12,442	11,058	.89	424

BARNSTABLE COUNTY — Continued.

TOWNS.	Whole No. of different male teachers in school-year.	Whole No. of different female teachers in school-year.	No. of teachers who have attended Normal Schools.	No. of teachers who have graduated from Normal Schools.	Av'ge wages per month of male teachers in Public Schools.	Av'ge wages per month of female teachers in Public Schools.	Aggregate of months all the Public Schools have been kept during the school-year.	Average No. of months the Public Schools have been kept for the entire year.	No. of Schools kept less than six months each.	HIGH SCHOOLS. No. of High Schools.	No. of teachers.	No. of pupils.	How supported.	LENGTH. Months.	Days.	Salary of Principal.
Barnstable,	8	25	9	9	$75 66	$36 72	192	8-11	—	1	1	35	Taxation,	9	—	$900 00
Bourne,	2	12	—	—	85 00	36 00	88	8-11	—	1	1	31	Taxation,	8	—	680 00
Brewster,	2	8	3	3	50 00	33 21	50	7-2	—	—	—	—	—	—	—	—
Chatham,	2	17	1	1	87 50	24 20	99	9	—	1	1	49	Taxation,	9	—	900 00
Dennis,	8	11	5	3	57 50	31 22	105-5	8-2	—	1	1	52	Taxation,	9	—	517 50
Eastham,	2	3	—	—	40 00	32 08	25-10	8-11	—	—	—	—	—	—	—	—
Falmouth,	4	22	6	3	55 00	39 00	136-10	8-11	—	1	2	65	Part tax,	9	—	1,000 00
Harwich,	6	13	1	1	52 00	31 50	121-10	7-12	—	1	1	46	Taxation,	9	—	900 00
Mashpee,	2	2	—	2	45 00	35 00	12-3	6	—	—	—	—	—	—	—	—
Orleans,	1	6	2	1	88 00	29 00	54	9	—	1	1	41	Taxation,	9	—	800 00
Provincetown,	3	18	2	1	93 00	30 00	152	9-10	—	1	3	120	Taxation,	9-10	—	1,000 00
Sandwich,	2	12	4	4	97 50	34 75	98	8-3	—	1	2	45	Taxation,	10	—	1,200 00
Truro,	3	7	3	2	48 00	31 00	49-20	8-6	—	—	—	—	—	—	—	—
Wellfleet,	1	9	4	2	100 00	34 25	78	8-9	—	1	2	60	Taxation,	10	—	1,000 00
Yarmouth,	5	8	—	—	67 83	30 70	89	8-18	—	1	1	30	Part tax,	9	—	841 64
Totals,	51	173	44	35	$65 85	$32 98	1,350-18	8-5	—	11	16	577	—	100-10	—	$9,739 14

BERKSHIRE COUNTY — Continued.

TOWNS.	Whole No. of different male teachers in school-year.	Whole No. of different female teachers in school-year.	No. of teachers who have attended Normal Schools.	No. of teachers who have graduated from Normal Schools.	Av'ge wages per month of male teachers in Public Schools.	Av'ge wages per month of female teachers in Public Schools.	Aggregate of months all the Public Schools have been kept during the school-year.	Average No. of months the Public Schools have been kept for the entire year.	No. of Schools kept less than six months each.	HIGH SCHOOLS. No. of High Schools.	No. of teachers.	No. of pupils.	How supported.	LENGTH. Months.	Days.	Salary of Principal.
Adams,	5	30	5	5	$97 44	$39 09	261-15	8-8	—	1	3	63	Taxation,	9-15	—	$1,500 00
Alford,	3	1	—	—	28 00	24 00	24-5	8	—	—	—	—	—	—	—	—

Becket,	1	8	2	1	30 00	20 66	48	6	1	–	–	47	Taxation,	8–10	566 29
Cheshire,	2	7	2	2	43 46	24 00	70–15	8	–	–	–	–	–	–	–
Clarksburg,	–	3	–	–	–	29 33	24–15	8–5	–	–	–	–	–	–	–
Dalton,	2	13	4	4	80 00	32 00	115–15	9–19	–	–	–	115	Taxation,	9–10	1,550 00
Egremont,	1	3	2	2	36 00	31 00	27–15	9–5	–	–	–	35	Taxation,	8–10	600 00
Florida,	–	9	1	–	–	23 83	36	6	–	–	2	–	–	–	–
Great Barrington,	5	25	–	1	71 00	27 00	207	9–9	–	2	–	–	–	–	–
Hancock,	–	10	2	–	–	22 57	42	7	–	–	–	–	–	–	–
Hinsdale,	1	14	2	1	30 00	28 33	99	8–6	–	1	1	–	–	–	–
Lanesborough,	–	11	2	2	–	25 22	66–5	7–7	–	–	–	–	–	–	–
Lee,	3	21	–	–	84 66	30 82	168–4	9–7	–	2	3	101	Taxation,	10	1,500 00
Lenox,	5	10	1	1	55 00	30 00	105	8	–	1	1	31	Taxation,	8–15	370 00
Monterey,	2	7	–	1	26 00	21 00	46	7–13	–	–	–	56	Taxation,	10	800 00
Mt. Washington,	2	2	–	–	32 00	20 00	18	9	–	–	–	–	–	–	–
New Ashford,	1	2	–	–	20 00	20 00	14	7	–	–	–	–	–	–	–
New Marlboro,	5	13	–	–	23 88	20 43	92–10	7–2	1	–	–	–	–	–	–
North Adams,	4	59	3	–	109 50	35 51	378–11	9	1	2	5	83	Taxation,	9–15	1,500 00
Otis,	1	10	–	–	22 00	19 71	48	6	–	–	–	21	Taxation,	9–10	–
Peru,	–	6	10	4	–	20 40	28–15	6	–	–	–	–	–	–	–
Pittsfield,	4	67	–	–	120 60	33 65	481–16	10	2	1	1	135	Taxation,	10	1,800 00
Richmond,	8	6	–	–	24 00	24 00	69	9–17	–	–	–	–	–	–	–
Sandisfield,	3	13	1	–	28 00	22 04	82–5	7–5	–	–	–	–	–	–	–
Savoy,	8	10	–	1	21 50	17 18	48–7	6	–	–	–	–	–	–	–
Sheffield,	7	14	2	–	41 00	27 00	116–5	8	–	1	1	57	Taxation,	9	632 00
Stockbridge,	3	13	–	1	170 00	31 50	87	9–13	–	1	2	48	Taxation,	9–15	1,200 00
Tyringham,	1	7	2	1	22 00	22 80	38–10	7–12	–	–	–	–	–	–	–
Washington,	1	7	–	–	24 00	22 00	42	7	–	–	–	–	–	–	–
West Stockbridge,	3	9	2	2	50 41	29 11	108–15	9–18	–	–	–	39	Taxation,	10	700 00
Williamstown,	2	18	1	2	40 00	29 27	129–5	8–1	–	1	3	–	–	–	–
Windsor,	1	13	–	1	20 00	17 98	55–10	6–18	–	1	–	–	–	–	–
Totals,	74	441	49	31	$57 95	$28 93	3,189–9	7–15	4	13	27	831	–	118–5	$12,698 29

BARNSTABLE COUNTY — Continued.

TOWNS.	Amount raised by taxes for Schools, including wages of teachers, board, fuel, care of fires and school-rooms, for the school-year 1885-86.	Expense of supervision by school committee.	Salary of Superintendent of Public Schools.	Expense of Printing reports, etc.	Expense of sundries,—books, stationery, etc.	Amount expended for new school-houses.	Amount expended for alterations and permanent improvements.	Amount expended for ordinary repairs.	Amount paid for all school purposes from money raised by taxation.	Amount of voluntary contributions for Public Schools.
Barnstable,	$11,000 00	$135 00	$389 00	$88 25	$1,764 80	$1,000 00	$674 50	$1,200 00	$16,251 55	—
Bourne,	4,550 00	100 00	—	25 00	450 00	1,000 00	75 00	303 15	6,503 15	—
Brewster,	2,200 00	100 00	—	15 00	276 69	—	—	150 00	2,741 69	—
Chatham,	3,300 00	150 00	75 00	20 00	300 00	—	200 00	100 00	4,170 00	—
Dennis,	5,000 00	—	65 00	25 00	776 11	—	—	161 35	6,037 46	—
Eastham,	800 00	—	—	10 00	183 18	—	—	20 67	1,028 85	—
Falmouth,	6,761 00	158 55	1,000 00	32 50	1,099 70	8,884 21	—	563 26	18,189 22	—
Harwich,	5,000 00	154 00	—	25 00	578 00	—	—	338 00	6,095 00	—
Mashpee,	500 00	10 00	—	10 00	—	—	—	47 00	567 00	—
Orleans,	2,200 00	5 00	100 00	22 00	187 76	—	—	189 67	2,704 43	—
Provincetown,	7,600 00	—	350 00	20 00	850 00	1,000 00	—	213 00	10,033 00	—
Sandwich,	5,800 00	—	200 00	45 00	446 33	2,160 65	60 00	98 53	8,750 51	—
Truro,	1,500 00	90 00	—	25 00	171 00	—	—	100 00	1,946 00	—
Wellfleet,	4,000 00	175 00	—	—	839 35	—	—	452 72	5,467 07	—
Yarmouth,	3,200 00	100 00	—	16 00	369 58	—	—	567 77	4,251 35	—
Totals,	$63,401 00	$1,177 55	$2,179 00	$378 75	$8,242 50	$14,044 86	$1,009 50	$4,505 12	$94,936 28	—

BERKSHIRE COUNTY — Continued.

TOWNS.										
Adams,	$14,423 20	$150 00	$1,000 00	$25 00	$2,239 62	—	$1,600 00	$1,589 04	$21,146 86	—
Alford,	367 00	20 00	—	10 00	20 00	—	—	7 00	404 00	—

Becker,	1,000 00	69 03	—	4 00	95 55	$176 03	913 69	7 75	2,566 05	—
Cheshire,	2,600 00	69 50	—	5 00	326 95	—		128 23	3,029 68	—
Clarksburg,	700 00		—	12 00	20 90	—	6 00	67 73	1,006 63	—
Dalton,	4,459 25	150 00	—		604 71	—	510 58	127 40	5,852 00	—
Egremont,	850 00	38 55	—	5 00	100 55	—			994 10	—
Florida,	800 00	45 00	—	10 00	114 00	—	72 00	10 43	1,051 43	—
Gt. Barrington,	9,600 00		—		737 00	—		26 00	10,363 00	—
Hancock,	500 00	50 00	—	8 00	91 99	—	47 00	63 82	760 81	—
Hinsdale,	3,100 00	44 00	—		532 94	—		130 45	3,807 89	—
Lanesborough,	1,600 00	35 00	—		126 66	—		24 78	1,786 44	—
Lee,	8,466 82	333 75	—	15 00	710 94	9,500 00		146 40	14,172 91	—
Lenox,	4,600 00	60 00	—	10 00	547 60	—	951 29	264 91	6,433 80	—
Monterey,	800 00	49 50	—	6 00	144 52	—	85 00	92 77	1,177 79	—
Mt. Washington,	130 00	16 00	—	5 00	15 83	—		5 00	171 83	—
New Ashford,	81 00	21 75	—	3 00	15 68	—		15 22	136 65	—
New Marlboro,	2,000 00	132 10	1,700 00		197 22	—	500 00		2,329 32	—
North Adams,	24,700 00	250 00	—	140 00	3,000 00	—	500 00	1,800 00	32,090 00	—
Otis,	1,000 00	76 50	—	3 75	43 33	—	8 00	7 00	1,138 58	—
Peru,	600 00	30 00	—	6 40	53 52	—	30 00	5 00	724 92	—
Pittsfield,	30,303 57	50 00	1,500 00	100 00	1,777 58	—	1,340 30	909 09	35,980 54	—
Richmond,	1,500 00	35 00	—	11 00	287 00	—	495 00	63 00	2,391 00	—
Sandisfield,	2,000 00	54 00	—	10 00	203 88	—		24 35	2,292 73	$70 00
Savoy,	660 00	57 00	—	10 00	100 00	475 00			1,242 00	—
Sheffield,	3,700 00	196 50	—	16 00	608 77	800 07	69 78	591 16	5,782 28	—
Stockbridge,	5,000 00	223 00	—	25 00	300 00	—	1,500 00	100 00	7,148 00	—
Tyringham,	700 00	22 00	—	6 00	96 00	—		42 00	866 00	—
Washington,	600 00	19 50	—	2 00	61 30	—	35 00		717 80	—
W. Stockbridge,	4,241 57	100 00	—	25 50	451 07	—		235 83	5,053 97	—
Williamstown,	5,200 00	111 50	—	36 00	470 62	—	4,486 56	268 11	10,592 79	—
Windsor,	800 00	40 00	—	11 00	34 35	—	13 25	7 48	906 08	—
Totals,	$136,922 41	$2,549 18	$4,200 00	$520 65	$14,250 08	$11,251 10	$12,663 45	$6,559 95	$184,117 38	$70 00

BARNSTABLE COUNTY — CONCLUDED.

TOWNS.	Amount of local funds the income of which can be appropriated only for the support of Schools and Academies.	Income of local funds.	Income of surplus revenue and other funds, including the dog tax, used at the option of the town.	ACADEMIES AND PRIVATE SCHOOLS.						Town's share of school fund payable Jan. 25, 1886.	How much of said fund was used for apparatus and books of reference.
				No. of Academies.	Whole No. attending for the year.	Amount of tuition paid.	No. of Private Schools.	Whole No. attending for the year.	Estimated amount of tuition.		
Barnstable,	$12,283 00	$409 32	$341 64							$185 32	$185 32
Bourne,			186 03							212 70	276 69
Brewster,							1	20	$300 00	309 58	
Chatham,			60 97				1	8	5,500 00	221 08	
Dennis,			72 10							179 11	
Eastham,			51 24	1	70	$800 00				305 13	
Falmouth,	10,000 00	600 00	277 75				1	10	100 00	18 63	
Harwich,			91 00							228 66	
Mashpee,			54 92							302 96	
Orleans,			58 63							309 92	50 43
Provincetown,										198 99	50 00
Sandwich,	5,100 00	200 00	277 73	1						221 93	
Truro,			58 63							309 23	
Wellfleet,										215 67	
Yarmouth,	16,000 00	900 00								167 95	218 00
Totals,	$43,383 00	$2,109 32	$1,529 64	2	70	$800 00	3	38	$5,900 00	$3,386 86	$780 44

BERKSHIRE COUNTY — CONCLUDED.

TOWNS.										Town's share	
Adams,										$94 57	—
Alford,										303 65	—

Becket,		$10 94	$168 00	28	1				$105 72	$36 62	$796 54
Cheshire,	$37 00	217 55									
Clarksburg,		309 12							56 66		
Dalton,		173 81									
Egremont,		307 23							48 30		
Florida,		307 07	4,500 00	35	2					57 64	960 67
Great Barrington,	18 27	197 85							252 80	12 00	200 00
Hancock,		305 81									
Hinsdale,		222 62								48 07	
Lanesborough,		214 93	150 00	187	2					89 24	775 00
Lee,		195 01	500 00	30	1			1	81 28		1,608 50
Lenox,	50 00	175 58					15		20 15	36 72	
Monterey,		306 38								6 00	612 01
Mt. Washington,		301 60							101 15		100 00
New Ashford,		301 88							403 47	327 52	
New Marlboro',		218 86	500 00	80	1						5,458 77
North Adams,		157 52									
Otis,		307 12								22 33	
Peru,		303 70									370 00
Pittsfield,		163 50	6,000 00	100	3				42 21		
Richmond,		314 07							88 98	77 40	
Sandisfield,		311 74							147 55	77 82	1,290 00
Savoy,		306 15								258 50	1,300 00
Sheffield,		223 30	105 00	11	2				58 56	400 00	5,131 58
Stockbridge,		168 40	300 00	20	3				52 86		4,000 00
Tyringham,		305 24									
Washington,		304 33							61 22		
West Stockbridge,		220 57									
Williamstown,		187 37	4,330 00	85	1						200 00
Windsor,		304 33								35 00	200 00
Totals,	$105 27	$8,041 80	$16,553 00	576	16	–	15	1	$1,520 91	$1,484 86	$22,803 07

BRISTOL COUNTY.

TOWNS.	Population — State Census, 1885.	Valuation — 1885.	No. of Public Schools.	No. of persons in town May 1, 1885, between 5 and 15 years of age.	No. of persons in town May 1, 1885, between 8 and 14 years of age.	No. of different pupils of all ages in the Public Schools during the school-year.	No. attending within the year under 5 years of age.	No. attending within the year over 15 years of age.	No. attending within the year between 8 and 14 years of age.	Average membership of all the Schools.	Average attendance in all the Public Schools during the school-year.	The per cent. of attendance based upon the average membership.	No. of teachers required by the Public Schools.
Acushnet,	1,071	$631,200	6	187	112	186	—	28	116	154	135	88	6
Attleborough,	13,175	6,108,715	50	2,191	1,251	2,604	11	154	1,577	2,041	1,812	89	56
Berkley,	941	410,319	7	147	105	158	5	14	99	142	130	92	7
Dartmouth,	3,448	1,905,250	22	570	435	583	10	31	429	486	402	83	22
Dighton,	1,782	725,355	11	269	175	327	2	11	220	265	237	89	11
Easton,	3,948	3,407,441	18	778	490	877	2	66	490	721	613	85	19
Fairhaven,	2,880	1,419,437	11	480	386	454	1	56	283	395	350	89	12
Fall River,	56,870	43,820,005	162	11,741	6,486	10,579	—	488	6,374	7,863	7,095	90	208
Freetown,	1,457	835,255	8	238	167	287	7	32	164	220	174	79	8
Mansfield,	2,939	1,144,265	13	473	296	533	5	12	309	442	384	87	13
New Bedford,	33,393	31,397,890	124	5,131	3,923	4,683	—	353	3,530	4,272	3,832	90	125
Norton,	1,718	764,275	10	287	210	283	2	12	197	201	171	85	8
Raynham,	1,535	860,059	10	265	171	281	8	11	166	226	205	90	10
Rehoboth,	1,788	734,040	15	285	159	309	7	38	159	262	234	89	15
Seekonk,	1,295	729,740	7	227	150	250	4	20	146	180	163	85	7
Somerset,	2,475	1,061,058	11	443	276	468	3	18	281	392	355	91	11
Swansea,	1,403	696,125	10	230	140	255	1	20	140	193	164	85	11
Taunton,	23,674	16,501,572	67	4,215	2,512	4,760	—	240	2,500	3,521	3,227	92	82
Westport,	2,706	1,344,275	19	502	312	496	8	56	273	389	326	84	19
Totals,	158,498	$114,486,276	579	28,660	17,706	28,373	70	1,660	17,543	22,365	19,999	.89	649

DUKES COUNTY.

Chilmark,	412	$218,780	3	58	46	62	2	5	40	51	46	.90	3
Cottage City,	709	1,363,275	4	112	89	144	–	9	89	114	96	.84	4
Edgartown,	1,165	735,883	6	144	97	167	3	22	95	143	128	.90	6
Gay Head,	186	19,904	1	32	20	40	1	8	20	29	21	.72	2
Gosnold,	122	187,263	1	19	10	12	–	3	6	12	10	.83	1
Tisbury,	1,541	690,180	8	173	122	218	4	34	133	173	168	.97	9
Totals,	4,135	$3,210,285	23	538	384	643	10	81	383	522	469	.90	25

BRISTOL COUNTY — CONTINUED.

TOWNS.	Whole No. of different male teachers in school-year.	Whole No. of different female teachers in school-year.	No. of teachers who have attended Normal Schools.	No. of teachers who have graduated from Normal Schools.	Av'ge wages per month of male teachers in Public Schools.	Av'ge wages per month of female teachers in Public Schools.	Aggregate of months have been kept during the school-year all the Public Schools.	Average No. of months the Public Schools have been kept for the entire year.	No. of Schools kept less than six months each.	HIGH SCHOOLS.						
										No. of High Schools.	No. of teachers.	No. of pupils.	How supported.	Length Months.	Length Days.	Salary of Principal.
Acushnet,	1	7	3	3	—	$33 28	54	9	—	—	—	—	—	—	—	—
Attleborough,	5	68	34	23	$115 80	42 46	420-18	8-5	—	2	4	122	Taxation,	9	7	$1,100 00
Berkley,	8	9	3	1	—	26 85	57-15	8-10	—	—	—	—	—	—	—	—
Dartmouth,	1	24	3	2	41 58	23 58	187-10	8-6	—	1	1	33	Taxation,	9	—	600 00
Dighton,	2	17	8	6	—	34 04	88-6	10-4	—	—	—	—	—	—	—	—
Easton,	12	25	4	4	150 00	41 05	183-10	9-10	—	1	1	90	Taxation,	10	4	1,500 00
Fairhaven,	—	15	10	10	110 00	33 45	104-15	10	—	1	2	56	Taxation,	9	15	1,200 00
Fall River,	4	205	20	18	136 55	46 65	1,585	—	—	1	9	467	Taxation,	10	—	2,700 00
Freetown,	8	11	4	—	—	30 26	67-15	8-9	—	—	—	—	—	—	—	—
Mansfield,	2	10	4	1	63 13	31 00	110-15	8-10	—	1	1	44	Taxation,	9	15	850 00
New Bedford,	—	117	35	35	153 12	50 68	1,240	10	—	1	9	323	Taxation,	10	—	1,900 00
Norton,	1	9	5	—	42 67	34 32	68-5	8-10	—	—	—	—	—	—	—	—
Raynham,	1	14	7	5	—	33 60	80	8	—	—	—	—	—	—	—	—
Rehoboth,	3	22	4	1	40 00	28 36	86-10	7-9	—	—	—	—	—	—	—	—
Seekonk,	4	12	3	—	—	30 05	58	8-5	—	—	—	—	—	—	—	—
Somerset,	9	12	7	5	53 33	35 33	90	8-3	—	1	1	32	Taxation,	—	—	$800 00
Swansea,	4	12	7	4	27 00	28 00	80	8	—	—	—	—	—	—	—	—
Taunton,	—	73	16	14	117 80	41 58	638	9-10	—	1	5	185	Taxation,	10	—	2,000 00
Westport,	—	28	4	3	41 00	24 00	161	9	1	1	1	35	Taxation,	9	—	595 00
Totals,	63	690	181	139	$95 48	$41 16	5,821-19	8-14	1	11	35	1,387	—	97	1	$13,245 00

DUKES COUNTY — Continued.

												Taxation,	8-10	
Chilmark, ·	2	3	—	—	$32 00	$28 00	19-21	6-17	—	—	—	—	—	—	—
Cottage City, ·	1	4	2	2	60 00	29 00	34-4	8-11	—	—	—	—	—	—	—
Edgartown, ·	2	8	—	—	50 00	32 33	46	7-10	—	1	1	28	—	8-10	$510 00
Gay Head, ·	1	1	—	—	40 00	16 66	8	8	—	—	—	—	—	—	—
Gosnold, ·	—	1	—	—	—	30 00	10	10	—	—	—	—	—	—	—
Tisbury, ·	2	10	8	6	50 00	27 80	64-5	8-1	—	—	—	—	—	—	—
Totals, ·	8	27	10	8	$45 50	$29 01	182-10	8-3	—	1	1	28	—	8-10	$510 00

BRISTOL COUNTY — Continued.

TOWNS.	Amount raised by taxes for Schools, including wages of teachers, board, fuel, care of fires and school-rooms, for the school-year 1885-86.	Expense of supervision by school committee.	Salary of Superintendent of Public Schools.	Expense of Printing reports, etc.	Expense of sundries,— books, stationery, etc.	Amount expended for new school-houses.	Amount expended for alterations and permanent improvements.	Amount expended for ordinary repairs.	Amount paid for all school purposes from money raised by taxation.	Amount of voluntary contributions for Public Schools.
Acushnet,	$1,700 00	$80 00	—	$7 00	$288 31	—	—	$103 45	$2,178 76	—
Attleborough,	25,000 00	300 00	$1,390 75	12 00	4,748 95	$13,005 28	—	5,363 36	49,820 34	$40 00
Berkley,	1,360 00	65 00	—	45 00	140 00	—	—	35 00	2,085 00	—
Dartmouth,	5,000 00	150 00	—	35 00	474 70	—	$500 00	364 85	6,023 75	—
Dighton,	3,000 00	—	125 00	10 25	229 45	4,299 95	106 21	161 42	7,932 28	—
Easton,	8,752 00	72 15	—	50 00	1,185 92	—	—	1,694 60	11,754 67	100 00
Fairhaven,	6,000 00	299 81	—	25 00	749 82	—	—	533 50	7,608 13	—
Fall River,	186,207 02	—	2,400 00	125 44	10,669 27	7,794 35	—	6,829 76	163,825 84	—
Freetown,	2,000 00	90 00	—	—	254 00	—	512 79	17 11	2,873 90	—
Mansfield,	5,500 00	175 15	—	38 19	877 76	—	331 48	67 04	6,989 62	—
New Bedford,	80,501 00	400 00	2,000 00	155 00	3,735 00	26,680 00	4,500 00	5,209 00	123,190 00	—
Norton,	2,717 36	—	125 00	30 00	265 94	—	142 33	126 61	3,907 24	—
Raynham,	3,000 00	18 00	150 00	15 00	259 00	—	1,527 00	48 28	5,167 28	—
Rehoboth,	3,200 00	90 00	—	25 00	675 00	—	—	20 00	4,010 00	—
Seekonk,	1,700 00	82 00	—	15 00	239 00	6,135 63	—	60 15	2,096 50	—
Somerset,	4,421 25	210 40	—	27 00	560 65	—	—	79 97	11,434 90	—
Swansea,	2,500 00	—	100 00	19 60	271 06	—	294 72	112 00	3,297 37	—
Taunton,	50,000 00	575 00	1,900 00	99 00	9,500 00	82,436 00	1,500 00	3,000 00	149,010 00	5 00
Westport,	4,000 00	227 00	—	14 69	550 92	—	309 93	400 00	5,502 54	—
Totals,	$346,298 63	$2,834 51	$8,190 75	$748 17	$35,674 74	$140,351 21	$9,724 46	$24,225 60	$568,708 12	$145 00

DUKES COUNTY — CONTINUED.

Chilmark,	$450 00	$14 00	—	$10 00	$136 17	—	$293 24	$123 80	$763 97	—
Cottage City,	1,243 50	75 00	—	25 00	177 82	—	—	78 42	1,892 98	—
Edgartown,	1,700 00	50 00	$10 00	19 00	404 05	—	—	100 00	2,273 05	—
Gay Head,	100 00	6 00	—	4 50	24 61	—	—	30 73	175 84	—
Gosnold,	200 00	30 00	—	2 50	15 00	—	130 00	—	377 50	—
Tisbury,	2,200 00	75 00	—	9 00	229 78	—	917 00	—	3,430 78	$70 00
Totals,	$5,893 50	$280 00	$10 00	$70 00	$987 43	—	$1,340 24	$332 95	$8,914 12	$70 00

BRISTOL COUNTY — CONCLUDED.

TOWNS.	Amount of local funds of Schools and Academies can be appropriated only for the support of which the income of	Income of local funds.	Income of surplus revenue and other funds, including the dog tax, used at the option of the town.	ACADEMIES AND PRIVATE SCHOOLS.						Town's share of school fund payable Jan. 23, 1886.	How much of said fund was used for apparatus and books of reference.
				No. of Academies.	Whole No. attending for the year.	Amount of tuition paid.	No. of Private Schools.	Whole No. attending for the year.	Estimated amount of tuition.		
Acushnet,			$144 40	—	—	—	—	—	—	$210 88	—
Attleborough,	$2,800 00	$115 00	867 62	—	—	—	3	70	$700 00	127 10	—
Berkley,	—	—	131 07	—	—	—	1	10	50 00	308 89	—
Dartmouth,	—	—	448 95	—	—	—	—	—	—	182 93	—
Dighton,	2,000 00	90 99	185 49	—	—	—	—	—	—	217 21	—
Easton,	50,000 00	4,000 00	519 27	—	—	—	5	20	200 00	45 58	$50 00
Fairhaven,	—	—		—	—	—	—	—	—	175 41	—
Fall River,	—	—	186 05	—	—	—	1	1,000	8,000 00		—
Freetown,	—	—	397 65	1	32	$3,300 00	—	—	—	212 99	—
Mansfield,	1,000 00	56 00	694 46	1	138	5,886 95	25	840	3,500 00	176 32	—
New Bedford,	50,000 00	3,000 00		—	—	—	—	—	—		—
Norton,	—	—	246 58	—	—	—	—	—	—	217 55	—
Raynham,	—	—	302 68	—	—	—	—	—	—	215 38	—
Rehoboth,	—	—		—	—	—	—	—	—	215 67	—
Seekonk,	—	—	203 82	—	—	—	—	—	—	212 93	—
Somerset,	—	—		—	—	—	—	—	—	176 95	—
Swansea,	—	—		—	—	—	—	—	—	212 87	15 00
Taunton,	—	8,000 00	277 13	1	155	5,000 00	1	20	200 00		52 00
Westport,	—	—		—	—	—	—	—	—	178 31	—
Totals,	$105,800 00	$15,261 99	$4,605 17	3	325	$14,186 95	36	1,960	$12,650 00	$3,086 97	$117 00

DUKES COUNTY — CONCLUDED.

Chilmark,	—	—	$67 20	—	—	—	—	—	—	$303 19	$24 00
Cottage City,	—	—	84 60	—	—	—	—	—	—	155 58	50 97
Edgartown,	—	—	—	—	—	—	—	—	—	208 37	50 00
Gay Head,	—	—	23 00	—	—	—	—	—	—	301 25	23 61
Gosnold,	—	—	106 10	—	—	—	—	—	—	301 21	—
Tisbury,	$5,000 00	$200 00	—	1	23	$125 00	—	—	—	211 40	—
Totals,	$5,000 00	$200 00	$280 90	1	23	$125 00	—	—	—	$1,481 00	$148 58

ESSEX COUNTY.

TOWNS.	Population—State Census, 1885.	Valuation — 1885.	No. of Public Schools.	No. of persons in town between May 1, 1885, 5 and 15 years of age.	No. of persons in town between May 1, 1885, 8 and 14 years of age.	No. of different pupils of all ages in the Public Schools during the school-year.	No. attending within the year under 5 years of age.	No. attending within the year over 15 years of age.	No. attending within the year between 8 and 14 years of age.	Average membership of all the Schools.	Average attendance in all the Public Schools during the school-year.	The per cent. of attendance based upon the average membership.	No. of teachers required by the Public Schools.
Amesbury,	4,403	$1,768,152	19	648	384	722	4	40	463	612	573	.94	20
Andover,	5,711	3,759,745	22	951	609	956	8	36	609	771	709	.92	24
Beverly,	9,186	10,633,425	35	1,578	864	1,388		84	836	1,518	1,220	.80	38
Boxford,	840	645,865	6	189	91	145	1	10	88	119	105	.89	6
Bradford,	3,106	1,466,484	11	535	368	656	1	47	393	513	456	.89	14
Danvers,	7,061	3,569,180	21	1,106	649	1,207	8	75	654	1,048	948	.91	27
Essex,	1,722	813,090	9	284	145	284	4	36	145	244	220	.90	9
Georgetown,	2,299	1,053,046	10	472	240	461	4	10	240	451	378	.84	12
Gloucester,	21,703	12,310,843	82	3,894	2,704	4,520	5	409	2,647	3,829	3,628	.95	100
Groveland,	2,272	856,068	10	407	239	391	1	33	221	328	276	.84	10
Hamilton,	851	626,795	4	113	77	125	5	12	77	97	82	.85	4
Haverhill,	21,795	14,325,988	77	3,600	2,110	4,346	8	305	2,536	3,374	2,939	.87	95
Ipswich,	4,207	2,069,071	16	616	409	676	8	68	409	559	526	.94	19
Lawrence,	38,862	27,144,050	102	6,947	4,265	6,077	44	327	4,168	4,772	4,529	.95	125
Lynn,	45,867	28,459,243	122	7,380	4,239	6,732		493	4,113	6,321	5,525	.87	138
Lynnfield,	766	548,485	3	115	80	120	7	8	80	91	86	.95	3
Manchester,	1,639	4,653,173	7	249	160	290		28	168	236	215	.91	7
Marblehead,	7,517	4,250,600	15	1,420	851	1,392		91	795	1,231	1,082	.88	27
Merrimac,	2,378	1,165,955	17	417	236	515	4	59	291	415	371	.89	15
Methuen,	4,507	2,731,946	19	787	513	827	3	20	619	778	614	.79	21
Middleton,	899	531,488	4	107	52	151	3	12	77	109	98	.90	4
Nahant,	637	4,878,624	4	147	80	144		12	80	134	111	.83	5
Newbury,	1,590	857,961	7	309	175	236	2	5	157	196	159	.81	7

Newburyport,	13,716	7,550,805	26	2,581	1,677	1,701	—	51	1,108	1,299	1,126	.87	42
North Andover,	3,425	2,168,841	10	681	401	725	4	28	413	646	571	.88	21
Peabody,	9,580	6,060,000	36	1,773	909	2,072	—	170	1,185	1,713	1,451	.85	37
Rockport,	3,888	2,034,166	14	815	490	790	4	95	440	696	624	.90	19
Rowley,	1,183	545,434	7	221	114	231	—	8	113	176	165	.88	7
Salem,	28,084	25,050,030	84	4,976	3,007	3,595	10	356	2,170	3,511	3,044	.87	94
Salisbury,	4,840	2,340,622	21	886	666	780	—	53	540	612	548	.90	22
Saugus,	2,855	1,474,360	13	486	298	524	—	41	310	513	416	.81	14
Swampscott,	2,471	3,496,140	10	348	213	435	5	31	295	378	337	.89	11
Topsfield,	1,141	717,183	5	179	131	175	4	14	122	138	118	.86	6
Wenham,	871	509,475	5	140	105	165	5	10	105	127	113	.89	5
West Newbury,	1,899	965,425	10	297	217	322		21	220	267	231	.86	10
Totals,	263,727	$182,631,698	872	45,654	27,868	43,876	143	3,098	26,887	37,822	33,584	.89	1,018

ESSEX COUNTY — CONTINUED.

TOWNS.	Whole No. of different male teachers in school-year.	Whole No. of different female teachers in school-year.	No. of teachers who have attended Normal Schools.	No. of teachers who have graduated from Normal Schools.	Av'ge wages per month of male teachers in Public Schools.	Av'ge wages per month of female teachers in Public Schools.	Aggregate of months all the Public Schools have been kept during the school-year.	Average No. of months the Public Schools have been kept for the entire year.	No. of Schools kept less than six months each.	HIGH SCHOOLS.				LENGTH.		Salary of Principal.
										No. of High Schools.	No. of teachers.	No. of pupils.	How supported.	Months.	Days.	
Amesbury,	1	20	—	1	$147 00	$30 63	133	9	7	1	2	35	Taxation,	9	10	$1,400 00
Andover,	1	26	8	5	36 00	37 78	188-6	9-11	—	1	3	93	Not by tax,	9		1,600 00
Beverly,	3	35	9	9	73 33	38 51	810	—	—	1	4	150	Taxation,	10		1,300 00
Boxford,	1	7	2	2	40 00	31 66	52	8-15	—	—	—	—	—			—
Bradford,	2	14	—	—	142 10	34 63	101-5	9-10	—	—	2	69	Taxation,	9	10	1,350 00
Danvers,	4	29	17	12	126 66	31 00	191-15	9-10	—	1	3	95	Taxation,	10		1,400 00
Essex,	4	7	5	2	65 00	25 00	76-10	8-10	—	—	—	—	—			—
Georgetown,	1	14	2	—	105 55	35 27	90	9	—	1	2	73	Taxation,	9		950 00
Gloucester,	6	109	53	1	144 00	37 70	784-16	9-11	—	1	6	312	Taxation,	9	15	2,000 00
Groveland,	1	9	2	1	70 00	34 67	90-15	9-2	—	1	1	41	Taxation,	10		700 00
Hamilton,	1	5	1	1	—	30 88	36	9	—	—	1	—	—			—
Haverhill,	5	90	14	12	135 00	48 00	744-8	9-11	—	1	6	217	Taxation,	10		1,800 00
Ipswich,	4	15	3	2	93 33	34 81	153	9-8	—	1	2	53	Taxation,	10		1,500 00
Lawrence,	8	117	9	8	127 50	45 42	1,020	10	—	1	9	275	Taxation,	10		1,800 00
Lynn,	10	128	79	52	144 00	54 00	1,280	9-12	—	1	10	290	Taxation,	9	14	2,000 00
Lynnfield,	1	6	6	6	—	38 25	27	9	—	—	—	—	—			—
Manchester,	1	8	5	5	80 00	33 00	63-5	9-10	—	1	1	55	Taxation,	9	10	760 00
Marblehead,	2	25	7	3	102 66	39 00	153-16	10-5	—	1	2	82	Taxation,	10	5	1,004 50
Merrimac,	4	13	—	—	75 00	33 25	112-10	8	—	1	2	54	Taxation,	9	10	950 00
Methuen,	2	19	2	2	83 00	37 00	171	9	—	1	2	38	Taxation,	9		1,100 00
Middleton,	1	7	5	5	—	36 00	38	9-10	—	—	—	—	—			—
Nahant,	1	4	3	3	123 07	51 12	39	9-15	—	1	2	33	Taxation,	9	15	1,200 00
Newbury,	1	7	1	—	28 00	28 00	56	8	—	—	—	—	—			—

Newburyport,	7	37	4	4	114 00	36 52	977-8	10-1	–	1	4	123	Taxation,	10-1	1,500 00
North Andover,	3	24	3	1	78 00	36 63	174-19	9-4	–	1	2	40	Taxation,	10	1,000 00
Peabody,	4	41	13	13	120 00	40 90	351	9-7	1	1	3	86	Taxation,	10	1,200 00
Rockport,	3	19	3	2	54 00	31 17	117	8-7	–	–	2	46	Taxation,	9	650 00
Rowley,	–	8	1	–	–	24 00	63	9	–	1	–	–	–	–	–
Salem,	7	86	66	61	164 30	54 59	850-15	10-1	–	1	8	214	Taxation,	10-1	2,200 00
Salisbury,	3	21	3	2	82 00	30 40	175	8-7	–	1	2	49	Taxation,	9-10	1,200 00
Saugus,	1	17	9	8	84 00	35 00	121-18	9-8	–	1	2	50	Taxation,	9-12	810 00
Swampscott,	1	13	11	9	110 00	44 00	100	10	–	1	2	49	Taxation,	10	1,100 00
Topsfield,	2	8	3	2	50 00	29 11	42-10	8-10	–	–	1	–	–	–	–
Wenham,	–	6	5	2	–	33 20	45	9	–	–	–	–	–	–	–
West Newbury,	3	10	–	–	64 45	28 00	80	8	–	1	1	31	Taxation,	8	631 25
Totals,	96	1,004	354	234	$108 43	$11 13	8,290-15	9-4	8	26	85	2,656	–	250-13	$33,105 75

ESSEX COUNTY — CONTINUED.

TOWNS.	Amount raised by taxes for Schools, including wages of teachers, board, fuel, care of fires and school-rooms, for the school-year 1885-86.	Expense of supervision by school committee.	Salary of Superintendent of Public Schools.	Expense of Printing reports, etc.	Expense of sundries,—books, stationery, etc.	Amount expended for new school-houses.	Amount expended for alterations and permanent improvements.	Amount expended for ordinary repairs.	Amount paid for all school purposes from money raised by taxation.	Amount of voluntary contributions for Public Schools.
Amesbury,	$7,200 00	$150 00	—	$45 00	$789 12	—	—	$108 22	$8,592 34	—
Andover,	9,800 00	525 00	—	75 81	1,156 38	—	$69 20	808 60	12,434 99	—
Beverly,	18,059 82	258 60	$100 00	50 00	2,997 85	$20,243 80	—	1,481 86	43,091 93	—
Boxford,	1,500 00	—	—	15 00	250 00	—	—	57 16	1,922 16	—
Bradford,	6,400 00	226 00	—	50 00	1,171 67	—	2,411 34	285 61	13,263 62	—
Danvers,	12,602 00	500 00	—	65 00	2,876 00	2,720 00	667 00	510 00	16,720 00	—
Essex,	3,000 00	180 00	—	27 00	433 00	—	100 00	118 00	3,858 00	—
Georgetown,	4,900 00	250 00	—	40 00	783 47	—	—	120 00	6,093 47	—
Gloucester,	47,462 70	792 00	2,500 00	255 00	5,883 71	8,524 56	415 04	5,627 33	71,460 34	—
Groveland,	3,677 00	160 00	—	30 00	507 72	—	—	183 76	4,558 48	—
Hamilton,	1,000 00	45 00	—	11 25	100 00	—	—	29 13	1,185 38	—
Haverhill,	59,288 14	2,066 00	400 00	—	6,897 34	3,906 91	1,790 00	3,786 68	78,135 07	—
Ipswich,	6,400 00	252 00	—	25 00	491 95	—	—	270 98	7,439 93	—
Lawrence,	72,707 07	800 00	2,200 00	352 00	9,744 42	20,000 00	5,000 00	4,000 00	114,808 49	—
Lynn,	95,259 78	800 00	2,250 00	327 00	11,129 61	—	11,217 30	6,974 96	127,958 65	—
Lynnfield,	800 00	85 00	—	25 00	—	—	—	75 00	985 00	—
Manchester,	3,000 00	232 00	—	24 50	339 85	—	—	297 21	3,893 56	—
Marblehead,	14,237 78	25 00	—	49 04	1,809 18	—	786 91	287 08	17,194 99	—
Merrimac,	5,800 00	150 00	—	—	450 00	—	50 00	25 00	5,900 00	—
Methuen,	9,000 00	400 00	—	34 80	940 36	—	—	986 78	11,361 94	—
Middleton,	1,200 00	84 70	—	13 00	170 71	—	—	67 91	1,536 32	—
Nahant,	3,980 35	275 00	—	75 00	317 76	—	—	65 85	4,713 46	—
Newbury,	1,654 18	60 00	—	15 00	177 66	—	—	74 00	1,980 81	—

Newburyport,	20,000 00	200 00	—	53 00	2,581 00	11,135 66	—	2,255 98	25,089 98	—
North Andover,	9,300 00	355 00	—	48 00	1,096 16	9,000 00	61 34	196 47	22,192 63	—
Peabody,	24,096 49	480 00	—	99 30	1,678 80	—	950 00	583 00	37,387 59	—
Rockport,	6,741 00	350 00	—	30 00	646 25	—	—	1,351 08	9,118 33	—
Rowley,	1,757 36	75 00	—	12 50	192 88	—	97 35	146 50	2,281 54	—
Salem,	68,817 79	1,000 00	—	112 43	7,950 64	—	5,785 80	2,883 91	86,550 57	—
Salisbury,	7,877 65	225 00	—	45 00	1,294 35	—	75 00	525 00	10,042 02	—
Saugus,	5,893 99	150 00	—	60 00	606 61	—	—	—	6,710 00	—
Swampscott,	6,750 00	300 00	—	—	1,000 00	—	50 00	374 22	8,474 22	—
Topsfield,	1,400 00	75 00	—	12 36	295 16	—	227 48	118 64	2,128 64	—
Wenham,	1,400 00	83 00	—	20 00	248 88	—	—	5 00	1,756 88	—
West Newbury,	3,014 32	145 00	—	45 00	368 18	—	—	128 46	3,700 96	$30 00
Totals,	$545,976 82	$11,753 30	$7,450 00	$2,141 99	$66,876 62	$75,530 93	$24,753 76	$35,108 88	$774,517 32	$30 00

ESSEX COUNTY — Concluded.

TOWNS.	Amount of local funds the income of which can be appropriated only for the support of Schools and Academies.	Income of local funds.	Income of surplus revenue and other funds, including the dog tax, at the option of the town.	ACADEMIES AND PRIVATE SCHOOLS.						Town's share of school fund payable Jan. 25, 1886.	How much of said fund was used for apparatus and books of reference.
				No. of Academies.	Whole No. attending for the year.	Amount of tuition paid.	No. of Private Schools.	Whole No. attending for the year.	Estimated amount of tuition.		
Amesbury,	$360,675 00	$12,595 00	$177 00	1			2	500	$400 00	$182 64	$50 00
Andover,	3,000 00	180 00	581 12	2	390	$24,212 80	3	25	600 00	50 25	—
Beverly,	3,467 58	179 47	50 00				1	20	250 00	86 19	—
Boxford,	—	—	217 80				1	20	—	207 80	—
Bradford,	—	—	413 00	1	135	6,925 00	1	18	1,698 00	177 74	—
Danvers,	—	—	96 19					20	300 00	60 90	—
Essex,	—	—	320 67				3		—	216 24	—
Georgetown,	—	—	—						—	171 65	—
Gloucester,	—	—	—				3	70	1,000 00	—	—
Groveland,	—	—	87 72						—	222 45	—
Hamilton,	4,300 00	430 00	—				2	38	1,500 00	206 27	—
Haverhill,	11,097 66	450 46	237 74				3	8	150 00	—	—
Ipswich,	—	—	—				6	1,400	5,000 00	187 09	—
Lawrence,	—	—	—					676	4,120 00	—	—
Lynn,	—	—	90 71						—	206 84	—
Lynnfield,	—	—	—				2		100 00	14 30	—
Manchester,	10,000 00	—	544 75					30	—	78 10	—
Marblehead,	—	—	175 94						—	174 67	—
Merrimac,	—	—	280 02						—	193 70	—
Methuen,	—	—	122 11						—	207 63	—
Middleton,	—	—	—						—	7 98	—
Nahant,	—	—	—						—	216 12	—
Newbury,	26,000 00	1,500 00	126 59	1	68	2,300 00	1	22	400 00	216 12	—

Newburyport,	15,000 00	675 00	—	—	1	—	4	500	—	153 08	—
North Andover,	—	—	—	—	—	—	1	8	200 00	189 99	—
Peabody,	10,000 00	610 00	687 29	—	—	—	2	33	418 00	108 98	—
Rockport,	—	—	—	—	—	—	1	10	200 00	195 69	25 00
Rowley,	—	—	96 98	—	—	—	—	—	—	212 87	—
Salem,	12,925 00	775 00	2,077 94	—	—	—	20	1,383	12,000 00	197 17	50 00
Salisbury,	—	—	258 67	—	—	—	1	10	50 00	178 48	30 00
Saugus,	—	—	58 50	—	—	—	—	—	—	21 99	—
Swampscott,	—	—	—	—	—	—	—	—	—	210 03	—
Topsfield,	—	—	132 08	—	—	—	—	—	—	207 63	—
Wenham,	—	—	101 51	—	—	—	—	—	—	207 63	—
West Newbury,	—	—	118 12	—	—	—	—	—	—	167 15	—
Totals,	$156,465 21	$17,424 93	$7,082 45	5	593	$33,437 80	56	4,791	$28,386 00	$4,711 62	$155 00

FRANKLIN COUNTY.

TOWNS.	Population—State Census, 1885.	Valuation—1885.	No. of Public Schools.	No. of persons in town between May 1, 1885, 5 and 15 years of age.	No. of persons in town between May 1, 1885, 8 and 14 years of age.	No. of different pupils of all ages in the Public Schools during the school-year.	No. attending within the year under 5 years of age.	No. attending within the year over 15 years of age.	No. attending within the year between 8 and 14 years of age.	Average membership of all the Schools.	Average attendance in all the Public Schools during the school-year.	The per cent. of attendance based upon the average membership.	No. of teachers required by the Public Schools.
Ashfield,	1,097	$449,500	12	150	125	211	6	34	120	166	153	.92	12
Bernardston,	930	396,535	6	148	99	153	4	4	99	122	113	.93	6
Buckland,	1,760	507,835	11	322	216	350	1	14	216	255	230	.90	11
Charlemont,	938	315,100	9	149	93	180	6	26	93	145	134	.92	10
Colrain,	1,605	567,360	14	340	245	380	4	37	245	322	290	.90	15
Conway,	1,573	739,524	15	320	187	332	4	36	186	265	243	.92	15
Deerfield,	3,042	1,189,418	20	606	316	620	5	20	313	595	570	.96	20
Erving,	873	328,182	5	143	111	197	5	19	111	154	130	.84	5
Gill,	860	435,469	7	165	95	142	4	10	89	113	106	.94	7
Greenfield,	4,869	3,141,741	22	871	638	1,052	—	148	619	837	760	.91	27
Hawley,	545	151,974	8	105	69	125	5	20	69	98	90	.92	8
Heath,	568	163,748	8	111	62	127	—	14	67	108	96	.89	8
Leverett,	779	288,838	6	131	71	166	—	18	81	120	109	.91	6
Leyden,	447	198,081	5	105	77	117	5	12	77	88	78	.89	6
Monroe,	176	44,048	3	52	39	63	—	15	34	45	39	.87	3
Montague,	5,629	2,891,753	26	1,422	978	1,278	3	53	863	1,126	1,016	.90	27
New Salem,	832	300,400	8	128	90	159	1	18	89	115	113	.93	8
Northfield,	1,705	624,905	9	254	159	287	1	30	159	211	162	.77	9
Orange,	3,650	1,709,985	21	629	368	745	1	72	406	617	580	.94	22
Rowe,	582	182,982	7	108	52	113	5	18	52	96	86	.90	7
Shelburne,	1,614	828,810	11	246	160	299	1	20	226	224	201	.90	11
Shutesbury,	485	149,122	6	99	56	115	3	14	56	92	84	.91	6
Sunderland,	700	423,880	5	130	82	148	1	36	82	119	109	.92	5

Warwick,	662	266,140	9	117	77	120	4	5	77	114	107	.94	9
Wendell,	509	192,935	5	82	53	105	2	12	53	70	63	.90	5
Whately,	999	401,501	6	203	97	191	5	17	88	138	122	.88	6
Totals,	37,449	$16,859,366	264	7,136	4,615	7,775	72	722	4,570	6,355	5,784	.91	274

HAMPDEN COUNTY.

Agawam,	2,357	$1,222,765	10	463	336	496	9	17	828	388	340	.88	11
Blandford,	954	345,720	13	213	143	215	9	19	143	182	161	.88	13
Brimfield,	1,137	483,750	9	196	98	199	1	12	126	158	146	.92	15
Chester,	1,318	507,529	10	231	167	252	3	21	149	191	169	.88	10
Chicopee,	11,516	5,604,040	30	2,391	1,425	1,649	20	85	919	1,185	1,074	.91	36
Granville,	1,193	349,232	10	228	149	282	12	41	151	198	174	.88	10
Hampden,	868	415,495	6	171	96	175	3	8	102	121	105	.87	6
Holland,	229	116,972	2	43	25	48	2	4	25	29	26	.90	2
Holyoke,	27,895	16,135,525	66	5,836	3,545	3,874	46	180	1,802	2,790	2,567	.92	85
Longmeadow,	1,677	921,140	11	232	138	304	6	31	165	249	216	.87	11
Ludlow,	1,649	790,328	13	370	245	441	8	30	282	297	264	.89	14
Monson,	3,958	1,303,736	19	625	415	680	18	39	406	481	439	.91	19
Montgomery,	278	134,917	5	46	29	55	1	8	29	50	44	.88	5
Palmer,	5,923	2,554,998	27	1,191	835	1,242	11	13	857	891	799	.90	28
Russell,	847	468,025	5	166	105	174	3	5	105	151	130	.86	5
Southwick,	982	559,867	10	187	113	227	2	29	119	214	187	.87	10
Springfield,	37,575	35,835,728	101	6,330	4,841	5,667	7	506	3,311	4,518	4,251	.94	125
Tolland,	422	174,202	7	69	54	72	8	10	45	66	60	.90	7
Wales,	853	291,077	6	152	98	168	—	2	93	121	115	.95	6
Westfield,	8,961	6,363,160	35	1,653	912	1,721	7	124	852	1,365	1,214	.89	44
West Springfield,	4,448	3,030,840	21	857	520	1,004	7	80	560	785	704	.90	22
Wilbraham,	1,724	703,815	9	252	150	309	3	17	163	221	196	.88	9
Totals,	116,764	$78,402,861	425	21,902	10,439	19,253	179	1,281	11,232	14,651	13,381	.91	493

FRANKLIN COUNTY — Continued.

TOWNS.	Whole No. of different male teachers in school-year.	Whole No. of different female teachers in school-year.	No. of teachers who have attended Normal Schools.	No. of teachers who have graduated from Normal Schools.	Av'ge wages per month of male teachers in Public Schools.	Av'ge wages per month of female teachers in Public Schools.	Aggregate of months all the Public Schools have been kept during the school-year.	Average No. of months the Public Schools have been kept for the entire year.	No. of Schools kept less than six months each.	HIGH SCHOOLS. No. of High Schools.	No. of teachers.	No. of pupils.	How supported.	LENGTH. Months.	LENGTH. Days.	Salary of Principal.
Ashfield,	—	18	1	1	$20 00	$21 33	81-15	6-16	1	—	—	—	—	—	—	—
Bernardston,	1	8	—	—	—	28 09	46-15	7-15	—	1	2	64	Part tax,	8	—	$833 22
Buckland,	5	14	—	—	37 50	24 45	81-2	7-8	—	—	—	—	—	—	—	—
Charlemont,	2	10	—	—	35 00	23 00	54	6	—	—	—	—	—	—	—	—
Colrain,	2	20	2	1	31 50	20 71	93-6	6-6	1	—	—	—	—	—	—	—
Conway,	—	22	3	3	—	26 17	103-10	6-18	—	—	—	—	—	—	—	—
Deerfield,	3	24	6	4	36 00	33 00	170-10	8-10	—	1	1	45	Taxation,	8-10	—	431 00
Erving,	3	8	—	—	39 15	28 22	41-10	8-6	—	1	1	31	Taxation,	9	—	432 00
Gill,	—	14	—	—	—	24 00	47	6-14	—	—	—	—	—	—	—	—
Greenfield,	5	31	6	3	57 62	36 31	183-3	8-6	—	1	6	101	Taxation,	9-3	—	1,200 00
Hawley,	1	10	—	—	27 00	29 00	48	6	—	—	—	—	—	—	—	—
Heath,	3	9	—	—	25 33	19 23	47-10	5-18	—	—	—	—	—	—	—	—
Leverett,	2	8	—	—	31 00	23 35	46-5	7-10	—	1	1	34	Taxation,	3	—	$100 00
Leyden,	1	6	—	—	—	26 00	30	6	—	—	—	—	—	—	—	—
Monroe,	—	3	—	—	—	17 53	18	8-10	—	—	—	—	—	—	—	—
Montague,	4	34	12	11	28 00	38 10	231	7	—	1	2	29	Taxation,	9	—	550 00
New Salem,	4	14	—	1	64 66	22 40	55-15	8-3	—	—	—	—	—	—	—	—
Northfield,	3	9	1	—	21 33	30 00	73-18	7-13	—	—	—	—	—	—	—	—
Orange,	1	31	4	4	36 00	28 26	160	6	—	1	2	75	Taxation,	9-10	—	1,000 00
Rowe,	2	8	—	—	66 63	16 36	42	8-10	—	—	—	—	—	—	—	—
Shelburne,	2	16	4	3	29 17	30 00	93	6	—	—	—	—	—	—	—	—
Shutesbury,	1	7	—	—	28 00	19 33	36	7-10	—	—	—	—	—	—	—	—
Sunderland,	1	7	3	—	26 00	26 40	37-10	6	—	—	—	—	—	—	—	—
Warwick,	1	9	9	3	40 00	20 47	54	6	1	—	—	—	—	—	—	—

Wendell,	2	6	1	—	22 66	22 67	36-10	7-6	—	—	—	—	—	—	—
Whately,	—	9	1	—	—	24 00	54	9	—	—	—	—	—	—	—
Totals,	46	350	54	35	$41 00	$27 40	1,964-14	7-3	4	7	15	379	—	56-3	$4,546 22

HAMPDEN COUNTY — CONTINUED.

Agawam,	1	15	3	2	$12 00	$35 25	83-10	8-7	—	—	—	—	—	—	—
Blandford,	1	17	2	2	22 00	22 08	72	6-13	—	—	—	98	Endowm't,	10	$1,200 00
Brimfield,	2	13	1	1	22 00	24 08	60	7-1	—	1	—	—	—	—	—
Chester,	—	15	—	1	—	25 60	70-10	9-10	1	—	4	—	—	—	—
Chicopee,	4	33	9	6	95 00	40 49	267-10	—	—	2	2 2	40	Taxation, Taxation,	9-15	1,400 00 / 1,200 00
Granville,	1	14	2	—	28 00	28 05	75	7-10	—	1	—	54	—	—	—
Hampden,	2	6	1	1	29 00	29 00	48	8	—	—	—	—	—	—	—
Holland,	1	3	—	—	20 00	19 33	15	7-10	—	—	—	—	—	—	—
Holyoke,	7	80	22	19	111 53	41 54	641-15	9-14	4	1	5	149	Taxation,	9-18	1,900 00
Longmeadow,	1	13	3	3	40 77	36 75	92-15	8-9	1	—	—	—	—	—	—
Ludlow,	1	19	4	3	—	28 00	92	8-1	—	—	—	—	—	—	—
Monson,	7	21	1	—	33 00	39 00	162	8-10	1	—	3	81	Part tax,	9-15	1,500 00
Montgomery,	—	8	—	2	—	20 00	37-10	7-10	—	—	—	—	—	—	—
Palmer,	4	30	4	1	62 50	33 44	243-10	9-7	—	1	2	59	Taxation,	10	1,000 00
Russell,	1	7	3	—	28 00	7 20	38	7-12	—	1	—	—	—	—	—
Southwick,	5	11	1	1	33 00	24 62	82-10	8-5	—	—	1	31	Taxation,	8-5	495 00
Springfield,	10	116	38	29	179 00	63 65	1,010	10	—	1	11	338	Taxation,	10	2,700 00
Tolland,	—	8	—	—	—	20 55	42	—	—	—	—	—	—	—	—
Wales,	—	13	1	1	—	22 50	41	6-10	2	—	—	—	—	—	—
Westfield,	6	55	44	32	104 90	37 60	311-15	9-2	—	1	5	188	Taxation,	9-2	1,700 00
West Springfield,	1	27	9	8	120 00	35 70	190	9	—	1	2	57	Taxation,	10	1,200 00
Wilbraham,	—	14	2	1	—	29 43	71	8	1	—	—	—	—	—	—
Totals,	54	538	149	110	$87 02	$38 07	3,747-5	8-11	9	10	37	1,095	—	86-15	$14,295 00

FRANKLIN COUNTY — Continued.

TOWNS.	Amount raised by taxes for schools, including wages of teachers, board, fuel, care of fires and school-rooms, for the school-year 1885-86.	Expense of supervision by school committee.	Salary of Superintendent of Public Schools.	Expense of Printing reports, etc.	Expense of sundries,—books, stationery, etc.	Amount expended for new school-houses.	Amount expended for alterations and permanent improvements.	Amount expended for ordinary repairs.	Amount paid for all school purposes from money raised by taxation.	Amount of voluntary contributions for Public Schools.
Ashfield,	$1,600 00	$105 50	—	$8 08	$289 49	$137 67	$86 20	$40 74	$2,567 68	—
Bernardston,	1,000 00	75 00	—	—	220 54	—	126 36	20 97	1,442 87	—
Buckland,	2,000 00	167 50	—	—	343 68	—	18 35	70 14	2,599 67	—
Charlemont,	1,000 00	71 00	—	15 00	150 00	—	4 78	25 00	1,661 00	—
Colrain,	2,300 00	142 25	—	8 55	272 62	400 00	—	11 40	2,739 60	—
Conway,	2,500 00	127 50	—	10 00	182 17	—	—	191 87	3,011 87	$39 00
Deerfield,	5,000 00	360 00	—	18 00	800 00	—	17 42	600 00	6,778 00	—
Erving,	1,200 00	39 64	—	8 40	206 61	—	—	59 80	1,531 87	—
Gill,	1,000 00	60 00	—	10 00	201 13	—	—	22 34	1,293 47	17 00
Greenfield,	11,350 00	332 00	—	—	1,474 98	10,106 22	428 19	589 66	24,281 05	—
Hawley,	900 00	47 00	—	9 20	50 00	—	—	5 71	956 20	—
Heath,	600 00	45 00	—	8 00	90 00	—	15 00	142 26	723 71	—
Leverett,	800 00	110 25	—	8 00	179 00	—	—	5 00	1,150 51	—
Leyden,	800 00	51 50	—	9 00	39 42	—	—	8 10	1,044 50	—
Monroe,	200 00	6 00	—	6 00	—	—	—	—	259 52	—
Montague,	10,386 61	300 00	—	20 00	1,582 52	15,000 00	—	1,255 91	28,545 91	—
New Salem,	1,000 00	61 50	—	8 75	201 00	—	—	16 30	1,287 55	—
Northfield,	2,200 00	162 00	—	30 40	240 00	—	—	200 00	2,832 40	—
Orange,	6,475 00	335 50	—	23 15	959 25	—	120 26	454 28	8,367 44	—
Rowe,	600 00	28 00	—	7 00	37 68	—	25 00	5 00	702 68	—
Shelburne,	3,000 00	100 00	—	18 00	303 00	—	—	64 00	3,485 00	—
Shutesbury,	500 00	35 00	—	4 00	89 32	—	—	113 58	741 90	—
Sunderland,	1,100 00	60 00	—	3 00	344 27	—	—	38 56	1,645 83	—

Warwick,	910 00	—	$60 00	12 25	180 60	—	—	32 20	1,195 05	—
Wendell,	700 00	48 00	—	5 00	57 07	—	—	20 22	825 29	—
Whately,	1,200 00	60 00	—	—	63 05	—	—	25 00	1,318 05	—
Totals,	$60,321 61	$2,925 14	$60 00	$249 78	$8,557 40	$25,943 89	$841 56	$4,018 04	$102,918 62	$56 00

HAMPDEN COUNTY — Continued.

Agawam,	$3,250 00	$125 00	—	$20 00	$445 06	—	—	$100 00	$3,940 06	—
Blandford,	1,600 00	51 03	—	12 00	819 28	—	$77 87	22 10	1,982 28	—
Brimfield,	1,600 00	100 00	—	6 30	124 73	—	—	82 57	1,913 60	—
Chester,	1,400 00	123 75	$1,536 71	—	196 85	—	—	38 76	1,759 36	—
Chicopee,	22,860 00	—	—	—	$1,632 10	—	1,079 57	900 00	27,998 98	—
Granville,	2,300 00	113 00	—	8 33	294 52	—	122 28	31 13	2,869 26	—
Hampden,	1,200 00	103 00	—	25 00	130 24	—	—	47 34	1,505 58	—
Holland,	200 00	15 00	—	6 00	25 00	—	—	15 00	261 00	—
Holyoke,	50,884 07	250 00	—	104 50	6,285 79	$15,477 98	4,205 60	1,751 73	80,809 67	—
Longmeadow,	3,200 00	178 85	1,900 00	30 00	327 40	—	—	174 91	3,911 16	—
Ludlow,	3,500 00	155 88	—	7 70	355 61	750 00	—	25 49	4,914 68	$149 00
Monson,	6,500 00	335 50	—	24 00	1,036 00	—	120 00	73 00	7,968 50	—
Montgomery,	500 00	15 50	—	—	43 80	—	—	—	559 30	—
Palmer,	11,700 00	600 00	—	—	1,266 50	—	—	176 47	13,742 97	—
Russell,	1,000 00	60 00	—	8 00	190 02	—	—	8 51	1,266 53	—
Southwick,	1,500 00	180 00	—	25 00	280 00	3,500 00	—	100 00	5,585 00	—
Springfield,	96,211 00	—	3,000 00	78 00	12,562 90	1,626 17	10,851 01	7,490 23	131,819 31	—
Tolland,	500 00	21 00	—	2 75	139 27	—	—	2 00	665 02	—
Wales,	700 00	73 75	—	5 00	135 00	—	—	5 00	918 75	—
Westfield,	21,200 00	700 00	—	77 76	2,824 90	—	1,350 52	1,702 57	27,865 75	—
W. Springfield,	9,000 00	370 49	—	3 00	1,122 83	—	—	442 29	10,938 61	—
Wilbraham,	2,200 00	118 75	—	18 00	262 17	2,500 00	—	22 32	5,121 24	—
Totals,	$242,895 07	$3,690 50	$6,436 71	$461 34	$29,949 97	$23,854 15	$17,806 85	$13,211 42	$338,306 01	$149 00

FRANKLIN COUNTY — Concluded.

TOWNS.	Amount of local funds the income of which can be appropriated only for the support of Schools and Academies.	Income of local funds.	Income of surplus revenue and other funds, including the dog tax, used at the option of the town.	ACADEMIES AND PRIVATE SCHOOLS.						Town's share of school fund payable Jan. 25, 1886.	How much of said fund was used for apparatus and books of reference.
				No. of Academies.	Whole No. attending for the year.	Amount of tuition paid.	No. of Private Schools.	Whole No. attending for the year.	Estimated amount of tuition.		
Ashfield,	$900 00	$54 00	$72 00	1	20	$200 00				$310 25	$23 70
Bernardston,	10,716 67	43 00	78 85							308 54	12 75
Buckland,	796 75	54 89	75 65							219 20	
Charlemont,	800 00	48 00	102 00							308 37	
Colrain,			72 00				1	17	200 00	219 94	
Conway,			74 00							217 38	
Deerfield,	50,000 00	3,000 00	250 00	1	80	200 00				185 15	
Erving,			65 00							308 16	
Gill,			33 00	1	120	2,000 00				309 17	
Greenfield,	400 00	23 72					1	53	2,700 00	46 83	
Hawley,			39 50							306 32	
Heath,			69 28							305 98	
Leverett,										307 01	20 00
Leyden,			14 00							306 95	
Monroe,										302 16	55 00
Montague,	5,000 00	250 00	42 90							226 74	
New Salem,			130 00	1	52	300 00				307 23	
Northfield,				1	222	13,018 78				214 07	12 00
Orange,			34 60							185 32	
Rowe,	200 00	12 00	101 00							304 67	
Shelburne,			54 00	2	153	1,202 00				214 30	
Shutesbury,							1	5	450 00	305 18	
Sunderland,	250 00	12 50								308 43	20 94

Warwick,	500 00	20 20	40 60	—	—	—	—	—	—	306 84	—
Wendell,	540 00	32 40	—	—	—	—	—	—	—	304 79	—
Whately,	—	—	—	—	—	—	—	—	—	311 39	—
Totals,	$70,103 42	$3,550 71	$1,348 38	7	647	$16,920 78	3	75	$3,350 00	$6,950 57	$143 94

HAMPDEN COUNTY — Concluded.

Agawam,	$3,000 00	$180 00	$188 55	—	—	—	—	—	—	$176 26	—
Blandford,	—	—	80 20	—	—	—	—	15	90 00	311 17	—
Brimfield,	—	—	—	—	—	—	—	—	—	309 97	—
Chester,	—	—	156 90	—	—	—	1	1,000	6,000 00	212 53	$124 48
Chicopee,	222 22	—	—	—	—	—	4	1,000	150 00	124 48	124 48
Granville,	—	13 33	76 40	—	—	—	3	40	—	313 11	—
Hampden,	—	—	27 64	—	—	—	—	—	—	309 40	—
Holland,	731 00	—	807 00	—	—	—	—	—	—	303 25	—
Holyoke,	—	48 17	123 10	—	—	—	4	2,300	11,000 00	—	—
Longmeadow,	—	—	219 65	—	—	—	1	6	75 00	213 73	—
Ludlow,	—	—	339 00	1	76	$2,052 00	—	—	—	219 65	43 80
Monson,	28,000 00	1,100 00	—	—	—	—	—	—	—	183 84	—
Montgomery,	—	—	—	—	—	—	—	—	—	303 02	—
Palmer,	—	—	—	—	—	—	—	—	—	216 94	—
Russell,	15,618 03	923 05	88 00	—	—	—	8	1,250	16,000 00	308 94	—
Southwick,	—	—	—	—	—	—	—	—	—	211 11	—
Springfield,	—	—	—	—	—	—	—	—	—	303 99	70 00
Tolland,	—	—	40 66	—	—	—	—	—	—	308 83	—
Wales,	100,000 00	3,500 00	41 20	1	—	—	1	26	350 00	88 70	135 30
Westfield,	14,000 00	728 00	332 24	—	—	—	1	10	120 00	198 14	14 50
West Springfield,	1,308 40	78 50	88 22	1	374	10,939 83	—	—	—	215 04	132 00
Wilbraham,	—	—	—	—	—	—	—	—	—	—	—
Totals,	$162,879 65	$6,571 05	$2,608 76	3	450	$12,991 83	23	5,647	$33,785 00	$4,832 10	$520 08

HAMPSHIRE COUNTY.

TOWNS.	Population—State Census, 1885.	Valuation—1885.	No. of Public Schools.	No. of persons in town between May 1, 1885, 5 and 15 years of age.	No. of persons in town between May 1, 1885, 5 and 14 years of age.	No. of different pupils of all ages in the Public Schools during the school-year.	No. attending within the year under 5 years of age.	No. attending within the year over 15 years of age.	No. attending within the year between 8 and 14 years of age.	Average membership of all the Schools.	Average attendance in all the Public Schools during the school-year.	The per cent. of attendance based upon the average membership.	No. of teachers required by the Public Schools.
Amherst,	4,199	$2,789,433	19	600	367	743	3	133	370	606	558	.92	23
Belchertown,	2,307	912,000	20	475	295	535	11	69	290	417	383	.92	20
Chesterfield,	698	284,463	7	131	94	145	7	14	94	122	107	.88	7
Cummington,	805	319,892	7	120	103	187	9	59	112	136	125	.92	10
Easthampton,	4,291	2,413,824	19	756	522	808	9	57	549	647	584	.90	21
Enfield,	1,010	549,340	7	171	83	167	3	8	81	152	139	.91	7
Goshen,	336	136,210	4	53	38	60		5	38	52	47	.90	4
Granby,	729	431,123	9	138	93	149		7	93	128	121	.95	9
Greenwich,	532	275,470	6	68	52	92	2	11	52	75	73	.97	13
Hadley,	1,747	1,119,710	13	338	200	387	9	28	233	322	303	.94	8
Hatfield,	1,367	872,310	8	262	167	268	3	10	170	211	182	.86	8
Huntington,	1,267	472,569	9	206	132	240	6	15	144	211	189	.90	9
Middlefield,	513	265,962	8	115	82	128	8	17	78	99	93	.94	2
Northampton,	12,896	8,444,325	57	2,241	1,480	2,365	19	132	1,476	1,957	1,787	.91	64
Pelham,	549	168,720	4	99	67	105		5	61	90	77	.85	4
Plainfield,	453	142,220	6	76	38	82	3	16	42	67	59	.88	6
Prescott,	448	180,999	5	88	62	95	2	18	62	78	75	.96	5
Southampton,	1,025	483,313	8	185	122	213	3	34	118	150	134	.89	8
South Hadley,	3,919	1,565,234	17	702	505	865	2	114	519	668	600	.90	20
Ware,	6,003	2,968,671	23	1,182	823	1,076	7	55	787	881	821	.93	24
Westhampton,	541	264,862	5	123	80	124	3	8	80	86	80	.93	5

Williamsburg,	17	86	298	348	261	14	9	438	261	421	16	861,857	2,044
Worthington,	9	90	110	122	83	17	2	130	83	118	9	333,537	763
Totals,	301	91	6,945	7,625	5,783	846	114	9,402	5,748	8,677	266	$26,166,074	48,472

HAMPSHIRE COUNTY — CONTINUED.

TOWNS	Whole No. of different male teachers in school-year.	Whole No. of different female teachers in school-year.	No. of teachers who have attended Normal Schools.	No. of teachers who have graduated from Normal Schools.	Av'ge wages per month of male teachers in Public Schools.	Av'ge wages per month of female teachers in Public Schools.	Aggregate of months all the Public Schools have been kept during the school-year.	Average No. of months the Public Schools have been kept for the entire year.	No. of Schools kept less than six months each.	HIGH SCHOOLS No. of High Schools.	No. of teachers.	No. of pupils.	How supported.	LENGTH Months.	Days.	Salary of Principal.
Amherst,	7	25	1		$64 05	$32 23	160 1	8-8		1	4	82	Taxation,	9-10		$1,000 00
Belchertown,	12	22	1		29 70	24 00	157 15	7-1	1	1	1	67	Taxation,	9		600 00
Chesterfield,	4	10	1		23 75	18 85	50 15	7-5								
Cummington,	3	7	3	3	36 44	22 87	39 5	6-1	2	1		42	Taxation,	3		200 00
Easthampton,		23	1	1		32 28	171	8-3		1	2	50	Taxation,	9-15		750 00
Enfield,	1	13	1	1	48 00	30 28	57	6-5								
Goshen,		8	4	2		21 75	25 5	8-9		1	1	28	Taxation,	8-10		500 00
Granby,	1	6	4	2	33 75	24 00	76 10	7-10								
Greenwich,	4	10	1	1		23 33	45	7-14					Not by tax.			
Hadley,		16	4	1	24 00	26 15	100	9		1	3	67		9-10		800 00
Hatfield,	1	11	4	1	-	28 00	72	8	1							
Huntington,		17	1	1		24 65	68 9	6-13								
Middlefield,	1	9			20 00	20 80	51 10	8-17	1							
Northampton,	2	69	10	8	113 95	36 22	505	7-10		1	5	116	Taxation,	10		1,600 00
Pelham,	4	5				25 00	30	6-15								
Plainfield,		7	1		26 00	17 14	40 10	7-5								
Prescott,	1	10	2			21 20	36 9	7-18								
Southampton,	1	11	3	1	-	26 66	61 5	9			1	30	Taxation,	6		216 00
South Hadley,	3	20	6	3	106 00	30 55	150	8-17		1	4	100	Taxation,	9		1,500 00 / 1,200 00
Ware,	4	33	6	2	73 33	35 00	188	9		1	2	45	Taxation,	8-17		1,000 00
Westhampton,	2	5			25 00	23 25	37 5	7-9	1							

							Taxation,								
Williamsburg,	4	18	1	1	62 67	24 45	130-15	8-3	–	1	1	20	–	8	512 00
Worthington,	2	10	1	–	27 00	21 00	63-5	7	2	–	–	–	–	–	–
Totals,	54	365	48	26	$50 07	$28 32	2,319-9	7-15	9	11	25	647	–	91-2	$9,878 00

HAMPSHIRE COUNTY — CONTINUED.

TOWNS.	Amount raised by taxes for Schools, including wages of teachers, board, fuel, care of fires and school-rooms, for the school-year 1885-86.	Expense of supervision by school committee.	Salary of Superintendent of Public Schools.	Expense of Printing reports, etc.	Expense of sundries,—books, stationery, etc.	Amount expended for new school-houses.	Amount expended for alterations and permanent improvements.	Amount expended for ordinary repairs.	Amount paid for all school purposes from money raised by taxation.	Amount of voluntary contributions for Public Schools.
Amherst,	$8,800 00	$150 00	$700 00	$16 50	$1,121 20		$536 21	$386 56	$11,740 47	$314 00
Belchertown,	3,800 00	275 00		41 70	440 22		34 33	88 52	4,679 77	18 00
Chesterfield,	900 00	60 00		10 00	125 00			15 00	1,110 00	75 00
Cummington,	800 00	42 00		7 50	135 66			48 38	1,033 54	60 00
Easthampton,	7,600 00	200 00		15 00	2,043 41			398 09	10,256 50	
Enfield,	1,700 00	107 43		9 00	320 42		123 22	116 16	2,376 23	
Goshen,	300 00	22 50		7 00	58 31			5 00	392 81	
Granby,	1,800 00	87 50		8 00	308 00			25 00	2,228 50	
Greenwich,	800 00		50 00	6 00	87 21			30 17	1,055 21	
Hadley,	2,850 00	161 75		6 81	447 17		81 83	219 26	4,045 17	
Hatfield,	1,950 00	150 00			331 88		360 18	136 95	3,090 18	
Huntington,	1,000 00	172 50		8 00	283 74	$521 35		231 34	1,695 58	
Middlefield,	800 00	50 00		10 00	160 00			15 00	1,035 00	
Northampton,	27,150 00		1,000 00	41 55	2,064 07		425 00	1,652 53	32,333 15	
Pelham,	700 00		50 00	2 00	121 19		54 68	14 50	942 87	
Plainfield,	500 00	25 85		4 74	77 37			45 63	653 59	
Prescott,	500 00		45 00	8 40	58 51			5 00	616 91	
Southampton,	1,450 00	80 00		15 00	177 38			73 00	1,795 38	
South Hadley,	8,000 00	110 00		21 73	671 00		718 27	551 97	9,357 70	
Ware,	10,000 00	525 00			1,100 82			728 52	13,072 61	
Westhampton,	1,000 00	94 00			261 82			246 72	1,602 54	

Williamsburg,	3,000 00	165 00	–	18 00	553 81	–	300 00	101 21	4,138 02	–
Worthington,	1,000 00	60 00	–	8 00	148 00	–	–	58 99	1,274 99	–
Totals,	$86,400 00	$2,538 53	$1,845 00	$294 93	$11,096 19	$591 36	$2,633 72	$5,106 50	$110,526 22	$492 00

HAMPSHIRE COUNTY — Concluded.

TOWNS.	Amount of local funds of Schools and Academies the income of which can be appropriated only for the support of Schools and Academies.	Income of local funds.	Income of surplus revenue and other funds, including the dog tax, used at the option of the town.	ACADEMIES AND PRIVATE SCHOOLS.						Town's share of school fund payable Jan. 25, 1886.	How much of said fund was used for apparatus and books of reference.
				No. of Academies.	Whole No. attending for the year.	Amount of tuition paid.	No. of Private Schools.	Whole No. attending for the year.	Estimated amount of tuition.		
Amherst,	$7,685 84	$400 00	$494 49				6	81	$6,706 00	$184 30	
Belchertown,	6,000 00	255 00	277 01							228 83	$20 00
Chesterfield,	1,100 00	60 00	32 65							306 95	550 00
Cummington,										306 89	
Easthampton,	256,000 00	13,000 00	128 08	1	175	$10,000 00				195 80	
Enfield,									60 00	209 57	
Goshen,			77 83							303 30	
Granby,			39 67							307 69	
Greenwich,	300 00	30 00								304 79	
Hadley,	37,300 00	2,275 28	89 38	1	67					170 00	
Hatfield,			90 00	1	49	365 75				216 80	
Huntington,			466 10							310 60	
Middlefield,			68 79							307 86	
Northampton,	3,077 93	180 00	40 67				4	169	9,000 00	135 76	
Pelham,			30 10							305 53	
Plainfield,			102 43							303 71	
Prescott,			205 87							304 73	
Southampton,	2,100 00	126 00		1						310 09	
South Hadley,				1	297	51,975 00				187 31	
Ware,			89 67				1	10	180 00	207 65	
Westhampton,							1	8	175 00	306 44	3 19

Williamsburg,	17,000 00	1,233 78	161 18	—	—	—	—	—	—	224 72	—
Worthington,	4,403 00	213 90	58 29	—	—	—	—	—	—	305 87	—
Totals,	$384,966 27	$17,773 96	$2,402 21	5	588	$62,340 75	12	187	$9,355 00	$5,945 19	$573 19

MIDDLESEX COUNTY.

TOWNS.	Population—State Census, 1885.	Valuation—1885.	No. of Public Schools.	No. of persons in town between May 1, 1885, 5 and 15 years of age.	No. of persons in town between May 1, 1885, 8 and 14 years of age.	No. of different pupils of all ages in the Public Schools during the school-year.	No. attending within the year under 5 years of age.	No. attending within the year over 15 years of age.	No. attending within the year between 8 and 14 years of age.	Average membership of all the Schools.	Average attendance in all the Public Schools during the school-year.	The per cent. of attendance based upon the average membership.	No. of teachers required by the Public Schools.
Acton,	1,785	$1,273,033	10	264	175	343	1	51	175	278	253	.91	10
Arlington,	4,673	4,737,378	22	958	590	984	–	112	567	901	806	.89	25
Ashby,	871	467,839	9	144	91	192	1	46	102	191	172	.90	10
Ashland,	2,633	1,361,653	13	450	270	553	1	40	326	431	395	.92	14
Ayer,	2,190	1,172,691	10	433	280	500	2	57	274	441	400	.91	10
Bedford,	930	767,158	6	139	92	152	–	51	88	182	122	.92	6
Belmont,	1,639	2,833,012	8	325	185	335	4	30	193	289	261	.90	12
Billerica,	2,161	1,573,965	10	427	284	418	4	15	282	326	293	.90	10
Boxborough,	348	257,826	4	44	35	55	2	16	36	50	33	–	4
Burlington,	604	478,232	10	125	88	98	3	8	80	112	104	.93	5
Cambridge,	59,658	55,346,555	207	10,957	6,858	10,213	8	695	6,657	8,650	7,915	.92	224
Carlisle,	526	403,900	4	80	56	86	–	11	56	80	61	.76	4
Chelmsford,	2,304	1,551,750	14	440	250	514	12	34	297	400	353	.88	15
Concord,	3,727	3,059,583	15	564	330	724	1	90	309	588	529	.90	18
Dracut,	1,927	1,204,617	11	330	213	368	–	15	215	265	239	.90	11
Dunstable,	431	308,845	5	65	42	94	1	21	44	70	65	.93	5
Everett,	5,825	5,133,600	24	1,039	623	1,350	5	96	807	987	894	.91	26
Framingham,	8,275	5,980,200	31	1,366	1,087	1,087	–	145	1,163	1,251	1,148	.92	35
Groton,	1,987	2,753,973	12	295	154	330	13	41	160	263	226	.86	13
Holliston,	2,926	1,668,975	15	575	316	570	3	56	313	480	442	.92	16
Hopkinton,	3,922	2,199,983	21	819	488	885	11	89	518	736	660	.90	22
Hudson,	3,968	2,074,132	16	816	511	880	9	63	523	772	706	.91	20
Lexington,	2,718	2,880,460	11	449	299	411	–	59	280	350	316	.90	12

Lincoln,	901	1,069,969	5	157	99	177	1	25	98	142	116	.82	5
Littleton,	1,067	758,269		191	126	206	2	17	123	181	169	.93	8
Lowell,	64,107	51,308,335	40	10,970	6,033	9,280		752	5,201	6,851	6,212	.91	180
Malden,	16,107	12,652,083	49	2,307	1,630	2,520		212	1,438	1,945	1,770	.90	58
Marlborough,	10,991	4,171,095	45	2,395	1,450	2,158	10	115	1,350	1,830	1,699	.88	51
Maynard,	2,703	1,941,341	9	515	207	553		51	283	402	355	.94	11
Medford,	9,042	8,121,211	32	1,653	1,229	1,760		118	903	1,501	1,404	.92	38
Melrose,	6,101	4,769,665	22	1,135	1,020	1,270		134	705	1,057	971	.92	25
Natick,	8,460	4,032,900	35	1,630	1,059	1,759		110	1,015	1,573	1,452	.91	40
Newton,	19,759	28,599,820	85	3,611	2,556	4,029	7	490	2,313	3,357	3,047	.86	93
North Reading,	878	506,826	6	140	94	173	3	21	94	132	113	.90	6
Pepperell,	2,587	1,462,758	11	443	267	483	6	46	258	399	860	.87	13
Reading,	3,639	2,363,042	15	557	357	659	3	76	374	554	483	.90	17
Sherborn,	1,391	821,470	7	201	120	194	5	1	130	140	125	.92	6
Shirley,	1,242	686,861		246	149	250	4	13	152	188	173	.91	7
Somerville,	29,971	24,878,400	102	5,608	3,641	6,276		659	2,558	4,904	4,627	.93	121
Stoneham,	5,659	3,110,010	20	906	528	1,079	8	73	633	856	797	.91	24
Stow,	976	955,721	6	181	181	236	2	15	134	158	144	.80	6
Sudbury,	1,165	1,017,990	8	194	136	207	4	13	131	171	136	.88	8
Tewksbury,	2,333	1,299,257	8	236	152	270		8	143	205	181	.89	8
Townsend,	1,846	908,011	14	337	249	343	6	52	186	272	243	.90	14
Tyngsborough,	604	333,664	7	97	97	117	8	16	69	111	100	.87	8
Wakefield,	6,069	3,726,800	24	1,260	810	1,135		112	737	1,055	920	.92	28
Waltham,	14,609	10,579,232	51	2,458	1,473	2,877	2	278	1,667	2,437	2,261	.94	59
Watertown,	6,238	6,482,350	24	1,104	794	1,293	1	122	777	1,061	994	.93	99
Wayland,	1,546	1,238,480	11	464	231	378		26	225	331	308	.91	11
Westford,	2,193	1,026,522	14	408	260	434	9	9	282	354	322	.97	14
Weston,	1,427	1,897,066	8	220	132	258	8	24	132	229	222	.89	8
Wilmington,	991	571,472	6	167	118	166	2	15	118	148	182	.90	6
Winchester,	4,390	4,151,077	14	620	472	869	2	90	502	736	659	.92	20
Woburn,	11,750	7,855,897	50	2,580	1,460	2,291	4	262	1,284	1,757	1,618		54
Totals,	357,311	$294,508,654	1,224	64,690	40,467	75,742	165	5,756	37,470	53,140	48,556	.92	1,503

MIDDLESEX COUNTY — CONTINUED.

TOWNS.	Whole No. of different male teachers in school-year.	Whole No. of different female teachers in school-year.	No. of teachers who have attended Normal Schools.	No. of teachers who have graduated from Normal Schools.	Av'ge wages per month of male teachers in Public Schools.	Av'ge wages per month of female teachers in Public Schools.	Aggregate of months all the Public Schools have been kept during the school-year.	Average No. of months the Public Schools have been kept for the entire year.	No. of Schools kept less than six months each.	No. of High Schools.	No. of teachers.	No. of pupils.	How supported.	Length Months.	Length Days.	Salary of Principal.
Acton,	2	12	4	2	$60 88	$38 00	90	9	—	1	1	47	Taxation,	9	—	$700 00
Arlington,	4	21	12	8	134 75	48 67	212-15	9-15	—	1	3	69	Taxation,	10	—	1,800 00
Ashby,	1	12	2	—	60 00	29 00	53	6-5	—	—	—	—	—	—	—	—
Ashland,	1	20	3	2	94 39	34 06	103	7-18	—	1	2	59	Taxation,	10	5	967 50
Ayer,	1	11	3	2	100 00	37 00	87-5	8-14	—	1	1	45	Taxation,	10	—	1,000 00
Bedford,	1	6	—	—	32 00	36 00	54	9	—	1	1	15	Taxation,	7	—	324 00
Belmont,	2	10	2	2	87 00	42 50	76-15	9-15	—	1	2	62	Taxation,	9	15	1,550 00
Billerica,	2	12	5	5	52 50	32 44	79-3	7-18	—	—	—	—	—	—	—	—
Boxborough,	—	—	1	—	—	29 66	28	7	—	—	—	—	—	—	—	—
Burlington,	—	5	—	—	—	28 00	39-10	7-18	—	1	1	24	Taxation,	8	15	210 00
Cambridge,	18	222	139	122	163 84	61 86	330	10	—	1	15	499	Taxation,	10	—	2,800 00
Carlisle,	1	6	2	—	30 00	30 00	34	8-10	—	—	—	—	—	—	—	—
Chelmsford,	1	19	6	4	90 00	34 86	117-5	8-8	—	1	1	39	Taxation,	9	—	765 00
Concord,	2	22	9	9	180 00	49 54	148-10	9-18	—	1	3	91	Taxation,	9	18	1,800 00
Dracut,	1	17	4	—	—	32 00	96-5	8-15	—	—	—	—	—	—	—	—
Dunstable,	—	10	1	1	—	25 96	98-15	7-15	—	—	—	—	—	—	—	—
Everett,	2	31	6	5	120 00	43 00	220-15	9	—	1	2	76	Taxation,	10	—	1,300 00
Framingham,	2	33	19	17	135 00	44 66	268	8-13	—	1	5	98	Taxation,	10	—	2,650 00
Groton,	2	11	3	3	70 00	36 72	99-11	8-6	—	1	2	60	Taxation,	10	—	1,000 00
Holliston,	2	21	7	4	62 97	38 65	125	8-4	—	1	2	50	Taxation,	9	10	968 41
Hopkinton,	2	23	6	6	100 00	37 19	172-5	8-6	—	1	2	75	Taxation,	9	15	1,000 00
Hudson,	2	22	6	6	111 11	37 97	133-10	8-6	1	1	2	60	Taxation,	9	—	1,000 00
Lexington,	1	12	7	5	150 00	63 80	110	10	—	1	2	51	Taxation,	10	—	1,500 00

Lincoln,	2	7	1	—	60 33	36 00	45	9	—	1	1	34	Taxation,	9	513 00
Littleton,	2	9	3	1	61 67	36 22	55-5	7-17	—	1	1	25	Taxation,	9	558 75
Lowell,	18	208	63	25	170 33	58 60	389-12	9-15	—	1	12	401	Taxation,	10	2,000 00
Malden,	2	56	25	18	58 00	57 00	430	10	—	1	5	181	Taxation,	10	2,200 00
Marlborough,	2	49	9	6	133 33	40 92	405	9	—	1	3	95	Taxation,	9	1,400 00
Maynard,	2	10	1	—	75 55	40 00	81	9	—	1	2	84	Taxation,	9	1,000 00
Medford,	9	34	10	8	148 50	51 00	294	9-15	—	1	5	114	Taxation,	9-16	2,200 00
Melrose,	1	25	13	9	170 00	49 75	214	10	—	1	3	116	Taxation,	10	1,700 00
Natick,	4	43	21	18	110 50	40 84	327	9-7	—	1	4	122	Taxation,	10	1,000 00
Newton,	14	96	37	31	190 77	62 76	847	10	—	1	13	389	Taxation,	10	2,800 00
North Reading,	1	8	5	5	58 66	28 80	53-2	8-17	—	1	1	32	Taxation,	8-17	528 00
Pepperell,	5	14	3	3	60 00	31 45	95	8-13	—	1	1	37	Taxation,	10	1,000 00
Reading,	1	20	9	9	126 30	38 25	142-10	9-10	—	1	3	138	Taxation,	9-10	1,200 00
Sherborn,	2	7	1	1	34 00	33 92	50-5	8-7	—	1	2	69	Taxation,	9-5	1,000 00
Shirley,		10	—	—	60 00	35 33	54-10	7-15	—	*	—	—		—	—
Somerville,	10	111	23	19	165 00	57 43	1,024	10	—	1	9	471	Taxation,	10	2,400 00
Stoneham,	2	31	12	11	170 00	43 16	183-2	9-2	—	1	3	79	Taxation,	10	1,700 00
Stow,	2	7	1	—	90 66	33 33	54	9	—	1	1	29	Part tax,	9	816 00
Sudbury,	—	11	2	8	—	36 00	63-15	7-19	—	1	—	—		—	—
Tewksbury,	3	14	8	2	36 66	37 00	67-2	9-15	—	1	1	84	Taxation,	10	600 00
Townsend,	1	15	2	3	50 00	29 22	100	7-3	—	1	1	28	Part tax,	3	150 00
Tyngsborough,	3	8	3	3	36 00	25 55	52-2	7-9	1	1	3	146	Taxation,	10	2,000 00
Wakefield,	3	25	13	13	126 67	40 50	234	10	—	1	6	186	Taxation,	10	1,800 00
Waltham,	8	63	27	22	117 50	53 08	476	9-10	—	1	3	97	Taxation,	9-17	2,000 00
Watertown,	4	29	9	8	160 00	48 00	210-12	9-16	—	1				—	—
Wayland,	2	13	4	4	80 00	35 52	99	9-5	—	1	2	44	Taxation,	9	1,200 00
Westford,	1	19	4	2	—	34 25	119-5	8-5	—	1	1	27	Taxation,	9	432 00
Weston,	1	9	2	3	133 33	46 00	72	9	—	1	1	44	Taxation,	9	1,200 00
Wilmington,	2	5	3	3	48 00	31 00	52-15	8	—	1	3	82	Taxation,	10	1,850 00
Winchester,	2	18	9	6	177 50	44 69	140	9	8	1	5	145	Taxation,	10	1,800 00
Woburn,	4	50	6	6	126 66	47 37	450	10							
Totals,	**158**	**1,588**	**578**	**441**	**$181 19**	**$49 41**	**9,658-1**	**8-17**	**13**	**43**	**132**	**4,625**		**400-3**	**$57,412 66**

* United with Sawin Academy.

MIDDLESEX COUNTY — CONTINUED.

TOWNS.	Amount raised by taxes for Schools, including wages of teachers, board, fuel, care of fires and school-rooms, for the school-year 1885-86.	Expense of supervision by school committee.	Salary of Superintendent of Public Schools.	Expense of Printing reports, etc.	Expense of sundries,—books, stationery, etc.	Amount expended for new school-houses.	Amount expended for alterations and permanent improvements.	Amount expended for ordinary repairs.	Amount paid for all school purposes from money raised by taxation.	Amount of voluntary contributions for Public Schools.
Acton,	$4,000 00	$125 00	—	$19 50	$1,060 09	—	$342 90	$596 75	$5,801 34	—
Arlington,	17,969 77	—	$100 00	12 00	2,251 93	—	198 50	456 13	21,020 73	—
Ashby,	1,830 00	—	—	11 00	209 24	—	219 32	158 54	2,478 28	—
Ashland,	5,800 00	120 00	—	10 00	485 76	—	—	123 78	6,759 86	—
Ayer,	4,000 00	141 66	—	30 00	881 91	—	—	117 33	5,151 90	—
Bedford,	2,300 00	200 00	—	30 00	300 00	—	50 00	25 00	2,905 00	—
Belmont,	6,000 00	240 00	—	40 00	542 15	—	241 46	853 94	7,907 55	—
Billerica,	3,000 00	240 00	—	20 00	543 73	$2,286 30	—	329 39	6,430 42	—
Boxborough,	970 03	35 00	—	18 00	44 42	—	53 08	4 00	1,131 53	—
Burlington,	1,010 00	57 00	—	—	108 52	—	—	26 37	1,209 89	—
Cambridge,	173,092 51	4,225 00	2,790 00	350 00	13,979 94	—	11,589 01	14,231 36	226,757 82	$326 75
Carlisle,	800 00	—	35 00	20 00	148 00	—	—	25 00	1,028 00	—
Chelmsford,	5,000 00	210 00	—	24 00	546 00	6,500 00	315 28	104 07	6,199 78	—
Concord,	12,000 00	193 50	—	—	1,046 00	—	611 80	511 94	14,364 04	20 00
Dracut,	3,000 00	150 00	—	31 25	227 63	—	97 67	43 81	3,550 36	—
Dunstable,	800 00	41 00	—	10 00	91 00	—	—	5 00	947 00	—
Everett,	14,712 00	275 00	300 00	10 62	1,494 00	6,995 00	—	774 00	24,560 62	—
Framingham,	18,500 00	800 00	—	25 00	2,200 00	11,400 00	—	1,500 00	34,425 00	—
Groton,	5,000 00	200 00	400 00	21 00	898 00	—	—	145 91	5,798 06	—
Holliston,	5,800 00	—	—	51 00	—	—	—	401 74	7,553 74	—
Hopkinton,	7,600 00	300 00	—	30 00	1,000 00	—	—	500 00	9,430 00	—
Hudson,	8,300 00	280 00	—	15 52	1,017 67	—	—	209 34	10,092 29	—
Lexington,	8,500 00	300 00	—	25 00	—	—	269 76	—	8,825 00	50 00

Lincoln,	2,500 00	45 00	—	25 00	428 32	—	—	227 88	3,226 20	—
Littleton,	2,400 00	80 00	—	28 00	413 91	—	—	210 65	3,132 56	12 00
Lowell,	148,375 96	—	2,550 00	581 90	17,539 15	—	14,802 52	11,904 26	195,753 79	—
Malden,	40,808 98	—	2,250 00	30 00	4,947 93	3,086 25	—	1,564 97	53,288 13	—
Marlborough,	20,046 54	300 00	1,700 00	100 00	1,571 37	—	—	548 07	24,265 98	—
Maynard,	5,500 00	225 00	—	29 75	848 30	—	—	43 24	6,616 29	—
Medford,	27,650 17	400 00	—	14 00	2,296 63	—	3,331 95	3,935 69	38,324 44	—
Melrose,	16,000 00	450 00	—	14 00	1,739 89	5,000 00	1,100 00	322 31	24,026 20	—
Natick,	21,500 00	425 00	—	—	1,800 00	—	750 00	1,000 00	25,475 00	—
Newton,	101,850 00	118 75	2,800 00	152 76	10,035 48	1,777 87	3,681 24	1,362 64	121,959 49	24 00
North Reading,	1,900 00	—	—	14 00	132 13	—	—	42 29	2,207 17	—
Pepperell,	4,400 00	375 00	180 00	21 80	298 20	—	—	119 49	5,019 49	—
Reading,	8,100 00	162 50	—	30 00	1,151 90	—	—	253 80	9,910 70	—
Sherborn,	2,125 00	98 00	—	35 00	285 63	—	—	24 60	2,682 73	—
Shirley,	2,000 00	—	—	15 00	374 37	—	74 99	132 58	2,694 94	—
Somerville,	86,053 29	400 00	2,000 00	—	6,318 43	14,249 00	—	7,452 68	116,073 40	—
Stoneham,	13,750 00	—	—	20 00	2,030 00	—	524 74	845 00	17,025 00	—
Stow,	2,019 47	—	100 00	10 00	658 71	—	—	151 34	3,474 26	—
Sudbury,	2,000 00	226 75	—	17 00	281 71	—	—	59 60	2,578 02	30 00
Tewksbury,	2,603 00	154 83	—	15 00	334 91	—	290 77	47 58	3,445 09	—
Townsend,	3,500 00	—	150 00	12 50	381 28	—	638 66	275 00	4,959 94	—
Tyngsborough,	1,150 00	250 00	75 00	100 00	176 54	—	—	15 02	1,429 00	—
Wakefield,	16,200 00	—	—	17 50	2,981 28	—	—	752 50	20,283 78	—
Waltham,	47,490 00	300 00	2,025 00	40 00	5,328 67	—	3,500 00	2,000 00	60,361 17	—
Watertown,	24,028 51	146 25	500 00	25 00	1,572 53	12,484 82	697 84	1,076 25	40,699 95	—
Wayland,	4,500 00	—	—	30 00	342 00	1,631 11	250 00	295 00	5,558 25	—
Westford,	4,000 00	—	150 00	—	573 87	—	185 16	75 10	6,645 24	—
Weston,	5,290 00	150 00	—	—	350 00	—	600 00	—	6,300 00	—
Wilmington,	1,750 00	80 00	—	8 00	296 24	14,000 00	—	44 21	2,178 45	—
Winchester,	15,000 00	150 00	—	—	2,869 68	—	—	1,143 24	33,162 92	—
Woburn,	28,672 66	—	1,350 00	101 60	2,973 11	—	—	2,157 16	35,251 53	—
Totals,	$973,014 89	$12,970 24	$19,455 00	$2,291 70	$101,535 31	$80,009 85	$44,416 65	$59,228 55	$1,292,929 38	$462 75

MIDDLESEX COUNTY — CONCLUDED.

TOWNS.	Amount of local funds the income of which can be appropriated only for the support of Schools and Academies.	Income of local funds.	Income of surplus revenue and other funds, including the dog tax, used at the option of the town.	ACADEMIES AND PRIVATE SCHOOLS.						Town's share of school fund payable Jan. 25, 1886.	How much of said fund was used for apparatus and books of reference.
				No. of Academies.	Whole No. attending for the year.	Amount of tuition paid.	No. of Private Schools.	Whole No. attending for the year.	Estimated amount of tuition.		
Acton,	$5,354 00	$321 24	$229 89	—	—	—	—	—	—	$164 99	—
Arlington,	—	—	107 09	—	—	—	—	—	—	53 27	—
Ashby,	—	—	187 98	—	—	—	—	—	—	308 43	—
Ashland,	—	—	—	—	—	—	—	—	—	177 40	—
Ayer,	—	—	—	—	—	—	1	5	$75 00	173 64	—
Bedford,	—	—	—	—	—	—	—	—	—	207 75	—
Belmont,	—	—	—	—	—	—	—	—	—	167 09	—
Billerica,	—	—	86 72	1	98	420 00	2	15	1,350 00	171 59	—
Boxborough,	—	—	—	—	—	—	1	41	2,870 00	302 52	—
Burlington,	10,000 00	777 20	—	—	—	—	—	—	—	307 02	—
Cambridge,	500 00	30 00	—	—	—	—	16	1,865	39,190 00	303 70	$28 00
Carlisle,.	—	—	74 00	—	—	—	1	26	—	171 25	—
Chelmsford,	4,300 00	268 25	332 32	—	—	—	—	—	—	29 62	—
Concord,	—	—	134 44	1	76	30 00	1	30	1,650 00	168 80	24 75
Dracut,	—	—	—	—	—	—	—	—	—	303 59	—
Dunstable,	—	—	—	—	—	—	—	—	—	54 97	—
Everett,	—	75 54	675 12	—	—	1,350 00	1	7	15,000 00	70 64	—
Framingham,	1,258 94	1,631 00	—	1	—	—	—	—	—	167 31	—
Groton, .	32,620 00	—	—	—	—	—	1	20	125 00	180 51	—
Holliston,	—	—	355 60	—	—	—	1	—	1,000 00	194 83	—
Hopkinton,	5,836 00	350 16	186 53	1	—	—	1	—	—	198 59	—
Hudson,..	—	—	—	—	—	—	—	—	—	173 47	—
Lexington,	—	—	—	—	—	—	—	—	—	159 74	—
Lincoln,	—	—	—	—	—	—	—	—	—		—

Littleton,	3,500 00	210 00	878 58				11	3,531	6,475 45	209 91	
Lowell,				1	60	700 00	8	670.	1,200 00		
Malden,	2,660 38	151 00					2	115.	400 00		61 53
Marlborough,										119 63	
Maynard,							3	50	2,500 00	176 78	
Medford,							1	10	100 00	81 86	70 00
Melrose,										64 49	
Natick,										89 50	
Newton,			1,841 45	2	180	12,000 00	13	303	18,482 00	207 58	22 15
North Reading,			133 00							174 15	50 00
Pepperell,							2	15	285 00	182 93	2 69
Reading,							1	5	50 00	210 37	
Sherborn,	19,910 00	1,081 51	80 90							211 96	
Shirley,	5,209 91	200 00	102 43							50 19	
Somerville,				1	69	32 00	*1	600	550 00	211 39	13 00
Stoneham,							2	20		160 71	
Stow,	15,727 53	899 75	123 97							162 99	
Sudbury,	304 00	10 00	122 22							219 31	
Tewksbury,										304 96	18 33
Townsend,	2,407 47	127 46	72 17							71 67	
Tyngsborough,							2	20	400 00		
Wakefield,							2	24	425 00	58 51	
Waltham,				1	60	4,500 00		27	675 00	169 54	
Watertown,			127 75							172 22	33 71
Wayland,	200 00	12 00								163 39	
Westford,	32,115 36	2,175 06					1	8	50 00	209 63	38 70
Weston,							1	10	435 00	38 80	
Wilmington,				1	111	563 00	2	475	600 00	137 92	
Winchester,											
Woburn,	12,000 00	600 00									
Totals,	$163,903 59	$8,920 17	$5,852 16	10	594	$19,595 00	63	7,892	$93,887 45	$8,070 91	$362 86

* Parochial school.

NANTUCKET COUNTY.

TOWNS.	Population—State Census, 1885.	Valuation—1885.	No. of Public Schools.	No. of persons in town between 5 and 15 years of age. May 1, 1885.	No. of persons in town between 5 and 14 years of age, May 1, 1885.	No. of different pupils of all ages in the Public Schools during the school-year.	No. attending within the year under 5 years of age.	No. attending within the year over 15 years of age.	No. attending within the year between 5 and 14 years of age.	Average membership of all the Schools.	Average attendance in all the Public Schools during the school-year.	The per cent. of attendance based upon the average membership.	No. of teachers required by the Public Schools.
Nantucket,	3,142	$2,667,784	12	565	460	400	—	18	290	392	355	.91	13

NORFOLK COUNTY.

TOWNS.	Population—State Census, 1885.	Valuation—1885.	No. of Public Schools.	No. of persons in town between 5 and 15 years of age. May 1, 1885.	No. of persons in town between 5 and 14 years of age, May 1, 1885.	No. of different pupils of all ages in the Public Schools during the school-year.	No. attending within the year under 5 years of age.	No. attending within the year over 15 years of age.	No. attending within the year between 5 and 14 years of age.	Average membership of all the Schools.	Average attendance in all the Public Schools during the school-year.	The per cent. of attendance based upon the average membership.	No. of teachers required by the Public Schools.
Bellingham,	1,198	$574,835	8	196	149	223	5	16	134	175	157	.90	8
Braintree,	4,040	2,849,725	19	705	430	835	3	58	517	612	542	.89	20
Brookline,	9,196	29,965,700	36	1,615	955	1,850	—	176	955	1,357	1,276	.94	43
Canton,	4,380	3,356,455	17	856	587	890	17	48	517	581	500	.94	25
Cohasset,	2,216	3,050,472	13	347	209	412	1	51	224	370	323	.82	14
Dedham,	6,641	5,232,551	35	1,135	771	1,347	1	116	755	1,127	1,052	.93	35
Dover,	664	742,591	4	86	51	102	—	7	59	76	68	.89	4
Foxborough,	2,814	1,482,192	11	391	230	473	1	60	266	377	345	.92	12
Franklin,	3,983	1,967,670	15	796	469	824	9	58	475	648	558	.86	17
Holbrook,	2,334	1,035,815	12	445	257	482	—	37	257	463	414	.89	13
Hyde Park,	8,376	5,202,085	34	1,606	994	2,000	—	194	1,106	1,584	1,447	.91	40
Medfield,	1,594	1,110,858	5	203	125	213	—	18	125	193	167	.87	6
Medway,	2,777	1,258,480	14	406	223	653	12	49	378	453	403	.89	15
Millis,	683	411,469	4	108	67	138	2	23	67	108	98	.90	4
Milton,	3,555	12,385,150	15	627	377	679	4	58	405	536	499	.93	17
Needham,	2,586	1,928,821	13	453	281	587	4	36	334	502	444	.88	13
Norfolk,	825	404,088	7	167	102	181	1	6	111	146	131	.90	6

Norwood,	2,921	2,065,942	12	501	334	535	2	54	337	469	424	.90	14
Quincy,	12,144	8,489,465	51	2,416	1,643	2,689	1	188	1,640	2,122	2,003	.94	53
Randolph,	3,807	1,998,200	16	660	443	695	9	52	443	695	591	.85	17
Sharon,	1,328	1,101,618	7	227	136	239	2	19	136	202	180	.89	7
Stoughton,	5,183	2,273,150	18	975	603	738	16	55	415	628	565	.90	19
Walpole,	2,443	1,571,387	13	452	293	430	3	28	287	349	314	.90	14
Wellesley,	3,013	4,552,841	11	379	216	457	–	60	216	365	335	.92	15
Weymouth,	10,740	5,669,535	49	1,993	1,312	2,203	–	189	1,293	1,944	1,705	.88	52
Wrentham,	2,710	1,382,473	15	427	266	479	2	87	266	400	364	.91	15
Totals,	102,142	$102,003,463	454	18,172	11,473	20,354	94	1,693	11,718	16,432	14,905	.91	498

NANTUCKET COUNTY — Continued.

TOWNS.	Whole No. of different male teachers in school-year.	Whole No. of different female teachers in school-year.	No. of teachers who have attended Normal Schools.	No. of teachers who have graduated from Normal Schools.	Av'ge wages per month of male teachers in Public Schools.	Av'ge wages per month of female teachers in Public Schools.	Aggregate of months have been kept during the school-year all the Public Schools.	Average No. of months have been kept for the entire year the Public Schools.	No. of Schools kept less than six months each.	No. of High Schools.	No. of teachers.	No. of pupils.	How supported.	Months.	Days.	Salary of Principal.
Nantucket,	1	12	2	—	$100 00	$28 16	113	9-8	—	1	2	45	Taxation,	10	—	$1,000 00

NORFOLK COUNTY — Continued.

TOWNS.	Whole No. of different male teachers in school-year.	Whole No. of different female teachers in school-year.	No. of teachers who have attended Normal Schools.	No. of teachers who have graduated from Normal Schools.	Av'ge wages per month of male teachers in Public Schools.	Av'ge wages per month of female teachers in Public Schools.	Aggregate of months have been kept during the school-year all the Public Schools.	Average No. of months have been kept for the entire year the Public Schools.	No. of Schools kept less than six months each.	No. of High Schools.	No. of teachers.	No. of pupils.	How supported.	Months.	Days.	Salary of Principal.
Bellingham,	1	11	1	1	$10 00	$31 81	64	8	—	—	—	—	—	—	—	—
Braintree,	6	21	6	5	76 00	32 00	187-13	9-18	—	1	2	106	Taxation,	10	—	$1,240 00
Brookline,	5	43	15	15	205 00	69 20	337-10	9-8	—	1	5	135	Taxation,	9-10	—	2,700 00
Canton,	4	23	6	6	103 53	36 32	170	10	—	1	2	54	Taxation,	10	—	1,200 00
Cohasset,	2	12	4	3	82 50	34 20	129-10	9-19	—	1	2	80	Taxation,	9-15	—	1,200 00
Dedham,	7	38	11	11	122 50	45 51	350	10	—	1	4	106	Taxation,	10	—	1,800 00
Dover,	1	5	—	1	—	38 00	35-10	8-17	—	—	—	—	—	—	—	—
Foxborough,	1	13	2	1	111 11	39 15	99	9	—	1	2	59	Taxation,	9	—	1,000 00
Franklin,	3	16	3	1	44 00	39 60	133-15	8-18	—	1	2	51	Taxation,	10	—	1,000 00
Holbrook,	2	21	1	—	110 00	36 87	113	9-5	—	1	2	96	Taxation,	10	—	1,100 00
Hyde Park,	7	39	10	8	123 00	45 00	336-12	9-18	—	1	4	145	Taxation,	10	—	1,800 00
Medfield,	1	5	4	3	84 49	46 62	46-5	9-5	—	—	—	—	—	—	—	—
Medway,	2	13	6	2	54 00	33 92	36	9-7	—	1	2	89	Taxation,	10	—	$1,000 00
Millis,	1	4	1	1	—	28 00	127	9	—	—	—	—	—	—	—	—
Milton,	5	12	5	4	131 00	55 00	150	10	—	1	2	63	Taxation,	10	—	1,800 00
Needham,	2	18	4	2	84 00	41 46	116-15	8-19	—	1	1	58	Taxation,	10	—	1,200 00
Norfolk,	1	6	1	—	37 00	30 60	47-2	6-17	—	—	—	—	—	—	—	—

Norwood,	2	18	10	10	122 00	42 50	114	9–10	–	1	2	56	Taxation,	9–10	1,159 00
Quincy,	5	48	9	9	108 00	46 61	510	10	–	1	3	165	Taxation,	10	1,400 00
Randolph,	3	14	5	5	119 00	39 00	152	9–10	–	1	2	81	Part tax,	9–10	1,500 00
Sharon,	1	8	1	1	80 00	32 33	62	8–17	–	1	1	37	Taxation,	9–10	760 00
Stoughton,	4	16	5	4	76 39	34 93	162	9	–	1	2	43	Taxation,	9	1,050 00
Walpole,	5	11	5	4	62 50	36 60	127	9–15	–	1	2	62	Taxation,	10	1,000 00
Wellesley,	1	32	17	14	150 00	54 00	105	9–11	–	1	3	69	Taxation,	10	1,500 00
Weymouth,	7	46	6	4	96 00	36 00	515	10	–	2	5	160	Taxation,	10	{ 1,200 00 / 1,200 00 }
Wrentham,	3	14	–	–	70 00	35 11	185	9	–	1	1	31	Taxation,	9	720 00
Totals,	80	507	147	124	$102 56	$43 04	4,361–12	9–8	–	22	51	1,746	–	204–15	$28,529 00

NANTUCKET COUNTY — CONTINUED.

TOWNS.	Amount raised by taxes for Schools, including wages of teachers, board, fuel, care of fires and school-rooms, for the school-year 1885-86.	Expense of supervision by school committee.	Salary of Superintendent of Public Schools.	Expense of Printing reports, etc.	Expense of sundries,— books, stationery, etc.	Amount expended for new school-houses.	Amount expended for alterations and permanent improvements.	Amount expended for ordinary repairs.	Amount paid for all school purposes from money raised by taxation.	Amount of voluntary contributions for Public Schools.
Nantucket,	$4,729 59	$100 00	—	$21 00	$546 54	—	—	$75 00	$5,472 13	—

NORFOLK COUNTY — CONTINUED.

TOWNS.	Amount raised by taxes for Schools, including wages of teachers, board, fuel, care of fires and school-rooms, for the school-year 1885-86.	Expense of supervision by school committee.	Salary of Superintendent of Public Schools.	Expense of Printing reports, etc.	Expense of sundries,— books, stationery, etc.	Amount expended for new school-houses.	Amount expended for alterations and permanent improvements.	Amount expended for ordinary repairs.	Amount paid for all school purposes from money raised by taxation.	Amount of voluntary contributions for Public Schools.
Bellingham,	$1,800 00	$66 00	$90 00	$17 00	$114 62	—	—	$144 00	$2,021 62	—
Braintree,	8,200 00	500 00	900 00	40 00	1,268 00	—	$628 00	750 00	11,246 00	—
Brookline,	42,600 08	—	2,500 00	23 00	1,997 51	—	9,499 95	596 40	57,870 54	—
Canton,	12,195 00	—	1,200 00	—	1,327 17	—	—	300 00	15,318 57	—
Cohasset,	6,200 00	—	275 00	30 00	500 00	—	—	—	7,305 00	—
Dedham,	24,168 59	—	1,600 00	60 00	2,821 17	$3,000 00	2,825 06	1,396 21	35,871 03	—
Dover,	1,400 00	—	50 00	15 00	138 83	—	—	35 00	1,638 83	$110 00
Foxborough,	5,000 00	275 00	—	34 67	890 55	—	1,534 00	66 69	7,800 00	—
Franklin,	6,500 00	481 13	—	35 00	—	—	—	363 99	7,380 12	—
Holbrook,	6,500 00	250 00	—	—	557 28	—	—	—	7,307 28	—
Hyde Park,	24,900 00	—	1,125 00	25 00	3,335 82	—	500 00	3,664 18	33,550 00	—
Medfield,	2,400 00	75 00	—	4 00	387 20	—	—	84 05	2,950 25	—
Medway,	5,500 00	185 00	—	10 00	844 73	—	—	480 52	7,020 25	—
Millis,	1,545 28	—	60 00	5 00	110 00	—	—	20 00	1,740 28	—
Milton,	15,105 92	—	—	86 00	1,661 31	—	—	1,228 56	19,281 79	—
Needham,	7,900 00	255 00	1,200 00	16 00	588 52	11,000 00	776 45	333 65	20,869 62	52 00
Norfolk,	1,200 00	111 86	—	9 00	292 42	2,110 79	74 48	24 18	3,822 73	—

Norwood,	8,300 00	180 00	1,500 00	19 00	669 75	—	—	964 39	10,114 14	—
Quincy,	34,679 47	—	—	—	6,788 87	—	—	2,083 17	45,070 51	—
Randolph,	9,500 00	320 00	—	5 00	910 00	—	512 00	—	11,247 00	—
Sharon,	2,400 00	25 00	88 00	40 00	191 60	—	—	104 87	2,849 47	—
Stoughton,	8,701 15	598 82	—	50 00	1,574 76	—	282 00	518 29	11,725 02	—
Walpole,	4,500 00	—	500 00	—	669 14	18,000 00	363 27	148 16	24,180 57	—
Wellesley,	9,700 00	225 00	—	—	1,029 76	—	—	1,076 01	12,030 77	—
Weymouth,	24,654 21	236 32	1,800 00	104 23	4,547 23	—	400 00	1,371 04	33,113 03	—
Wrentham,	6,000 00	325 20	—	70 00	407 03	—	—	280 30	7,082 53	—
Totals,	$281,549 70	$4,109 33	$12,888 00	$697 90	$38,623 27	$34,110 79	$17,395 21	$16,033 66	$400,406 95	$162 00

NANTUCKET COUNTY — Concluded.

TOWNS.	Amount of local funds the income of which can be appropriated only for the support of Schools and Academies.	Income of local funds.	Income of surplus revenue and other funds, including the dog tax, used at the option of the town.	ACADEMIES AND PRIVATE SCHOOLS.						Town's share of school fund payable Jan. 25, 1886.	How much of said fund was used for apparatus and books of reference.
				No. of Academies.	Whole No. attending for the year.	Amount of tuition paid.	No. of Private Schools.	Whole No. attending for the year.	Estimated amount of tuition.		
Nantucket,	—	—	—	1	80	$640 00	—	—	—	$180 75	—

NORFOLK COUNTY — Concluded.

TOWNS.	Amount of local funds the income of which can be appropriated only for the support of Schools and Academies.	Income of local funds.	Income of surplus revenue and other funds, including the dog tax, used at the option of the town.	No. of Academies.	Whole No. attending for the year.	Amount of tuition paid.	No. of Private Schools.	Whole No. attending for the year.	Estimated amount of tuition.	Town's share of school fund payable Jan. 25, 1886.	How much of said fund was used for apparatus and books of reference.
Bellingham,	$6,700 00	$250 00	$293 71	—	—	—	—	—	—	$211 22	—
Braintree,	—	—	489 00	1	79	$1,100 00	—	—	—	189 48	—
Brookline,	—	—	—	—	—	—	—	—	—	—	—
Canton,	1,000 00	45 50	230 00	—	—	—	—	—	—	51 61	—
Cohasset,	—	—	—	—	—	—	—	—	—	19 54	$50 00
Dedham,	—	—	75 92	—	—	—	8	150	$900 00	59 70	50 00
Dover,	—	—	300 50	—	—	—	*1	350	—	205 13	—
Foxborough,	—	—	323 06	—	—	—	3	30	—	171 76	—
Franklin,	—	—	228 94	1	145	4,719 27	1	24	260 00	194 66	—
Holbrook,	—	—	—	—	—	—	—	—	—	173 76	18 00
Hyde Park,	—	—	—	—	—	—	—	—	—	96 62	76 93
Medfield,	3,760 20	150 23	280 86	—	—	—	—	—	—	161 34	—
Medway,	—	—	—	1	46	3,780 00	—	—	—	181 56	—
Millis,	100 00	6 00	—	—	—	—	—	—	—	—	—
Milton,	—	—	307 17	—	—	—	—	—	—	—	—
Needham,	1,000 00	—	96 00	—	—	—	—	—	—	179 45	—
Norfolk,	—	—	—	—	—	—	—	—	—	308 89	—

Norwood,	121,000 00	—	—	1	—	—	2	—	600 00	174 90	50 00
Quincy,	11,700 00	5,789 18	—	—	—	—	1	48	2,000 00	155 75	—
Randolph,	2,350 00	733 43	474 53	—	—	—	—	6	550 00	188 51	—
Sharon,	—	141 60	153 00	—	—	—	—	—	—	162 48	—
Stoughton,	—	—	—	—	—	—	†2	†320	*300 00	204 46	—
Walpole,	—	—	—	—	—	—	—	—	—	174 55	—
Wellesley,	6,000 00	275 00	688 39	—	—	—	2	80	6,000 00	22 27	—
Weymouth,	1,818 26	109 08	246 00	—	—	—	2	40	600 00	116 27	—
Wrentham,	—	—	—	—	—	—	—	—	—	176 72	—
Totals,	$155,438 46	$7,500 02	$4,187 08	4	260	$9,599 27	22	1,048	$11,210 00	$3,580 63	$244 93

* Parochial school. † One parochial school.

PLYMOUTH COUNTY.

TOWNS.	Population—State Census, 1885.	Valuation — 1886.	No. of Public Schools.	No. of persons in town May 1, 1885, between 5 and 15 years of age.	No. of persons in town May 1, 1885, between 8 and 14 years of age.	No. of different pupils of all ages in the Public schools during the school-year.	No. attending within the year under 5 years of age.	No. attending within the year over 15 years of age.	No. attending within the year between 8 and 14 years of age.	Average membership of all the Schools.	Average attendance in all the Public Schools during the school-year.	The per cent. of attendance based upon the average membership.	No. of teachers required by the Public Schools.
Abington,	3,699	$1,905,283	17	629	450	686	—	36	417	657	574	.87	21
Bridgewater,	3,827	2,098,685	18	522	343	608	2	123	354	533	460	.86	22
Brockton,	20,783	12,989,214	66	3,477	2,173	3,956	5	347	2,104	3,170	2,841	.90	70
Carver,	1,091	581,815	8	196	119	210	3	17	126	165	189	.90	8
Duxbury,	1,924	1,103,312	10	296	194	338	1	54	194	270	232	.86	11
East Bridgewater,	2,812	1,464,485	15	486	311	539	1	42	315	437	406	.93	16
Halifax,	530	246,409	4	73	42	77	—	3	40	63	57	.90	4
Hanover,	1,966	1,087,632	9	322	229	349	1	30	249	294	260	.88	10
Hanson,	1,227	536,266	7	217	136	233	2	13	136	179	155	.87	7
Hingham,	4,375	3,341,687	16	666	417	713	8	60	409	642	580	.90	19
Hull,	451	2,157,316	2	71	37	80	1	6	41	62	54	.87	2
Kingston,	1,570	1,504,244	6	224	132	258	2	45	156	228	210	.92	7
Lakeville,	980	450,281	8	167	107	172	4	9	107	136	103	.76	8
Marion,	965	807,410	7	143	94	175	—	15	108	160	141	.88	7
Marshfield,	1,649	1,031,580	9	217	135	250	4	30	132	197	174	.88	9
Mattapoisett,	1,215	1,439,429	6	183	113	192	1	34	173	182	151	.83	6
Middleborough,	5,163	2,714,577	24	864	567	932	3	126	484	775	702	.91	29
Pembroke,	1,318	621,135	8	209	138	227	7	11	144	185	154	.83	8
Plymouth,	7,239	4,521,176	34	1,231	743	1,461	10	146	743	1,136	1,043	.92	37
Plympton,	600	281,502	3	91	51	96	3	6	47	75	64	.85	3
Rochester,	1,021	469,100	7	162	118	197	3	11	118	158	135	.85	7
Rockland,	4,785	2,319,133	20	880	503	1,002	—	63	571	883	797	.90	22
Scituate,	2,350	1,410,535	13	506	288	484	5	40	310	411	371	.90	15

South Abington,	3,595	2,584,720	12	611	426	667	4	68	364	593	543	.92	14
South Scituate,	1,589	871,179	11	259	192	281	4	20	182	226	192	.84	11
Wareham,	3,254	1,337,465	16	691	451	702	23	54	408	540	489	.91	19
West Bridgewater,	1,707	921,042	10	312	183	289	5	6	174	237	215	.91	10
Totals,	81,680	$50,786,612	366	13,708	8,092	14,174	99	1,115	8,601	12,584	11,242	.89	402

SUFFOLK COUNTY.

Boston,	390,393	$685,679,072	519	68,702	—	65,000	91	5,099	38,871	57,180	51,662	.90	1,234
Chelsea,	25,709	18,454,694	77	4,709	2,872	4,913	—	424	2,641	3,893	3,532	.91	85
Revere,	3,637	3,427,550	13	636	560	775	1	20	504	541	468	.86	13
Winthrop,	1,370	2,245,605	4	201	111	265	2	30	89	228	196	.86	5
Totals,	421,109	$709,706,921	613	74,268	—	70,953	94	5,573	42,105	61,842	55,858	.90	1,337

PLYMOUTH COUNTY — CONTINUED.

TOWNS.	Whole No. of different male teachers in school-year.	Whole No. of different female teachers in school-year.	No. of teachers who have attended Normal School.	No. of teachers who have graduated from Normal Schools.	Av'ge wages per month of male teachers in Public Schools.	Av'ge wages per month of female teachers in Public Schools.	Aggregate of months all the Public Schools have been kept during the school-year.	Average No. of months the Public Schools have been kept for the entire year.	No. of Schools kept less than six months each.	HIGH SCHOOLS — No. of High Schools.	No. of teachers.	No. of pupils.	How supported.	Length Months.	Days.	Salary of Principal.
Abington,	4	23	9	6	$85 00	$18 14	159	9-12		2	4	79	Taxation,	10		$1,000 00
Bridgewater,	6	27	21	20	78 81	34 84	153-10	8-11	1	1	3	109	Taxation,	9-10		1,000 00
Brockton,	12	85	31	25	105 71	41 73	640	10		1	4	222	Taxation,	10		1,800 00
Carver,	2	9		1	29 50	29 77	60	7-10	1							
Duxbury,	2	11	3	2	67 50	33 00	92-10	9-5		1	2	68	Part tax,	10		1,000 00
East Bridgewater,	1	20	8	8	100 00	35 00	136	9		1	2	60	Taxation,	10		1,000 00
Halifax,		6	3	1		26 50	32-14	8								
Hanover,		12	4	4	72 00	29 00	88	9		1	2	69	Taxation,	10		720 00
Hanson,		10	4	2		31 10	59-17	8-11								
Hingham,	9	16	8	7	96 00	42 30	160	10		1	3	81	Taxation,	10		1,600 00
Hull,	2	1	1	1	76 00	32 00	18	9								
Kingston,	2	8	6	4	112 00	41 41	54	7-6		1	2	50	Taxation,	9		1,035 00
Lakeville,	2	11	6	6	25 50	29 33	58-10	7-17	1							
Marion,	5	4	1	1	39 00	29 00	55	9								
Marshfield,	1	12	3	2	36 00	28 50	81	9								
Mattapoisett,	1	5	4	4	70 00	32 00	54	9-10		1	1	40	Part tax,	9-15		700 00
Middleborough,	1	39	19	16	120 00	35 26	216-10	8-5		1	3	102	Taxation,	9-15		1,200 00
Pembroke,	2	8	1		36 00	6 86	66	9-17								
Plymouth,	6	38	10	8	98 33	33 80	335	9	2	1	4	150	Taxation,	10		1,500 00
Plympton,	1	4				31 00	27	8-10								
Rochester,	2	11	6		31 70	31 70	59-10	9-5								
Rockland,	5	19	7	2	75 17	37 53	185			1	3	64	Taxation,	10		1,260 00

Scituate,	1	19	6	4	105 26	30 00	118	9	–	1	2	56	Taxation,	9–10	1,000 00
South Abington,	1	16	6	3	120 00	38 00	100	9–2	–	1	2	90	Taxation,	10	1,200 00
South Scituate,	3	10	5	5	37 00	29 00	100–5	9	–	1	2	63	Taxation,	–	–
Wareham,	3	21	1	–	71 00	31 00	129	8	–	1	2	–	Taxation,	9	1,100 00
W. Bridgewater,	–	11	5	5	–	36 72	80	8	–	–	–	–	–	–	–
Totals,	74	456	177	136	$78 38	$35 17	3,327–6	8–16	4	16	39	1,303	–	146–10	$18,115 00

SUFFOLK COUNTY — CONTINUED.

Boston,	115	1,089	750	750	$254 26	$72 95	5,120	10–1	–	11	105	2,561	Taxation,	10	$22,680 00 〔 6,336 00 5,760 00 2,860 00
Chelsea,	5	80	23	19	175 00	55 00	750	10	–	1	7	250	Taxation,	10	
Revere,	1	12	6	5	105 00	41 97	121	9–4	1	–	–	–	Taxation,	–	600 00
Winthrop,	1	4	1	–	64 85	39 78	38	9–5	1	1	1	45		9–5	
Totals,	162	1,185	780	774	$249 95	$71 31	6,029	9–7	1	13	113	2,856	–	29–5	$38,176 00

PLYMOUTH COUNTY — Continued.

TOWNS.	Amount raised by taxes for schools, including wages of teachers, board, fuel, care of fires and school-rooms, for the school-year, 1885-86.	Expense of supervision by school committee.	Salary of Superintendent of Public Schools.	Expense of Printing reports, etc.	Expense of sundries,—books, stationery, etc.	Amount expended for new school-houses.	Amount expended for alterations and permanent improvements.	Amount expended for ordinary repairs.	Amount paid for all school purposes from money raised by taxation.	Amount of voluntary contributions for Public Schools.
Abington,	$8,800 00	$311 00	–	$25 00	$948 18	–	$1,947 69	$1,597 36	$13,629 23	–
Bridgewater,	8,500 00	531 14	–	56 00	1,100 00	–	100 00	500 00	10,787 14	–
Brockton,	36,602 14	–	$2,000 00	–	3,272 35	$14,895 11	4,850 58	1,947 83	63,568 01	–
Carver,	1,200 00	73 45	–	22 00	168 83	–	–	59 81	1,524 09	–
Duxbury,	2,800 00	171 40	–	15 00	335 21	–	258 70	64 32	3,644 63	–
E Bridgewater,	5,600 00	200 12	500 00	40 00	1,329 00	–	1,158 55	425 68	9,253 25	–
Halifax,	700 00	–	40 00	16 00	50 00	–	–	15 00	821 00	–
Hanover,	3,300 00	165 00	–	35 00	400 00	–	–	300 00	4,100 00	–
Hanson,	1,700 00	157 50	–	30 00	314 77	–	200 00	64 71	2,466 98	–
Hingham,	11,978 89	–	1,000 00	–	1,490 22	–	1,890 64	437 99	16,797 24	–
Hull,	1,400 00	45 00	–	17 50	88 33	–	–	14 98	1,565 61	–
Kingston,	2,950 00	175 00	–	–	725 21	–	–	139 46	3,989 67	–
Lakeville,	1,500 00	125 00	–	15 00	165 00	–	865 00	50 00	2,710 00	–
Marion,	1,450 00	90 00	–	–	193 00	–	–	59 00	4,553 00	–
Marshfield,	2,500 00	128 00	–	19 32	437 37	2,761 00	572 91	59 21	3,716 81	–
Mattapoisett,	2,100 00	80 00	–	9 00	321 69	–	6 00	114 83	2,631 52	–
Middleborough,	10,000 00	228 15	833 33	–	1,560 00	–	–	570 00	14,131 48	–
Pembroke,	1,750 00	121 74	–	21 60	150 00	1,000 00	–	180 30	2,223 64	–
Plymouth,	19,839 50	–	1,000 00	15 00	2,000 00	–	89 82	1,055 68	24,000 00	–
Plympton,	800 00	50 00	–	20 00	68 10	–	142 25	2 60	1,082 95	–
Rochester,	1,500 00	94 00	–	2 50	410 54	–	–	212 15	2,219 19	–
Rockland,	10,500 00	291 75	–	75 00	964 20	260 00	250 00	125 00	12,465 95	–
Scituate,	4,500 00	123 54	–	30 00	594 96	–	–	117 53	5,696 03	–

South Abington,	5,000 00	381 00	—	42 00	800 00	—	—	1,000 00	7,181 00	—
South Scituate,	2,900 00	129 00	—	25 00	—	—	—	30 00	3,101 00	—
Wareham,	6,000 00	280 86	—	—	593 44	1,231 69	—	365 71	8,496 70	—
W. Bridgewater,	3,000 00	37 36	89 89	—	222 80	—	—	227 06	3,577 11	—
Totals,	$158,870 03	$3,990 01	$5,463 22	$530 92	$18,643 20	$20,147 80	$12,332 14	$10,066 11	$229,933 23	—

SUFFOLK COUNTY.—Continued.

Boston,	$1,387,640 36	$54,710 00	$4,200 00	$2,500 00	$86,186 84	$333,555 52	—	$217,676 26	$2,036,468 98	—
Chelsea,	58,476 20	—	2,200 00	83 50	8,084 08	9,112 25	$22,698 13	3,900 00	104,549 16	—
Revere,	6,555 60	75 00	—	23 00	684 62	17,300 00	195 00	200 00	24,958 22	—
Winthrop,	2,200 00	—	—	10 00	312 21	—	—	182 28	2,779 49	—
Totals,	$1,404,872 16	$54,785 00	$6,400 00	$2,616 50	$95,267 75	$359,967 77	$22,888 13	$221,958 54	$3,068,755 85	—

PLYMOUTH COUNTY — Concluded.

TOWNS.	Amount of local funds the income of which can be appropriated only for the support of Schools and Academies.	Income of local funds.	Income of surplus revenue and other funds, including the dog tax, used at the option of the town.	ACADEMIES AND PRIVATE SCHOOLS.						Town's share of school fund payable Jan. 25, 1880.	How much of said fund was used for apparatus and books of reference.
				No. of Academies.	Whole No. attending for the year.	Amount of tuition paid.	No. of Private Schools.	Whole No. attending for the year.	Estimated amount of tuition.		
Abington,	$6,300 00	$353 64	$125 25							$184 24	$184 24
Bridgewater,	—	—	607 10				1	20	$560 00	181 62	—
Brockton,	6,300 00	345 30	141 80				1	12	1,200 00	210 94	—
Carver,	21,000 00	1,667 00	287 17							167 09	—
Duxbury,	—	—	296 62	1	68	$1,400 00				175 58	—
E. Bridgewater,	—	—	—							304 56	—
Halifax,	1,700 00	50 00	145 91							168 97	—
Hanover,	—	—	140 96	1	31	600 00				212 13	—
Hanson,	—	—	—	1	65	534 00	3	40	500 00	38 11	—
Hingham,	30,000 00	1,800 00	—							154 27	—
Hull,	—	—	175 88							161 96	—
Kingston,	—	—	198 97				1	25	150 00	310 20	—
Lakeville,	—	—	—							208 77	—
Marion,	—	—	187 95							162 99	—
Marshfield,	—	—	379 84				1	25	1,000 00	160 03	—
Mattapoisett,	—	—	—	1	45					195 97	—
Middleborough,	28,000 00	1,500 00	136 67				1	25	1,000 00	211 39	—
Pembroke,	—	—	—							66 88	—
Plymouth,	—	—	117 60				2	35	3,000 00	305 41	—
Plympton,	—	—	146 47							310 20	—
Rochester,	—	—	—							195 24	—
Rockland,	—	—	190 00							178 49	—
Scituate,	—	—	—								—

South Abington,			427 86				1	10	—	184 07
South Scituate,			169 05				—	—	—	216 12
Wareham,			354 90				—	—	—	182 64
West Bridgewater,			-				2	18	—	216 24
Totals,	$93,300 00	$5,715 94	$4,530 00	4	209	$2,534 00	12	185	$6,410 00	$5,064 11

SUFFOLK COUNTY — CONCLUDED.

Boston,	$47,373 22	$2,964 84	$47,673 30	22	5,000	$290,000 00	70	2,050	$160,000 00	-	-
Chelsea,			-				1	35	400 00	-	-
Revere,			-				-	-	-	$184 41	$20 00
Winthrop,			207 87				-	-	-	158 89	-
Totals,	$47,373 22	$2,964 84	$47,881 17	22	5,000	$290,000 00	71	2,085	$160,400 00	$343 30	$20 00

WORCESTER COUNTY.

TOWNS.	Population—State Census, 1885.	Valuation—1885.	No. of Public Schools.	No. of persons in town between May 1, 1885, 5 and 15 years of age.	No. of persons in town between May 1, 1885, 8 and 14 years of age.	No. of different pupils of all ages in the Public Schools during the school-year.	No. attending within the year under 5 years of age.	No. attending within the year over 15 years of age.	No. attending within the year between 8 and 14 years of age.	Average membership of all the Schools.	Average attendance in all the Public Schools during the school-year.	The per cent. of attendance based upon the average membership.	No. of teachers required by the Public Schools.
Ashburnham,	2,658	$964,800	12	343	265	378	2	17	265	341	268	.79	12
Athol,	4,758	2,555,770	22	842	526	1,003	6	99	577	723	688	.95	23
Auburn,	1,268	487,795	7	254	144	270		14	140	183	165	.90	7
Barre,	2,093	1,414,810	15	293	184	335	5	51	192	295	276	.94	16
Berlin,	899	485,102	5	161	108	183	1	21	111	162	136	.84	5
Blackstone,	5,436	2,316,345	18	1,033	712	1,133	6	51	655	820	715	.87	22
Bolton,	876	484,364	7	128	69	170	4	26	84	121	111	.92	7
Boylston,	884	409,945	6	160	98	171	8	18	97	130	122	.94	6
Brookfield,	3,013	1,223,125	15	465	338	651	4	54	385	507	451	.89	24
Charlton,	1,823	954,620	12	303	176	336	5	37	250	263	232	.88	12
Clinton,	8,945	5,143,726	32	1,774	1,095	1,787	6	92	1,098	1,565	1,422	.91	34
Dana,	695	283,912	5	107	63	125	3	13	76	116	110	.95	5
Douglas,	2,205	1,022,400	13	406	239	440	4	52	239	283	268	.95	13
Dudley,	2,742	939,925	12	564	356	475	11	41	227	339	310	.91	13
Fitchburg,	15,375	11,494,562	56	2,889	1,721	3,187	2	251	1,783	2,540	2,305	.90	64
Gardner,	7,283	3,309,616	23	1,248	930	1,206	7	91	916	1,079	866	.80	26
Grafton,	4,498	2,242,800	22	820	541	983	15	15	453	794	682	.86	24
Hardwick,	3,145	1,218,520	15	512	322	593	4	35	373	439	390	.89	16
Harvard,	1,184	911,061	10	146	84	192	3	17	112	156	145	.93	10
Holden,	2,471	1,013,317	13	530	347	541		26	278	388	347	.89	15
Hubbardston,	1,803	714,882	10	216	127	269	1	48	189	209	189	.90	10
Lancaster,	2,050	2,329,803	11	334	210	364	6	35	213	279	253	.91	13
Leicester,	2,923	1,724,193	15	583	344	599	7	53	359	501	460	.92	18
Leominster,	5,297	3,797,471	21	882	510	962	4	83	517	913	842	.92	25
Lunenburg,	1,071	684,849	8	143	91	167	3	26	90	158	132	.84	8

Mendon,	8	.87	150	172	92	40	3	199	92	162	8	560,612	945
Milford,	44	.93	1,238	1,327	935	159	1	1,728	1,006	1,707	37	5,201,529	9,513
Millbury,	18	.93	603	749	606	58	—	916	572	920	17	2,115,711	4,655
New Braintree,	6	.92	85	92	61	7	4	124	61	97	6	431,564	558
Northborough,	10	.91	257	283	218	23	3	351	216	249	8	1,080,058	1,853
Northbridge,	16	.92	572	624	515	54	—	828	464	769	16	2,057,105	3,786
North Brookfield,	21	.87	577	662	498	74	1	805	730	800	19	1,834,194	4,201
Oakham,	6	.89	112	126	77	30	3	144	81	123	6	369,123	749
Oxford,	13	.86	267	311	295	76	—	427	269	311	13	1,303,253	2,555
Paxton,	5	.92	75	82	57	16	2	116	57	95	5	281,098	561
Petersham,	9	.91	127	139	92	13	2	163	90	148	9	571,876	1,052
Phillipston,	6	.85	69	81	56	21	2	108	58	91	6	201,054	530
Princeton,	8	.93	151	103	105	30	2	231	94	159	8	843,093	1,038
Royalston,	10	.93	168	180	126	61	6	237	126	202	10	662,335	1,153
Rutland,	10	.91	164	170	127	37	4	237	127	175	10	467,070	963
Shrewsbury,	10	.92	250	271	162	41	7	308	165	260	9	991,730	1,450
Southborough,	9	.89	281	259	185	34	2	341	196	323	9	1,373,643	2,100
Southbridge,	94	.88	606	687	496	60	18	867	833	1,358	22	3,074,084	6,500
Spencer,	36	.93	1,359	1,458	1,098	89	4	1,845	1,075	1,790	32	3,887,284	8,247
Sterling,	12	.93	200	214	173	50	4	276	177	228	11	873,407	1,331
Sturbridge,	15	.89	320	359	270	25	5	483	231	382	15	971,019	1,980
Sutton,	15	—	315	542	310	—	—	542	310	707	15	1,272,661	3,101
Templeton,	16	.93	401	433	245	78	1	617	302	509	7	1,093,202	2,627
Upton,	12	.91	270	297	189	38	1	333	211	312	11	867,059	2,265
Uxbridge,	18	.91	333	432	269	51	4	586	294	685	18	1,941,701	2,948
Warren,	21	.93	604	651	420	41	2	903	471	762	20	2,221,973	4,032
Webster,	17	.75	405	542	447	22	12	827	532	1,145	21	2,178,167	6,220
Westborough,	24	.91	678	747	—	85	5	992	653	845	13	2,567,742	4,880
West Boylston,	14	.92	416	452	328	46	5	596	380	555	13	1,102,020	2,997
West Brookfield,	10	.93	217	233	196	22	12	309	240	347	10	812,886	1,747
Westminster,	13	.95	239	251	205	35	7	347	182	274	13	755,524	1,556
Winchendon,	19	.92	539	590	419	59	5	726	416	689	18	1,953,119	3,872
Worcester,	267	.90	9,598	10,757	9,240	987	—	12,981	9,810	13,269	234	52,714,391	68,389
Totals,	1,170	.89	33,621	37,640	28,136	3,737	242	46,963	30,101	45,474	1,026	$146,891,400	244,039

WORCESTER COUNTY — CONTINUED.

TOWNS.	Whole No. of different male teachers in school-year.	Whole No. of different female teachers in school-year.	No. of teachers who have attended Normal Schools.	No. of teachers who have graduated from Normal Schools.	Av'ge wages per month of male teachers in Public Schools.	Av'ge wages per month of female teachers in Public Schools.	Aggregate of months all the Public Schools have been kept during the school-year.	Average No. of months the Public Schools have been kept for the entire year.	No. of Schools kept less than six months each.	No. of High Schools.	No. of teachers.	No. of pupils.	How supported.	Months.	Days.	Salary of Principal.
Ashburnham,	—	14	—	—	—	$30 50	81-11	6-7	—	—	—	—	—	—	—	—
Athol,	1	27	3	3	$119 56	33 91	156-11	7-2	—	1	2	58	Taxation,	9	—	$1,076 00
Auburn,	1	11	1	—	—	28 00	52-10	7-10	—	—	—	—	—	—	—	—
Barre,	4	19	2	2	72 00	32 00	98-15	6-12	5	1	2	50	Taxation,	9	—	1,000 00
Berlin,	—	8	6	4	—	32 80	40	8	—	—	—	—	—	—	—	—
Blackstone,	3	25	3	1	70 37	30 40	162	9	—	1	2	72	Taxation,	9	—	1,000 00
Bolton,	2	11	4	3	60 00	29 00	64	9-3	—	1	—	34	Not by tax,	10	—	600 00
Boylston,	—	22	2	1	—	32 00	46	8	—	—	—	—	—	—	—	—
Brookfield,	2	20	1	2	105 79	33 17	135-10	9	—	1	2	41	Taxation,	9	10	1,000 00
Charlton,	3	39	5	5	9 33	7 60	91-5	9-8	—	—	—	—	—	—	—	—
Clinton,	1	—	11	1	160 00	43 80	291-2	7-12	—	1	3	117	Taxation,	9	8	1,600 00
Dana,	2	6	2	2	28 00	24 30	39-15	9-8	—	—	—	—	—	—	—	—
Douglas,	1	15	1	14	60 00	30 50	102-5	7-19	—	1	1	53	Taxation,	10	—	600 00
Dudley,	—	10	2	3	52 00	33 00	94-15	8-15	—	1	2	42	Taxation,	10	—	1,000 00
Fitchburg,	4	74	17	3	115 00	40 00	557	7-18	—	1	6	269	Taxation,	10	—	1,800 00
Gardner,	6	26	9	3	81 00	45 00	187	9-16	—	1	3	98	Taxation,	10	—	1,300 00
Grafton,	2	29	5	1	100 00	35 92	171-15	8	—	1	3	66	Taxation,	9	—	1,200 00
Hardwick,	1	19	2	3	36 94	32 15	132	7-17	—	1	—	—	—	9	—	—
Harvard,	3	12	4	2	31 25	30 00	72	8-16	—	—	—	—	—	—	—	—
Holden,	4	14	2	1	57 30	28 00	95	7-2	—	—	—	—	—	—	—	—
Hubbardston,	6	11	1	1	31 00	26 00	75	7-3	—	1	2	51	Taxation,	9	—	900 00
Lancaster,	7	11	4	—	59 00	33 00	79-16	7-10	—	1	2	44	Taxation,	9	—	1,300 00
Leicester,	4	16	4	1	89 92	38 07	133-5	7-5	—	1	3	70	Part tax,	9	6	1,700 00
Leominster,	5	24	4	—	150 00	35 00	189	9	1	1	4	85	Taxation,	9	15	1,500 00
Lunenburg,	1	10	4	2	29 00	27 91	60	7-10	—	—	—	—	—	10	—	—

Town															
Mendon,	9	8	4	2	60 00	25 21	58-10	7-7	—	1	1	43	Taxation,	6	360 00
Milford,	6	51	32	16	102 22	39 65	322-10	8-19	—	1	5	228	Taxation,	10	1,700 00
Millbury,	3	21	7	8	87 50	38 66	153	9	—	1	2	77	Taxation,	9-10	1,325 00
New Braintree,	—	11	5	4	—	30 78	45	7-10	—	—	—	—	—	—	—
Northborough,	1	11	8	3	108 10	33 35	290	8-1	—	1	—	82	Taxation,	9-5	1,000 00
Northbridge,	1	16	12	12	120 00	42 13	155-15	9-15	—	1	2	32	Taxation,	10	1,200 00
North Brookfield,	2	21	—	1	120 00	34 08	171-10	9-2	—	1	1	74	Taxation,	9	1,200 00
Oakham,	4	8	1	—	34 00	26 60	45	7-6	—	1	—	—	—	—	—
Oxford,	3	12	—	—	62 00	31 20	106	8-15	—	1	1	50	Taxation,	10	900 00
Paxton,	—	7	3	1	—	29 00	29	5-16	—	1	—	—	—	—	—
Petersham,	3	11	—	—	40 00	24 66	64	7-6	—	1	1	34	Taxation,	5-15	287 50
Phillipston,	1	8	1	—	28 00	24 00	35-10	6	—	1	—	—	—	—	—
Princeton,	4	10	—	—	37 20	25 71	62-5	6-13	—	1	—	—	—	—	—
Royalston,	2	17	5	4	28 66	29 63	72-10	7-5	—	1	1	—	—	—	—
Rutland,	2	11	—	—	35 00	25 25	60	6	—	1	—	—	—	—	—
Shrewsbury,	1	12	3	1	25 00	32 60	77	8-5	2	1	2	63	Taxation,	9	900 00
Southborough,	—	9	5	2	100 00	39 58	82	9-2	—	1	1	38	Taxation,	10	1,000 00
Southbridge,	3	29	4	4	92 83	36 87	207	9-8	—	1	3	58	Taxation,	10	1,100 00
Spencer,	7	40	21	7	62 50	42 50	289	9-15	—	1	3	119	Taxation,	10	700 00
Sterling,	1	14	1	1	94 74	30 25	84-10	7-13	—	1	2	44	Taxation,	9-10	900 00
Sturbridge,	1	19	3	—	—	27 33	112	8-8	—	1	—	—	—	—	—
Sutton,	—	15	1	—	115 00	31 20	110-10	7-10	2	1	1	31	Taxation,	9	700 00
Templeton,	1	15	2	1	74 00	29 97	111-10	7-6	—	1	2	104	Taxation,	10	1,150 00
Upton,	3	13	5	2	73 00	35 60	86-10	7-5	2	1	2	55	Taxation,	8-15	900 00
Uxbridge,	2	22	6	3	62 00	33 00	136-1	7-12	1	1	—	37	Taxation,	10	1,100 00
Warren,	3	22	—	1	100 00	37 00	162-5	8-11	—	1	2	60	Taxation,	9-5	900 00
Webster,	—	17	10	1	100 00	37 00	137	8	—	1	2	49	Taxation,	10	1,000 00
Westborough,	2	24	5	9	102 50	39 36	191	9	—	1	3	98	Taxation,	10	1,500 00
West Boylston,	1	19	5	4	111 11	33 00	101	8	—	1	2	34	Taxation,	9-15	1,000 00
West Brookfield,	—	12	5	4	66 66	30 00	82-10	8	—	1	—	—	—	—	—
Westminster,	2	19	4	2	100 00	28 00	99	7-10	—	1	1	29	Taxation,	9	600 00
Winchendon,	1	19	—	1	136 82	33 81	145-10	8-2	—	1	2	53	Taxation,	9	1,000 00
Worcester,	22	245	184	184	—	54 03	2,281	10	—	1	17	898	Taxation,	10	2,700 00
Totals,	149	1,274	430	327	$76 21	$37 71	9,373-17	8-19	22	39	99	3,490	—	365-14	$12,698 50

WORCESTER COUNTY — CONTINUED.

TOWNS.	Amount raised by taxes for Schools, including wages of teachers, board, fuel, care of fires and school-rooms, for the school-year 1885-86.	Expense of supervision by school committee.	Salary of Superintendent of Public Schools.	Expense of Printing reports, etc.	Expense of sundries,—books, stationery, etc.	Amount expended for new school-houses.	Amount expended for alterations and permanent improvements.	Amount expended for ordinary repairs.	Amount paid for all school purposes from money raised by taxation.	Amount of voluntary contributions for Public Schools.
Ashburnham,	$3,500 00	$135 00	–	$15 30	$564 95	–	–	$113 95	$4,329 20	–
Athol,	7,000 00	300 00	–	10 00	1,066 22	–	–	273 37	8,649 59	$30 00
Auburn,	1,300 00	100 00	–	20 00	280 00	–	–	80 00	2,980 00	–
Barre,	4,800 00	255 75	–	18 00	500 00	–	$1,200 00	381 54	5,555 29	–
Berlin,	1,100 00	48 00	–	9 50	186 84	–	–	149 99	1,492 33	–
Blackstone,	8,000 00	300 00	–	50 00	1,282 12	–	–	505 81	10,137 93	–
Bolton,	1,300 00	99 00	–	11 00	84 76	–	–	80 45	1,775 21	–
Boylston,	1,600 00	124 23	–	14 00	159 95	–	–	42 60	1,940 78	–
Brookfield,	4,450 00	150 00	–	18 00	622 04	–	–	126 00	5,366 04	–
Charlton,	3,000 00	212 35	–	–	678 22	–	–	355 41	4,245 98	–
Clinton,	19,292 62	–	$1,600 00	37 15	3,674 27	–	1,253 89	361 13	26,219 06	–
Dana,	800 00	66 75	–	10 50	122 00	–	–	24 00	1,023 25	–
Douglas,	3,900 00	100 00	–	–	439 81	–	–	40 00	4,571 81	–
Dudley,	4,300 00	146 00	–	20 00	300 00	–	92 00	300 00	6,366 00	–
Fitchburg,	38,761 46	–	2,000 00	20 00	6,577 38	$1,300 00	–	1,398 24	–	–
Gardner,	12,000 00	375 00	–	39 00	3,468 00	8,114 05	1,170 00	322 00	17,374 00	–
Grafton,	8,100 00	759 50	–	20 80	1,132 33	–	680 86	991 38	11,684 87	–
Hardwick,	4,500 00	200 00	–	26 00	381 68	–	–	307 99	5,415 67	–
Harvard,	2,500 00	132 50	–	21 80	274 50	–	–	39 93	2,968 73	–
Holden,	4,541 08	–	200 00	17 10	884 53	–	235 00	97 09	5,974 80	–
Hubbardston,	2,000 00	121 25	–	18 00	279 73	–	–	226 94	2,645 92	–
Lancaster,	4,605 00	176 00	–	25 00	503 00	–	–	86 00	5,485 00	–
Leicester,	6,000 00	250 12	–	20 00	854 43	–	–	225 75	7,350 30	–
Leominster,	12,000 00	–	1,500 00	100 00	1,400 00	–	2,000 00	1,199 94	18,199 94	–
Lunenburg,	1,700 00	82 00	–	20 00	246 00	–	346 00	129 00	2,523 00	–

Mendon,	1,500 00	—	75 00	20 00	70 00	—	230 00	30 00	1,925 00	—
Milford,	18,400 00	50 00	1,500 00	91 00	1,454 12	—	776 53	962 78	23,234 43	—
Millbury,	9,000 00	400 00	—	25 00	1,500 00	—	—	500 00	11,425 00	—
New Braintree,	1,559 11	98 00	—	18 00	183 96	—	20 00	57 26	1,936 33	—
Northborough,	3,500 00	165 00	—	9 00	286 63	—	—	214 31	4,174 94	—
Northbridge,	8,800 00	250 00	—	50 00	703 13	—	—	898 52	10,611 65	—
N. Brookfield,	8,000 00	286 20	—	55 00	926 08	—	—	672 75	9,940 03	—
Oakham,	950 00	107 90	—	5 00	260 00	—	—	—	1,322 90	—
Oxford,	5,000 00	156 50	—	—	366 00	—	126 00	226 00	5,874 60	—
Paxton,	1,100 00	95 00	—	16 00	134 73	—	200 97	21 77	1,568 47	—
Petersham,	1,600 00	130 00	—	5 00	221 79	—	—	160 37	2,117 16	—
Phillipston,	800 00	70 00	—	12 00	134 34	—	—	20 00	1,036 34	—
Princeton,	2,000 00	115 69	—	4 00	250 00	—	32 00	8 00	2,409 69	—
Royalston,	1,500 00	124 50	—	10 50	427 52	—	—	44 48	2,107 00	—
Rutland,	1,200 00	95 50	—	9 00	366 24	—	—	26 32	1,697 06	—
Shrewsbury,	4,000 00	215 00	—	20 00	578 91	—	200 00	255 08	5,268 99	—
Southborough,	4,300 00	150 00	816 66	21 00	387 94	—	—	646 14	5,505 08	—
Southbridge,	10,500 00	466 50	—	40 00	1,130 72	—	210 00	479 05	13,642 93	—
Spencer,	16,250 00	—	1,000 00	69 75	1,832 20	—	923 39	1,225 94	21,301 28	—
Sterling,	2,400 00	182 50	—	32 00	583 47	—	160 00	62 62	4,420 59	—
Sturbridge,	3,200 00	184 24	—	17 00	278 81	—	1,054 45	238 92	4,973 42	—
Sutton,	4,500 00	150 00	—	10 00	341 59	—	150 00	120 00	5,271 59	—
Templeton,	4,700 00	177 50	—	23 80	1,100 73	—	—	277 83	6,279 56	—
Upton,	4,142 31	201 50	—	12 50	514 72	—	183 59	149 56	5,204 18	225 00
Uxbridge,	6,715 19	150 00	—	89 25	1,264 30	3,496 58	378 00	511 83	12,605 15	—
Warren,	8,100 00	—	400 00	—	1,087 60	—	828 27	431 27	10,847 14	—
Webster,	6,350 00	225 00	—	40 00	—	—	—	440 00	7,055 00	—
Westborough,	10,500 00	1,450 00	—	—	1,148 81	—	100 00	500 00	13,698 81	—
West Boylston,	4,600 00	188 50	—	10 00	578 76	—	—	332 66	5,709 92	—
West Brookfield,	3,300 00	150 00	—	20 00	473 00	—	159 00	55 00	4,157 00	42 00
Westminster,	3,350 75	148 00	—	9 00	440 08	—	682 31	10 00	4,640 14	—
Winchendon,	6,195 20	292 00	—	36 96	818 44	—	—	339 01	7,681 61	—
Worcester,	176,130 88	—	4,250 00	186 69	16,852 06	65,467 72	955 38	9,624 64	273,467 37	—
Totals,	$506,283 60	$10,608 48	$13,341 66	$1,528 60	$62,059 44	$78,378 35	$14,347 64	$27,310 62	$657,784 96	$297 00

WORCESTER COUNTY — Concluded.

TOWNS.	Amount of local funds the income of which can be appropriated only for the support of Schools and Academies.	Income of local funds.	Income of surplus revenue and other funds, including the dog tax, used at the option of the town.	ACADEMIES AND PRIVATE SCHOOLS.						Town's share of school fund payable Jan. 25, 1886.	How much of said fund was used for apparatus and books of reference.
				No. of Academies.	Whole No. attending for the year.	Amount of tuition paid.	No. of Private Schools.	Whole No. attending for the year.	Estimated amount of tuition.		
Ashburnham,	$120,000 00	$7,007 00	$133 53	1	122	$2,500 00	1	15	$50 00	$217 20	$103 27
Athol,	—	—	—	—	—	—	—	—	—	197 68	—
Auburn,	—	—	—	—	—	—	—	—	—	313 79	—
Barre,	2,000 00	120 00	170 96	—	—	—	—	—	—	170 96	—
Berlin,	12,000 00	655 99	92 00	—	—	—	—	—	—	310 20	—
Blackstone,	—	—	228 62	—	—	—	—	—	—	206 63	51 66
Bolton,	—	—	—	—	—	—	—	—	—	308 33	25 00
Boylston,	1,000 00	60 00	160 84	—	—	—	—	—	—	308 77	10 00
Brookfield,	—	—	—	—	—	—	—	—	—	182 81	25 00
Charlton,	—	—	—	—	—	—	—	—	—	216 01	—
Clinton,	—	—	—	—	—	—	1	20	—	100 72	—
Dana,	941 33	56 48	63 22	—	—	—	—	—	—	306 22	50 00
Douglas,	8,000 00	420 00	136 57	—	—	—	—	—	—	174 84	—
Dudley,	—	—	54 00	—	—	—	—	—	—	236 06	25 00
Fitchburg,	—	—	—	—	—	—	—	—	—	78 50	—
Gardner,	1,000 00	50 00	—	—	—	—	—	—	—	199 68	—
Grafton,	1,000 00	65 00	—	—	—	—	1	38	500 00	180 88	—
Hardwick,	200 00	12 00	—	—	—	—	—	—	—	208 77	—
Harvard,	—	—	256 44	—	—	—	—	—	—	176 32	30 00
Holden,	3,366 66	202 00	—	1	75	1,485 00	1	8	120 00	212 76	30 00
Hubbardston,	1,200 00	72 00	—	1	15	350 00	—	—	—	168 17	—
Lancaster,	—	—	278 19	—	—	—	—	—	—	184 30	42 04
Leicester,	51,000 00	3,060 00	—	—	—	—	—	—	—	54 23	—
Leominster,	13,000 00	620 00	128 00	—	—	—	—	—	—	207 98	—
Lunenburg,	—	—	—	—	—	—	—	—	—	—	25 00

Mendon,	—	—	98 63	—	—	—	—	—	—	—	45 64
Milford,	5,000 00	300 00	299 44	—	—	—	2	265	500 00	97 42	—
Millbury,	—	—	—	—	—	—	1	10	200 00	201 16	—
New Braintree,	—	—	66 26	—	—	—	—	—	—	305 87	50 00
Northborough,	—	—	—	—	—	—	1	14	925 00	164 87	—
Northbridge,	—	—	—	—	—	—	—	—	—	194 04	—
North Brookfield,	—	—	236 67	—	—	—	—	—	—	196 03	—
Oakham,	—	—	—	—	—	—	—	—	—	307 35	50 00
Oxford,	735 00	19 14	—	—	—	—	—	—	—	170 28	—
Paxton,	—	—	182 08	—	—	—	—	—	—	305 24	—
Pedersham,	—	—	—	—	—	—	—	—	—	208 77	—
Phillipston,	—	—	35 48	—	—	—	—	—	—	305 07	—
Princeton,	6,500 00	480 05	106 95	—	—	—	—	—	—	207 86	—
Royalston,	—	—	71 57	—	—	—	—	—	—	211 11	22 67
Rutland,	1,000 00	30 00	—	—	—	—	—	—	—	211 17	19 40
Shrewsbury,	—	—	116 33	1	63	4,600 00	2	38	1,250 00	215 38	55 20
Southborough,	—	—	—	—	—	—	2	550	185 00	166 35	—
Southbridge,	—	—	—	—	—	—	2	95	—	77 59	—
Spencer,	—	—	—	—	—	—	—	—	—	100 49	12 25
Sterling,	—	—	—	—	—	—	—	—	—	212 76	46 60
Sturbridge,	2,000 00	120 00	202 83	—	—	—	—	—	—	221 53	46 16
Sutton,	—	—	130 18	—	—	—	—	—	—	180 19	—
Templeton,	—	—	217 77	—	—	—	1	17	250 00	180 31	—
Upton,	—	—	—	—	—	—	*	—	—	217 77	25 00
Uxbridge,	—	—	—	—	—	—	—	—	—	181 05	57 00
Warren,	—	—	—	—	—	—	—	—	—	192 67	63 12
Webster,	—	—	256 44	—	—	—	2	700	5,000 00	215 80	—
Westborough,	—	—	—	—	—	—	1	15	150 00	196 89	—
West Boylston,	—	—	—	—	—	—	—	—	—	182 93	—
West Brookfield,	—	—	—	—	—	—	—	—	—	220 11	—
Westminster,	—	—	—	—	—	—	3	45	120 00	216 35	—
Winchendon,	1,504 76	59 63	—	2	150	4,000 00	9	1,800	2,000 00	189 02	45 00
Worcester,	—	—	—	—	—	—	—	—	—	—	—
Totals,	$231,447 75	$13,359 29	$3,723 00	6	425	$12,935 00	31	3,630	$11,250 00	$11,385 84	$955 01

* Parochial schools.

RECAPITULATION.

COUNTIES.	Population—State Census, 1885.	Valuation—1885.	No. of Public Schools.	No. of persons in town between May 1, 1885, 5 and 15 years of age.	No. of persons in town between May 1, 1885, 8 and 14 years of age.	No. of different pupils of all ages in the Public Schools during the school-year.	No. attending within the year under 5 years of age.	No. attending within the year over 15 years of age.	No. attending within the year between 8 and 14 years of age.	Average membership of all the Schools.	Average attendance in all the Public Schools during the school-year.	The per cent. of attendance based upon the average membership.
Barnstable,	29,845	$16,768,848	162	5,062	3,342	5,936	5	831	3,389	4,838	4,351	.90
Berkshire,	73,828	37,238,951	381	14,498	9,615	15,773	146	1,261	8,933	12,442	11,058	.89
Bristol,	158,498	114,486,276	579	28,659	17,706	28,373	70	1,660	17,543	22,365	19,999	.89
Dukes,	4,135	3,210,235	23	538	384	643	10	81	383	522	469	.90
Essex,	263,727	182,631,698	872	45,554	27,868	43,876	143	3,098	26,887	37,892	33,584	.89
Franklin,	37,449	16,889,366	264	7,136	4,615	7,775	72	722	4,570	6,355	5,784	.91
Hampden,	116,764	78,402,861	425	21,902	10,439	19,253	179	1,281	11,232	14,651	13,381	.91
Hampshire,	48,472	26,156,074	286	8,677	5,748	9,402	114	846	5,783	7,025	6,945	.91
Middlesex,	357,311	294,508,654	1,224	64,690	40,467	75,742	165	5,756	37,470	53,140	48,536	.92
Nantucket,	3,142	2,667,784	12	565	460	400	—	18	290	392	355	.91
Norfolk,	102,142	102,003,463	454	18,172	11,473	20,354	94	1,693	11,718	16,432	14,905	.91
Plymouth,	81,680	50,786,612	366	13,708	8,692	14,174	99	1,415	8,601	12,684	11,242	.89
Suffolk,	421,109	709,706,921	613	74,268	47,302	70,953	94	5,573	42,105	61,842	55,858	.90
Worcester,	244,039	146,891,400	1,056	45,474	30,101	46,963	242	3,737	28,136	37,640	33,621	.89
Totals,	1,912,141	$1,782,340,143	6,717	348,903	228,202	359,617	1,433	27,972	207,040	288,640	260,088	.90

RECAPITULATION — CONTINUED.

COUNTIES.	No. of teachers required by the Public Schools.	Whole No. of different male teachers in school-year.	Whole No. of different female teachers in school-year.	No. of teachers who have attended Normal Schools.	No. of teachers who have graduated from Normal Schools.	Av'ge wages per month of male teachers in Public Schools.	Av'ge wages per month of female teachers in Public Schools.	Aggregate of months all the Public Schools have been kept during the school-year.	Average No. of months the Public Schools have been kept for the entire year.	No. of Schools kept less than six months each.	HIGH SCHOOLS No. of High Schools.	No. of teachers.	No. of pupils.	Salary of Principal.
Barnstable,	168	51	173	44	35	$65 85	$32 98	1,350-18	8-5	—	11	16	577	$9,739 14
Berkshire,	424	74	441	49	31	57 95	28 93	3,189-9	7-15	4	13	27	831	12,698 29
Bristol,	649	63	690	181	139	95 48	41 16	5,821-19	8-14	1	11	35	1,387	13,245 00
Dukes,	25	8	27	10	8	45 50	29 01	182-10	8-3	7	1	1	28	510 00
Essex,	1,018	96	1,004	354	234	108 43	41 13	8,290-15	9-4	8	26	85	2,656	33,105 75
Franklin,	274	46	350	54	35	41 00	27 40	1,964-14	7-3	4	7	15	379	4,546 22
Hampden,	493	54	538	149	110	87 02	38 07	3,747-5	8-11	9	10	37	1,095	14,295 00
Hampshire,	301	54	365	48	26	50 07	28 32	2,319-9	7-15	9	11	25	647	9,878 00
Middlesex,	1,503	158	1,588	578	441	131 09	49 41	9,658-1	8-17	13	43	132	4,625	57,412 66
Nantucket,	13	1	12	2	—	100 00	28 16	113	9-8	—	1	2	45	1,000 00
Norfolk,	498	80	507	147	124	102 56	43 04	4,361-12	9-8	1	22	51	1,746	28,529 00
Plymouth,	402	74	456	177	136	78 38	35 17	3,327-6	8-16	4	16	39	1,303	18,115 00
Suffolk,	1,337	152	1,185	780	774	249 95	71 31	6,029	9-7	1	13	113	2,561	38,176 00
Worcester,	1,170	149	1,274	430	327	76 21	37 71	9,373-17	8-19	22	39	99	3,490	42,698 50
Totals,	8,275	1,060	8,610	3,003	2,420	$111 23	$43 97	59,729-15	8-12	82	224	677	21,370	$283,948 56

RECAPITULATION — Continued.

COUNTIES.	Amount raised by taxes for Schools, including wages of teachers, board, fuel, care of fires and school-rooms, for the school-year 1885-86.	Expense of supervision by school committee.	Salary of Superintendent of Public Schools.	Expense of Printing reports, etc.	Expense of sundries, — books, stationery, etc.	Amount expended for new school-houses.	Amount expended for alterations and permanent improvements.	Amount expended for ordinary repairs.	Amount paid for all school purposes from money raised by taxation.	Amount of voluntary contributions for Public Schools.
Barnstable,	$63,401 00	$1,177 55	$2,179 00	$378 75	$8,242 50	$14,044 86	$1,009 50	$4,505 12	$94,936 28	—
Berkshire,	136,922 41	2,549 18	4,200 00	520 65	14,260 08	11,251 10	12,663 45	6,559 95	184,117 38	$70 00
Bristol,	316,298 63	2,834 51	8,190 00	748 17	35,674 74	140,361 21	9,724 46	24,225 60	568,708 12	145 00
Dukes,	5,893 50	280 00	10 00	70 00	987 43	—	1,340 24	382 95	8,914 12	70 00
Essex,	545,976 82	11,753 30	7,450 00	2,141 99	66,876 62	75,530 93	24,753 76	35,108 88	774,517 32	30 00
Franklin,	60,321 61	2,925 14	60 00	249 78	8,557 40	25,943 89	841 56	4,018 04	102,918 62	56 00
Hampden,	242,895 07	3,690 50	6,436 71	461 34	29,949 97	23,854 15	17,806 85	13,211 42	338,306 01	149 00
Hampshire,	86,400 00	2,538 53	1,845 00	294 93	11,096 19	521 35	2,633 72	5,196 50	110,526 22	492 00
Middlesex,	973,014 89	12,970 24	19,455 00	2,291 70	101,535 31	80,009 85	44,416 65	59,228 55	1,292,929 38	462 75
Nantucket,	4,729 59	100 00	—	21 00	546 54	—	—	75 00	5,472 13	—
Norfolk,	281,649 70	4,109 33	12,888 00	697 90	33,623 27	34,110 79	17,395 21	16,033 66	400,406 95	162 00
Plymouth,	158,870 03	3,990 01	5,463 22	530 92	18,643 20	20,147 80	12,332 14	10,066 11	229,983 23	—
Suffolk,	1,404,872 16	54,785 00	6,400 00	2,616 50	95,267 75	359,967 77	22,888 13	221,958 54	3,068,755 85	—
Worcester,	506,283 60	10,608 48	13,331 66	1,528 60	162,959 44	78,378 35	14,347 64	27,310 62	667,784 96	297 00
Totals,	$4,817,499 01	$114,311 77	$87,918 59	$12,552 23	$188,210 44	$864,122 05	$182,153 31	$427,830 94	$7,838,226 57	$1,933 75

RECAPITULATION — Concluded.

COUNTIES.	Amount of local funds the income of which can be appropriated only for the support of Schools and Academies.	Income of local funds.	Income of surplus revenue and other funds, including the dog tax, used at the option of the town.	ACADEMIES AND PRIVATE SCHOOLS.						Town's share of school fund payable Jan. 25, 1886.	How much of said fund was used for apparatus and books of reference.
				No. of Academies.	Whole No. attending for the year.	Amount of tuition paid.	No. of Private Schools.	Whole No. attending for the year.	Estimated amount of tuition.		
Barnstable,	$43,333 00	$2,109 32	$1,529 64	2	70	$800 00	3	38	$5,900 00	$3,386 86	$780 44
Berkshire,	22,803 07	1,484 86	1,520 91	1	15		16	576	16,553 00	8,041 80	105 27
Bristol,	105,800 00	15,261 99	4,606 17	3	325	14,186 95	36	1,960	12,650 00	3,086 97	117 00
Dukes,	5,000 00	200 00	280 90	1	23	125 00				1,481 00	148 58
Essex,	456,465 24	17,424 93	7,082 45	5	593	33,437 80	56	4,791	28,386 00	4,711 62	155 00
Franklin,	70,103 42	3,550 71	1,348 38	7	647	16,920 78	3	75	3,350 00	6,950 37	143 94
Hampden,	162,879 65	6,571 05	2,608 76	3	450	12,991 83	23	5,647	33,785 00	4,832 10	520 08
Hampshire,	834,966 27	17,773 96	2,402 21	5	588	62,340 75	12	187	9,355 00	5,945 19	573 19
Middlesex,	153,903 59	8,920 17	5,852 16	10	594	19,595 00	63	7,892	93,887 45	8,070 91	862 86
Nantucket,				1	80	640 00				180 76	
Norfolk,	155,438 46	7,500 02	4,187 08	4	260	9,599 27	22	1,048	11,210 00	3,580 63	244 93
Plymouth,	93,300 00	5,715 94	4,580 00	4	209	2,584 00	12	185	6,410 00	5,064 11	
Suffolk,	47,373 22	2,964 84	47,881 17	22	5,000	290,000 00	71	2,085	160,400 00	343 30	20 00
Worcester,	231,447 75	13,359 29	3,723 00	6	425	12,935 00	31	3,630	11,250 00	11,385 84	955 01
Totals,	$1,882,813 67	$102,887 08	$87,551 83	74	9,279	$476,106 38	348	28,114	$393,136 45	$67,061 46	$4,126 30

EVENING SCHOOLS.

CITIES AND TOWNS.	No. of Schools.	ATTENDANCE.			TIME. No. of Evenings.	No. of Teachers.	Expense.
		Males.	Females.	Average.			
Boston,	19	3,079	*	2,932	1,719	142	$47,193 99
Brockton,	4	171	31	67	52	4	471 02
Brookline,	1	54	13	27	64	2	354 61
Cambridge,	6	546	167	250	50	25	2,616 67
Chelsea,	2	376	*	191	50	10	1,060 65
Chicopee,	2	172	250	205	42	23	1,690 00
Clinton,	1	192	124	176	46	11	427 84
Dedham,	1	34	16	19	52	2	400 00
Fall River,	20	1,085	227	615	64	41	3,039 11
Fitchburg,	2	204	142	113	53	18	964 50
Haverhill,	1	90	86	80	60	8	836 00
Holyoke,	6	559	247	294	40	29	1,927 50
Hyde Park,	2	50	10	28	75	3	400 00
Lawrence,	4	300	100	325	40	25	1,311 42
Lowell,	9	1,634	755	838	91	66	10,740 35
Lynn,	7	474	*	108	56	45	2,950 41
Malden,	2	143	*	99	85	5	1,293 78
Maynard,	3	108	55	–	70	5	410 81
Milford,	2	34	–	16	69	2	377 45
New Bedford,	3	197	157	175	140	15	1,801 13
Newburyport,	1	26	*	27	50	5	136 25
Newton,	1	89	63	53	45	9	332 83
North Adams,	4	69	60	78	29	4	326 00
Pittsfield,	1	132	12	–	68	4	649 86
Rockland,	2	64	35	30	53	2	238 45
Salem,	3	396	166	221	178	16	1,425 00
Somerville,	4	293	71	241	21	18	1,230 04
Spencer,	1	149	100	108	36	9	408 35
Springfield,	1	320	142	138	85	15	1,498 50
Stow,	1	15	5	17	25	1	100 00
Sutton,	1	40	23	34	80	1	100 00
Taunton,	2	278	134	217	141	11	1,558 00
Waltham,	3	150	133	95	140	9	1,125 60
Warren,	2	40	10	25	24	4	58 00
Warwick,	1	20	23	42	39	1	87 88
Westfield,	1	71	32	40	35	5	243 72
W. Springfield,	1	17	25	27	33	2	33 50
Winchester,	1	47	20	30	40	27	233 00
Woburn,	1	53	13	40	50	4	643 56
Worcester,	9	335	41	233	75	39	4,210 36
Totals,	138	12,106	3,488	8,254	4,165	667	$94,906 14

* With males.

RETURNS OF SCHOOLS IN STATE INSTITUTIONS FOR THE YEAR ENDING JULY 31, 1886.

STATE INSTITUTIONS.	No. of Schools in the Institution.	No. of different Scholars of all ages during the year.	Average attendance during the year.	No. under 5 years of age attending School.	No. over 15 years of age attending School.	No. between 5 and 15 years of age remaining in the Institution July 31, 1886.	NO. OF TEACHERS DURING THE YEAR.		WAGES OF TEACHERS PER MONTH.		Length of each School in Months.
							Males.	Females.	Males.	Females.	
State Industrial School at Lancaster,	3	148	72	–	59	14	–	8	–	$25 00*	12 months.
State Primary School at Monson,	8	515	347	17	12	322	–	10	–	23 83*	11¾ months.
Lyman School for Boys at Westborough,	3	198	92	–	1	89	–	7	–	25 00*	12 months.

* With board.

GRADUATED TABLES — First Series.

The following Table shows the sums appropriated by the several cities and towns in the State, for the education of each child between five and fifteen years of age. The income of the surplus revenue and of other funds held in a similar way, when appropriated to schools, is added to the sum raised by taxes; and these sums constitute the amount reckoned as appropriations. The income of such school funds as were given and are held on the express condition that their income shall be appropriated to schools, is not included. Such an appropriation of their income, being necessary to retaining the funds, is no evidence of the liberality of those holding the trust. But if a town appropriates the income of any fund to its public schools, which may be so appropriated or not, at the option of the voters, or when the town has a legal right to use such income in defraying its ordinary expenses, then such an appropriation is as really a contribution to common schools as an equal sum raised by taxes. On this account the surplus revenue, and sometimes other funds, are to be distinguished from local school funds as generally held. The income of the one *may* be appropriated to schools, or not, at the pleasure of the town; the income of the other *must* be appropriated to schools by the condition of the donation. Funds of the latter kind are usually donations made to furnish means of education in addition to those provided by a reasonable taxation. Committees are expected, in their annual returns, to make this distinction in relation to school funds.

Voluntary contributions are not included in the amount which is divided in order to ascertain the sum appropriated to each child. In many towns such contributions, however liberal, are not permanent, and cannot be relied upon as a stated provision. They are often raised and applied to favor particular schools, or classes of scholars, and not to benefit equally all that attend the public schools. Besides, the value of board and fuel gratuitously furnished is determined by the mere estimate of individuals, and is therefore uncertain; while the amount raised by taxes, being in money, has a fixed and definite value, and is a matter of record. Still the contributions voluntarily made are exhibited in a separate column of the Table, as necessary to a complete statement of the provision made by the towns for the education of their children.

The Table exhibits the rank of each city or town in the State, in respect to its liberality in the appropriation of money to its schools, as compared with other cities and towns for the year 1885-86, also its rank in a similar scale for 1884-85. It presents the sum appropriated to each child between five and fifteen.

GRADUATED TABLES—(For the State)—First Series.

Table showing the Comparative Amount of Money appropriated by the different Towns in the State for the Education of each Child in the Town, between the Ages of 5 and 15 Years.

For 1884-85.	For 1885-86.	TOWNS.	Sum appropriated by towns for each child between 5 and 15 yrs. of age.	Amount raised by taxes for the support of schools.	Income of Funds, with Dog Tax, appropriated to Schools.	TOTAL.	No. of Children between 5 and 15 years of age.	Amount contributed for board and fuel.
4	1	NEWTON,	$28 71.5	$101,850 00	$1,841 45	$103,691 45	3,611	—
2	2	Nahant,	27 07.7	3,980 35	—	3,980 35	147	—
1	3	Brookline,	26 37.8	42,600 08	—	42,600 08	1,615	—
3	4	Wellesley,	25 59.4	9,700 00	—	9,700 00	379	—
13	5	Winchester,	24 19.4	15,000 00	—	15,000 00	620	—
5	6	Milton,	24 09.2	15,105 92	—	15,105 92	627	—
14	7	Weston,	23 63.6	5,200 00	—	5,200 00	220	—
91	8	Boxborough,	22 04.6	970 03	—	970 03	44	—
23	9	Watertown,	21 76.5	24,028 51	—	24,028 51	1,104	—
7	10	Dedham,	21 29.4	24,168 59	—	24,168 59	1,135	—
6	11	Concord,	21 27.7	12,000 00	—	12,000 00	564	—
11	12	Boston,	20 16.4	1,387,640 36	47,673 30	1,385,313 66	68,702	—
77	13	Hull,	19 71.8	1,400 00	—	1,400 00	71	—
21	14	Swampscott,	19 89.7	6,750 00	—	6,750 00	348	—
16	15	Waltham,	19 36	47,490 00	—	47,490 00	2,453	—
12	16	Lexington,	18 93.1	8,500 00	—	8,500 00	449	—
8	17	Arlington,	18 75.8	17,969 77	—	17,969 77	968	—
17	18	Cohasset,	18 53	6,200 00	230 00	6,430 00	347	—

Showing the Comparative Amount of Money appropriated by the different Towns in the State — Continued.

For 1884-85.	For 1885-86.	TOWNS.	Sum appropriated by towns for each child between 5 and 15 yrs. of age.	Amount raised by taxes for the support of Schools.	Income of Funds, with Dog Tax, appropriated to Schools.	TOTAL.	No. of Children between 5 and 15 years of age.	Amount contributed for board and fuel.
165	19	Mashpee,	$18 49.7	$500 00	$54 92	$554 92	30	—
9	20	Belmont,	18 46.2	6,000 00	—	6,000 00	325	—
10	21	Falmouth,	18 35.2	6,751 00	277 75	7,028 75	383	—
31	22	Bourne,	18 21.2	4,550 00	185 03	4,735 03	260	—
33	23	Needham,	18 11.7	7,900 00	307 17	8,207 17	453	—
22	24	Hingham,	17 98.6	11,978 39	—	11,978 39	666	—
19	25	Barnstable,	17 28.9	11,000 00	341 64	11,341 64	656	—
42	26	Littleton,	17 16.5	2,400 00	878 58	3,278 58	191	$12 00
26	27	Dover,	17 16.2	1,400 00	75 92	1,475 92	86	—
47	28	Harvard,	17 12.3	2,500 00	—	2,600 00	146	—
30	29	Bridgewater,	17 03.8	8,500 00	425 25	8,925 25	522	—
68	30	Barre,	16 96.6	4,800 00	170 96	4,970 96	293	—
25	31	Groton,	16 94.9	5,000 00	—	5,000 00	295	50 00
43	32	New Braintree,	16 75.6	1,559 11	66 26	1,625 37	97	—
18	33	Medford,	16 72.7	27,650 17	—	27,650 17	1,653	—
15	34	Norwood,	16 56.7	8,300 00	—	8,300 00	501	—
99	35	Bedford,	16 54.7	2,300 00	—	2,300 00	139	—
29	36	Haverhill,	16 46.9	59,288 14	—	59,288 14	3,600	—
64	37	Oxford,	16 07.7	5,000 00	—	5,000 00	311	—
20	38	Plymouth,	16 07.7	19,839 50	—	19,839 50	1,234	—
28	39	Acton,	16 02.2	4,000 00	229 89	4,229 89	264	—
72	40	Lincoln,	15 92.4	2,500 00	—	2,500 00	157	—
37	41	New Bedford,	15 82.4	80,501 00	694 46	81,195 46	5,131	—
34	42	Cambridge,	15 79.7	173,092 51	—	173,092 51	10,957	326 75
50	43	Hyde Park,	15 50.4	24,900 00	—	24,900 00	1,606	—
89	44	Amherst,	15 49.1	8,800 00	494 49	9,294 49	600	344 00

62	45	Sandwich,		15 46.5	5,800 00	277 73	6,077 73	393	—
90	46	Shrewsbury,		15 38.5	4,000 00	—	4,000 00	260	—
73	47	Somerville,		15 34.5	86,053 99	—	86,053 29	5,608	—
49	48	Springfield,		15 19.9	96,211 00	—	96,211 00	6,330	—
32	49	Stoneham,		15 17.7	13,750 00	—	13,750 00	906	—
24	50	Holbrook,		15 12.1	6,500 00	228 94	6,728 94	446	—
54	51	Randolph,		15 11.3	9,500 00	474 53	9,974 53	660	—
39	52	Sterling,		14 91.2	3,400 00	—	3,400 00	228	—
66	53	Wrentham,		14 62.8	6,000 00	246 00	6,246 00	427	—
52	54	Reading,		14 54.2	8,100 00	—	8,100 00	567	—
38	55	North Reading,		14 52.1	1,900 00	133 00	2,033 00	140	24 00
121	56	Quincy,		14 35.4	34,679 47	—	34,679 47	2,416	—
86	57	Merrimac,		14 33.1	5,800 00	175 94	5,975 94	417	—
85	58	Longmeadow,		14 32.4	3,200 00	123 10	3,323 10	232	—
—	59	Millis,		14 30.8	1,545 28	—	1,545 28	108	52 00
67	60	Salem,		14 24.8	68,817 79	2,077 94	70,895 73	4,976	—
75	61	Canton,		14 24.6	12,195 00	—	12,195 00	856	—
106	62	Medway,		14 28.9	5,500 00	280 86	5,780 86	466	—
63	63	Everett,		14 16	14,712 00	—	14,712 00	1,039	—
61	64	Melrose,		14 09.7	16,000 00	—	16,000 00	1,135	—
48	65	Wellfleet,		14 08.5	4,000 00	—	4,000 00	284	—
35	66	Lancaster,		14 05.7	4,695 00	—	4,695 00	334	—
74	67	Northborough,		14 05.6	3,600 00	—	3,500 00	249	—
59	68	Malden,		14 03.8	40,808 98	—	40,808 98	2,907	—
44	69	Framingham,		14 03.7	18,500 00	675 12	19,175 12	1,366	—
46	70	Abington,		13 99	8,800 00	—	8,800 00	629	—
112	71	Peabody,		13 97.8	24,096 49	687 29	24,783 78	1,773	225 00
45	72	Upton,		13 97.5	4,142 31	217 77	4,360 08	312	—
27	73	Kingston,		13 95.5	2,950 00	175 88	3,125 88	224	—
95	74	Orleans,		13 68.9	2,200 00	58 63	2,258 63	165	—
41	75	Southborough,		13 67.3	4,300 00	116 33	4,416 33	323	—
96	76	North Andover,		13 65.6	9,300 00	—	9,300 00	681	—

Showing the Comparative Amount of Money appropriated by the different Towns in the State — Continued.

For 1884-85.	For 1885-86.	TOWNS.	Sum appropriated by towns for each child between 5 and 15 yrs. of age.	Amount raised by taxes for the support of Schools.	Income of Funds, with Dog Tax, appropriated to Schools.	TOTAL.	No. of Children between 5 and 15 years of age.	Amount contributed for board and fuel.
123	77	West Stockbridge,	$13 63.8	$4,241 57		$4,241 57	311	—
58	78	Granby,	13 60.3	1,800 00	$77 83	1,877 83	138	—
87	79	Leominster,	13 60.5	12,000 00		12,000 00	882	$110 00
55	80	Foxborough,	13 55.6	5,000 00	300 50	5,300 50	391	—
158	81	Mattapoisett,	13 55.1	2,100 00	379 84	2,479 84	183	—
110	82	Lowell,	13 52.6	148,375 96		148,375 96	10,970	—
105	83	Fitchburg,	13 43.6	38,761 46	54 00	38,815 46	2,889	—
179	84	Tisbury,	13 33	2,200 00	106 10	2,306 10	173	—
81	85	Worcester,	13 27.4	176,130 88		176,130 88	13,269	70 00
53	86	Natick,	13 27.2	21,500 00		21,500 00	1,620	—
71	87	Ashby,	13 24.4	1,800 00	107 09	1,907 09	144	—
57	88	Greenfield,	13 03.1	11,350 00		11,350 00	871	—
79	89	Lynn,	12 90.8	95,259 78		95,259 78	7,380	—
260	90	Ashland,	12 88.9	5,800 00		5,800 00	450	—
93	91	Wakefield,	12 85.7	16,200 00		16,200 00	1,260	—
65	92	Westfield,	12 82.5	21,200 00		21,200 00	1,653	—
104	93	Princeton,	12 80.2	2,000 00	35 48	2,035 48	159	—
82	94	Brewster,	12 79.1	2,200 00		2,200 00	172	—
92	95	Lunenburg,	12 78.3	1,700 00	128 00	1,828 00	143	—
36	96	Stockbridge,	12 72.3	5,000 00		5,000 00	393	—
76	97	Weymouth,	12 71.6	24,654 21	688 39	25,342 60	1,993	—
102	98	Shelburne,	12 60.6	3,000 00	101 00	3,101 00	246	—
80	99	Tyngsborough,	12 60	1,150 00	72 17	1,222 17	97	—
83	100	Fairhaven,	12 50	6,000 00		6,000 00	480	100 00
126	101	Mansfield,	12 46.9	5,500 00	397 65	5,897 65	473	—
113	102	Westborough,	12 42.6	10,500 00		10,500 00	845	—

100	103	Chelsea	12 41.8	58,476 20	—	58,476 20	4,709	—
129	104	Edgartown	12 39.3	1,700 00	84 60	1,784 60	144	—
130	105	Marshfield	12 38.7	2,500 00	187 95	2,687 95	217	—
146	106	Bradford	12 37	6,400 00	217 80	6,617 80	535	—
218	107	Middleton	12 35.6	1,200 00	122 11	1,322 11	107	—
191	108	Greenwich	12 34.8	800 00	39 67	839 67	68	—
97	109	Braintree	12 32.5	8,200 00	489 00	8,689 00	705	—
143	110	Northampton	12 32.3	27,150 00	466 10	27,616 10	2,241	—
125	111	Dunstable	12 30.8	800 00	—	800 00	65	—
103	112	Rehoboth	12 29	3,200 00	302 68	3,502 68	285	—
124	113	Raynham	12 25.1	3,000 00	246 58	3,246 58	265	—
118	114	Saugus	12 24.7	5,893 39	58 50	5,951 89	486	—
170	115	Westminster	12 22.9	3,350 75	—	3,350 75	274	—
114	116	Gloucester	12 18.9	47,462 70	—	47,462 70	3,894	20 00
84	117	East Bridgewater	12 13.3	5,600 00	296 62	5,896 62	486	—
98	118	Chelmsford	12 11.9	5,000 00	332 32	5,332 32	440	—
161	119	Manchester	12 04.8	3,000 00	—	3,000 00	249	—
135	120	Petersham	12 04.1	1,600 00	182 08	1,782 08	148	—
219	121	Peru	12 00	600 00	—	600 00	50	—
40	122	Winthrop	11 97.9	2,200 00	207 87	2,407 87	201	—
122	123	Rockland	11 93.2	10,500 00	—	10,500 00	880	—
144	124	Easton	11 91.7	8,752 00	519 27	9,271 27	778	—
157	125	Pittsfield	11 89.8	30,303 57	—	30,303 57	2,547	—
119	126	Taunton	11 86.2	50,000 00	—	50,000 00	4,215	—
156	127	South Scituate	11 85	3,000 00	169 05	3,069 05	259	—
202	128	Dighton	11 84.2	3,000 00	185 49	3,185 49	269	—
229	129	Stow	11 84.2	2,019 47	123 97	2,143 44	181	—
117	130	Medfield	11 82.3	2,400 00	—	2,400 00	203	—
108	131	Beverly	11 81.3	18,059 82	581 12	18,640 94	1,578	40 00
94	132	Attleborough	11 80.6	25,000 00	867 62	25,867 62	2,191	—
116	133	Danvers	11 79.5	12,602 00	443 00	13,045 00	1,106	—
128	134	Methuen	11 79.2	9,000 00	280 02	9,280 02	787	—

Showing the Comparative Amount of Money appropriated by the different Towns in the State — Continued.

For 1884-85.	For 1885-86.	TOWNS.	Sum appropriated by towns for each child between 5 and 15 yrs. of age.	Amount raised by taxes for the support of Schools.	Income of Funds, with Dog Tax, appropriated to Schools.	TOTAL.	No. of Children between 5 and 15 years of age.	Amount contributed for board and fuel.
174	135	Great Barrington,	$11 77.2	$9,600 00	$252 80	$9,852 80	837	—
131	136	Gosnold,	11 73.7	200 00	23 00	223 00	19	—
88	137	Cottage City,	11 70.3	1,243 50	67 20	1,310 70	112	—
60	138	South Hadley,	11 68.9	8,000 00	205 87	8,205 87	702	—
181	139	Fall River,	11 58.4	136,007 02	—	136,007 02	11,741	—
154	140	Paxton,	11 57.9	1,100 00	—	1,100 00	95	—
109	141	Middleborough,	11 57.4	10,000 00	—	10,000 00	864	—
137	142	Uxbridge,	11 47.9	6,715 19	—	6,715 19	585	—
132	143	Northbridge,	11 44.3	8,800 00	—	8,800 00	769	—
70	144	Amesbury,	11 38.4	7,200 00	177 00	7,377 00	648	—
133	145	Sharon,	11 24.7	2,400 00	153 00	2,553 00	227	—
192	146	Boxford,	11 15.1	1,500 00	50 00	1,550 00	139	—
228	147	Ashfield,	11 14.7	1,600 00	72 00	1,672 00	150	—
56	148	Woburn,	11 11.3	28,672 66	—	28,672 66	2,580	—
115	149	Georgetown,	11 06.1	4,900 00	320 67	5,220 67	472	—
127	150	Sherborn,	10 97.5	2,125 00	80 90	2,205 90	201	—
155	151	Milford,	10 95.5	18,400 00	299 44	18,699 44	1,707	—
214	152	Monson,	10 94.2	6,500 00	339 00	6,839 00	625	—
141	153	Sudbury,	10 93.9	2,000 00	122 22	2,122 22	194	—
78	154	Carlisle,	10 92.5	800 00	74 00	874 00	80	—
159	155	Essex,	10 90.2	3,000 00	96 19	3,096 19	284	—
142	156	West Springfield,	10 88.9	9,000 00	332 24	9,332 24	857	—
193	157	Clinton,	10 87.5	19,292 62	—	19,292 62	1,774	—
319	158	Montgomery,	10 87	500 00	—	500 00	46	—
148	159	Swansea,	10 87	2,500 00	—	2,500 00	230	$5 00
209	160	Ipswich,	10 77.5	6,400 00	237 74	6,637 74	616	—

	No.	Town							
180	161	Warren,	10 77.1	8,100 00	—	8,100 00	752		
168	162	Leicester,	10 76.9	6,000 00	278 19	6,278 19	583		
145	163	Wenham,	10 72.5	1,400 00	101 51	1,601 51	140		
186	164	Brockton,	10 70.2	36,602 14	607 10	37,209 24	3,477		
178	165	Hanover,	10 70.2	3,300 00	145 91	3,445 91	322		
173	166	Bellingham,	10 68.2	1,800 00	293 71	2,093 71	196		
164	167	Maynard,	10 68	5,500 00		5,500 00	515		
147	168	Yarmouth,	10 66.7	3,200 00		3,200 00	300		
162	169	Lee,	10 63.7	8,466 82		8,466 82	796	30 00	
234	170	Lenox,	10 62.4	4,600 00		4,600 00	433		
172	171	Ashburnham,	10 59.3	3,500 00	133 53	3,633 53	343		
184	172	West Newbury,	10 54.7	3,014 32	118 12	3,132 44	297		
140	173	Dalton,	10 54.2	4,459 25		4,459 25	423		
189	174	Wilmington,	10 47.9	1,750 00		1,750 00	167		
184	175	Lawrence,	10 46.6	72,707 07		72,707 07	6,947		
254	176	Somerset,	10 44	4,421 25	203 82	4,625 07	443		
183	177	Duxbury,	10 43	2,800 00	287 17	3,087 17	296		
153	178	Marblehead,	10 41	14,237 78	544 75	14,782 53	1,420		
211	179	Hudson,	10 40	8,300 00	186 53	8,486 53	816		
194	180	Harwich,	10 39	5,000 00	91 00	5,091 00	490		
176	181	Townsend,	10 38.6	3,500 00		3,500 00	337		
318	182	Egremont,	10 32.5	850 00	48 30	898 30	87		
160	183	Andover,	10 30.5	9,800 00		9,800 00	951		
207	184	North Brookfield,	10 29.6	8,000 00	236 67	8,236 67	800		
167	185	Orange,	10 29.4	6,475 00		6,475 00	629		
177	186	Easthampton,	10 22.2	7,600 00	128 08	7,728 08	756		
69	187	Wayland,	10 19.3	4,500 00	127 75	4,627 75	454		
149	188	Lakeville,	10 17.3	1,500 00	198 97	1,698 97	167		
264	189	Rochester,	10 16.3	1,500 00	146 47	1,646 47	162		
142	190	Bolton,	10 15.6	1,300 00		1,300 00	128		
111	191	Tewksbury,	10 15.6	2,600 00		2,600 00	256		30 00
189	192	Marion,	10 14	1,450 00		1,450 00	143		

Showing the Comparative Amount of Money appropriated by the different Towns in the State — Continued.

For 1885-86.	For 1884-85.	TOWNS.	Sum appropriated by towns for each child between 5 and 15 yrs. of age.	Amount raised by taxes for the support of Schools.	Income of Funds, with Dog Tax, appropriated to Schools.	TOTAL.	No. of Children between 5 and 15 years of age.	Amount contributed for board and fuel.
193	200	Sandisfield,	$10 11	$2,000 00	$42 21	$2,042 21	202	
194	171	Granville,	10 08.8	2,300 00	—	2,300 00	228	$70 00
195	152	Holliston,	10 08.7	5,800 00	—	5,800 00	575	—
196	169	Plympton,	10 08.4	800 00	117 60	917 60	91	—
197	185	Ludlow,	10 05.3	3,500 00	219 65	3,719 65	370	—
198	120	Boylston,	10 00	1,600 00	—	1,600 00	160	149 00
199	101	Revere,	9 99.3	6,555 60	—	6,555 60	656	—
200	227	Walpole,	9 95.6	4,500 00	—	4,500 00	452	—
201	187	Enfield,	9 94.2	1,700 00	—	1,700 00	171	—
202	175	Pepperell,	9 93.2	4,400 00	—	4,400 00	443	—
203	226	Brookfield,	9 91.6	4,450 00	160 84	4,610 84	465	—
204	195	Dennis,	9 90.6	5,000 00	72 10	5,072 10	512	—
205	163	Charlton,	9 90.1	3,000 00	—	3,000 00	303	—
206	222	Grafton,	9 87.8	8,100 00	—	8,100 00	820	—
207	257	Mendon,	9 86.8	1,500 00	98 63	1,598 63	162	—
208	220	Acushnet,	9 86.3	1,700 00	144 40	1,844 40	187	—
209	196	Palmer,	9 82.4	11,700 00	—	11,700 00	1,191	—
210	232	Westford,	9 80.4	4,000 00	—	4,000 00	408	—
211	190	Millbury,	9 78.3	9,000 00	—	9,000 00	920	—
212	210	Berkley,	9 73.5	1,300 00	131 07	1,431 07	147	—
213	223	Salisbury,	9 73.2	7,877 65	258 67	8,136 32	826	—
214	225	Hopkinton,	9 71.4	7,600 00	355 60	7,955 60	819	—
215	197	Ayer,	9 67.2	4,000 00	187 98	4,187 98	433	—
216	314	Hamilton,	9 62.6	1,000 00	87 72	1,087 72	113	—
217	275	Gardner,	9 61.5	12,000 00	—	12,000 00	1,248	—
218	166	West Bridgewater,	9 61.5	3,000 00	—	3,000 00	312	—

		Town					
214	219	Douglas,	9 60.6	3,900 00	—	3,900 00	406
251	220	Halifax,	9 58.9	700 00	—	700 00	73
277	221	Dartmouth,	9 56	5,000 00	448 95	5,448 95	570
198	222	Chicopee,	9 55.6	22,850 00	—	22,850 00	2,391
239	223	Chatham,	9 54.8	3,300 00	60 97	3,360 97	352
261	224	West Brookfield,	9 51	3,300 00	—	3,300 00	347
206	225	Dracut,	9 49.8	3,000 00	134 44	3,134 44	330
236	226	Templeton,	9 48.9	4,700 00	130 18	4,830 18	509
305	227	Norton,	9 46.8	2,717 36	—	2,717 36	287
221	228	Eastham,	9 45.8	800 00	51 24	851 24	90
216	229	Truro,	9 44.6	1,500 00	58 63	1,558 63	165
238	230	Provincetown,	9 38.3	7,600 00	—	7,600 00	810
208	231	Sheffield,	9 36.1	3,700 00	147 55	3,847 55	411
308	232	North Adams,	9 28	24,700 00	403 47	25,103 47	2,705
224	233	Scituate,	9 26.9	4,500 00	190 00	4,690 00	506
245	234	Hubbardston,	9 25.9	2,000 00	—	2,000 00	216
230	235	Wareham,	9 19.7	6,000 00	354 90	6,354 90	691
213	236	Freetown,	9 18.5	2,000 00	186 05	2,186 05	238
199	237	Northfield,	9 17.3	2,200 00	130 00	2,330 00	254
253	238	Wilbraham,	9 08	2,200 00	88 22	2,288 22	252
266	239	Spencer,	9 07.8	16,250 00	—	16,250 00	1,790
231	240	Holden,	9 05.2	4,541 08	256 44	4,797 52	530
248	241	Groveland,	9 03.4	3,677 00	—	3,677 00	407
255	242	Wendell,	9 03.2	700 00	40 60	740 60	82
252	243	Pembroke,	9 02.7	1,750 00	136 67	1,886 67	209
263	244	Winchendon,	8 99.2	6,195 20	—	6,195 20	689
107	245	Worthington,	8 96.9	1,000 00	58 29	1,058 29	118
204	246	Stoughton,	8 92.4	8,701 15	—	8,701 15	975
242	247	South Abington,	8 88.4	5,000 00	427 86	8,427 86	611
274	248	Holyoke,	8 85.7	50,884 07	807 00	51,691 07	5,836
249	249	Erving,	8 84.6	1,200 00	65 00	1,265 00	143
217	250	Phillipston,	8 79.1	800 00	—	800 00	91

Showing the Comparative Amount of Money appropriated by the different Towns in the State — Continued.

For 1885-86.	For 1884-85.	TOWNS.	Sum appropriated by towns for each child between 5 and 15 yrs. of age.	Amount raised by taxes for the support of Schools.	Income of Funds, with Dog Tax, appropriated to Schools.	TOTAL.	No. of Children between 5 and 15 years of age.	Amount contributed for board and fuel.
251	301	Hardwick,	$8 78.9	$1,500 00	—	$4,500 00	512	—
252	203	Burlington,	8 69.4	1,000 00	$86 72	1,086 72	125	—
253	246	Deerfield,	8 66.3	5,000 00	250 00	5,250 00	606	—
254	271	Belchertown,	8 58.3	3,800 00	277 01	4,077 01	475	$13 00
255	265	Franklin,	8 57.2	6,500 00	323 06	6,823 06	796	—
256	240	Hawley,	8 57.1	900 00	—	900 00	105	—
257	256	Topsfield,	8 55.9	1,400 00	132 08	1,532 08	179	—
258	188	Shirley,	8 54.6	2,000 00	102 43	2,102 43	246	—
259	259	Westport,	8 52	4,000 00	277 13	4,217 13	502	—
260	278	Southwick,	8 49.2	1,500 00	88 00	1,588 00	187	—
261	281	Hanson,	8 48.4	1,700 00	140 96	1,840 96	217	—
262	262	Sunderland,	8 46.2	1,100 00	—	1,100 00	130	—
263	237	Ware,	8 46	10,000 00	—	10,000 00	1,182	—
264	235	Westhampton,	8 45.3	1,000 00	39 67	1,039 67	123	—
265	293	Hadley,	8 43.2	2,850 00	—	2,850 00	338	—
266	258	Southampton,	8 39.2	1,450 00	102 43	1,552 43	185	—
267	280	Rowley,	8 39.1	1,757 36	96 98	1,854 34	221	—
268	241	Sturbridge,	8 37.7	3,200 00	—	3,200 00	382	—
269	150	Marlborough,	8 37	20,046 54	—	20,046 54	2,395	—
270	243	Nantucket,	8 36.7	4,727 59	—	4,727 59	565	—
271	201	Athol,	8 31.4	7,000 00	—	7,000 00	842	—
272	287	Adams,	8 29.9	14,423 20	—	14,423 20	1,738	30 00
273	295	West Boylston,	8 28.8	4,600 00	—	4,600 00	555	—
274	267	Rockport,	8 27.1	6,741 00	—	6,741 00	815	—
275	233	Brimfield,	8 16.3	1,600 00	—	1,600 00	196	—
276	205	New Salem,	8 14.8	1,000 00	42 90	1,042 90	128	—

	No.	Town			Rate				
288	277	Williamstown,			8 13.8	5,200 00	—	5,200 00	639	—
309	278	Dana,			8 06.7	800 00	63 22	863 22	107	—
279	279	Conway,			8 04.4	2,500 00	74 00	2,574 62	320	39 00
276	280	Blackstone,			7 96.6	8,000 00	228 62	8,228 62	1,033	—
151	281	Royalston,			7 95.5	1,500 00	106 95	1,606 95	202	—
322	282	Dudley,			7 86.6	4,300 00	136 57	4,436 57	564	—
328	283	Tolland,			7 83.6	500 00	40 66	540 66	69	—
138	284	Windsor,			7 82.9	800 00	61 22	861 22	110	—
299	285	Hinsdale,			7 80.9	8,100 00	—	3,100 00	397	—
212	286	Warwick,			7 77.8	910 00	—	910 00	117	—
315	287	Pelham,			7 76.6	700 00	68 79	768 79	99	—
296	288	Norfolk,			7 76	1,200 00	96 00	1,296 00	167	—
282	289	Chilmark,			7 75.9	450 00	—	450 00	58	—
272	290	Newburyport,			7 74.5	20,000 00	—	20,000 71	2,581	—
325	291	Lynnfield,			7 73.9	800 00	90 71	890 71	115	—
316	292	Middlefield,			7 73.2	800 00	90 00	890 00	115	—
310	293	Southbridge,			7 72.4	10,500 00	—	10,500 00	1,358	—
273	294	Oakham,			7 66.3	950 00	—	950 00	123	—
291	295	Monterey,			7 61.9	800 00	81 28	881 28	115	—
320	296	Leyden,			7 50.9	800 00	—	800 00	105	—
306	297	Williamsburg,			7 48.9	3,000 00	161 18	3,161 18	421	—
270	298	Seekonk,			7 46.4	1,700 00	—	1,700 00	227	—
247	299	Hampden,			7 44.3	1,200 00	76 40	1,276 40	171	—
285	300	Hatfield,			7 42.7	1,950 00	—	1,950 00	262	—
314	301	Agawam,			7 41.9	3,250 00	188 55	3,438 55	463	—
283	302	Blandford,			7 40.4	1,500 00	80 20	1,580 20	213	—
332	303	Berlin,			7 39.6	1,100 00	92 00	1,192 00	161	—
-294	304	Charlemont,			7 35.3	1,000 00	102 00	1,102 00	149	—
268	305	Otis,			7 30.4	1,000 00	—	1,000 00	136	—
303	306	Montague,			7 29	10,386 61	—	10,386 61	1,422	—
51	307	Bernardston,			7 26.6	1,000 00	78 85	1,078 85	148	—
317	308	Rutland,				1,200 00	71 57	1,271 57	175	—

Showing the Comparative Amount of Money appropriated by the different Towns in the State — Concluded.

For 1884-85.	For 1885-86.	TOWNS.	Sum appropriated by towns for each child between 5 and 15 yrs. of age.	Amount raised by taxes for the support of Schools.	Income of Funds, with Dog Tax, appropriated to Schools.	TOTAL.	No. of Children between 5 and 15 years of age.	Amount contributed for board and fuel.
298	309	Chesterfield,	$7 11.9	$900 00	$32 65	$932 65	131	$75 00
286	310	Plainfield,	7 11.4	500 00	40 67	640 67	76	—
289	311	Billerica,	7 02.6	3,000 00	—	3,000 00	427	—
330	312	Colerain,	6 97.6	2,300 00	72 00	2,372 00	340	—
340	313	Richmond,	6 84.9	1,500 00	—	1,600 00	219	—
300	314	Carver,	6 84.6	1,200 00	141 80	1,341 80	196	—
338	315	Becket,	6 82.5	1,000 00	105 72	1,105 72	162	—
269	316	Cheshire,	6 75.7	2,500 00	—	2,500 00	370	—
290	317	Chester,	6 74.	1,400 00	156 90	1,556 90	231	—
284	318	Tyringham,	6 65.4	700 00	58 56	758 56	114	—
250	319	Sutton,	6 65.2	4,500 00	202 83	4,702 83	707	—
311	320	Leverett,	6 63.6	800 00	69 28	869 28	131	—
327	321	New Marlborough,	6 60.7	2,000 00	101 15	2,101 15	318	—
302	322	Washington,	6 46.4	600 00	52 86	652 86	101	—
329	323	Buckland,	6 44.6	2,000 00	75 65	2,075 65	322	—
342	324	Gill,	6 26.1	1,000 00	33 00	1,033 00	165	—
186	325	Cummington,	6 20.2	800 00	—	800 00	129	17 00
325	326	Lanesborough,	6 03.8	1,600 00	—	1,600 00	265	60 00
323	327	Prescott,	6 02.4	500 00	30 10	530 10	88	—
326	328	Russell,	6 02.4	1,000 00	—	1,000 00	166	—
337	329	Savoy,	5 93.9	600 00	88 98	688 98	116	—
343	330	Florida,	5 92.6	800 00	—	800 00	135	—
294	331	Whately,	5 91.1	1,200 00	—	1,200 00	203	—
333	332	Rowe,	5 87.6	600 00	34 60	634 60	108	—
297	333	Alford,	5 82.5	867 00	—	867 00	63	—
321	334	Clarksburg,	5 77.6	700 00	56 66	756 66	131	—

331	335	Webster,	·	5 77	6,350 00	256 44	6,606 44	1,145	—
312	336	Newbury,	·	5 76.3	1,654 18	126 59	1,780 77	309	—
335	337	Heath,	·	5 76.1	600 00	39 50	639 50	111	—
341	338	Goshen,	·	5 66	300 00	—	300 00	53	—
336	339	Shutesbury,	·	5 59.6	500 00	54 00	554 00	99	—
307	340	Mount Washington,	·	5 56.1	130 00	20 15	150 15	27	—
345	341	Holland,	·	5 29.4	200 00	27 64	227 64	43	—
215	342	Huntington,	·	5 28.8	1,000 00	89 38	1,089 38	206	—
334	343	Auburn,	·	5 11.8	1,300 00	—	1,300 00	254	—
313	344	Wales,	·	4 87.6	700 00	41 20	741 20	152	—
292	345	Hancock,	·	4 16 7	500 00	—	500 00	120	—
339	346	Monroe,	·	4 11.5	200 00	14 00	214 00	52	—
347	347	Gay Head,	·	3 12.5	100 00	—	100 00	82	—
346	348	New Ashford,	·	3 00	81 00	—	81 00	27	—

GRADUATED TABLES.—(COUNTY TABLES).—FIRST SERIES.

Table showing the Comparative Amount of Money appropriated by the different Towns in each of the Counties in the State for the Education of each Child in the Town, between the Ages of 5 and 15 years.

BARNSTABLE COUNTY

For 1884-85.	For 1885-86.	TOWNS.	Sum appropriated by towns for each child between 5 and 15 yrs. of age.	Amount raised by taxes for the support of Schools.	Income of Funds, with Dog Tax, appropriated to Schools.	TOTAL.	No. of Children between 5 and 15 years of age.	Amount contributed for board and fuel.
9	1	MASHPEE,	$18 49.7	$500 00	$54 92	$554 92	30	—
1	2	Falmouth,	18 35.2	6,751 00	277 75	7,028 75	383	—
3	3	Bourne,	18 21.2	4,550 00	185 03	4,735 03	260	—
2	4	Barnstable,	17 28.9	11,000 00	341 64	11,341 64	656	—
5	5	Sandwich,	15 46.5	5,800 00	277 73	6,077 73	393	—
4	6	Wellfleet,	14 08.5	4,000 00	—	4,000 00	284	—
7	7	Orleans,	13 68.9	2,200 00	58 63	2,258 63	165	—
6	8	Brewster,	12 79.1	2,200 00	—	2,200 00	172	—
8	9	Yarmouth,	10 66.7	3,200 00	—	3,200 00	300	—
10	10	Harwich,	10 39	5,000 00	91 00	5,091 00	490	—
11	11	Dennis,	9 90.6	5,000 00	72 10	5,072 10	512	—
15	12	Chatham,	9 54.8	3,300 00	60 97	3,360 97	352	—
13	13	Eastham,	9 45.8	800 00	51 24	851 24	90	—
12	14	Truro,	9 44.6	1,500 00	58 63	1,558 63	165	—
14	15	Provincetown,	9 38.3	7,600 00	—	7,600 00	810	—

BERKSHIRE COUNTY.

For 1884-85.	For 1885-86.	TOWNS.	Sum appropriated by towns for each child between 5 and 15 yrs. of age.	Amount raised by taxes for the support of Schools.	Income of Funds, with Dog Tax, appropriated to Schools.	TOTAL.	No. of Children between 5 and 15 years of age.	Amount contributed for board and fuel.
2	1	WEST STOCKBRIDGE,	$13 63.8	$4,241 57	—	$4,241 57	311	—
1	2	Stockbridge,	12 72.3	5,000 00	—	5,000 00	393	—

10	3	Peru,	12 00	600 00	—	600 00	50	—
5	4	Pittsfield,	11 89.8	30,303 57	—	30,303 57	2,547	—
7	5	Great Barrington,	11 77.2	9,852 80	252 80	9,600 00	837	—
6	6	Lee,	10 63.7	8,466 82	—	8,466 82	796	—
11	7	Lenox,	10 62.4	4,600 00	—	4,600 00	433	—
4	8	Dalton,	10 54.2	4,459 25	—	4,459 25	423	—
23	9	Egremont,	10 32.5	898 30	48 30	850 00	87	—
8	10	Sandisfield,	10 11	2,042 21	42 21	2,000 00	202	$70 00
9	11	Sheffield,	9 36.1	3,847 55	147 55	3,700 00	411	—
22	12	North Adams,	9 28	25,103 47	403 47	24,700 00	2,706	—
15	13	Adams,	8 29.9	14,423 20	—	14,423 20	1,738	—
16	14	Williamstown,	8 13.8	5,200 00	—	5,200 00	639	—
3	15	Windsor,	7 82.9	861 22	61 22	800 00	110	—
19	16	Hinsdale,	7 80.9	3,100 00	—	3,100 00	397	—
17	17	Monterey,	7 66.3	881 28	81 28	800 00	115	—
12	18	Otis,	7 35.3	1,000 00	—	1,000 00	136	—
29	19	Richmond,	6 84.9	1,500 00	—	1,500 00	219	—
28	20	Becket,	6 82.5	1,105 72	105 72	1,000 00	162	—
13	21	Cheshire,	6 75.7	2,500 00	—	2,500 00	370	—
14	22	Tyringham,	6 65.4	758 56	58 56	700 00	114	—
27	23	New Marlborough,	6 60.7	2,101 15	101 15	2,000 00	318	—
20	24	Washington,	6 46.4	662 86	52 86	610 00	101	—
25	25	Lanesborough,	6 03.8	1,600 00	—	1,600 00	265	—
30	26	Savoy,	5 93.9	688 98	88 98	600 00	116	—
26	27	Florida,	5 92.6	800 00	—	800 00	135	—
24	28	Alford,	5 82.5	367 00	—	367 00	63	—
31	29	Clarksburg,	5 77.6	756 66	56 66	700 00	131	—
21	30	Mt. Washington,	5 56.1	150 15	20 15	130 00	27	—
18	31	Hancock,	4 16.7	500 00	—	500 00	120	—
32	32	New Ashford,	3 00	81 00	—	81 00	27	—

BRISTOL COUNTY.

For 1884-85.	For 1885-86.	TOWNS.	Sum appropriated by towns for each child between 5 and 15 yrs. of age.	Amount raised by taxes for the support of Schools.	Income of Funds, with Dog Tax, appropriated to Schools.	TOTAL.	No. of Children between 5 and 15 years of age.	Amount contributed for board and fuel.
1	1	NEW BEDFORD,	$15 82.4	$80,501 00	$694 46	$81,195 46	5,131	
2	2	Fairhaven,	12 50	6,000 00	—	6,000 00	480	$100 00
7	3	Mansfield,	12 46.9	5,500 00	397 65	5,897 65	473	—
4	4	Rehoboth,	12 29	3,200 00	302 68	3,502 68	285	—
6	5	Raynham,	12 25.1	3,000 00	246 58	3,246 58	265	—
8	6	Easton,	11 91.7	8,752 00	519 27	9,271 27	778	—
5	7	Taunton,	11 86.2	50,000 00	—	50,000 00	4,215	—
11	8	Dighton,	11 84.2	3,000 00	185 49	3,185 49	269	—
3	9	Attleborough,	11 80.6	25,000 00	867 62	25,867 62	2,191	40 00
10	10	Fall River,	11 58.4	136,007 02	—	136,007 02	11,741	—
9	11	Swansea,	10 87	2,500 00	—	2,500 00	230	5 00
15	12	Somerset,	10 44	4,421 25	203 82	4,625 07	443	—
14	13	Acushnet,	9 86.3	1,700 00	144 40	1,844 40	187	—
12	14	Berkley,	9 73.5	1,300 00	131 07	1,431 07	147	—
18	15	Dartmouth,	9 56	5,000 00	448 95	5,448 95	570	—
19	16	Norton,	9 46.8	2,717 36	—	2,717 36	287	—
13	17	Freetown,	9 18.5	2,000 00	186 05	2,186 05	238	—
16	18	Westport,	8 52	4,000 00	277 13	4,277 13	502	—
17	19	Seekonk,	7 48.9	1,700 00	—	1,700 00	227	—

DUKES COUNTY.

For 1884-85.	For 1885-86.	TOWNS.	Sum appropriated by towns for each child between 5 and 15 yrs. of age.	Amount raised by taxes for the support of Schools.	Income of Funds, with Dog Tax, appropriated to Schools.	TOTAL.	No. of Children between 5 and 15 years of age.	Amount contributed for board and fuel.
4	1	TISBURY,	$13 33	$2,200 00	$106 10	$2,306 10	173	$70 00
2	2	Edgartown,	12 39.3	1,700 00	84 60	1,784 60	144	—

3	3	Gosnold,	11 73.7	200 00	23 00	223 00	19	—
4	1	Cottage City,	11 70.3	1,243 50	67 20	1,310 70	112	—
5	5	Chilmark,	7 75.9	450 00	—	450 00	58	—
6	6	Gay Head,	3 12.5	1c 00	—	100 00	32	—

ESSEX COUNTY.

1	1	Nahant,	$27 07.7	$3,980 35	—	$3,980 35	147	—
2	2	Swampscott,	19 39.7	6,750 00	—	6,750 00	348	—
3	3	Haverhill,	16 46.9	59,288 14	—	59,288 14	3,600	—
4	4	Merrimac,	14 33.1	5,800 00	$175 94	5,975 94	417	—
10	5	Salem,	14 24.8	68,817 79	2,077 94	70,895 73	4,976	—
8	6	Peabody,	13 97.8	24,096 49	687 29	24,783 78	1,773	—
6	7	North Andover,	13 65.6	9,300 00	—	9,300 00	681	—
18	8	Lynn,	12 90.8	95,259 78	—	95,259 78	7,380	—
26	9	Bradford,	12 87	6,400 00	217 80	6,617 80	555	—
14	10	Middleton,	12 35.6	1,200 00	122 11	1,322 11	107	—
11	11	Saugus,	12 24.7	5,893 39	58 50	5,951 89	486	—
12	12	Gloucester,	12 18.9	47,462 70	—	47,462 70	3,894	—
22	13	Manchester,	12 04.8	3,000 00	—	3,000 00	249	—
9	14	Beverly,	11 81.3	18,059 82	581 12	18,640 94	1,578	—
13	15	Danvers,	11 79.5	12,602 00	443 00	13,045 00	1,106	—
15	16	Methuen,	11 79.2	9,000 00	280 02	9,280 02	787	—
5	17	Amesbury,	11 38.4	7,2c0 00	177 00	7,377 00	648	—
24	18	Boxford,	11 15.1	1,500 00	50 00	1,550 00	139	—
12	19	Georgetown,	11 06.1	4,900 00	320 67	5,220 67	472	—
20	20	Essex,	10 90.2	3,000 00	96 19	3,096 19	284	—
25	21	Ipswich,	10 77.5	6,400 00	237 74	6,637 74	616	—
17	22	Wenham,	10 72.5	1,4c0 00	101 51	1,501 51	140	$30 00
16	23	West Newbury,	10 54.7	3,014 32	118 12	3,182 44	297	—
23	24	Lawrence,	10 46.6	72,707 07	—	72,7C7 07	6,947	—

ESSEX COUNTY — Concluded.

For 1884-85.	For 1885-86.	TOWNS.	Sum appropriated by towns for each child between 5 and 15 yrs. of age.	Amount raised by taxes for the support of Schools.	Income of Funds, with Dog Tax, appropriated to Schools.	TOTAL.	No. of Children between 5 and 15 years of age.	Amount contributed for board and fuel.
19	25	Marblehead,	$10 41	$14,237 78	$544 75	$14,782 53	1,420	—
21	26	Andover,	10 30.5	9,800 00	—	9,800 00	951	—
27	27	Salisbury,	9 73.2	7,877 65	258 67	8,136 32	836	—
33	28	Hamilton,	9 62.6	1,000 00	87 72	1,087 72	113	—
28	29	Groveland,	9 03.4	3,677 00	—	3,677 00	407	—
29	30	Topsfield,	8 55.9	1,400 00	132 08	1,582 08	179	—
32	31	Rowley,	8 39.1	1,757 36	96 98	1,854 34	221	—
30	32	Rockport,	8 27.1	6,741 00	—	6,741 00	815	—
31	33	Newburyport,	7 74.9	20,000 00	—	20,000 00	2,581	—
35	34	Lynnfield,	7 74.5	800 00	90 71	890 71	115	—
34	35	Newbury,	5 76.3	1,654 18	126 59	1,780 77	309	—

FRANKLIN COUNTY.

For 1884-85.	For 1885-86.	TOWNS.	Sum appropriated by towns for each child between 5 and 15 yrs. of age.	Amount raised by taxes for the support of Schools.	Income of Funds, with Dog Tax, appropriated to Schools.	TOTAL.	No. of Children between 5 and 15 years of age.	Amount contributed for board and fuel.
2	1	GREENFIELD,	$13 03.1	$11,350 00	$101 00	$11,850 00	871	—
3	2	Shelburne,	12 60.6	3,000 00	72 00	3,101 00	246	—
8	3	Ashfield,	11 14.7	1,600 00	—	1,672 00	150	—
4	4	Orange,	10 29.4	6,475 00	—	6,475 00	629	—
5	5	Northfield,	9 17.3	2,200 00	130 00	2,330 00	254	—
12	6	Wendell,	9 03.2	700 00	40 60	740 60	82	—
11	7	Erving,	8 84.6	1,200 00	65 00	1,265 00	143	—
10	8	Deerfield,	8 66.3	5,000 00	250 00	5,250 00	606	—
9	9	Hawley,	8 57.1	900 00	—	900 00	105	—
13	10	Sunderland,	8 46.2	1,100 00	—	1,100 00	130	—

6	11	New Salem,	8 11.8	1,000 00	42 90	1,042 90	128	$39 00
14	12	Conway,	8 01.4	2,500 00	74 00	2,574 00	320	—
7	13	Warwick,	7 77.8	910 00	—	910 00	117	—
19	14	Leyden,	7 61.9	800 00	—	800 00	105	—
15	15	Charlemont,	7 39.6	1,000 00	102 00	1,102 00	149	—
17	16	Montague,	7 30.4	10,386 61	—	10,386 61	1,422	—
1	17	Bernardston,	7 29	1,000 00	78 85	1,078 85	148	—
21	18	Colerain,	6 97.6	2,300 00	72 00	2,372 00	340	—
18	19	Leverett,	6 63.6	800 00	69 28	869 28	131	—
20	20	Buckland,	6 44.6	2,000 00	75 65	2,075 65	322	—
22	21	Gill,	6 26.1	1,000 00	33 00	1,033 00	165	—
16	22	Whately,	5 91.1	1,200 00	—	1,200 00	203	—
23	23	Rowe,	5 87.6	600 00	34 60	634 60	108	17 00
24	24	Heath,	5 76.1	600 00	39 50	639 50	111	—
25	25	Shutesbury,	5 59.6	500 00	51 00	554 00	99	—
	26	Monroe,	4 11.5	200 00	14 00	214 00	52	—

HAMPDEN COUNTY.

1	1	SPRINGFIELD,	$15 19.9	$96,211 00	$123 10	$96,211 00	6,330	—
3	2	Longmeadow,	14 32.4	3,200 00	—	3,323 10	232	—
2	3	Westfield,	12 82.5	21,200 00	—	21,200 00	1,653	—
9	4	Monson,	10 94.2	6,500 00	339 00	6,839 00	625	—
4	5	West Springfield,	10 88.9	9,000 00	382 24	9,332 24	857	—
19	6	Montgomery,	10 87	500 00	—	500 00	46	—
5	7	Granville,	10 08.8	2,300 00	—	2,300 00	228	—
6	8	Ludlow,	10 05.3	3,560 00	219 65	3,719 65	370	—
7	9	Palmer,	9 82.4	11,700 00	—	11,700 00	1,191	—
10	10	Chicopee,	9 55.6	22,850 00	—	22,850 00	2,391	—
12	11	Wilbraham,	9 08	2,200 00	88 22	2,288 22	252	—
13	12	Holyoke,	8 85.7	50,884 07	807 00	51,691 07	5,886	$149 00

HAMPDEN COUNTY — Concluded.

For 1885-86.	For 1884-85.	TOWNS.	Sum appropriated by towns for each child between 5 and 15 yrs. of age.	Amount raised by taxes for the support of Schools.	Income of Funds, with Dog Tax, appropriated to Schools.	TOTAL.	No. of Children between 5 and 15 years of age.	Amount contributed for board and fuel.
13	14	Southwick,	$8 49.2	$1,500 00	$88 00	$1,588 00	187	—
14	10	Brimfield,	8 16.3	1,600 00	—	1,600 00	196	—
15	20	Tolland,	7 83.6	500 00	40 66	540 66	69	—
16	11	Hampden,	7 46.4	1,200 00	76 40	1,276 40	171	—
17	18	Agawam,	7 42.7	3,250 00	188 55	3,438 55	463	—
18	15	Blandford,	7 41.9	1,500 00	80 20	1,580 20	213	—
19	16	Chester,	6 74	1,400 00	156 90	1,556 90	231	—
20	21	Russell,	6 02.4	1,000 00	—	1,000 00	166	—
21	22	Holland,	5 29.4	200 00	27 64	227 64	48	—
22	17	Wales,	4 87.6	700 00	41 20	741 20	152	—

HAMPSHIRE COUNTY.

For 1885-86.	For 1884-85.	TOWNS.	Sum appropriated by towns for each child between 5 and 15 yrs. of age.	Amount raised by taxes for the support of Schools.	Income of Funds, with Dog Tax, appropriated to Schools.	TOTAL.	No. of Children between 5 and 15 years of age.	Amount contributed for board and fuel.
1	3	Amherst,	$15 49.1	$8,800 00	$494 49	$9,294 49	600	$344 00
2	1	Granby,	13 60.8	1,800 00	77 83	1,877 83	138	—
3	9	Greenwich,	12 34.8	800 00	39 67	839 67	68	—
4	5	Northampton,	12 32.3	27,150 00	466 10	27,616 10	2,241	—
5	2	South Hadley,	11 68.9	8,000 00	205 87	8,205 87	702	—
6	6	Easthampton,	10 22.2	7,600 00	128 08	7,728 08	756	—
7	8	Enfield,	9 94.2	1,700 00	—	1,700 00	171	—
8	4	Worthington,	8 96.9	1,000 00	58 29	1,058 29	118	—
9	14	Belchertown,	8 58.3	3,800 00	277 01	4,077 01	475	13 00
10	12	Ware,	8 46	10,000 00	—	10,000 00	1,182	—

	Town							
11	Westhampton,	.	8 45.3	1,000 00	39 67	1,039 67	123	—
17	Hadley,	.	8 43.2	2,850 00	—	2,850 00	338	—
13	Southampton,	.	8 39.2	1,450 00	102 43	1,552 43	185	—
20	Pelham,	.	7 76.6	700 00	68 79	768 79	99	—
21	Middlefield,	.	7 73.9	800 00	90 00	890 00	115	—
19	Williamsburg,	.	7 50.9	3,000 00	161 18	3,161 18	421	—
15	Hatfield,	.	7 44.3	1,950 00	—	1,950 00	262	—
18	Chesterfield,	.	7 11.9	900 00	32 65	932 65	131	—
16	Plainfield,	.	7 11.4	500 00	40 67	540 67	76	—
7	Cummington,	.	6 20.2	800 00	—	800 00	129	75 00
22	Prescott,	.	6 02.4	500 00	30 10	530 10	88	—
23	Goshen,	.	5 66	300 00	—	300 00	53	60 00
10	Huntington,	.	5 28.8	1,000 00	89 38	1,089 38	206	—

MIDDLESEX COUNTY.

	Town							
1	NEWTON,	.	$28 71.5	$101,850 00	$1,841 45	$103,691 45	3,611	—
6	Winchester,	.	24 19.4	15,000 00	—	15,000 00	620	—
7	Weston,	.	23 63.6	5,200 00	—	5,200 00	220	—
30	Boxborough,	.	22 04.6	970 03	—	970 03	44	—
10	Watertown,	.	21 76.5	24,028 51	—	24,028 51	1,104	—
2	Concord,	.	21 27.7	12,000 00	—	12,000 00	564	—
8	Waltham,	.	19 36	47,490 00	—	47,490 00	2,453	—
5	Lexington,	.	18 93.1	8,500 00	—	8,500 00	449	—
3	Arlington,	.	18 75.8	17,969 77	—	17,969 77	958	—
4	Belmont,	.	18 46.2	6,000 00	—	6,000 00	325	—
16	Littleton,	.	17 16.5	2,400 00	878 58	3,278 58	191	$12 00
11	Groton,	.	16 94.9	5,000 00	—	5,000 00	295	50 00
9	Medford,	.	16 72.7	27,650 17	—	27,650 17	1,653	—
33	Bedford,	.	16 54.7	2,300 00	—	2,300 00	139	—
12	Acton,	.	16 02.2	4,000 00	229 89	4,229 89	264	—

MIDDLESEX COUNTY — Concluded.

For 1884-85.	For 1885-86.	TOWNS.	Sum appropriated by towns for each child between 5 and 15 yrs. of age.	Amount raised by taxes for the support of Schools.	Income of Funds, with Dog Tax, appropriated to Schools.	TOTAL.	No. of Children between 5 and 15 years of age.	Amount contributed for board and fuel.
26	16	Lincoln,	$15 92.4	$2,500 00	—	$2,500 00	157	—
14	17	Cambridge,	15 79.7	173,092 51	—	173,092 51	10,957	$326 75
27	18	Somerville,	15 34.5	86,053 29	—	86,053 29	5,608	—
18	19	Stoneham,	15 17.7	13,750 00	—	13,750 00	906	—
18	20	Reading,	14 54.2	8,100 00	—	8,100 00	557	—
15	21	North Reading,	14 52.1	1,900 00	$133 00	2,033 00	140	24 00
22	22	Everett,	14 16	14,712 00	—	14,712 00	1,039	—
23	23	Melrose,	14 09.7	16,000 00	—	16,000 00	1,135	—
21	24	Malden,	14 03.8	40,808 98	—	40,808 98	2,907	—
17	25	Framingham,	14 03.7	18,500 00	675 12	19,175 12	1,366	—
34	26	Lowell,	13 52.6	148,375 96	—	148,375 96	10,970	—
19	27	Natick,	13 27.2	21,500 00	—	21,500 00	1,620	—
25	28	Ashby,	13 24.4	1,800 00	107 09	1,907 09	144	—
63	29	Ashland,	12 88.9	5,890 00	—	5,890 00	450	—
31	30	Wakefield,	12 85.7	16,200 00	—	16,200 00	1,260	—
29	31	Tyngsborough,	12 60	1,150 00	72 17	1,222 17	97	—
36	32	Dunstable,	12 30.8	800 00	—	800 00	65	—
32	33	Chelmsford,	12 11.9	5,000 00	332 32	5,332 32	440	20 00
51	34	Stow,	11 84.2	2,019 47	123 97	2,143 44	181	—
20	35	Woburn,	11 11.3	28,672 66	—	28,672 66	2,580	—
37	36	Sherborn,	10 97.5	2,125 00	80 90	2,205 90	201	—
37	37	Sudbury,	10 93.9	2,000 00	122 22	2,122 22	194	—
28	38	Carlisle,	10 92.5	800 00	74 00	874 00	80	—
42	39	Maynard,	10 68	5,500 00	—	5,500 00	515	—
38	40	Wilmington,	10 47.9	1,750 00	—	1,750 00	167	—
49	41	Hudson,	10 40	8,300 00	186 53	8,486 53	816	—

44	42	Townsend,	10 38.6	3,500 00	—	3,500 00	337	—	
24	43	Wayland,	10 19.3	4,500 00	127 75	4,627 75	454	$30 00	
35	44	Tewksbury,	10 15.6	2,600 00	—	2,600 00	256	—	
41	45	Holliston,	10 08.7	5,800 00	—	5,800 00	575	—	
43	46	Pepperell,	9 93.2	4,400 00	—	4,400 00	443	—	
52	47	Westford,	9 80.4	4,000 00	—	4,000 00	408	—	
50	48	Hopkinton,	9 71.4	7,600 00	355 60	7,955 60	819	—	
46	49	Ayer,	9 67.2	4,000 00	187 98	4,187 98	433	—	
48	50	Dracut,	9 49.8	3,000 00	134 44	3,134 44	330	—	
47	51	Burlington,	8 69.4	1,000 00	86 72	1,086 72	125	—	
45	52	Shirley,	8 54.6	2,000 00	102 43	2,102 43	246	—	
40	53	Marlborough,	8 37	20,046 54	—	20,046 54	2,395	—	
54	54	Billerica,	7 02.6	3,000 00	—	3,000 00	427	—	

NANTUCKET COUNTY.

	NANTUCKET,	$8 36.7	$4,727 59	—	$4,727 59	565	—

NORFOLK COUNTY.

1	BROOKLINE,	$26 37.8	$42,600 08	—	$42,600 08	1,615	—	
2	Wellesley,	25 59.4	9,700 00	—	9,700 00	379	—	
3	Milton,	24 09.2	15,105 92	—	15,105 92	627	—	
4	Dedham,	21 29.4	24,168 59	—	24,168 59	1,135	—	
5	Cohasset,	18 53	6,200 00	$230 00	6,430 00	347	—	
6	Needham,	18 11.7	7,900 00	307 17	8,207 17	453	—	
7	Dover,	17 16.2	1,400 00	75 92	1,475 92	86	—	
8	Norwood,	16 56.7	8,300 00	—	8,300 00	501	—	

NORFOLK COUNTY — Concluded.

For 1885-86.	For 1884-85.	TOWNS.		Sum appropriated by towns for each child between 5 and 15 yrs. of age.	Amount raised by taxes for the support of Schools.	Income of Funds, with Dog Tax, appropriated to Schools.	TOTAL.	No. of Children between 5 and 15 years of age.	Amount contributed for board and fuel.
9	10	Hyde Park,		$15 50.4	$24,900 00	—	$24,900 00	1,606	—
10	7	Holbrook,		15 12.1	6,500 00	$228 94	6,728 94	445	—
11	11	Randolph,		15 11.3	9,500 00	474 53	9,974 53	660	—
12	13	Wrentham,		14 62.8	6,000 00	246 00	6,246 00	427	—
13	19	Quincy,		14 35.4	34,679 47	—	34,679 47	2,416	—
14	—	Millis,		14 30.8	1,545 28	—	1,545 28	108	$52 00
15	14	Canton,		14 24.6	12,195 00	—	12,195 00	856	—
16	17	Medway,		14 23.9	5,500 00	280 86	5,780 86	406	—
17	12	Foxborough,		13 55.6	5,000 00	300 50	5,300 50	391	110 00
18	15	Weymouth,		12 71.6	24,654 21	688 39	25,342 60	1,993	—
19	16	Braintree,		12 32.5	8,200 00	489 00	8,689 00	705	—
20	18	Medfield,		11 82.3	2,400 00	—	2,400 00	203	—
21	20	Sharon,		11 24.7	2,400 00	153 00	2,553 00	227	—
22	21	Bellingham,		10 68.2	1,800 00	293 71	2,093 71	196	—
23	23	Walpole,		9 95.6	4,500 00	—	4,500 00	452	—
24	22	Stoughton,		8 92.4	8,701 15	—	8,701 15	975	—
25	24	Franklin,		8 57.2	6,500 00	323 06	6,823 06	796	—
26	25	Norfolk,		7 76	1,200 00	96 00	1,296 00	167	—

PLYMOUTH COUNTY.

For 1885-86.	For 1884-85.	TOWNS.		Sum appropriated by towns for each child between 5 and 15 yrs. of age.	Amount raised by taxes for the support of Schools.	Income of Funds, with Dog Tax, appropriated to Schools.	TOTAL.	No. of Children between 5 and 15 years of age.	Amount contributed for board and fuel.
1	6	Hull,		$19 71.8	$1,400 00	—	$1,400 00	71	—
2	2	Hingham,		17 98.6	11,978 39	—	11,978 39	666	—
3	4	Bridgewater,		17 09.8	8,500 00	$425 25	8,925 25	522	—

1	4	Plymouth,	16 07.7	19,839 50	—	19,839 50	1,234	—
5	5	Abington,	13 99	8,800 00	—	8,800 00	629	—
3	6	Kingston,	13 95.5	2,950 00	175 88	3,125 88	224	—
14	7	Mattapoisett,	13 55.1	2,100 00	379 84	2,479 84	183	—
10	8	Marshfield,	12 38.7	2,500 00	187 95	2,687 95	217	—
10	9	East Bridgewater,	12 13.3	5,600 00	296 62	5,896 62	486	—
7	10	Rockland,	11 93.2	10,500 00	—	10,500 00	880	—
9	11	South Scituate,	11 85	2,900 00	169 05	3,069 05	259	—
13	12	Middleborough,	11 57.4	10,000 00	—	10,000 00	864	—
8	13	Brockton,	10 70.2	36,602 14	607 10	37,209 24	3,477	—
11	14	Hanover,	10 70.2	3,300 00	145 91	3,445 91	322	—
17	15	Duxbury,	10 43	2,800 00	287 17	3,087 17	296	—
18	16	Lakeville,	10 17.3	1,500 00	198 97	1,698 97	167	—
12	17	Rochester,	10 16.3	1,500 00	146 47	1,646 47	162	—
25	18	Marion,	10 14	1,450 00	—	1,450 00	143	—
19	19	Plympton,	10 08.4	800 00	117 60	917 60	91	—
16	20	West Bridgewater,	9 61.5	3,000 00	—	3,000 00	312	—
23	21	Halifax,	9 58.9	700 00	—	700 00	73	—
20	22	Scituate,	9 26.9	4,500 00	190 00	4,690 00	506	—
21	23	Wareham,	9 19.7	6,000 00	354 90	6,354 90	691	—
24	24	Pembroke,	9 02.7	1,750 00	136 67	1,886 67	209	—
22	25	South Abington,	8 88.4	5,000 00	427 86	5,427 86	611	—
26	26	Hanson,	8 48.4	1,700 00	140 96	1,840 96	217	—
27	27	Carver,	6 84.6	1,200 00	141 80	1,341 80	196	—

SUFFOLK COUNTY.

1	1	BOSTON,	$20 16.4	$1,337,640 36	$47,673 30	$1,385,313 66	68,702	—
3		Chelsea,	12 41.8	58,476 20	—	58,476 20	4,709	—
2	3	Winthrop,	11 97.9	2,200 00	207 87	2,407 87	201	—
4	4	Revere,	9 99.3	6,555 60	—	6,555 60	656	—

WORCESTER COUNTY.

For 1885-86.	For 1884-85.	TOWNS.	Sum appropriated by towns for each child between 5 and 15 yrs. of age.	Amount raised by taxes for the support of Schools.	Income of Funds, with Dog Tax, appropriated to Schools.	TOTAL.	No. of Children between 5 and 15 years of age.	Amount contributed for board and fuel.
1	6	HARVARD,	$17 12.3	$2,500 00		$2,500 00	146	
2	8	Barre,	16 96.0	4,800 00	$170 96	4,970 96	298	—
3	4	New Braintree,	16 75.6	1,559 11	66 26	1,625 37	97	—
4	7	Oxford,	16 07.7	5,000 00	—	5,000 00	311	—
5	12	Shrewsbury,	15 38.5	4,000 00	—	4,000 00	260	—
6	2	Sterling,	14 91.2	3,400 00	—	3,400 00	228	—
7	1	Lancaster,	14 05.7	4,695 00		4,695 00	334	—
8	9	Northborough,	14 05.6	3,500 00		3,500 00	249	—
9	5	Upton,	13 97.5	4,142 31	217 77	4,360 08	312	—
10	3	Southborough,	13 67.3	4,300 00	116 33	4,416 33	323	$225 00
11	11	Leominster,	13 60.5	12,000 00		12,000 00	882	—
12	15	Fitchburg,	13 43.6	38,761 46	54 00	38,815 46	2,889	—
13	10	Worcester,	18 27.4	176,130 88		176,130 88	13,269	—
14	14	Princeton,	12 80.2	2,000 00	35 48	2,035 48	159	—
15	13	Lunenburg,	12 78.3	1,700 00	128 00	1,828 00	143	—
16	16	Westborough,	12 42.6	10,500 00		10,500 00	845	—
17	26	Westminster,	12 22.9	3,350 75		3,350 75	274	—
18	19	Petersham,	12 04.1	1,600 00	182 08	1,782 08	148	—
19	22	Paxton,	11 57.9	1,100 00		1,100 00	95	—
20	20	Uxbridge,	11 47.9	6,715 19		6,715 19	585	—
21	18	Northbridge,	11 44.3	8,800 00		8,800 00	769	—
22	23	Milford,	10 95.5	18,400 00	299 44	18,699 44	1,707	—
23	31	Clinton,	10 87.5	19,292 62		19,292 62	1,774	—
24	28	Warren,	10 77.1	8,100 00		8,100 00	752	—
25	25	Leicester,	10 76.9	6,000 00	278 19	6,278 19	683	—
26	27	Ashburnham,	10 59.3	8,500 00	183 53	3,633 53	343	—

No.	No.	Town						
33	27	North Brookfield,	10 29.6	8,000 00	236 67	8,236 67	800	
29	28	Bolton,	10 15.6	1,300 00	—	1,300 00	128	
17	29	Boylston,	10 00	1,600 00		1,600 00	160	
36	30	Brookfield,	9 91.6	4,450 00	160 84	4,610 84	465	
24	31	Charlton,	9 90 1	3,000 00	—	3,000 00	303	
35	32	Grafton,	9 87.8	8,100 00		8,100 00	820	
43	33	Mendon,	9 86.8	1,500 00	98 63	1,598 63	162	
30	34	Millbury,	9 78.3	9,000 00	—	9,000 00	920	
48	35	Gardner,	9 61.5	12,000 00		12,000 00	1,248	
40	36	Douglas,	9 60.6	3,900 00		3,900 00	406	42 00
44	37	West Brookfield,	9 51	3,300 00		3,300 00	347	
38	38	Templeton,	9 48.9	4,700 00	130 18	4,830 18	509	
41	39	Hubbardston,	9 25.9	2,000 00	—	2,000 00	216	
46	40	Spencer,	9 07 8	16,250 00		16,250 00	1,790	
37	41	Holden,	9 05.2	4,541 08	256 44	4,797 52	530	
45	42	Winchendon,	8 99.2	6,195 20	—	6,195 20	689	30 00
34	43	Phillipston,	8 79.1	800 00		800 00	91	
51	44	Hardwick,	8 78.9	4,500 00		4,500 00	512	
39	45	Sturbridge,	8 37.7	3,200 00		3,200 00	382	
32	46	Athol,	8 31.4	7,000 00		7,000 00	842	
50	47	West Boylston,	8 28.8	4,600 00	—	4,600 00	555	
52	48	Dana,	8 06.7	800 00	63 22	863 22	107	
49	49	Blackstone,	7 96.6	8,000 00	228 62	8,228 62	1,033	
21	50	Royalston,	7 95.5	1,500 00	105 95	1,605 95	202	
55	51	Dudley,	7 86.6	4,300 00	186 57	4,436 57	564	
53	52	Southbridge,	7 73.2	10,500 00	—	10,500 00	1,358	
47	53	Oakham,	7 72.4	950 00		950 00	123	
57	54	Berlin,	7 40.4	1,100 00	92 00	1,192 00	161	
54	55	Rutland,	7 26.6	1,200 00	71 57	1,271 57	175	
42	56	Sutton,	6 65.2	4,500 00	202 83	4,702 83	707	
56	57	Webster,	5.77	6,350 00	256 44	6,606 44	1,145	
58	58	Auburn,	5 11 8	1,300 00	—	1,300 00	254	

GRADUATED TABLES — FIRST SERIES.

Showing the Comparative Amount of Money appropriated by the different Counties in the State for the Education of each Child between the Ages of 5 and 15 Years in the County.

For 1884-85.	For 1885-86.	COUNTIES.	Sum appropriated by towns for each child between 5 and 15 yrs. of age.	Amount raised by taxes for the support of Schools.	Income of Funds, with Dog Tax, appropriated to Schools.	TOTAL.	No. of Children between 5 and 15 years of age.	Amount contributed for board and fuel.
1	1	Suffolk,	$19 56.1	$1,404,872 16	$47,881 17	$1,452,753 33	74,268	—
2	2	Norfolk,	15 72.4	281,549 70	4,187 08	285,736 78	18,172	$162 00
3	3	Middlesex,	15 13	973,014 89	5,852 16	978,767 05	64,690	462 75
4	4	Barnstable,	12 82.7	63,401 00	1,529 64	64,930 64	5,062	—
7	7	Bristol,	12 24.4	346,298 63	4,605 17	350,903 80	28,669	145 00
6	6	Essex,	12 14.1	545,976 82	7,082 45	553,059 27	45,554	30 00
5	5	Plymouth,	11 92	158,870 03	4,530 00	163,400 03	13,708	—
10	10	Dukes,	11 47.7	5,893 50	280 90	6,174 40	538	70 00
9	9	Worcester,	11 21.5	506,283 60	3,723 00	510,006 60	45,474	297 00
8	8	Hampden,	11 20.9	212,895 07	2,608 76	245,503 83	21,902	149 00
11	11	Hampshire,	10 23.4	86,400 00	2,402 21	88,802 21	8,677	492 00
14	14	Berkshire,	9 54.9	136,922 41	1,520 91	138,443 32	14,498	70 00
13	13	Franklin,	8 64.2	60,321 61	1,348 38	61,669 99	7,136	56 00
12	12	Nantucket,	8 37.1	4,729 59	—	4,729 59	565	—

AGGREGATE FOR THE STATE.

		THE STATE,	$14 05.8	$4,817,429 01	$87,551 83	$4,904,880 84	348,903	$1,933 75

GRADUATED TABLES — First Series.

Showing the Comparative Amount of Money, including Voluntary Contributions, appropriated by the different Counties in the State, for the Education of each Child between the Ages of 5 and 15 Years in the County.

For 1884-85.	For 1885-86.	COUNTIES.	Totals.
1	1	Suffolk, ...	$19 56.1
2	2	Norfolk, ...	15 73.3
3	3	Middlesex, ...	15 13.9
4	4	Barnstable, ...	12 82.7
7	5	Bristol, ...	12 28.2
6	6	Essex, ...	12 14.1
5	7	Plymouth, ...	11 92
10	8	Dukes, ...	11 60.7
9	9	Worcester, ...	11 22.1
8	10	Hampden, ...	11 21.6
11	11	Hampshire, ...	10 29.1
14	12	Berkshire, ...	9 55.4
13	13	Franklin, ...	8 65
12	14	Nantucket, ...	8 37.1
		State, ...	$14 06.4

GRADUATED TABLES — Second Series.

The next Table exhibits the appropriation of the cities and towns, as compared with their respective valuation in 1885.

The first column shows the rank of the cities and towns in a similar Table for 1884–85, according to their valuation in 1884.

The second column indicates, in numerical order, the precedence of the cities and towns in respect to the liberality of their appropriations for 1885–86, according to their valuation in 1885.

The third consists of the names of the cities and towns, as numerically arranged.

The fourth shows the percentage of taxable property appropriated to the support of the public schools. The result is equivalent in value to mills and hundredths of mills. The decimals are carried to three figures, in order to indicate more perfectly the distinction between the different towns. The first figure (mills) expresses the principal value, and is separated from the last two figures by a dash.

The appropriations for schools are not given in the following Table, as they may be found by referring to the previous Tables; also in the Abstract of School Returns, commencing on page ii. These appropriations include the sum raised by taxes, the income of the surplus revenue, and of such other funds as the towns may appropriate at their option, either to support common schools, or to pay ordinary municipal expenses. The income of other local funds, and the voluntary contributions, are not included in the estimate. The appropriations are reckoned the same as in the first series of Tables, and for the same reasons.

The amount of taxable property, in each city and town, according to the last State valuation, is also omitted, as it is already given in the foregoing Abstract of School Returns.

If the rank assigned to towns in the next Tables is compared with the rank of the same town in the former series, it will be seen that they hold, in many instances, a very different place in the scale.

GRADUATED TABLES — Second Series.

[FOR THE STATE.]

A Graduated Table in which all the Towns in the State are numerically arranged according to the Percentage of their Taxable Property appropriated to the Support of Public Schools for the Year 1885–86.

For 1884-85, by the State Valuation of 1884	For 1885-86, by the State Valuation of 1885	TOWNS.	Percentage of Valuation appropriated to Public Schools—equivalent to mills and hundredths of mills.	For 1884-85, by the State Valuation of 1884	For 1885-86, by the State Valuation of 1885	TOWNS.	Percentage of Valuation appropriated to Public Schools—equivalent to mills and hundredths of mills.
1	1	GRANVILLE, .	$.006–59	43	34	Ludlow,	$.004–71
7	2	Sandwich,	6–51	40	35	Wellfleet,	4–69
2	3	Holbrook,	6–50	24	36	Wrentham,	4–69
4	4	W. Stockb'ge,	6–08	39	37	Dedham,	4–62
5	5	Truro, .	5–98	29	38	Abington,	4–61
3	6	Hawley,	5–95	138	39	Medway,	4–59
11	7	Chatham,	5–40	37	40	Palmer, .	4–58
6	8	S. Hadley,	5–24	53	41	Adams, .	4–57
14	9	Sandisfield, .	5–21	36	42	Blandford,	4–57
19	10	Harwich,	5–15	98	43	Pelham,	4–56
21	11	Mansfield,	5–15	65	44	Rockland,	4–53
20	12	Merrimac,	5–12	66	45	Bradford,	4–51
16	13	Orleans,	5–09	64	46	N. Brookfield,	4–49
111	14	Bourne,	5–04	38	47	Belchertown,	4–47
85	15	N. Adams,	5–03	22	48	Weymouth,	4–47
12	16	Upton, .	5–03	86	49	Westminster,	4–44
128	17	Gay Head,	5–02	32	50	Dennis, .	4–43
18	18	Florida, .	4–99	34	51	Stoneham,	4–42
79	19	Hudson,	4–99	44	52	Templeton,	4–42
15	20	Peru, .	4–98	31	53	Deerfield,	4–41
48	21	Mashpee,	4–97	103	54	Somerset,	4–40
59	22	Georgetown, .	4–96	73	55	Dighton,	4–39
8	23	Brewster,	4–91	33	56	Plymouth,	4–39
80	24	Monson,	4–91	84	57	Waltham,	4–37
30	25	Randolph,	4–91	45	58	Granby,	4–36
25	26	Monroe,	4–86	27	59	Natick, .	4–36
10	27	Marlborough,	4–81	35	60	Wakefield,	4–35
26	28	Hyde Park, .	4–79	42	61	Lee, .	4–33
28	29	Rehoboth,	4–77	174	62	Littleton,	4–32
50	30	Wareham,	4–75	71	63	Groveland,	4–30
23	31	Otis, .	4–74	100	64	Hinsdale,	4–30
70	32	Holden, .	4–73	67	65	N. Andover, .	4–29
47	33	Dudley, .	4–72	49	66	Northbridge, .	4–28

For 1884-85, by the State Valuation of 1881.	For 1885-86, by the State Valuation of 1885.	TOWNS.	Percentage of Valuation appropriated to Public Schools—equivalent to mills and hundredths of mills.	For 1884-85, by the State Valuation of 1881.	For 1885-86, by the State Valuation of 1885.	TOWNS.	Percentage of Valuation appropriated to Public Schools—equivalent to mills and hundredths of mills.
242	67	Ashland,	$.004-26	305	117	Boxborough,	$.003-76
41	68	Needham,	4-26	88	118	Provincetown,	3-76
52	69	Sheffield,	4-26	160	119	Clinton,	3-75
54	70	Bridgewater,	4-25	–	120	Millis,	3-75
93	71	Millbury,	4-25	106	121	Shelburne,	3-74
17	72	Attleborough,	4-23	87	122	Wayland,	3-74
69	73	Fairhaven,	4-23	91	123	Northfield,	3-73
109	74	Colerain,	4-18	104	124	Ashfield,	3-72
13	75	Amesbury,	4-17	148	125	Peabody,	3-72
89	76	Barnstable,	4-17	147	126	Shutesbury,	3-72
74	77	W. Boylston,	4-17	284	127	Montgomery,	3-71
78	78	Haverhill,	4-14	256	128	Savoy,	3-71
63	79	Spencer,	4-11	293	129	Watertown,	3-71
68	80	Buckland,	4-09	141	130	Sutton,	3-70
76	81	Quincy,	4-09	155	131	Hardwick,	3-69
96	82	Westboro'	4-09	123	132	Middleboro',	3-68
60	83	Ashby	4-08	158	133	Williamsburg,	3-67
90	84	Chicopee,	4-08	142	134	Tyngsboro',	3-66
77	85	Windsor,	4-08	132	135	Danvers,	3-65
120	86	W.Brookfield,	4-06	168	136	Warren,	3-65
75	87	Leyden,	4-04	62	137	Woburn,	3-65
46	88	Saugus,	4-04	131	138	Bellingham,	3-64
92	89	E. Bridgew'r,	4-03	119	139	Leicester,	3-64
105	90	Eastham,	4-03	127	140	Canton,	3-63
139	91	Shrewsbury,	4-03	137	141	Gardner,	3-62
57	92	Norwood,	4-02	182	142	Hopkinton,	3-62
83	93	N. Reading,	4-01	121	143	Grafton,	3-61
94	94	Clarksburg,	3-96	122	144	Greenfield,	3-61
82	95	Westhampton,	3-93	154	145	Longmeadow,	3-61
101	96	Concord,	3-92	133	146	Winchester,	3-61
107	97	Heath,	3-91	146	147	Milford,	3-59
143	98	Paxton,	3-91	162	148	Montague,	3-59
150	99	Westford,	3-90	153	149	Swansea,	3-59
99	100	Sterling,	3-89	118	150	Foxborough,	3-58
102	101	Monterey,	3-88	145	151	Hingham,	3-58
55	102	Gloucester,	3-86	210	152	Newton,	3-58
136	103	Erving,	3-85	126	153	Ayer,	3-57
129	104	Oxford,	3-84	114	154	Cheshire,	3-56
130	105	Wendell,	3-84	241	155	Norton,	3-56
61	106	Stoughton,	3-83	135	156	Blackstone,	3-55
117	107	Douglas,	3-81	125	157	Pittsfield,	3-53
115	108	Essex,	3-81	169	158	S. Scituate,	3-52
134	109	Plainfield,	3-80	179	159	Barre,	3-51
72	110	Arlington,	3-79	187	160	Rochester,	3-51
97	111	Orange,	3-79	149	161	Townsend,	3-51
178	112	Ashburnham,	3-77	116	162	Charlemont,	3-50
51	113	Brookfield,	3-77	124	163	Berkley,	3-49
56	114	Lakeville,	3-77	197	164	Ware,	3-49
157	115	N'w Braintree,	3-77	170	165	Conway,	3-48
108	116	Raynham,	3-77	180	166	Holliston,	3-48

For 1884-85, by the State Valuation of 1884.	For 1885-86, by the State Valuation of 1885.	TOWNS.	Percentage of Valuation appropriated to Public Schools—equivalent to mills and hundredths of mills.	For 1884-85, by the State Valuation of 1884.	For 1885-86, by the State Valuation of 1885.	TOWNS.	Percentage of Valuation appropriated to Public Schools—equivalent to mills and hundredths of mills.
161	167	Marblehead, .	$.003-48	233	217	Winchendon,	$ 003-17
165	168	Franklin, .	3-47	95	218	Worthington,	3-17
81	169	New Salem, .	3-47	198	219	Leominster, .	3-16
151	170	Rowe, .	3-47	219	220	Charlton, .	3-14
177	171	Salisbury, .	3-47	214	221	Cambridge, .	3-13
215	172	G. Barrington,	3-46	221	222	Petersham, .	3-12
206	173	Uxbridge, .	3-46	261	223	Fall River, .	3-10
184	174	Somerville, .	3-45	274	224	Tolland, .	3-10
204	175	Chelmsford, .	4-44	239	225	Becket, .	3-09
192	176	Hanson, .	3-43	244	226	Enfield, .	3-09
166	177	Reading, .	3-43	211	227	W. Springfi'd,	3-08
225	178	Southbridge, .	3-42	159	228	Chester, .	3-07
202	179	Medford, .	3-40	183	229	Hampden, .	3-07
172	180	Methuen, .	3-40	200	230	Phillipston, .	3-06
140	181	Rowley, .	3-40	235	231	Shirley, .	3-06
209	182	Fitchburg, .	3-38	173	232	Wilmington, .	3-06
171	183	Lynn, .	3-35	224	233	Braintree, .	3-05
156	184	Melrose, .	3-35	223	234	Williamstown.	3-05
227	185	Middlefield, .	3-35	249	235	Dana, .	3-04
230	186	Tisbury, .	3-34	250	236	Greenwich, .	3-04
186	187	Worcester, .	3-34	259	237	Pembroke, .	3-04
255	188	Amherst, .	3-33	58	238	Warwick, .	3-04
163	189	Westfield, .	3-33	251	239	Taunton, .	3-03
175	190	Acton, .	3-32	185	240	Webster, .	3-03
190	191	N. Marlboro',	3-32	216	241	Leverett, .	3-01
181	192	Scituate, .	3-32	248	242	Pepperell .	3-01
188	193	Brimfield, .	3-31	299	243	Bedford, .	3-00
176	194	Rockport, .	3-31	253	244	Lenox, .	2-99
152	195	Sturbridge, .	3-30	246	245	Whately, .	2-99
199	196	Chesterfield, .	3-28	195	246	Lexington, .	2-95
220	197	Northampton,	3-27	238	247	Wenham. .	2-95
144	198	Plympton, .	3-26	272	248	Richmond, .	2-94
222	199	Tyringham, .	3-26	245	249	Prescott, .	2-93
208	200	W. Bridgew'r,	3-26	248	250	Acushnet, .	2-92
194	201	Wilbraham, .	3-25	252	251	Brockton, .	2-89
203	202	Northboro', .	3-24	264	252	Lowell, .	2-89
164	203	W. Newbury,	3-24	269	253	Everett, .	2-87
189	204	Malden, .	3-23	229	254	Lanesboro', .	2-87
196	205	Southboro', .	3-22	287	255	Dartmouth, .	2-86
201	206	Framingham,	3-21	281	256	Walpole, .	2-86
205	207	Ipswich, .	3-21	258	257	Mendon, .	2-85
232	208	Norfolk, .	3-21	257	258	Halifax, .	2-84
226	209	Southampton,	3-21	247	259	Southwick, .	2-84
267	210	Washington, .	3-21	262	260	Maynard, .	2-83
112	211	Boylston, .	3-20	260	261	Salem, .	2-83
193	212	Easthampton,	3-20	280	262	Agawam, .	2-81
234	213	Holyoke, .	3-20	254	263	Duxbury, .	2-80
213	214	Westport, .	3-18	263	264	Hubbardston,	2-80
217	215	Chelsea, .	3-17	231	265	Dalton, .	2-76
212	216	Hanover, .	3-17	191	266	Athol, .	2-74

cxiv BOARD OF EDUCATION.

For 1884-85, by the State Valuation of 1884.	For 1885-86, by the State Valuation of 1885	TOWNS.	Percentage of Valuation appropriated to Public Schools—equivalent to mills and hundredths of mills.	For 1884-85, by the State Valuation of 1884.	For 1885-86, by the State Valuation of 1885.	TOWNS.	Percentage of Valuation appropriated to Public Schools—equivalent to mills and hundredths of mills.
290	267	Harvard,	$.002-74	308	308	Medfield,	$.002-16
197	268	Weston,	2-74	322	309	Egremont,	2-15
9	269	Bernardston,	2-72	329	310	Russell,	2-14
275	270	Easton,	2-72	315	311	Topsfield,	2-14
277	271	Rutland,	2-72	298	312	Wellesley,	2-13
228	272	Oakham,	2-70	307	313	Belmont,	2-12
265	273	Sherborn,	2-69	316	314	Chilmark,	2-11
218	274	Bolton,	2-68	318	315	Cohasset,	2-11
270	275	Lawrence,	2-68	300	316	S. Abington,	2-10
266	276	Springfield,	2-68	304	317	Newbury,	2-08
237	277	Auburn,	2-67	312	318	Stockbridge,	2-06
271	278	Lunenburg,	2-67	320	319	Sudbury,	2-03
240	279	Newburyport,	2-65	321	320	Boston,	2-02
276	280	Freetown,	2-62	302	321	Lancaster,	2-01
282	281	Andover,	2-61	291	322	Tewksbury,	2-00
279	282	Marshfield,	2-61	324	323	Dover,	1-99
268	283	Dracut,	2-60	309	324	Kingston,	1-96
236	284	Sunderland,	2-60	326	325	Falmouth,	1-95
288	285	Dunstable,	2-59	323	326	Holland,	1-95
289	286	New Bedford,	2-59	327	327	Swampscott,	1-93
294	287	Hadley,	2-55	330	328	Billerica,	1-91
167	288	Wales,	2-55	283	329	Revere	1-91
110	289	Cummington,	2-50	333	330	Groton,	1-82
295	290	Middleton,	2-49	325	331	Marion,	1-80
303	291	Berlin,	2-46	334	332	Nantucket,	1-77
306	292	Edgartown,	2-43	328	333	Beverly,	1-75
207	293	Royalston,	2-43	339	334	Hamilton,	1-74
319	294	Princeton,	2-41	342	335	Mattapoisett,	1-72
313	295	Boxford,	2-40	338	336	Lynnfield,	1-62
331	296	Gill,	2-37	335	337	Alford,	1-59
317	297	Lincoln,	2-34	336	338	Brookline,	1-42
273	298	Seekonk,	2-33	286	339	Mt. Wash'ton,	1-40
301	299	Sharon,	2-32	314	340	Hancock,	1-35
278	300	Carver,	2-31	341	341	Milton	1-22
113	301	Huntington,	2-31	340	342	Gosnold,	1-19
292	302	Burlington,	2-27	343	343	Winthrop,	1-07
285	303	Hatfield,	2-24	337	344	N'w Ashford,	0-97
332	304	Stow,	2-24	344	345	Cottage City,	0-96
296	305	Yarmouth,	2-21	345	346	Nahant,	0-82
310	306	Goshen,	2-20	347	347	Hull,	0-65
311	307	Carlisle,	2-16	346	348	Manchester,	0-64

GRADUATED TABLES — SECOND SERIES.

[COUNTY TABLES.]

*In which all the Towns in the respective Counties in·the State are
numerically arranged according to the Percentage of their Taxable
Property appropriated for the Support of Public Schools for the
Year 1885–86.*

BARNSTABLE COUNTY.

For 1884–85, by the State Valuation of 1884.	For 1885–86, by the State Valuation of 1885.	TOWNS.	Percentage of Valuation appropriated to Public Schools—equivalent to mills and hundredths of mills.	For 1884–85, by the State Valuation of 1884.	For 1885–86, by the State Valuation of 1885.	TOWNS.	Percentage of Valuation appropriated to Public Schools—equivalent to mills and hundredths of mills.
2	1	SANDWICH, .	$.006–51	8	9	Wellfleet, .	$.004–69
1	2	Truro, .	5–98	7	10	Dennis, .	4–43
4	3	Chatham,	5–40	11	11	Barnstable, .	4–17
6	4	Harwich,	5–15	12	12	Eastham,	4–03
5	5	Orleans,	5–09	10	13	Provincetown,	3–76
13	6	Bourne,.	5–04	14	14	Yarmouth, .	2–21
9	7	Mashpee,	4–97	15	15	Falmouth, .	1–95
3	8	Brewster,	4–91				

BERKSHIRE COUNTY.

1	1	WEST STOCKBRIDGE,	$.006–08	17	17	Gt.Barrington,	$.003–46
2	2	Sandisfield, .	5–21	16	18	N. Marlboro',	3–32
10	3	North Adams,	5–03	18	19	Tyringham, .	3–26
4	4	Florida,.	4–99	25	20	Washington, .	3–21
3	5	Peru, .	4–98	22	21	Becket, .	3–09
5	6	Otis, .	4–74	19	22	Williamstown,	3–05
8	7	Adams, .	4–57	23	23	Lenox, .	2–99
6	8	Lee, .	4–33	26	24	Richmond, .	2–94
12	9	Hinsdale, .	4–30	20	25	Lanesboro', .	2–87
7	10	Sheffield,	4–26	21	26	Dalton, .	2–76
9	11	Windsor,	4–08	30	27	Egremont,	2–15
11	12	Clarksburg, .	3–96	28	28	Stockbridge, .	2–06
13	13	Monterey,	3–88	31	29	Alford, .	1–59
24	14	Savoy, .	3–71	27	30	Mt.W'hingt'n,	1–40
14	15	Cheshire,	3–56	29	31	Hancock, .	1–35
15	16	Pittsfield,	3–53	32	32	New Ashford,	0–97

BRISTOL COUNTY.

For 1884-85, by the State Valuation of 1884.	For 1885-86, by the State Valuation of 1885.	TOWNS.	Percentage of Valuation appropriated to Public Schools—equivalent to mills and hundredths of mills.	For 1884-85, by the State Valuation of 1884.	For 1885-86, by the State Valuation of 1885.	TOWNS.	Percentage of Valuation appropriated to Public Schools—equivalent to mills and hundredths of mills.
2	1	MANSFIELD, .	$.005–15	10	11	Westport, .	$.003–18
3	2	Rehoboth,	4–77	14	12	Fall River, .	3–10
6	3	Somerset, .	4–40	13	13	Taunton, .	3–03
5	4	Dighton, .	4–39	12	14	Acushnet, .	2–92
1	5	Attleboro', .	4–23	18	15	Dartmouth, .	2–86
4	6	Fairhaven, .	4–23	16	16	Easton, .	2–72
7	7	Raynham, .	3–77	17	17	Freetown, .	2–62
9	8	Swansea, .	3–59	19	18	New Bedford,	2–59
11	9	Norton, .	3–56	15	19	Seekonk, .	2–33
8	10	Berkley, .	3–49				

DUKES COUNTY.

1	1	GAY HEAD, . .	$.005–02	4	4	Chilmark, .	$.002–11
2	2	Tisbury, .	3–34	5	5	Gosnold, . .	1–19
3	3	Edgartown, .	2–43	6	6	Cottage City,	0–96

ESSEX COUNTY.

2	1	MERRIMAC, . .	$.005–12	15	19	W. Newbury,	$.003–24
5	2	Georgetown, .	4–96	20	20	Ipswich, .	3–21
6	3	Bradford, .	4–51	21	21	Wenham, .	2–95
8	4	Groveland, .	4–30	23	22	Salem, . .	2–83
7	5	No. Andover, .	4–29	24	23	Lawrence, .	2–68
1	6	Amesbury, .	4–17	22	24	Newburyport,	2–65
9	7	Haverhill, .	4–14	25	25	Andover, .	2–61
3	8	Saugus, .	4–04	26	26	Middleton, .	2–49
4	9	Gloucester, .	3–86	28	27	Boxford, .	2–40
10	10	Essex, .	3–81	29	28	Topsfield, .	2–14
13	11	Peabody, .	3–72	27	29	Newbury, .	2–08
11	12	Danvers, .	3–65	30	30	Swampscott, .	1–93
14	13	Marblehead, .	3–48	31	31	Beverly, .	1–75
19	14	Salisbury, .	3–47	33	32	Hamilton, .	1–74
17	15	Methuen, .	3–40	32	33	Lynnfield, .	1–62
12	16	Rowley, .	3–40	34	34	Nahant, .	0–82
16	17	Lynn, .	3–35	35	35	Manchester, .	0–64
18	18	Rockport, .	3–31				

FRANKLIN COUNTY.

For 1884-85, by the State Valuation of 1884.	For 1885-86, by the State Valuation of 1885.	TOWNS.	Percentage of Valuation appropriated to Public Schools — equivalent to mills and hundredths of mills.	For 1884-85, by the State Valuation of 1884.	For 1885-86, by the State Valuation of 1885.	TOWNS.	Percentage of Valuation appropriated to Public Schools — equivalent to mills and hundredths of mills.
1	1	HAWLEY, .	$.005-95	19	14	Shutesbury, .	$.003-72
3	2	Monroe,	4-86	16	15	Greenfield, .	3-61
4	3	Deerfield, .	4-41	21	16	Montague, .	3-59
14	4	Colerain, .	4-18	15	17	Charlemont, .	3-50
6	5	Buckland, .	4-09	22	18	Conway, .	3-48
7	6	Leyden, .	4-04	8	19	New Salem, .	3-47
13	7	Heath, .	3-91	20	20	Rowe, .	3-47
18	8	Erving, .	3-85	5	21	Warwick, .	3-04
17	9	Wendell, .	3-84	23	22	Leverett, .	3-01
10	10	Orange, .	3-79	25	23	Whately, .	2-99
12	11	Shelburne, .	3-74	2	24	Bernardston, .	2-72
9	12	Northfield, .	3-73	24	25	Sunderland, .	2-60
11	13	Ashfield, .	3-72	26	26	Gill, . .	2-37

HAMPDEN COUNTY.

1	1	GRANVILLE, .	$.006-59	15	12	Holyoke, .	$.003-20
5	2	Monson, .	4-91	18	13	Tolland, .	3-10
4	3	Ludlow, .	4-71	14	14	W. Springfield,	3-08
3	4	Palmer, .	4-58	8	15	Chester, .	3-07
2	5	Blandford, .	4-57	11	16	Hampden, .	3-07
6	6	Chicopee, .	4-08	16	17	Southwick, .	2-84
20	7	Montgomery,	3-71	19	18	Agawam, .	2-81
7	8	Longmeadow,	3-61	17	19	Springfield, .	2-68
9	9	Westfield, .	3-33	10	20	Wales, . .	2-55
12	10	Brimfield, .	3-31	22	21	Russell, .	2-14
13	11	Wilbraham, .	3-25	21	22	Holland, .	1-95

HAMPSHIRE COUNTY.

1	1	SOUTH HADLEY, .	$.005-24	15	13	Southampton,	$.003-21
6	2	Pelham, .	4-56	11	14	Easthampton,	3-20
2	3	Belchertown,	4-47	5	15	Worthington,	3-17
3	4	Granby, .	4-36	17	16	Enfield, .	3-09
4	5	Westhampton,	3-93	19	17	Greenwich, .	3-04
9	6	Plainfield, .	3-80	18	18	Prescott, .	2-93
10	7	Williamsburg,	3-67	22	19	Hadley, .	2-55
12	8	Ware, . .	3-49	7	20	Cummington,	2-50
16	9	Middlefield, .	3-35	8	21	Huntington, .	2-31
20	10	Amherst, .	3-33	21	22	Hatfield, .	2-24
13	11	Chesterfield, .	3-28	23	23	Goshen, .	2-20
14	12	Northampton,	3-27				

MIDDLESEX COUNTY.

For 1884-85, by the State Valuation of 1884.	For 1885-86, by the State Valuation of 1885.	TOWNS.	Percentage of Valuation appropriated to Public Schools—equivalent to mills and hundredths of mills.	For 1884-85, by the State Valuation of 1884.	For 1885-86, by the State Valuation of 1885.	TOWNS.	Percentage of Valuation appropriated to Public Schools—equivalent to mills and hundredths of mills.
8	1	HUDSON, . .	$.004-99	29	28	Medford, .	$.003-40
1	2	Marlborough,	4-81	18	29	Melrose, .	3-35
3	3	Stoneham, .	4-42	22	30	Acton, . .	3-32
10	4	Waltham, .	4-37	26	31	Malden, .	3-23
2	5	Natick, . .	4-36	28	32	Framingham,	3-21
4	6	Wakefield, .	4-35	32	33	Cambridge, .	3-13
21	7	Littleton, .	4-32	33	34	Shirley, . .	3-06
34	8	Ashland, .	4-26	20	35	Wilmington, .	3-06
5	9	Ashby, . .	4-08	35	36	Pepperell, .	3-01
9	10	No. Reading,	4-01	46	37	Bedford, .	3-00
12	11	Concord, .	3-92	27	38	Lexington, .	2-95
17	12	Westford, .	3-90	37	39	Lowell, . .	2-89
7	13	Arlington, .	3-79	40	40	Everett, .	2-87
47	14	Boxborough,	3-76	36	41	Maynard, .	2-83
11	15	Wayland, .	3-74	45	42	Weston, .	2-74
44	16	Watertown, .	3-71	38	43	Sherborn, .	2-69
15	17	Tyngsboro', .	3-66	39	44	Dracut, . .	2-60
6	18	Woburn, .	3-65	41	45	Dunstable, .	2-59
24	19	Hopkinton, .	3-62	50	46	Lincoln, .	2-34
14	20	Winchester, .	3-61	43	47	Burlington, .	2-27
31	21	Newton, .	3-58	53	48	Stow, . .	2-24
13	22	Ayer, . .	3-57	49	49	Carlisle, .	2-16
16	23	Townsend, .	3-51	48	50	Belmont, .	2-12
23	24	Holliston, .	3-48	51	51	Sudbury, .	2-03
25	25	Somerville, .	3-45	42	52	Tewksbury, .	2-00
30	26	Chelmsford, .	3-44	52	53	Billerica, .	1-91
19	27	Reading, .	3-43	54	54	Groton, .	1-82

NANTUCKET COUNTY.

NANTUCKET, ...	$.001-77

NORFOLK COUNTY.

1	1	HOLBROOK, . .	$.006-50	8	10	Norwood, .	$.004-02
5	2	Randolph, .	4-91	9	11	Stoughton, .	3-83
4	3	Hyde Park, .	4-79	–	12	Millis, . .	3-75
3	4	Wrentham, .	4-69	13	13	Bellingham, .	3-64
6	5	Dedham, .	4-62	12	14	Canton, . .	3-63
14	6	Medway, .	4-59	11	15	Foxborough, .	3-58
2	7	Weymouth, .	4-47	15	16	Franklin, .	3-47
7	8	Needham, .	4-26	17	17	Norfolk, .	3-21
10	9	Quincy, . .	4-09	16	18	Braintree, .	3-05

NORFOLK COUNTY — Concluded.

For 1884-85, by the State Valuation of 1884.	For 1884-86, by the State Valuation of 1885.	TOWNS.	Percentage of Valuation appropriated to Public Schools—equivalent to mills and hundredths of mills.	For 1884-85, by the State Valuation of 1884.	For 1885-86, by the State Valuation of 1885.	TOWNS.	Percentage of Valuation appropriated to Public Schools—equivalent to mills and hundredths of mills.
18	19	Walpole,	$.002–86	22	23	Cohasset,	$.002–11
20	20	Sharon,	2–32	23	24	Dover,	1–99
21	21	Medfield,	2–16	24	25	Brookline,	1–42
19	22	Wellesley,	2–13	25	26	Milton,	1–22

PLYMOUTH COUNTY.

		TOWNS.				TOWNS.	
3	1	WAREHAM,	$.004–75	15	15	W. Bridgew'r,	$.003–26
1	2	Abington,	4–61	16	16	Hanover,	3–17
6	3	Rockland,	4–53	20	17	Pembroke,	3–04
2	4	Plymouth,	4–39	17	18	Brockton,	2–89
4	5	Bridgewater,	4–25	19	19	Halifax,	2–84
7	6	E. Bridgew'r,	4–03	18	20	Duxbury,	2–80
5	7	Lakeville,	3–77	22	21	Marshfield,	2–61
8	8	Middleboro',	3–68	21	22	Carver,	2–31
10	9	Hingham,	3–58	23	23	So. Abington,	2–10
11	10	So. Scituate,	3–52	24	24	Kingston,	1–96
13	11	Rochester,	3–51	25	25	Marion,	1–80
14	12	Hanson,	3–43	26	26	Mattapoisett,	1–72
12	13	Scituate,	3–32	27	27	Hull,	0–65
9	14	Plympton,	3–26				

SUFFOLK COUNTY.

1	1	CHELSEA,	$.003–17	2	3	Revere,	$.001–91
3	2	Boston,	2–02	4	4	Winthrop,	1–07

WORCESTER COUNTY.

1	1	UPTON,	$.005–03	12	11	Westborough,	$.004–09
8	2	Holden,	4–73	17	12	W. Brookfield,	4–06
3	3	Dudley,	4–72	22	13	Shrewsbury,	4–03
7	4	N. Brookfield,	4–49	24	14	Paxton,	3–91
10	5	Westminster,	4–44	13	15	Sterling,	3–89
2	6	Templeton,	4–42	19	16	Oxford,	3–84
4	7	Northbridge,	4–28	15	17	Douglas,	3–81
11	8	Millbury,	4–25	31	18	Ashburnham,	3–77
9	9	W. Boylston,	4–17	5	19	Brookfield,	3–77
6	10	Spencer,	4–11	28	20	N. Braintree,	3–77

WORCESTER COUNTY — CONCLUDED.

For 1884-85, by the State Valuation of 1884.	For 1885-86, by the State Valuation of 1885.	TOWNS.	Percentage of Valuation appropriated to Public Schools equivalent to mills and hundredths of mills.	For 1884-85, by the State Valuation of 1884.	For 1885-86, by the State Valuation of 1885.	TOWNS.	Percentage of Valuation appropriated to Public Schools equivalent to mills and hundredths of mills.
29	21	Clinton, .	$.003–75	37	40	Leominster, .	$.003–16
23	22	Sutton, .	3–70	44	41	Charlton,	3–14
27	23	Hardwick,	3–69	45	42	Petersham,	3–12
30	24	Warren,	3–65	38	43	Phillipston,	3–06
16	25	Leicester,	3–64	50	44	Dana, .	3–04
21	26	Gardner,	3–62	33	45	Webster,	3–03
18	27	Grafton,	3–61	51	46	Mendon,	2–85
25	28	Milford,	3–59	52	47	Hubbardston,	2–80
20	29	Blackstone,	3–55	35	48	Athol, .	2–74
32	30	Barre, .	3–51	55	49	Harvard,	2–74
40	31	Uxbridge,	3–46	54	50	Rutland,	2–72
46	32	Southbridge,	3–42	47	51	Oakham,	2–70
42	33	Fitchburg,	3–38	43	52	Bolton, .	2–68
34	34	Worcester,	3–34	49	53	Auburn,	2–67
26	35	Sturbridge,	3–30	53	54	Lunenburg,	2–67
39	36	Northboro',	3–24	57	55	Berlin, .	2–46
36	37	Southboro',	3–22	41	56	Royalston,	2–43
14	38	Boylston,	3–20	58	57	Princeton,	2–41
48	39	Winchendon,	3–17	56	58	Lancaster,	2–01

GRADUATED TABLES—SECOND SERIES.

Showing the different Counties in the State, numerically arranged, according to the Percentage of their Taxable Property appropriated for the Support of Public Schools for the Year 1885–86.

For 1885-86, by the State Valuation of 1885.	For 1884-85, by the State Valuation of 1884.	COUNTIES.	Percentage of Valuation appropriated to Public Schools—equivalent to mills and hundredths of mills.	Amount of money raised by taxes for the support of Public Schools.	Income of surplus Revenue and of similar funds appropriated for Public Schools.	TOTALS.	Valuation of 1885.	Amount contributed for board and fuel.
1	1	BARNSTABLE,	$0 03·87	$63,401 00	$1,529 64	$64,930 64	$16,768,848	—
2	3	Berkshire,	3·72	136,922 41	1,520 91	138,443 32	87,238,951	$70 00
3	2	Franklin,	3·65	60,321 61	1,348 38	61,669 99	16,889,366	56 00
4	4	Worcester,	3·47	506,288 60	3,723 00	510,016 60	146,591,400	297 00
5	5	Hampshire,	3·40	86,400 00	2,402 21	88,802 21	26,156,074	492 00
6	6	Middlesex,	3·32	973,014 89	5,852 16	978,767 05	294,508,654	462 75
7	7	Plymouth,	3·22	158,870 03	4,530 00	163,400 03	50,786,612	—
8	8	Hampden,	3·13	242,895 07	2,608 76	245,503 83	78,402,861	149 00
9	11	Bristol,	3·07	346,298 63	4,605 17	350,903 80	114,486,276	145 00
10	9	Essex,	3·03	545,976 82	7,082 45	553,059 27	182,631,698	30 00
11	10	Norfolk,	2·80	281,549 70	4,187 08	285,736 78	102,903,463	162 00
12	12	Suffolk,	2·05	1,404,872 16	47,881 17	1,452,753 33	709,766,921	
13	14	Dukes,	1·92	5,893 50	280 90	6,174 40	3,210,235	70 00
14	13	Nantucket,	1·77	4,729 59		4,729 59	2,667,784	—

AGGREGATE FOR THE STATE.

		STATE,	$0 02·75	$4,817,429 01	$87,551 83	$4,904,880 84	$1,782,349,143	$1,933 75

GRADUATED TABLES — Second Series.

*Showing the Arrangement of Counties according to their Appropria-
tions, including Voluntary Contributions.*

If the counties are numerically arranged, according to the percentage of
their valuations appropriated for public schools, voluntary contributions of
board and fuel being added to the sum raised by tax and to the income of
the surplus revenue and other funds, as severally given in the previous
table, the order of precedence will be as follows: —

For 1884-85, by the State Valuation of 1884.	For 1885-86, by the State Valuation of 1885.	COUNTIES.	Percentage of Valuation appropriated to Public Schools—equivalent to mills and hundredths of mills.
1	1	BARNSTABLE, ...	$.003-87
3	2	Berkshire, ...	3-72
2	3	Franklin, ...	3-65
4	4	Worcester, ...	3-54
5	5	Hampshire, ...	3-41
6	6	Middlesex, ...	3-32
7	7	Plymouth, ...	3-22
8	8	Hampden, ...	3-13
11	9	Bristol, ...	3-07
9	10	Essex, ...	3-03
10	11	Norfolk, ...	2-80
12	12	Suffolk, ...	2-05
14	13	Dukes, ...	1-95
13	14	Nantucket, ...	1-77
		STATE, ...	$.002-75

GRADUATED TABLES — Third Series.

The following table exhibits the ratio of the average attendance for the year in each town to the whole number of children between 5 and 15, according to the returns.

The ratio is expressed in decimals, continued to four figures, the first two of which are separated from the last two by a point, as only the two former are essential to denote the real per cent. Yet the ratios of many towns are so nearly equal, or the difference is so small a fraction, that the first two decimals with the appropriate mathematical sign appended, indicate no distinction. The continuation of the decimals, therefore, is simply to indicate a priority in cases where, without such continuation, the ratios would appear to be precisely similar.

In several cases the ratio of attendance exhibited in the Table is over 100 per cent. These results, supposing the registers to have been properly kept and the returns correctly made, are to be thus explained: The average attendance upon all Public Schools being compared with the whole number of children in the town between 5 and 15, the result may be over 100 per cent., because the attendance of children under 5 and over 15 may more than compensate for the absence of children between those ages. The rank of the towns standing highest in the following Table is in accordance with the returns. As the returns are often incorrect, the rank may be too high in some cases.

GRADUATED TABLES — Third Series.

[for the state.]

In which all the Towns in the State are numerically arranged according to the Average Attendance *of the Children upon the Public Schools for the Year 1885–86.*

	TOWNS.	No. of children between 5 and 15 years of age in each town.	Average attendance upon School.	Ratio of attendance to the whole No. of children between 5 and 15, expressed in decimals.		TOWNS.	No. of children between 5 and 15 years of age in each town.	Average attendance upon School.	Ratio of attendance to the whole No. of children between 5 and 15, expressed in decimals.
1	MASHPEE, .	30	47	1.56–67	33	Deerfield, .	606	570	.94–06
2	Savoy, .	116	152	1.31–03	34	Concord, .	564	529	.93–79
3	Ashby, .	144	172	1.19–44	35	Kingston, .	224	210	.93–75
4	Greenwich, .	68	73	1.07–35	36	Worthington,	118	110	.93–22
5	Winchester, .	620	659	1.06–29	37	Gloucester, .	3,894	3,628	.93–17
6	Northboro', .	249	257	1.03–21	38	Longm'dow,	232	216	.93–10
7	Tyngsboro', .	97	100	1.03–09	39	Cohasset, .	347	323	.93–08
8	Dana, .	107	110	1.02–80	40	Holbrook, .	445	414	.93–03
9	Ashfield, .	150	153	1.02–00	41	Amherst, .	600	558	.93–00
10	Weston, .	220	222	1.00–91	42	Dedham, .	1,135	1,052	.92–69
11	Dunstable, .	65	65	1.00–00	43	Mendon, .	162	150	.92–59
12	Southwick, .	187	187	1.00–00	44	Ayer, .	433	400	.92–38
13	W. St'kb'dge,	311	310	99–68	45	Provincet'on,	810	748	.92–35
14	Mattapoisett,	183	182	99–45	46	Lunenburg, .	143	132	.92–31
15	Harvard, .	146	145	99–32	47	Orange, .	629	580	.92–21
16	Medway, .	406	403	99–26	48	Waltham, .	2,453	2,261	.92–17
17	Methuen, .	787	778	98–86	49	Huntington, .	206	189	.91–75
18	Marion, .	143	141	98–60	50	Middleton, .	107	98	.91–59
19	Needham, .	453	444	98–01	51	Warwick, .	117	107	.91–45
20	Winthrop, .	201	196	97–51	52	Abington, .	629	574	.91–26
21	Tisbury, .	173	168	97–11	53	Wellfleet, .	284	259	.91–20
22	Brookfield, .	465	451	96–99	54	Oakham, .	123	112	.91–06
23	Cummingt'n,	129	125	96–90	55	Erving, .	143	130	.90–91
24	Swampscott,	348	337	96–84	56	Millis, .	108	98	.90–74
25	Pittsfield, .	2,547	2,453	96–31	57	Barnstable, .	656	595	.90–70
26	Shrewsbury,	260	250	96–15	58	Rockland, .	880	797	.90–57
27	Acton, .	264	253	95–83	59	Hyde Park, .	1,606	1,447	.90–10
28	Montgomery,	46	44	95 65	60	Watertown, .	1,104	994	.90–04
29	Leominster, .	882	842	95–46	61	Charlemont,	149	134	.89–93
30	Harwich, .	490	467	95–31	62	Egremont, .	87	78	.89–66
31	Princeton, .	159	151	94–97	63	Hadley, .	338	303	.89–64
32	Barre, .	293	276	94–20	64	Natick, .	1,620	1,452	.89–63

TOWNS.	No. of children between 5 and 15 years of age in each town.	Average attendance upon School.	Ratio of attendance to the whole No. of children between 5 and 15, expressed in decimals.		TOWNS.	No. of children between 5 and 15 years of age in each town.	Average attendance upon School.	Ratio of attendance to the whole No. of children between 5 and 15, expressed in decimals.
65 Randolph,	660	591	.89–55	113	Shutesbury,	99	84	.84–85
66 Merrimac,	417	371	.88–97	114	Sandwich,	393	333	.84–73
67 Otis,	136	121	.88–97	115	Norwood,	501	424	.84–63
68 Edgartown,	144	128	.88–89	116	Plymouth,	1,234	1,043	.84–52
69 S. Abington,	611	543	.88–87	117	Berlin,	161	136	.84–47
70 Goshen,	53	47	.88–68	118	Newton,	3,611	3,047	.84–38
71 Dennis,	512	453	.88–48	119	Arlington,	958	806	.84–13
72 Littleton,	191	169	.88–48	120	Framingh'm,	1,366	1,148	.84–04
73 Berkley,	147	130	.88–44	121	No. Andover,	681	571	.83–85
74 Amesbury,	648	573	.88–43	122	Sunderland,	130	109	.83–85
75 New Salem,	128	113	.88–28	123	Sturbridge,	382	320	.83–77
76 Foxborough,	391	345	.88–24	124	E. Bridgew'r,	486	406	.83–54
77 Bridgewater,	522	460	.88–12	125	Rochester,	162	135	.83–38
78 Dighton,	269	237	.88–10	126	Leverett,	131	109	.83–21
79 Rutland,	175	154	.88–00	127	Burlington,	125	104	.83–20
80 Stoneham,	906	797	.87–97	128	Grafton,	820	682	.83–17
81 Ashland,	450	395	.87–78	129	Royalston,	202	168	.83–17
82 Bedford,	139	122	.87–77	130	Quincy,	2,416	2,003	.82–89
83 Sterling,	228	200	.87–72	131	Wellesley,	379	314	.82–85
84 Granby,	138	121	.87–68	132	Windsor,	110	91	.82–73
85 N. Braintree,	97	85	.87–63	133	Attleboro',	2,191	1,812	.82–70
86 Hubbardst'n,	216	189	.87–50	134	Somerville,	5,608	4,627	.82–51
87 Greenfield,	871	760	.87–26	135	Medfield,	203	167	.82–26
88 Westminster,	274	239	.87–23	136	Lee,	796	654	.82–16
89 Hingham,	666	580	.87–09	137	W.Springfi'd,	857	704	.82–15
90 Tolland,	69	60	.86–96	138	Rehoboth,	285	234	.82–11
91 Bolton,	128	111	.86–72	139	Peabody,	1,773	1,451	.81–84
92 Reading,	557	483	.86 71	140	Athol,	842	688	.81–71
93 Upton,	312	270	.86–54	141	Brockton,	3,477	2,841	.81–71
94 Hudson,	816	706	.86–52	142	Shelburne,	246	201	.81–71
95 Heath,	111	96	.86–49	143	Chesterfield,	131	107	.81–68
96 Manchester,	249	215	.86–35	144	Haverhill,	3,600	2,989	.81–64
97 Everett,	1,039	894	.85–95	145	Enfield,	171	139	.81–29
98 Oxford,	311	267	.85–85	146	Pepperell,	443	360	.81–26
99 Petersham,	148	127	.85–81	147	Middleboro',	864	702	.81–25
100 Cottage City,	112	96	.85–71	148	Mansfield,	473	384	.81–18
101 Danvers,	1,106	948	.85–71	149	Eastham,	90	73	.81–11
102 Hawley,	105	90	.85–71	150	Falmouth,	383	310	.80–94
103 Saugus,	486	416	.85–60	151	Middlefield,	115	93	.80–87
104 Melrose,	1,135	971	.85–55	152	Hanover,	322	260	.80–75
105 Weymouth,	1,993	1,705	.85–55	153	N. Reading,	140	113	.80–71
106 So. Hadley,	702	600	.85–47	154	Wenham,	140	113	.80–71
107 Ipswich,	616	526	.85–39	155	Belchertown,	475	383	.80–63
108 Colerain,	340	290	.85–29	156	Hopkinton,	819	660	.80–59
109 Wrentham,	427	364	.85–25	157	Warren,	752	604	.80–32
110 Bradford,	535	456	.85–23	158	Belmont,	325	261	.80–31
111 Prescott,	88	75	.85–23	159	Westboro',	845	678	.80–24
112 Medford,	1,653	1,401	.84–94	160	Chelmsford,	440	353	.80–23

	TOWNS.	No. of children between 5 and 15 years of age in each town.	Average attendance upon School.	Ratio of attendance to the whole No. of children between 5 and 15, expressed in decimals.		TOWNS.	No. of children between 5 and 15 years of age in each town.	Average attendance upon school.	Ratio of attendance to the whole No. of children between 5 and 15, expressed in decimals.
161	Marshfield, .	217	174	.80–18	209	Bernardston,	148	113	.76–35
162	Clinton, .	1,774	1,422	.80–16	210	Granville,	228	174	.76–32
163	Somerset, .	443	355	.80–14	211	Boylston, .	160	122	.76–25
164	Bellingham, .	196	157	.80–10	212	Carlisle, .	80	61	.76–25
165	Georgetown,	472	378	.80–08	213	Marblehead,.	1,420	1,082	.76–20
166	Fitchburg, .	2,889	2,305	.79–79	214	Alford, . .	63	48	.76–19
167	Northampt'n,	2,241	1,787	.79–74	215	Hardwick, .	512	390	.76–17
168	Brewster, .	172	137	.79–65	216	Hull, . .	71	54	76–06
169	Rowe, . .	108	86	.79–63	217	Peru, . .	50	38	.76–00
170	Milton, . .	627	499	.79–59	218	Conway, .	320	243	.75–94
171	Gt.Barr'gton,	837	666	.79–57	219	Spencer, .	1,790	1,359	.75–92
172	Stow, . .	181	144	.79–56	220	Phillipston, .	91	69	.75–82
173	Chilmark, .	58	46	.79–31	221	Lancaster, .	334	253	.75–75
174	Sharon, .	227	180	.79–30	222	Wales, . .	152	115	.75–66
175	Dover, . .	86	68	.79–07	223	Blandford, .	213	161	.75–59
176	Wilmington,	167	132	.79–04	224	Boxford, .	139	105	.75–54
177	Brookline, .	1,615	1,276	.79–01	225	Nahant, .	147	111	.75–51
178	Paxton, .	95	75	.78–95	226	Millbury, .	920	693	.75–33
179	Westford, .	408	322	.78–92	227	Chatham, .	352	265	.75–28
180	Leicester, .	583	460	.78–90	228	Boston, .	68702	51662	.75–20
181	Easton, .	778	613	.78–79	229	Chelsea, .	4,709	3,532	.75–01
182	Truro, . .	165	130	.78–79	230	Bourne, .	260	195	.75–00
183	Templeton, .	509	401	.78–78	231	Boxborough,	44	33	.75–00
184	Norfolk, .	167	131	.78–44	232	Monroe, .	52	39	.75–00
185	Duxbury, .	296	232	.78–38	233	W. Boylston,	555	416	.74–95
186	Russell, .	166	130	.78–31	234	Lynn, . .	7,380	5,525	.74–86
187	Winchendon,	689	539	.78–23	235	Lynnfield, .	115	86	.74–78
188	Ashburnham,	343	268	.78–13	236	N'w Bedford,	5,131	3,832	.74–68
189	Halifax, .	73	57	.78–08	237	Yarmouth, .	300	224	.74–67
190	New Ashford,	27	21	.77–78	238	Hinsdale, .	397	296	.74–56
191	Pelham, .	99	77	.77–78	239	Andover, .	951	709	.74–55
192	W. Newbury,	297	231	.77–78	240	Brimfield, .	196	146	.74–49
193	Wilbraham, .	252	196	.77–78	241	Northbridge,	769	572	.74–38
194	Sandisfield, .	202	157	.77–73	242	Leyden, .	105	78	.74–29
195	Plainfield, .	76	59	.77–63	243	So. Scituate,.	259	192	.74–13
196	Essex, . .	284	220	.77–46	244	Lincoln, .	157	116	.73–89
197	Raynham, .	265	205	.77–36	245	Pembroke, .	209	154	.73–68
198	Beverly, .	1,578	1,220	.77–31	246	Becket, . .	162	119	.73–46
199	Easthampt'n,	756	584	.77–25	247	Westfield, .	1,653	1,214	.73–44
200	Braintree, .	705	542	.76–88	248	Agawam, .	463	340	.73–43
201	Holliston, .	575	442	.76–87	249	Scituate, .	506	371	.73–32
202	Wendell, .	82	63	.76–83	250	Chester, .	231	169	.73–16
203	Groton, .	295	226	.76–61	251	Freetown, .	238	174	.73–11
204	Dalton, .	423	324	.76–60	252	Monterey, .	115	84	.73–04
205	Charlton, .	303	232	.76–57	253	Wakefield, .	1,260	920	.73–02
206	Rockport, .	815	624	.76–56	254	Fairhaven, .	480	350	.72–92
207	Taunton, .	4,215	3,227	.76–56	255	Lanesboro', .	265	193	.72–83
208	N. Marlboro',	318	243	.76–42	256	Hamilton, .	113	82	.72–57

No.	TOWNS.	No. of children between 5 and 15 years of age in each town.	Average attendance upon School.	Ratio of attendance to the whole No. of children between 5 and 15, expressed in decimals.	No.	TOWNS.	No. of children between 5 and 15 years of age in each town.	Average attendance upon School	Ratio of attendance to the whole No. of children between 5 and 15, expressed in decimals.
257	Milford,	1,707	1,238	.72-53	303	Uxbridge,	585	393	.67-18
258	Southampt'n,	185	134	.72-48	304	Springfield,	6,330	4,251	.67-16
259	Dracut,	330	239	.72-42	305	Palmer,	1,191	799	.67-09
260	Worcester,	13269	9,598	.72-53	306	Sheffield,	411	273	.66-42
261	Cambridge,	10957	7,915	.72-24	307	Douglas,	406	268	.66-01
262	Acushnet,	187	135	.72-19	308	Topsfield,	179	118	.65-92
263	N. Brookfi'ld,	800	577	.72-13	309	Hancock,	120	79	.65-83
264	Townsend,	337	243	.72-11	310	Gay Head,	32	21	.65-63
265	Tyringham,	114	82	.71-93	311	Salisbury,	836	548	.65-55
266	Southboro',	323	231	.71-52	312	Holden,	530	347	.65-47
267	Montague,	1,422	1,016	.71-45	313	Washington,	101	66	.65-35
268	Buckland,	322	230	.71-43	314	No. Adams,	2,705	1,766	.65-20
269	Hanson,	217	155	.71-43	315	Lawrence,	6,947	4,529	.65-19
270	Lenox,	433	309	.71-36	316	Westhampt'n,	123	80	.65-04
271	Ludlow,	370	264	.71-35	317	Auburn,	254	165	.64-96
272	Revere,	656	468	.71-34	318	Westport,	502	326	.64-94
273	Swansea,	230	164	.71-30	319	Gill,	165	106	.64-24
274	Marlboro',	2,395	1,699	.70-94	320	Northfield,	254	162	.63-78
275	Carver,	196	139	.70-92	321	Nantucket,	565	355	.62-83
276	Adams,	1,738	1,232	.70-89	322	Woburn,	2,580	1,618	.62-71
277	Williamsb'g,	421	298	.70-78	323	W. Brookfi'd,	347	217	.62-54
278	Wareham,	691	489	.70-77	324	Sherborn,	201	125	.62-19
279	Tewksbury,	256	181	.70-70	325	Lakeville,	167	103	.61-62
280	Dartmouth,	570	402	.70-53	326	Hampden,	171	105	.61-40
281	Lexington,	449	316	.70-38	327	Salem,	4,976	3,044	.61-18
282	Plympton,	91	64	.70-33	328	Malden,	2,907	1,770	.60-89
283	Shirley,	246	173	.70-33	329	Holland,	43	26	.60-47
284	Monson,	625	439	.70-24	330	Fall River,	11741	7,095	.60-43
285	Rowley,	221	155	.70-14	331	Clarksburg,	131	79	.60-31
286	Franklin,	796	558	.70-10	332	Whately,	203	122	.60-10
287	Sudbury,	194	136	.70-10	333	Norton,	287	171	.59-58
288	Cheshire,	370	259	.70-00	334	Mt. Wash't'n,	27	16	.59-26
289	Orleans,	165	115	.69-70	335	Canton,	856	500	.58 41
290	Florida,	135	94	.69-63	336	Richmond,	219	127	.57-99
291	Hatfield,	262	182	.69-47	337	Stoughton,	975	565	.57-95
292	Stockbridge,	393	273	.69-47	338	Lowell,	10970	6,242	.56-90
293	Walpole,	452	314	.69-47	339	Williamsto'n,	639	355	.55-56
294	Ware,	1,182	821	.69-46	340	Dudley,	564	310	.54-96
295	Gardner,	1,248	866	.69-39	341	Gosnold,	19	10	.52-63
296	Blackstone,	1,033	715	.69-22	342	Newbury,	309	159	.51-46
297	Maynard,	515	355	.68-93	343	Chicopee,	2,391	1,074	.44-92
298	W. Bri'gew'r,	312	215	.68-91	344	Southbridge,	1,358	606	.44-62
299	Billerica,	427	293	.68-62	345	Sutton,	707	315	.44-55
300	Wayland,	454	308	.67-84	346	Holyoke,	5,836	2,567	.43-99
301	Groveland,	407	276	.67-81	347	Newburyp'rt,	2,581	1,126	.43-63
302	Seekonk,	227	153	.67-40	348	Webster,	1,145	405	.35-37

GRADUATED TABLES — Third Series.

[COUNTY TABLES.]

In which all the Towns in the respective Counties in the State are numerically arranged according to the AVERAGE ATTENDANCE of their Children upon the Public Schools for the Year 1885–86.

[For an explanation of the principles on which the Tables are constructed, see *ante*, p. cxxiii.]

BARNSTABLE COUNTY.

	TOWNS.	No. of children between 5 and 15 years of age in each town.	Average attendance upon School.	Ratio of attendance to the whole No. of children between 5 and 15, expressed in decimals.		TOWNS.	No. of children between 5 and 15 years of age in each town.	Average attendance upon School.	Ratio of attendance to the whole No. of children between 5 and 15, expressed in decimals.
1	MASHPEE, .	30	47	1.56–67	9	Falmouth, .	383	310	.80–94
2	Harwich,	490	467	.95–31	10	Brewster, .	172	137	.79–65
3	Provinceto'n,	810	748	.92–35	11	Truro, .	165	130	.78–79
4	Wellfleet, .	284	259	.91–20	12	Chatham, .	352	265	.75–28
5	Barnstable, .	656	595	.90–70	13	Bourne, .	260	195	.75–00
6	Dennis, .	512	453	.88–48	14	Yarmouth, .	300	224	.74–67
7	Sandwich, .	393	333	.84–73	15	Orleans, .	165	115	.69–70
8	Eastham, .	90	73	.81–11					

BERKSHIRE COUNTY.

	TOWNS.	No. of children between 5 and 15 years of age in each town.	Average attendance upon School.	Ratio of attendance to the whole No. of children between 5 and 15, expressed in decimals.		TOWNS.	No. of children between 5 and 15 years of age in each town.	Average attendance upon School.	Ratio of attendance to the whole No. of children between 5 and 15, expressed in decimals.
1	SAVOY, .	116	152	1.31–03	17	Monterey, .	115	84	.73–04
2	W. Stockb'ge.	311	310	.99–68	18	Lanesboro', .	265	193	.72–83
3	Pittsfield, .	254	245	.96–31	19	Tyringham, .	114	82	.71–93
4	Egremont, .	87	78	.89–66	20	Lenox, .	433	309	.71–36
5	Otis, .	136	121	.88–97	21	Adams, .	1,738	1,232	.70–89
6	Windsor, .	110	91	.82–73	22	Cheshire, .	370	259	.70–00
7	Lee, .	796	654	.82–16	23	Florida, .	135	94	.69–63
8	G Barringt'n,	837	666	.79–57	24	Stockbridge,	393	273	.69–47
9	N'w Ashford,	27	21	.77–78	25	Sheffield, .	411	273	.66–42
10	Sandisfield, .	202	157	.77–73	26	Hancock, .	120	79	.65–83
11	Dalton, .	423	324	.76–60	27	Washington,	101	66	.65–35
12	N. Marlboro',	318	243	.76–42	28	No. Adams, .	2,705	1,766	.65–29
13	Alford, .	63	48	.76–19	29	Clarksburg, .	131	79	.60–31
14	Peru, .	50	38	.76–00	30	Mt.Wash'g'n,	27	16	.59–26
15	Hinsdale, .	397	296	.74–56	31	Richmond, .	219	127	.57–99
16	Becket, .	162	119	.73–46	32	Williamsto'n,	639	355	.55–56

BRISTOL COUNTY.

	TOWNS.	No. of children between 5 and 15 years of age in each town.	Average attendance upon School.	Ratio of attendance to the whole No. of children between 5 and 15, expressed in decimals.		TOWNS.	No. of children between 5 and 15 years of age in each town.	Average attendance upon School.	Ratio of attendance to the whole No. of children between 5 and 15, expressed in decimals.
1	BERKLEY,	147	130	.88–44	11	Freetown,	238	174	.73–11
2	Dighton,	269	237	.88–10	12	Fairhaven,	480	350	.72–92
3	Attleboro',	2,191	1,812	.82–70	13	Acushnet,	187	135	.72–19
4	Rehoboth,	285	234	.82–11	14	Swansea,	230	164	.71–30
5	Mansfield,	473	384	.81–18	15	Dartmouth,	570	402	.70–53
6	Somerset,	443	355	.80–14	16	Seekonk,	227	153	.67–40
7	Easton,	778	613	.78–79	17	Westport,	502	326	.64–94
8	Raynham,	265	205	.77–36	18	Fall River,	11741	7,095	.60–43
9	Taunton,	4,215	3,227	.76–56	19	Norton,	287	171	.59–58
10	N'w Bedford,	5,131	3,832	.74–68					

DUKES COUNTY.

	TOWNS.					TOWNS.			
1	TISBURY,	173	168	.97–11	4	Chilmark,	58	46	.79–31
2	Edgartown,	144	128	.88–89	5	Gay Head,	32	21	.65–63
3	Cottage City,	112	96	.85–71	6	Gosnold,	19	10	.52–63

ESSEX COUNTY.

	TOWNS.					TOWNS.			
1	METHUEN,	787	778	.98–86	19	Beverly,	1,578	1,220	.77–31
2	Swampscott,	348	337	.96–84	20	Rockport,	815	624	.76–56
3	Gloucester,	3,894	3,628	.93–17	21	Marblehead,	1,420	1,082	.76–20
4	Middleton,	107	98	.91–59	22	Boxford,	139	105	.75–54
5	Merrimac,	417	371	.88–97	23	Nahant,	147	111	.75–51
6	Amesbury,	648	573	.88–43	24	Lynn,	7,380	5,525	.74–86
7	Manchester,	249	215	.86–35	25	Lynnfield,	115	86	.74–78
8	Danvers,	1,106	948	.85–71	26	Andover,	951	709	.74–55
9	Saugus,	486	416	.85–60	27	Hamilton,	113	82	.72–57
10	Ipswich,	616	526	.85–39	28	Rowley,	221	155	.70–14
11	Bradford,	535	456	.85–23	29	Groveland,	407	276	.67–81
12	N. Andover,	681	571	.83–85	30	Topsfield,	179	118	.65–92
13	Peabody,	1,773	1,451	.81–84	31	Salisbury,	836	548	.65–55
14	Haverhill,	3,600	2,939	.81–64	32	Lawrence,	6,947	4,529	.65–19
15	Wenham,	140	113	.80–71	33	Salem,	4,976	3,044	.61–18
16	Georgetown,	472	378	.80–08	34	Newbury,	309	159	.51–46
17	W.Newbury,	297	231	.77–78	35	Newbu'yp'rt,	2,581	1,126	.43–63
18	Essex,	284	220	.77–46					

FRANKLIN COUNTY.

	TOWNS.	No. of children between 5 and 15 years of age in each town.	Average attendance upon School.	Ratio of attendance to the whole No. of children between 5 and 15, expressed in decimals.		TOWNS.	No. of children between 5 and 15 years of age in each town.	Average attendance upon School.	Ratio of attendance to the whole No. of children between 5 and 15, expressed in decimals.
1	ASHFIELD,	150	153	1.02-00	14	Leverett,	131	109	.83-21
2	Deerfield,	606	570	.94-06	15	Shelburne,	246	201	.81-71
3	Orange,	629	580	.92-21	16	Rowe,	108	86	.79-63
4	Warwick,	117	107	.91-45	17	Wendell,	82	63	.76-83
5	Erving,	143	130	.90-91	18	Bernardston,	148	113	.76-35
6	Charlemont,	149	134	.89-93	19	Conway,	320	243	.75-94
7	New Salem,	128	113	.88-28	20	Monroe,	52	39	.75-00
8	Greenfield,	871	760	.87-26	21	Leyden,	105	78	.74-29
9	Heath,	111	96	.86-49	22	Montague,	1,422	1,016	.71-45
10	Hawley,	105	90	.85-71	23	Buckland,	322	230	.71-43
11	Colerain,	340	290	.85-29	24	Gill,	165	106	.64-24
12	Shutesbury,	99	84	.84-85	25	Northfield,	254	162	.63-78
13	Sunderland,	130	109	.83-85	26	Whately,	203	122	.60-10

HAMPDEN COUNTY.

	TOWNS.					TOWNS.			
1	SOUTHWICK,	187	187	1.00-00	12	Westfield,	1,653	1,214	.73-44
2	Montgom'ry,	46	44	.95-65	13	Agawam,	463	340	.73-43
3	Longm'dow,	232	216	.93-10	14	Chester,	231	169	.73-16
4	Tolland,	69	60	.86-96	15	Ludlow,	370	264	.71-35
5	W. Springfi'd,	857	704	.82-15	16	Monson,	625	439	.70-24
6	Russell,	166	130	.78-31	17	Springfield,	6,330	4,251	.67-16
7	Wilbraham,	252	196	.77-78	18	Palmer,	1,191	799	.67-09
8	Granville,	228	174	.76-32	19	Hampden,	171	105	.61-40
9	Wales,	152	115	.75-66	20	Holland,	43	26	.60-47
10	Blandford,	213	161	.75-59	21	Chicopee,	2,391	1,074	.44-92
11	Brimfield,	196	146	.74-49	22	Holyoke,	5,836	2,567	.43-99

HAMPSHIRE COUNTY.

	TOWNS.					TOWNS.			
1	GREENWICH,	68	73	1.07-35	13	Middlefield,	115	93	.80-87
2	Cummingt'n,	129	125	.96-90	14	Belchertown,	475	383	.80-63
3	Worthingt'n,	118	110	.93-22	15	Northampt'n,	2,241	1,787	.79-74
4	Amherst,	600	558	.93-00	16	Pelham,	99	77	.77-78
5	Huntington,	206	189	.91-75	17	Plainfield,	76	59	.77-63
6	Hadley,	338	303	.89-64	18	Easthampt'n,	756	584	.77-25
7	Goshen,	53	47	.88-68	19	Southampt'n,	185	134	.72-43
8	Granby,	138	121	.87-68	20	Williamsb'g,	421	298	.70-78
9	So. Hadley,	702	600	.85-47	21	Hatfield,	262	182	.69-47
10	Prescott,	88	75	.85-23	22	Ware,	1,182	821	.69-46
11	Chesterfield,	131	107	.81-68	23	Westh'mpt'n,	123	80	.65-04
12	Enfield,	171	139	.81-29					

MIDDLESEX COUNTY.

	TOWNS.	No. of children between 5 and 15 years of age in each town.	Average attendance upon School.	Ratio of attendance to the whole No. of children between 5 and 15, expressed in decimals.		TOWNS.	No. of children between 5 and 15 years of age in each town.	Average attendance upon School.	Ratio of attendance to the whole No. of children between 5 and 15, expressed in decimals.
1	ASHBY, . .	144	172	1.19–44	28	Hopkinton, .	819	660	.80–59
2	Winchester, .	620	659	1.06–29	29	Belmont, .	325	261	.80–31
3	Tyngsboro', .	97	100	1.03–09	30	Chelmsford,	440	353	.80–23
4	Weston, .	220	222	1.00–91	31	Stow, . .	181	144	.79–56
5	Dunstable, .	65	65	1.00–00	32	Wilmington,	167	132	.79–04
6	Acton, . .	264	253	.95–83	33	Westford, .	408	322	.78–92
7	Concord, .	564	529	.93–79	34	Holliston, .	575	442	.76–87
8	Ayer, . .	433	400	.92–38	35	Groton, .	295	226	.76–61
9	Waltham, .	2,453	2,261	.92–17	36	Carlisle, .	80	61	.76–25
10	Watertown, .	1,104	994	.90–04	37	Boxborough,	44	33	.75–00
11	Natick, .	1,620	1,452	.89–63	38	Lincoln, .	157	116	.73–89
12	Littleton, .	191	169	.88–48	39	Wakefield, .	1,260	920	.73–02
13	Stoughton, .	906	797	.87–97	40	Dracut, .	330	239	.72–42
14	Ashland, .	450	395	.87–78	41	Cambridge, .	10957	7,915	.72–24
15	Bedford, .	139	122	.87–77	42	Townsend, .	337	243	.72–11
16	Reading, .	557	483	.86–71	43	Marlboro', .	2,395	1,699	.70–94
17	Hudson, .	816	706	.86–52	44	Tewksbury, .	256	181	.70–70
18	Everett, .	1,039	894	.85–95	45	Lexington, .	449	316	.70–38
19	Melrose, .	1,135	971	.85–55	46	Shirley, .	246	173	.70–33
20	Medford, .	1,653	1,404	.84–94	47	Sudbury, .	194	136	.70–10
21	Newton, .	3,611	3,047	.84–88	48	Maynard, .	515	355	.68–93
22	Arlington, .	958	806	.84–13	49	Billerica, .	427	293	.68–62
23	Framingh'm,	1,366	1,148	.84–04	50	Wayland, .	454	308	.67–84
24	Burlington, ,	125	104	.83–20	51	Woburn, .	2,580	1,618	.62–71
25	Somerville, .	5,608	4,627	.82–51	52	Sherborn, .	201	125	.62–19
26	Pepperell, .	443	360	.81–26	53	Malden, .	2,907	1,770	.60–89
27	No. Reading,	140	113	.80–71	54	Lowell, .	10970	6,242	.56–90

NANTUCKET COUNTY.

1	NANTUCKET,	. . . .	565	355	.62–83

NORFOLK COUNTY.

	TOWNS.					TOWNS.			
1	MEDWAY, . .	406	403	.99–26	7	Hyde Park, .	1,606	1,447	.90–10
2	Needham, .	453	444	.98–01	8	Randolph, .	660	591	.89–55
3	Cohasset, .	347	323	.93–08	9	Foxborough,	391	345	.88–24
4	Holbrook, .	445	414	.93–03	10	Weymouth, .	1,993	1,705	.85–55
5	Dedham, .	1,135	1,052	.92–69	11	Wrentham, .	427	364	.85–25
6	Millis, . .	108	98	.90–74	12	Norwood, .	501	424	.84–63

NORFOLK COUNTY — Concluded.

	TOWNS.	No. of children between 5 and 15 years of age in each town.	Average attendance upon School.	Ratio of attendance to the whole No. of children between 5 and 15, expressed in decimals.		TOWNS.	No. of children between 5 and 15 years of age in each town.	Average attendance upon School.	Ratio of attendance to the whole No. of children between 5 and 15, expressed in decimals.
13	Quincy,	2,416	2,003	.82–89	20	Brookline,	1,615	1,276	.79–01
14	Wellesley,	379	314	.82–85	21	Norfolk,	167	131	.78–44
15	Medfield,	203	167	.82–26	22	Braintree,	705	542	.76–88
16	Bellingham,	196	157	.80–10	23	Franklin,	796	558	.70–10
17	Milton,	627	499	.79–59	24	Walpole,	452	314	.69–47
18	Sharon,	227	180	.79–30	25	Canton,	856	500	.58–41
19	Dover,	86	68	.79–07	26	Stoughton,	975	565	.57–95

PLYMOUTH COUNTY.

1	MATTAPOISETT,	183	182	.99–45	15	Marshfield,	217	174	.80–18
2	Marion,	143	141	.98–60	16	Duxbury,	296	232	.78–38
3	Kingston,	224	210	.93–75	17	Halifax,	73	57	.78–08
4	Abington,	629	574	.91–26	18	Hull,	71	54	.76–06
5	Rockland,	880	797	.90–57	19	So. Scituate,	259	192	.74–13
6	So. Abington,	611	543	.88–87	20	Pembroke,	209	154	.73–68
7	Bridgewater,	522	460	.88–12	21	Scituate,	506	371	.73–32
8	Hingham,	666	580	.87–09	22	Hanson,	217	155	.71–43
9	Plymouth,	1,234	1,043	.84 52	23	Carver,	196	139	.70–92
10	E. Bridgew'r,	486	406	.83–54	24	Wareham,	691	489	.70–77
11	Rochester,	162	135	.83–33	25	Plympton,	91	64	.70–33
12	Brockton,	3,477	2,841	.81–71	26	W.Bridgew'r,	312	215	.68–91
13	Middleboro',	864	702	.81–25	27	Lakeville,	167	103	.61–62
14	Hanover,	322	260	.80–75					

SUFFOLK COUNTY.

1	WINTHROP,	201	196	.97–51	3	Chelsea,	4,709	3,532	.75–01
2	Boston,	68702	51662	.75–20	4	Revere,	656	468	.71–34

WORCESTER COUNTY.

1	NORTHBOROUGH,	249	257	1.03–21	7	Princeton,	159	151	.94–97
2	Dana,	107	110	1.02–80	8	Barre,	293	276	.94–20
3	Harvard,	146	145	.99–32	9	Mendon,	162	150	.92–59
4	Brookfield,	465	451	.96–99	10	Lunenburg,	143	132	.92–31
5	Shrewsbury,	260	250	.96–15	11	Oakham,	123	112	.91–06
6	Leominster,	882	842	.95–46	12	Rutland,	175	154	.88–00

WORCESTER COUNTY — Concluded.

	TOWNS.	No. of children between 5 and 15 years of age in each town.	Average attendance upon School.	Ratio of attendance to the whole No. of children between 5 and 15, expressed in decimals.		TOWNS.	No. of children between 5 and 15 years of age in each town.	Average attendance upon School.	Ratio of attendance to the whole No. of children between 5 and 15, expressed in decimals.
13	Sterling,	228	200	.87–72	36	Boylston,	160	122	.76–25
14	N. Braintree,	97	85	.87–63	37	Hardwick,	512	390	.76–17
15	Hubbardston,	216	189	.87–50	38	Spencer,	1,790	1,359	.75–92
16	Westminster,	274	239	.87–23	39	Phillipston,	91	69	.75–82
17	Bolton,	128	111	.86–72	40	Lancaster,	334	253	.75–75
18	Upton,	312	270	.86–54	41	Millbury,	920	693	.75–33
19	Oxford,	311	267	.85–85	42	W. Boylston,	555	416	.74–95
20	Petersham,	148	127	.85–81	43	Northbridge,	769	572	.74–38
21	Berlin,	161	136	.84–47	44	Milford,	1,707	1,238	.72–53
22	Sturbridge,	382	320	.83–77	45	Worcester,	13269	9,598	.72–33
23	Grafton,	820	682	.83–17	46	N. Brookfield,	800	577	.72–13
24	Royalston,	202	168	.83–17	47	Southboro',	323	231	.71–52
25	Athol,	842	688	.81–71	48	Gardner,	1,248	866	.69–39
26	Warren,	752	604	.80–32	49	Blackstone,	1,033	715	.69–22
27	Westboro',	845	678	.80–24	50	Uxbridge,	585	393	.67–18
28	Clinton,	1,774	1,422	.80–16	51	Douglas,	406	268	.66–01
29	Fitchburg,	2,889	2,305	.79–79	52	Holden,	530	347	.65–47
30	Paxton,	95	75	.78–95	53	Auburn,	254	165	.64–96
31	Leicester,	583	460	.78–90	54	W. Brookfield	347	217	.62–54
32	Templeton,	509	401	.78–78	55	Dudley,	564	310	.54–96
33	Winchendon,	689	539	.78–23	56	Southbridge,	1,358	606	.44–62
34	Ashburnh'm,	343	268	.78–13	57	Sutton,	707	315	.44–55
35	Charlton,	303	232	.76–57	58	Webster,	1,145	405	.35–37

TABLE *in which all the Counties are numerically arranged, according to the* AVERAGE ATTENDANCE *of their Children upon the Public Schools for the Year 1885–86.*

1884-85.	1885-86.	COUNTIES.	Ratio of Attendance.
3	1	DUKES, ...	.87–17
2	2	Barnstable, ...	.85–95
6	3	Norfolk, ...	.82–02
2	4	Plymouth, ...	.82–01
4	5	Franklin, ...	.81–05
5	6	Hampshire, ...	.80–04
10	7	Berkshire, ...	.76–27
9	8	Suffolk, ...	.75–21
7	9	Middlesex, ...	.75–03
8	10	Worcester, ...	.73–93
11	11	Essex, ...	.73–72
12	12	Bristol, ...	.69–78
13	13	Nantucket, ...	.62–83
14	14	Hampden, ...	.61–10
	STATE, ...		.77–03

GENERAL INDEX

TO THE

REPORTS OF THE STATE BOARD OF EDUCATION

(VOLUMES 1 TO 50)

From 1838 to 1887.

GENERAL INDEX.

Abbot Academy, Andover, **40**, 285.

Abstracts of reports of school committees : —

    normal schools, teachers' institutes and qualifications of teachers, **21**, 217–243.

    physical and moral education, **21**, 3–134.

    primary schools and elementary education, **21**, 135–216.

    private schools and academies, **21**, 244–252.

    studies and methods of teaching, **22**, 3–250.

    subjects of, **21**, 6; **23**, 2.

    value of, **29**, 6.

Academies, seminaries and institutions : —

    Abbot, Andover, **40**, 285.

    Adams, Quincy, **40**, 278.

    Amesbury and Salisbury, **40**, 345.

    Amherst, **40**, 339.

    Arms, Shelburne Falls, **40**, 345.

    Asylum, American, Hartford, **40**, 350.

    Belcherton Classical School, **40**, 343.

    Belmont Institute, Boston, **40**, 343.

    Berkshire, Lenox, **40**, 337.

    Bradford, **40**, 262.

    Bridgewater, **40**, 262.

    Bristol, Taunton, **40**, 241.

    centennial report on, compiled by G. A. Walton, **40** (Appendix), 174–360.

    Central Village, Dracut, **40**, 343.

    Charlestown Seminary, female, **40**, 343.

    Chauncy Hall School, Boston, **40**, 333.

    Clarke Institution, Northampton, **40**, 352.

    Coffin School, Nantucket, **40**, 282.

    Conway, **40**, 344.

    Cushing, Ashburnham, **40**, 324.

    Day's, Wrentham, **40**, 339.

    Dean, Franklin, **40**, 328.

    Deerfield, **40**, 261.

    Deerfield Academy and Dickinson High School, **40**, 336.

    Derby, Hingham, **40**, 238.

    Drury, North Adams, **40**, 344.

Academies, etc. — *Continued.*

    Dukes County, West Tisbury, **40**, 291.

    Dummer, Byfield, **40**, 229.

    Egremont, **40**, 342.

    Elliot School, Jamaica Plain, **40**, 217.

    English and Classical, West Newton, **40**, 317.

    Fellenburg, Greenfield, **40**, 343.

    Framingham, **40**, 337.

    Franklin, North Andover, **40**, 339.

    Friends, New Bedford, **40**, 270.

    Greylock Institute, Williamstown, **40**, 346.

    Hammond, Charles, paper on New England academies and classical schools, **40** (Appendix), 182.

    Hanover, **40**, 287.

    Haverhill, **40**, 341.

    Hinsdale, **40**, 344.

    Hitchcock Free High School, Brimfield, **40**, 320.

    Hollis Institute, South Braintree, **40**, 344.

    Holyrood, Lowell, **40**, 345.

    Hopkins School, Cambridge, **40**, 280.

    Hopkins School, Hadley, **40**, 271.

    Hopkinton High School, **40**, 344.

    Horace Mann School for the Deaf, Boston, **40**, 354.

    Howe's School, Billerica, **40**, 316.

    Ipswich Female Seminary, **40**, 283.

    Ipswich Grammar School, **40**, 238.

    Jubilee Hill, Pittsfield, **40**, 344.

    Lancaster, **40**, 341.

    Lasell Seminary, Auburndale, **40**, 313.

    Lawrence, Falmouth, **40**, 296.

    Lawrence, Groton, **40**, 250.

    Lawson Classical and Scientific Institute, **40**, 344.

    Lawson, Shelburne Falls, **40**, 343.

    Lee, **40**, 344.

    Leicester, **40**, 234.

    Lexington, **40**, 340.

    Lynn, **40**, 339.

    Maplewood Institute, Pittsfield, **40**, 311.

    Marblehead, **40**, 337.

    Massachusetts School for Feeble-Minded, South Boston, **40**, 357.

    Merrimac, Groveland, **40**, 273.

    Milford, **40**, 341.

    Millbury, **40**, 343.

    Milton, **40**, 337.

    Monson, **40**, 264.

    Mt. Hollis, Holliston, **40**, 344.

    Mount Holyoke Female Seminary, South Hadley, **40**, 299.

    Nantucket, **40**, 337.

    New Church School, Waltham, **40**, 322.

    New England academies and classical schools, paper on, by Charles Hammond, **40** (Appendix), 182.

    New England, Cohasset, **40**, 344.

Academies, etc. — *Continued.*

New Salem, **40**, 258.

Nichols, Dudley, **40**, 272.

normal classes in, **32**, 63–64; **34**, 98, 113.

Northampton Female Seminary, **40**, 343.

Northfield, **40**, 342.

number attending, **50**, 80.

Oread Institute, Worcester, **40**, 315.

Partridge, Duxbury, **40**, 287.

Peirce, Middleborough, **40**, 297.

Pepperell, **40**, 344.

Perkins Institution for the Blind, **40**, 355.

Phillips, Andover, **40**, 220.

Pine Grove Seminary, Harwich, **40**, 344.

plan for normal classes in New York, **32**, 63, 64.

Powers Institute, Bernardston, **40**, 323.

Pratt Free School, North Middleborough, **40**, 323.

Prospect Hill School, Greenfield, **40**, 330.

Punchard Free School, Andover, **40**, 312.

Putnam Free School, Newburyport, **40**, 306.

Quaboag Seminary, Warren, **40**, 344.

Riverside, Newton, **40**, 344.

Roxbury Latin School, Boston Highlands, **40**, 210.

Sanderson, Ashfield, **40**, 339.

Sandwich, **40**, 339.

Sawin, Sherborn, **40**, 332.

Sheffield, **40**, 344.

Sheldon, Southampton, **40**, 342.

Smith, Hatfield, **40**, 331.

South Berkshire Institute, New Marlborough, **40**, 322.

South Reading, **40**, 340.

Springfield Female Seminary, **40**, 342.

statistics of, **40** (Appendix), 176–181.

St. Mark's School, Southborough, **40**, 326.

Stockbridge, **40**, 311.

Thayer, **40**, 345.

Topsfield, **40**, 340.

training classes in, **32**, 62; **33**, 91; **34**, 113.

Walton, George A., report on, **40** (Appendix), 174–181.

Warren, Woburn, **40**, 288.

Wellesley Seminary, **40**, 345.

Wesleyan, Wilbraham, **40**, 273.

West Brookfield Female Seminary, **40**, 340.

Westfield, **40**, 247.

Westford, **40**, 242.

Westminster, **40**, 343.

Weymouth and Braintree, **40**, 341.

Wheaton Female Seminary, Norton, **40**, 303.

Williamstown, **40**, 340.

Williamstown Free School, **40**, 337.

Williston Seminary, Easthampton, **40**, 306.

Winchendon Academy, **40**, 344.

Academies, etc. — *Concluded*.
　　Woodbridge School, Hadley, **40**, 342.
　　Worcester, **40**, 292.
　　Worcester County Free Institute, **40**, 348.
Adams Academy, Quincy, **40**, 278.
Address to the people of Massachusetts, **1**, 71.
Adults, school for. *See* Evening schools.
Agassiz, Louis, permanent instructor in normal schools, **16**, 53; **17**, 70.
Agents of Board of Education, acquaintance of, with the people, necessary, **20**, 60.
　　additional, appointed, **46**, 9.
　　additional one suggested, **32**, 47.
　　appointment of, **14**, 5; **15**, 11, 12.
　　appropriation for, refused, **20**, 59; **24**, 25, 52.
　　authority for appointment of, **40**, 98.
　　Banks, N. P., appointed, 1850, **14**, 48.
　　Bristol County, report of schools on, by George A. Walton, **45**, 203.
　　Crosby, Prof. Alpheus, agent, **18**, 73.
　　　　summary of work of, **19**, 78.
　　distinguished men, **24**, 68.
　　duties of, **40**, 99, 102; **46**, 9.
　　Edwards, Richard, Jr., employed, **18**, 70.
　　examination of schools in Hampden and Franklin Counties, **45**, 225.
　　examination of schools of Norfolk County, by George A. Walton, **43**, 99.
　　　　report on, **43**, 123–248.
　　general report of, **37**, 91.
　　Greene, S. S., appointed, 1850, **14**, 48.
　　Guyot, Prof. Arnold, lectures of, **15**, 18.
　　history of, and value of, **34**, 114, 116.
　　history of plan of, **29**, 17.
　　Hubbard, E. A., resigned, 1883, notice of, **47**, 98.
　　importance of, **14**, 53.
　　larger number needed, **38**, 10, 126; **44**, 138; **45**, 114.
　　Leach, D., appointed, 1851, **15**, 12.
　　Martin, G. H., appointed, 1882, **46**, 9, 89.
　　　　work of, in examination of schools, **47**, 171.
　　meetings of Secretary with, **17**, 68.
　　　　character of work, **17**, 72.
　　object of, and labors of, **14**, 6, 47–49.
　　opportunities of, for observation, **26**, 8.
　　names of, from 1848–60, **24**, 68.
　　　- in order of service, **46**, 99.
　　Northrop, B. G., appointed, 1857, **21**, 59; **22**, 9.
　　　　resigned, 1867, **30**, 7, 73.
　　　　work of, in examination of schools, **20**, 73; **29**, 51.
　　number of, limited to two, **41**, 96.
　　Oliver, H. K., appointed, 1858, **22**, 9.
　　persons employed as, since 1850, **50**, 90.
　　Phipps, A. J., appointed, 1867, **31**, 66,
　　plan of work of, **41**, 104.
　　Prince, John T., appointed, 1883, **47**, 101.
　　qualifications of, **39**, 134.
　　question of necessity of, considered, **20**, 59–65.

Agents of Board of Education, etc. — *Concluded.*

 received with favor, **42**, 74.

 reference of board to, **50**, 13.

 report of J. T. Prince on supervision, **48**, 221.

 report on high schools by G. H. Martin, **48**, 175.

 results of examinations, **48**, 166.

 Secretary's reference to work of, **50**, 145.

 small cost of, **24**, 69.

 success of plan of, **39**, 131.

 their value, **48**, 94.

 towns visited by G. H. Martin, **50**, 189.

 Upham, C. W., appointed, 1851, **15**, 12.

 usefulness of, **16**, 58–62; **23**, 10; **38**, 10.

  discussed, **24**, 25–29.

 value of work of, **26**, 12, 42; **41**, 96.

 Walker, Cornelius, appointed, 1857, **21**, 59.

 Walton, George A., appointed special, for western counties, **35**, 6, 109.

  report of, **37**, 85.

  work of, in examination of schools, **47**, 159.

 work assigned to each, **16**, 6.

 work of, **18**, 50, 54, 69, 70; **21**, 59; **22**, 35; **28**, 4; **29**, 7, 17; **31**, 66–71; **32**, 47; **35**, 80; **36**, 166–169; **39**, 103, 134; **40**, 8, 9, 48, 63; **42**, 69; **48**, 11.

  review of, **16**, 58.

  systematized, **41**, 7.

  too great, **45**, 11.

Aldrich, Hon. P. E., address, **41**, 152.

American Academy of Arts and Sciences, **40**, 92.

American Antiquarian Society, **40**, 98.

American Asylum at Hartford for the Education of the Deaf and Dumb. *See* Deaf-mutes.

American Institute of Instruction, **18**, 51.

 aid from state to, **10**, 229.

Amesbury and Salisbury Academy, **40**, 345.

Amherst Academy, Amherst, **40**, 339.

Amherst College, **40**, 67.

Amusements, character of, **19**, 46.

Andover Theological Seminary, **40**, 102.

Anthony, Francis W., paper by, on the Bradford High School Library, **48**, 257.

Apparatus, deficiency of, **39**, 113; **40**, 61, 66.

 how to secure, **29**, 18.

 improvements in, **10**, 70–72.

 in foreign schools, **7**, 55, 60.

 lack of, **29**, 18; **1**, 67.

 laws respecting, **10**, 216.

 needed, most schools destitute, **24**, 80.

 report of G. H. Prince on, **48**, 196.

 value of, in 1848, **12**, 29; **4**, 63.

 what needed, **50**, 213.

Appleton, William, answers of, to questions respecting religious instruction in the common schools, **18**, 92.

Appropriations, School, **6,** 20; **7,** 15; **8,** 51, 62–65; **9,** 23; **23,** 37.
    comparison of, for different years, **18,** 61; **21,** 47.
    decrease of, **43,** 59.
        valuation fallen off, **43,** 59.
    distribution of, **16,** 35.
    effect of war on, **26,** 68, 70.
    failure to appropriate for agents, **24,** 25.
    for School for Feeble-Minded, **24,** 171.
    improvement slight from year to year, **12,** 23.
    inconvenience arising from time of making, **24,** 24.
    increased, **10,** 68; **11,** 21; **19,** 5; **34,** 106.
    increase of, 1837–48, **12,** 20.
        in amount of, tabular statement of, **34,** 106.
    in different years, **20,** 37.
    largely advanced for 1863–64, **28,** 56.
    large, needed, **38,** 11.
    per child by cities and towns.   *See* Returns in 10th–50th reports.
    reductions of, feared, **26,** 69.
    small fraction of valuation, **29,** 20.
    tables giving average amount of, for ten years, **27,** 57.
    yearly increase of, **37,** 109.
Architecture, School.   *See* School-houses.
Arithmetic, causes of failure in, **22,** 66.
    Colburn's Intellectual, **22,** 65.
    in grammar schools, **15,** 61.
    intermediate course in, **44,** 124.
    manner of teaching, **47,** 108; **48,** 98.
    method of teaching, in foreign schools, **7,** 100; **9,** 115.
        in Germany, **49,** 261.
    numbers, primary work in, **44,** 105.
Arms Academy, Shelburne, **40,** 345.
Arnold, James, donation of books by, to State Normal School at Bridgewater, **25,** 11.
Art education, commercial value of. **36,** 9.
    course of study for primary and grammar schools, **48,** 214–221.
    director of.   *See* Director.
    evening classes, course in industrial drawing, **38,** 55.
        exhibition of, report of committee, **38,** 65–76.
    exhibition of work, and report of judges, **43,** 289.
    history and progress of, **40,** 6.
    history of English effort in, report of Mr. Rapet, **38,** 8, 9.
    industrial education.   *See* Industrial.
    synopsis of course of study in public schools for thirteen years, **38,** 53–55.
Articulation.   *See* Deaf-mutes.
Art School, Normal, aim of, **50,** 49.
    appropriation for, **39,** 17.
    Bartlett, G. H., appointed principal of, 1883, **47,** 47.
        notice of, **47,** 47.
    building for, **48,** 10.
        necessary, **38,** 7, 46; **39,** 56; **40,** 11; **43,** 288; **48,** 50.
        new, description of, **50,** 51.
            plans of, **50,** 53–56.
        new plans of, report of G. H. Bartlett on, **47,** 213.

Art School, etc. — *Concluded*.
  Centennial Exposition, **43**, 284.
  condition of, in 1884, **47**, 213.
  Deacon House, a year at, **45**, 243.
    leased, **44**, 11–39.
  Director of. *See* Director.
  enlargement of curriculum of, **48**, 46.
  exhibit of, at Centennial, **40**, 36, 37.
    value of, **40**, 38.
  forward steps of, **50**, 50.
  Fuchs, Otto, acting principal of, 1883, **47**, 46.
  good results of, **43**, 10.
  grant of land for building for, **44**, 11.
  influence of, **40**, 36, 37.
  law respecting, **37**, 145.
  letter of Richard Redgrave, **38**, 48.
  need of, **36**, 108; **38**, 6; **42**, 105.
  object of, **37**, 33; **43**, 282.
  opened, 1873, **37**, 10.
  origin and history of, **43**, 279.
  organization of, **37**, 35.
  papers relating to, **37**, 40–48.
  prospectus of, **37**, 45.
  reasons for support of, **43**, 40.
  recommended, **36**, 10, 32, 34, 168.
  regulations of, **37**, 46.
  removed to School Street, **39**, 19.
  report of, **43**, 39; **46**, 40.
  report of A. G. Boyden on, **40**, 169–173.
  report of C. M. Carter, **49**, 209.
  report of visitors, **38**, 34; **39**, 54–57; **41**, 39; **42**, 39; **44**, 39
  resolves relating to, **37**, 34.
  results of, **43**, 283–285, 287.
  results of examinations, **38**, 51, 52.
  rooms of, in Pemberton Square, **39**, 18.
  scheme of work in, **48**, 47–49.
  successful beginning of, **37**, 38, 39.
  successful work in, **39**, 82–84.
  successful year, **47**, 10.
  success of, **39**, 18.
    under difficulties, **38**, 46.
  teachers and lecturers of, **37**, 45, 46.
  visitors and teachers of, **40**, 173.
Ashley, J. B., generosity of, **27**, 28.
Assistant Secretary, Dr. S. C. Jackson, **27**, 10.
    appointed, 1848, **13**, 51.
    value of work of, **26**, 12.
    resignation of, 1876, **40**, 10.
  O. Warner appointed, 1876, **40**, 11.
  C. B. Tillinghast appointed, 1879, **43**, 12.

Associations, advantages of, **22**, 9.
    aid for, **22**, 9.
    county, **1**, 68.
        aid to and management of, **24**, 73.
        assisted by state, **23**, 10.
        history of the several associations that have received state aid, **25**, 14–19.
    productive of good, **26**, 11.
    school committees', **41**, 111; **42**, 73, 74; **44**, 12, 95; **45**, 69.
    state and county, uniting of, **29**, 12.
    teachers', object of, **17**, 11, 72.
        of invaluable service, **8**, 71; **13**, 47.
        resolve of Board of Education concerning, **25**, 13.
    town, short lived, **25**, 19.
        suggested, **1**, 68.
Astronomical Observatory, **40**, 61.
Attendance (*see also* Truancy), abstracts of committees' reports on, **1**, 37, 169;
    4, 65; **5**, 33; **6**, 20–24; **7**, 12–14; **8**, 14; **9**, 24–30; **23** (Abstracts),
    111–209; **25** (Abstracts), 94.
    agents' report upon, **50**, 163.
    attention of Legislature called to the large number of children kept from
    school, **14**, 10, 11.
    basis of per cent. of, **43**, 58.
    cheerful obedience, **47**, 15.
    comparison of, for different years, **10**, 84–93.
    complaints of non-attendance and irregularity in reports of school committees,
    37, 127.
    compulsory, **34**, 84, 91, 120; **36**, 19; **46**, 64; **47**, 15.
        law not enforced, **34**, 85; **41**, 114.
        weak point in our school system, **34**, 120.
    decrease in number between five and fifteen, **23**, 37.
    diminished, **21**, 7, 47.
    discussed, **46**, 61.
    employment of children in manufacturing establishments, **20**, 48.
    exclusion from school, **24**, 134.
    increased, **11**, 31; **22**, 31.
    increase of, comparison, **26**, 6, 7; **39**, 110, 122.
    irregularity and tardiness, **19**, 52; **20**, 51; **25** (Abstracts), 193, 208.
    laws respecting, and comments, **20**, 49; **24**, 131–135; **37**, 136; **38**, 182;
        44, 139–144; **46**, 129–138; **50**, 107.
        early laws concerning, **50**, 163.
    laws and execution, **37**, 137–139.
    laws explained, **48**, 86.
    local interruptions, **48**, 184.
    non-attendance and irregularity, **14**, 29, 19, 52.
        from religious and social considerations, **20**, 50.
        involves loss of appropriations, **20**, 48.
        no remedy found for, **20**, 46, 47.
    number not attending any school, **20**, 54.
    objections to regular, **11**, 109.
    parents, teachers and committees must co-operate, **13**, 33; **20**, 52.
    rank of towns of state in. *See* Returns in 10th–50th reports.
    regular and punctual, required, **45**, 75, 76.

Attendance, etc. — *Concluded.*

    regularity of, must be secured, **36,** 18 ; **48,** 69.

    responsibility of parents concerning, **22,** 31.

    right of children in one town to attend school in another, law respecting, and comments, **24,** 133.

    rules for, may be enforced, **48,** 75.

    school time of children in manufacturing establishments should be increased, **20,** 50.

    slight falling off, **29,** 13, 14.

    statistical tables, showing the advance in education compared with growth in population, etc., **25,** 102–109.

    tendency to abridge the time of, **13,** 32.

    test of utility of schools, **23,** 65.

    vaccination, law respecting, **24,** 134.

    wrong impressions received from returns, **13,** 32.

Auchmuty, Richard T., paper by, on New York trade schools, **47,** 195–200.

Back Bay, sales of land in, receipts from, paid to school fund, **25,** 49.

Bail, Louis, letter from, on industrial drawing, **34,** 186–192.

Bancroft, George, answers of, to questions respecting religious instruction in the, common schools, **18,** 91–92.

Banks, N. P., agent, appointed, 1851, **14,** 48.

Barnard, Henry, letter from, on industrial drawing, **34,** 213–217.

Barre, State Normal School at. *See* Westfield.

Barry, Charles A., letter from, on industrial drawing, **34,** 209–212.

Bartholomew, William N., letter from, on industrial drawing, **34,** 192–198.

Bartlett, George H., principal of Normal Art School, appointed, 1883, **47,** 47.

Bates, William G., address by, at dedication of Bridgewater Normal School, **10,** 6, 12.

Belchertown Classical School, **40,** 343.

Belmont Institute, Boston, **40,** 343.

Beneficiaries of special institutions, statistics of, **50,** 71.

Berkshire Academy, Lenox, **40,** 337.

Bible history, etc., method of teaching, in foreign schools, **7,** 125.

Bible in schools (*see also* Religious instruction), **8,** 15–17, 75 ; **18,** 66.

    daily reading of the, **21,** 67 ; **50,** 106.

        law respecting, and comments, **24,** 104 ; **46,** 120–122.

Bigelow, George N., principal of State Normal School at Framingham, resigned, 1866, **30,** 20.

Bigelow, Dr. H., **30,** 119.

    in memoriam, **30,** 107–109.

Blackboards, directions for making, **17,** 101.

    multiplied, **28,** 47.

Blind, Schools for the, account of, **46,** 56.

    aid from state to, **10,** 230.

    appeal for printing fund for, **45,** 57.

    condition of, **41,** 60.

    kindergarten, **48,** 63 ; **50,** 73.

    object teaching in, **48,** 63.

    Perkins Institution, **24,** 169 ; **39,** 163 ; **40,** 355 ; **42,** 61 ; **50,** 72.

        industrial work in, **50,** 75.

        methods of teaching in, **44,** 64–66.

        progress of pupils in, **48,** 64.

Blind, Schools for the — *Concluded.*
    report of, **43,** 55; **44,** 63.
    state of school, **45,** 58–61.
    terms of admission to, **24,** 170; **39,** 176.
    working of, "means and methods," **47,** 73.
Boarding round, **19,** 75.
Board of Education, address ot, to the people of Massachusetts, **1,** 71.
    agents of. *See* Agents.
    almoner of state, **26,** 13.
    committee of, to act with Secretary before the legislative committee, **17,** 65.
    conformity to law, **11,** 10.
    constitution of, **24,** 62.
    duties of, **24,** 67, 68; **45,** 66.
        prescribed by law, **36,** 6.
    elements of weakness and strength, **45,** 8.
    established by act of Legislature, 1837, **1,** 5; **45,** 66.
    executive committee, **17,** 64.
    history of, in brief, by Secretary, **50,** 76.
    influence of, **18,** 46–48.
    instrumentalities of, **29,** 7.
    laws respecting, **10,** 191, 214; **24,** 61–70; **38,** 132; **46,** 95–100; **50,** 88.
    limit of power of, **11,** 7–10; **36,** 5.
    meetings of, **44,** 7.
        first, **1,** 5.
    members of, **24,** 67.
        list of, in order of service, to 1883, **46,** 95, 96.
        names of, from its organization to 1861, **24,** 62, 63.
            from 1837 to 1874, **38,** 135.
            from 1838 to 1886, **50,** 89.
        original, **50,** 76.
    need of, **8,** 8.
    need of an office for, **12,** 149.
    no direct control over schools, **37,** 5.
    normal schools intrusted to, **37,** 5.
    of Maine, **10,** 10.
    organization and efficiency of, **17,** 63; **24,** 61.
    oversight of schools required, **45,** 10.
    relation of. to schools, **45,** 7.
    report of, **1,** 5.
        how far valuable, **20,** 62.
        what it is required to contain, **16,** 5.
    results of labors of, **8,** 9–15; **45,** 9, 68.
    Secretary of. *See* Secretary.
    select committees, **17,** 67.
    unpaid, **8,** 3.
    usefulness of, **24,** 67, 68; **41,** 8.
    value of the organization, **19,** 50.
    work of, **20,** 5; **21,** 5.
Books, School, changes of law respecting, **31,** 46.
        and comments, **24,** 105–107.
    commission of examination of, proposed, **31,** 6
    defects of, and remedies, **1,** 14, 15; **2,** 62, 66.

Books, School — *Concluded.*

    diversity of, **28**, 49.

    failure of committees to supply destitute children, **28**, 71.

        to provide, **24**, 107.

    free text-books. *See* Free.

    laws respecting, **1**, 33, 35; **10**, 183–187; **28**, 70; **40**, 84, 90; **46**, 120–122; **50**, 105.

    multitude of, an evil, **31**, 6.

    reading, **7**, 51–55.

    recommending, **2**, 76.

    selection of, and evils attending, **1**, 32; **2**, 76; **14**, 29.

    should be condensed, **48**, 18.

    uniformity of, **4**, 61–63; **5**, 37; **25**, 121.

Boston, city normal school established in, 1853, **17**, 11.

Boston College, **40**, 79.

Boston Public Library, law respecting, **12**, 29.

Boston Society of Natural History, **40**, 88.

    grant of land for use of, **25**, 50.

Boston University, **40**, 76.

    School of Theology of, **40**, 106.

Botany, scientific course of study in, **44**, 137.

Boutwell, George S., Secretary of the Board of Education, address by, at dedication of State Normal School at Salem, **18**, 10, 25.

    appointed, 1855, **19**, 8.

    reports as Secretary (appended to 20th–24th annual reports of the Board).

    resignation of, 1860, **24**, 19.

Bowditch, Nathaniel Ingersoll, bequest of, to State Normal School at Salem, **25**, 11, 39.

Boyden, A. G., paper by, **40** (Appendix), 146.

Bradford Academy, Bradford, **40**, 262.

Bradford High School Library, paper by F. W. Anthony on, **48**, 257.

Bridgewater, school of observation at, **48**, 25; **50**, 23.

Bridgewater, State Normal School at : —

    Arnold, James, donation to, of books by, **25**, 11.

    assistant teachers from, **50**, 22.

    boarding hall and park, **50**, 25.

    Boyden, A. G., appointed principal of, **24**, 7.

    building at, dedication of, **10**, 6, 9–12.

        address of William G. Bates at, **10**, 6, 12.

        enlargement of, **35**, 24, 99.

        plans of, **10**, 241–245, 253.

    Conant, Marshall, appointed principal of, 1854, **18**, 6.

        resigned, 1860, **24**, 7.

    contributions to libraries and cabinets of, **30**, 31.

    donations to, **12**, 8; **25**, 35.

    donors to library at, **26**, 26; **27**, 20.

    Emerson, George B., donation by, to, **19**, 21.

    London Encyclopædia presented to, by Hon. John Davis, **9**, 21.

    physical science and methods in, **50**, 22.

    reports of visitors to (appended to the annual reports of the Board).

    sewerage in, investigation of, **47**, 23.

    Sharpe, Professor, lectures by, at, **19**, 21.

Bridgewater, State Normal School at — *Concluded.*
    Tillinghast, Nicholas, first principal of, 1840, **4, 5**; **7,** 5.
        resigned, 1853, **17, 15**.
        notice of, **18,** 6.
    visitors and teachers of, 1840–76, **40,** 154–156.
Bridgewater Academy, Bridgewater, **40,** 262.
Bristol Academy, Taunton, **40,** 241.
Bristol County, report of G. A. Walton on schools in, **45,** 203.
Brooks, Rev. Charles, died July 7, 1872, notice of, **36,** 194–196.
Brussels Congress for the amelioration of the condition of deaf-mutes, **47,** 63.
Bureau of Education, national, **30,** 14.
    benefits of, **30,** 14.
Bussey Institution, **40,** 60.

Cartée, Cornelius S., letter of, on the construction of school-houses, **17,** 76–78.
Carter, Charles M., paper on drawing by, **46,** 261–301.
    report of, **49,** 209.
Centennial Exposition, appropriation for inadequate, **40,** 6.
    art school exhibit. **40,** 5, 6, 36, 37, 42.
        value of, **40,** 38.
    drawing in, **43,** 287.
    educational exhibit, very complete, **41,** 5.
    extract from circular of commissioners, **39,** 2.
    preparation for, **39,** 21, 22.
Central Village Academy, Dracut, **40,** 343.
Charitable institutions, **48,** 13.
Charlestown Female Seminary, Charlestown, **40,** 343.
Chauncy Hall School, Boston, **40,** 343.
Children, age of, **23,** 56.
    conveyance of, to school, **50,** 107.
    constant vigilance required, **29,** 65.
    disregard of law concerning, **29,** 65.
    employment of, in factories. *See* Factories.
    foreign parentage of, in schools in 1848, **12,** 135.
    generosity of M. H. Simpson, Saxonville, **28,** 52.
    ignorance an obstacle to progress, **23,** 57.
    laws respecting, **40,** 86.
        and comments, **23,** 135–137; **28,** 50.
    neglected or abused, **46,** 139–141; **50,** 109.
        act concerning the care and education of, **31,** 41; **42,** 257.
    number of, attending school, **50,** 61, (Abstracts) iii–cxxxiv.
        employed in 1858, **23,** 57.
    officers to see that laws are obeyed, **31,** 49.
    should be required to attend school from fifteen to eighteen weeks in the year, **23,** 56.
    truant. *See* Truancy.
Circular letters. *See* Laborers, Libraries, Physiology, Schools.
Civil war, advance in education during the, **29,** 50.
    effects on education, **26,** 5, 7, 14, 18, 38, 60; **29,** 46, 47.
    facts developed by the, **26,** 5.
    first, second, third and fourth year of the, **29,** 47, 48.
    increase of appropriations during the, **29,** 49.
    school system of Massachusetts tested by the, **26,** 18; **27,** 10, 11.

Clarke, John, founder of Clarke Institution, **33**, 9, 44; **34**, 35.
Clarke Institution for Deaf-Mutes at Northampton. *See* Deaf-mutes.
Clerc, Laurent, death of, **34**, 68.
Coffin School, Nantucket, **40**, 282.
Colleges and historical societies : —
   American Academy of Arts and Sciences, **40**, 92.
   American Antiquarian Society, **40**, 98.
   Amherst College, **40**, 67.
   Andover Theological Seminary, **40**, 102.
   Boston College, **40**, 79.
   Boston Society of Natural History, **40**, 88.
   Boston University, **40**, 76.
   Episcopal Theological School, **40**, 105.
   Essex Institute, **40**, 100.
   Harvard College, **40**, 48.
      Divinity School, 55.
      Law School, 56.
      Medical School, 57.
      Dental School, 58.
      Lawrence Scientific School, 59.
      Bussey Institution, 60.
      Astronomical Observatory, 61.
      Botanic Garden, 62.
      Museum of Comparative Zoölogy, 62.
   Holy Cross, **40**, 78.
   Massachusetts Agricultural College, **40**, 80.
   Massachusetts Historical Society, **40**, 85.
   Massachusetts Institute of Technology, **40**, 94.
   Museum of Fine Arts, **40**, 96.
   New Church Theological School, **40**, 104.
   New England Historic Genealogical Society, **40**, 90.
   Newton Theological Institution, **40**, 103.
   Paper on, by O. Warner, **40** (Appendix), 48, 107.
   School of Theology of Boston University, **40**, 106.
   Smith College, **40**, 83.
   Tufts College, **40**, 72.
   Tufts Divinity School, **40**, 107.
   Wellesley College, **40**, 85.
   Williams College, **40**, 63.
Committees, School, action of, **19**, 74.
   appointment and powers of, **14**, 94.
   associations of, **41**, 111; **42**, 73, 74; **44**, 12, 95; **45**, 69.
   centralization of power feared, **13**, 37.
   changes in, detrimental, **18**, 66.
   choice of, **18**, 66; **19**, 73.
      manner of, **24**, 98.
      laws respecting, and comments, **24**, 98–108.
   compensation of, **1**, 10, 41; **2**, 22; **46**, 122.
      laws respecting, and comments, **24**, 107; **37**, 131.
   discretionary powers of, large, **50**, 114.
   duties of, **1**, 29; **2**, 22; **46**, 68–76; **48**, 77.
      laws respecting, **10**, 159; **24**, 98; **33**, 127–138.

Committees, School — *Concluded.*

    engaging teachers, **1,** 29.

    evils arising from having two sets of, **13,** 36; **18,** 54.

    examination of teachers, laws respecting, **10,** 160–166.

    examination of teachers by printed questions, **10,** 74–80.

    failure in duties of, **1,** 44.

    importance of, **1,** 8; **3,** 19; **4,** 75; **22,** 51; **27,** 44; **47,** 17

    law prescribing duties of, defects in, **18,** 68.

        respecting, **46,** 115.

    not sufficient for work needed, **48,** 173.

    obstacles in the way of, **1,** 10, 41, 45.

    organization of, **41,** 70.

    powers and duties, **13,** 36; **24,** 98.

    prudential. *See* Prudential.

    reports of, **8,** 52; **10,** 93–97; **33,** 136.

        abstracts of (appended to Secretary's reports).

        attention invited to, **26,** 50.

        complaints of non-attendance and irregularity n, **37,** 127.

        details required, **28,** 69.

        discreditable, **22,** 38.

        improvement in, **24,** 67; **28,** 68.

        laws respecting, **10,** 207, 214, 180, 200, 228; **33,** 136.

        objections to, answered, **28,** 67.

        remarks of Mr. Mann on, **28,** 68.

        valuable, **25,** 94.

        wide range of subjects in, **31,** 74.

    shall the town or prudential, elect teachers? **13,** 38.

        question carefully considered, **13,** 38–46.

    vacancies, how filled, laws respecting, and comments, **24,** 98.

    visitation of schools, laws respecting, **10,** 180–183; **24,** 104.

    when required to elect, **45,** 65.

    women as members of, **35,** 107.

Common schools. *See* Schools.

Composition, elementary, **44,** 103.

    methods of teaching, **47,** 107.

        in foreign schools, **7,** 105.

Compulsory attendance. *See* Attendance.

Compulsory education. *See* Education.

Conant, Marshall, appointed principal of State Normal School at Bridgewater, 1854
    18, 6.

    resigned, 1860, **24,** 7.

Connell, W., paper by, on free text-books, **45,** 257.

Constitution of the United States, methods of studying the, **48,** 132.

Contagious diseases, laws respecting, **48,** 79.

    rules for preventing the spread of, **42,** 143.

Conventions, county, organized, **1,** 7.

    plan and purpose of, **1,** 72, 73.

    report of, **1,** 8, 22; **2,** 27; **3,** 3–5; **4,** 9.

    substitute for, proposed, **5,** 25.

Conveyance of pupils, **33,** 107.

Conway Academy, Conway, **40,** 344.

Corporal punishment. *See* Punishment.

County associations. *See* Association.

Course of studies. *See* Studies.

Cousin, Victor, article on supervision in the Netherlands, **41,** 67.

 extract from his account of schools in Germany, **37,** 7.

Cramming, remedy for, **31,** 10–12.

 in grammar, **31,** 11, 12.

Crime, criminal class most expensive, **23,** 65.

 England and Scotland, experience of, in regard to, **21,** 63–68.

 prevention of, easier than reformation, **21,** 69.

 relation of education to, **1,** 65; **11,** 52; **21,** 62–65; **23,** 59, 64; **46,** 62.

Crocker, Miss Lucretia, opinion of, concerning the present condition of schools, **44,** 229–230.

 paper by, lessons on color in primary schools, **46,** 247–258.

Crosby, Prof. Alpheus, agent, 1855, **18,** 73.

 appointed principal of State Normal School at Salem, 1857, **21,** 7, 31.

 resigned, 1865, **29,** 10.

 summary of work of, **19,** 78.

Cushing, Thomas P. *See* Todd, H.

Cushing Academy, Ashburnham, **40,** 324.

Davis, Emerson, address of, **10,** 8.

Davis, John, London Encyclopædia presented by, to State Normal School at Bridgewater, **9,** 21.

Day's Academy, Wrentham, **40,** 339,

Deacon House. *See* Art School, Normal.

Deaf-mutes, aid from state for, **10,** 230.

 articulation, **33,** 9, 43, 45, 75, 79; **34,** 37.

 in schools in Europe, **7,** 25–36.

 Brussels Congress, **47,** 63.

 claims of, on the state, **40,** 82.

 earlier education required, **31,** 55.

 European institutions for, report of Miss Rogers on, **36,** 162, 163.

 foreign schools for, **34,** 38.

 institutions doing noble work for, **39,** 145.

 institutions for : —

  American Asylum at Hartford, **40,** 350; **50,** 67.

   aim and policy of, **47,** 58, 59.

   appropriation for education of pupils of, **31,** 52.

   appropriations for, **24,** 169.

   change of name of, **31,** 52.

   comments upon, **31,** 51.

   Connecticut, new American Asylum, **31,** 51, 53.

   drawing, free schools to be established in, **33,** 10.

   duty of Board of Education, **31,** 13.

   expatriation, **31,** 55.

   extract from report of committee, **31,** 54, 58.

   extracts from reports of, **31,** 82–93; **37,** 117; **39,** 150; **41,** 52.

   extracts from report of Mr. Stone, on visible speech, **38,** 114.

   improved methods, **48,** 56.

   list of beneficiaries, **32,** 66–71; **33,** 68, 72.

   methods of teaching in, **44,** 49–54; **46,** 50.

   report of, **35,** 60; **42,** 54; **43,** 50; **44,** 49.

Deaf-mutes, institutions for, etc. — *Concluded.*
  sign language, argument for, **45**, 48–52.
   chief medium, **48**, 55; **49**, 54.
  terms of admission to, **34**, 64; **35**, 65.
  two methods discussed, **47**, 59, 62.
 Clarke Institution, **32**, 41, 84; **33**, 43; **33**, 9; **40**, 352; **50**, 68.
  claim of, for state support, **50**, 69.
  Clarke, John, founder and benefactor of, **33**, 9, 44; **34**, 35.
  Clerc, Laurent, death of, **34**, 68.
  course of study and methods in, **50**, 68.
  domestic training, **37**, 122.
  extracts from report of, **37**, 120; **38**, 120; **39**, 156; **41**, 55.
  incorporated, 1867, **31**, 57.
  introduction of articulation in, **39**, 156.
  Jacobs, John A., death of, 34, 69.
  methods of teaching in, **44**, 55–56; **46**, 52.
  oral method vindicated, **47**, 62, 66–68.
  principal of, change of, **50**, 68.
  report of committee, **35**, 47.
   of president, **32**, 85–93; **34**, 35–41; **35**, 41.
   of principal, **32**, 94–111; **33**, 51; **34**, 46–57.
   of teachers, **31**, 106–110.
  terms of admission to, **31**, 111; **32**, 112; **33**, 65; **34**, 59; **35**, 55.
  two methods of teaching, **32**, 42, 76–83.
  visible speech in, **45**, 53, 54.
  workshop, **37**, 121.
 Horace Mann School (formerly the Boston School), **34**, 74; **35**, 70; **41**, 58; **42**, 57; **43**, 53; **44**, 59; **46**, 53; **50**, 69.
  a day school, **48**, 59.
  character and method of, **47**, 69.
  expenditures of state for, **34**, 77.
  extracts from report of committee, **38**, 118.
  grant of land for building, **49**, 60.
  methods of teaching, **44**, 59.
  new building needed, **47**, 71.
  report of school committee on, **34**, 75; **45**, 55.
  work of, **48**, 60.
 instruction of, in drawing, **37**, 118.
 laws concerning the education of, **31**, 50; **33**, 111; **35**, 77; **38**, 194.
  and comments, **39**, 147–149; **43**, 48.
 meeting of commissioners of New England states, **31**, 53.
 method of teaching, in Germany, **47**, 64.
 number of, estimated, **41**, 54.
  in state in 1865, **32**, 42.
 provision for, address of governor, **31**, 54.
 resolve of committee of Legislature concerning, **31**, 51.
 special attention given to, **43**, 10.
 state provision for, **43**, 47.
 statistics of institutions for, **36**, 156, 157.
 terms of admission to institutions, **36**, 159, 164.
 two methods of teaching, **31**, 56, 58, 59, 101.

Deaf-mutes — *Concluded.*

    vigilance urged upon school committees, **35,** 97.

    visible speech, **35,** 72–76; **36,** 158, 159, 161; **37,** 118, 121; **38,** 114.

        report of committee on, **35, 7**4.

Dean Academy, Franklin, **40,** 328.

Deerfield Academy, Deerfield, **40,** 261.

Deerfield Academy and Dickinson High School, Deerfield, **40,** 336.

Defacing school-houses. *See* School-houses.

Defective classes. *See* Blind, Deaf-mutes, Feeble-minded.

Derby Academy, Hingham, **40,** 338.

Dickinson, John W., principal of State Normal School at Westfield, appointed, 1856,

    20, 9, 19.

    notice of, **41,** 8–16.

    resigned, 1877, **41,** 16.

    Secretary of Board of Education, appointed, 1877, **41,** 8.

    reports as Secretary (appended to the 41st–50th annual reports of the Board).

Dickinson, Mrs. J. W., letter from, on industrial drawing, **34,** 204–208.

Dictionaries, distribution of, ceased in 1858, **25,** 51.

    furnished to all schools, **14,** 61; **22,** 32.

    much used, **28,** 53.

Director of art education, address of, **35,** 134.

    appointment of Walter Smith, **35,** 9, 110.

    change of work from year to year, **40,** 45.

    circular of, **36,** 47.

    notice of, **36,** 8, 168.

    recommendations of, **37,** 36.

    report of, **36,** 22–37; **37,** 56–62; **38,** 39–50; **39,** 72–84; **40,** 42–45; **44,**

        189–219; **45,** 243–253.

    work of, **35,** 110; **36,** 24.

Discipline (*see also* Punishment, Corporal).

    emulation, **9,** 138–144.

    expediency of a code of laws, **9,** 90.

    government of schools, moral power needed, **26,** 79.

        should not be despotic, **30,** 15.

    improvements in, **10,** 80–84.

    improving, **20,** 54.

    management of school, **48,** 76.

    mistakes in, **19,** 59–65.

    motives, **9,** 96.

    refractory pupils, should they be dismissed? **9,** 99.

    requisites of good, **4,** 92–96; **6,** 38, 39.

    rigid forms to be avoided, **30,** 15.

    self-government, **9,** 94.

    two extremes to be avoided, **28,** 7, 8.

    whispering, means to prevent, **9,** 116–125.

Districts, School, abolishment of, advantages of, **20,** 81; **23,** 8; **25** (Abstracts),

    53; **29,** 15.

    bill passed, 1869, **33,** 120.

    by the Legislature of Massachusetts, 1883, **46,** 8.

    in other states, by law, **18,** 56.

    law for the, **33,** 112.

        made permissive, **34,** 81.

Districts, School — *Concluded.*

   abolishment of, law for the, repealed, **23**, 74.

      respecting, and comments, **24**, 114.

   partial, **18**, 55.

   report of committee on education on, **33**, 115–120.

      school committees on, **23** (Abstracts), 3.

   will not be gradual, **20**, 81.

  action of, **19**, 74–78.

  act of 1870, to authorize towns to re-establish the district system, **34**, 121.

  a hindrance, **40**, 58, 64, 66.

  assessment of taxes, laws respecting, **24**, 120–123.

  circular letter of B. Sears in respect to, **16**, 37.

      answers to, from J. J. Babson, D. Leach, Jr., R. A. Merriam, N. N. Withington, N. Hall, E. O. Pinney, George Packard, S. B. Perry, H. Bigelow, Augustus Pope, **16**, 37–48.

  circulars to towns on, **20**, 78.

  clerk to be chosen, **24**, 118.

  contiguous, in adjoining towns, **10**, 155, 156.

      laws respecting, and comments, **24**, 125.

  distribution of school money among, **8**, 77–101; **10**, 144; **16**, 35.

  evils connected with, **3**, 94; **4**, 17–24; **5**, 29; **16**, 26–51; **26**, 62–68; **27**, 49, 50; **29**, 15; **39**, 98.

  history, evils, **44**, 91–95.

  history of, **24**, 112.

  how can evil be lessened? **20**, 82–85.

  laws respecting, **10**, 129–132, 146–148, 160; **46**, 125; **50**, 114.

      and comments, **24**, 111, 127; **31**, 44; **38**, 164.

  may raise money for school-houses, **24**, 119.

  meetings, laws respecting, and comments, **24**, 117.

  number of, **19**, 76.

  origin of, **29**, 84, 85.

  penalty for not providing school-houses, laws respecting, **24**, 120.

  redistricting, **19**, 74.

  serious evil, **21**, 49–55.

      suggestions to mitigate, **21**, 49–52.

  state of population favorable to an improved system, **16**, 25.

  subdivision of, **28**, 78.

  subject discussed, **23**, 74–80.

  suggestion for change of plans, **20**, 82.

  system of, observations on, **16**, 24.

  taxes, laws respecting, **10**, 153, 155; **38**, 194.

  town the unit of our political system, **26**, 67.

  towns where restored, **40**, 95.

  union districts, laws respecting, **10**, 157, 158.

  union, laws respecting, and comments, **24**, 124.

  when established, **45**, 65.

Dog tax, law relating to, **34**, 121; **46**, 142.

Drawing. *See also* Art School, Director.

  act concerning free instruction in, **34**, 143, 163.

  agents wanted to promote instruction in, **34**, 159.

  appendix to Secretary's report, **34**, 163–217.

  appointment of Walter Smith as art master, **35**, 109.

Drawing — *Concluded.*

    appropriation for agent, **35,** 108.

    benefits of, **34,** 6.

    circulars of information, **35,** 148.

    claims of law and testimony of eminent men, **34,** 143–159.

    commercial value of, **36,** 9.

    course of study in, for primary and grammar schools. **49,** 214–221.

    evening classes in, **35,** 149; **36,** 30; **37,** 66, 68; **38,** 80; **39,** 73.

    exhibition of, in Boston, **36,** 31.

        report of, **36,** 47. '

        state. **45,** 252.

    exhibition of drawings, from evening classes. report of, **39,** 78–81.

    favor accorded, **36,** 7.

    free schools in, to be established for the deaf and dumb, **33,** 10.

    hints on teaching, **47,** 109.

    history of movement to introduce free instruction in common schools, **34,** 143–159; **36,** 7.

    "travelling museum," **36,** 22.

    in day schools, **39,** 74–77.

    industrial. *See* Industrial.

    in normal schools, **34,** 158; **39,** 77, 78; **41,** 3; **45,** 246; **48,** 15.

    introduction of, **45,** 67.

    list of towns having, **40,** 93.

    paper on, by C. M. Carter, **46,** 261–301.

    papers on, **35,** 134–153.

       . by C. O. Thompson, George Gladwin, William R. Ware, Louis Bail, Wm. N. Bartholomew, J. S Woodman, Mrs. J. W. Dickinson, Charles A. Barry, Henry Barnard, **34,** 170–217.

    plan for first year's course in schools where drawing has not been taught, by C. M. Carter, **47,** 201–210.

    plans for teaching in different grades, **35,** 140–147.

    practical uses of, **26,** 84, 85.

    programme of, for public schools, **43,** 294.

        synopsis of, **43,** 296–345.

    purchase of casts by cities, **36,** 34.

        models, **35,** 110.

    required to be taught, **35,** 8; **41,** 4.

    school of art at South Boston, **36,** 35.

    spread of, in state, **43,** 293.

    synopsis for thirteen years' course, **38,** 53–55.

    teachers' class at Worcester, **35,** 152.

Drury Academy, North Adams, **40,** 344.

Dukes Academy, West Tisbury, **40,** 291.

Dummer Academy, Byfield, **40,** 229.

Dunton, Larkin, paper by, on methods of teaching in German schools, **49,** 259–283.

Dwight, Hon Edmund, died April 5, 1849, **13,** 14.

    donation of, for teachers' institutes, **9,** 45.

    efforts of, for the establishment of the Board of Education and normal schools, **13,** 14.

Dwight School, Boston, report on industrial instruction in the, **46,** 217–223.

Eastburn, Bishop, answers of, to questions respecting religious instruction in the common schools, **18**, 92.

Education, ability to read and write a low standard on which to base the estimate of the intelligence of a people, **11**, 52–55.

     aids and encouragements to, laws, **10**, 226.

     a means of removing poverty and securing abundance, **12**, 53.

     argument on obligation to educate children, **10**, 111–128.

     a science and an art, **10**, 43.

     attention of, to elements enjoined, **25**, 96.

     Board of.   *See* Board of Education.

     character of reading and amusements, **19**, 46.

     circular to officers of penal institutions, **23**, 60.

         answers to same, **23**, 62, 63.

     civil war, effects, etc., of the, on.   *See* Civil war.

     compulsory, **11**, 121; **27** (Abstracts), 16; **34**, 110; **46**, 64.

     courses of study too extended, **15**, 32.

     Cousin, Victor, account of German schools, **37**, 7.

     crime in relation to.   *See* Crime.

     cultivation of memory, **19**, 55.

     customs of society changing, **19**, 42.

     direction of, divided, **41**, 6.

     distribution of studies in different grades, **15**, 43.

     educational statistics, **31**, 46, 47.

     expenditures for, compared with appropriations for other purposes, **22**, 55.

     greater unity desirable, **28**, 20.

     gymnastics.   *See* Gymnastics.

     health dependent upon obedience to physical laws, **12**, 44–53.

     higher, of women, **21**, 54.

     hindrances to, **48**, 167.

     history of, in Massachusetts, **10**, 14; **39**, 5.

     important advance in, **48**, 9.

     important decisions to be made, **20**, 61, 62.

     important in every condition, **20**, 53.

     importance of, to government, **22**, 11.

     industrial.   *See* Industrial.

     inequality in means of, **5**, 69; **46**, 13.

     influence on, of increase of manufacturing, **19**, 43.

     influences on, from a foreign race, **19**, 42.

     in foreign countries, **19**, 37.

     intelligence the condition of a wealthy people, **12**, 67.

     is all, demoralizing? **21**, 62.

     key to knowledge, **12**, 62.

     lectures on, **2**, 32.

     legislation in behalf of, in 1848, **12**, 29.   *See also* Legislation.

     low estimate of the value of, **19**, 51.

     military.   *See* Military drill.

     modern, more practical, **31**, 11.

     moral.   *See* Moral instruction.

     more generous provision for, needed, **38**, 11.

     more thorough training in elements needed, **25** (Abstracts), 90.

     necessary to the existence of state, **46**, 63.

     new impulse given to, **18**, 48.

Education — *Concluded.*
   not acquisition of knowledge, **15**, 30.
   of childhood, **15**, 35.
   outside of school-houses needed, **20**, 61.
   part only of, belongs to the school-room, **19**, 41.
   penalties for not providing means of, laws, **10**, 223–226.
   physical. *See* Physical.
   policy of the state in relation to, **10**, 232.
   political, necessity of, **12**, 76.
   practical, **15**, 29.
   progress of, **48**, 162.
   progressive system of, needed, **15**, 38.
   prosperity of state dependent upon, **23**, 40.
   provisions for, have not kept progress with growth of state in wealth and
      population, **39**, 17.
   relation of, to manufacturing interests, **23**, 39–59.
      to state, **10**, 21.
   right of a child to, **10**, 124.
   science of, in Germany, **48**, 279.
   sentiment and policy of western states on, **21**, 44.
   taxation the only means by which universal, can be secured, **21**, 69.
   should not have special reference to the future occupation of pupil, **15**, 29, 30.
   signs of advance in public mind, **17**, 62.
   state to supply the means of, **37**, 7.
   testimony concerning, **21**, 63.
   the equalizer of conditions, **12**, 59.
   universal, **18**, 28; **37**, 7; **39**, 6–11.
   value of, in manufacturing establishments, **11**, 44, 117.
      to laborers, **5**, 100–120; **11**, 42–44, 117.
Educational map, **40**, 122.
Educational survey of Europe, **7**, 36–183.
Edwards, Richard, Jr., agent of Board and principal of normal school at Salem,
      18, 70; **19**, 24; **21**, 7, 31.
Egremont Academy, South Egremont, **40**, 342.
Elementary instruction (*see also* Primary schools), attention to, urged, **26**, 19.
   branches to be taught, **50**, 104.
   need of improvement in, **42**, 9.
   neglect of, **21**, 57.
   thoroughness in, advised, **27**, 13.
   what it should be, **22**, 58, 64.
Elliot School, Jamaica Plain, **40**, 217.
Elocution. *See* Reading. Vocal culture.
Emerson, George B., treasurer of Board of Education, address of, **17**, 29.
   circular of, on reading, **27**, 62, 65.
   donation by, to State Normal School at Bridgewater, **19**, 21.
   letter from, on acceptance of Lee prizes, **25**, 10.
Emerson, Thomas, report of, on common schools, **36**, 201.
Employment of children in factories. *See* Factories.
Encyclopædia Britannica presented to State Normal School at Westfield, **11**, 39.
   to State Normal School at West Newton, by Hon. J. Phillips, **10**, 102.
English and Classical School, West Newton, **40**, 317.
Episcopal Theological School, **40**, 105.

Essex Institute, **40**, 100.

Europe, educational survey of, **7**, 36–183.

Evening schools, **21**, 14; **32**, 54–56.
    Boston, **27** (Abstracts), 5.
    circular for information on, **25**, 75.
        answer to same, **25**, 76–92.
    conclusions warranted from information, **25**, 93.
    high, to be maintained in cities of 50,000 inhabitants, **50**, 101.
    laws respecting, **24**, 94; **25**, 75; **33**, 110; **47**, 13; **50**, 101.
        no provision for enforcement of, **48**, 19.
    maintenance of, justified, **48**, 20.
    paper on, by A. P. Marble, **47**, 187–191.
    reference of Board to, **50**, 17.
    required in towns and cities of 10,000 inhabitants, **50**, 101.
    results of, most satisfactory, **25**, 92.
    teachers and lecturers, **37**, 45, 46.

Everett, Edward, answers of, to questions respecting religious instruction in the common schools, **18**, 90, 91.

Examination of teachers by printed questions, **10**, 74–80.

Examinations, class, discussed, **48**, 87.
    school, **9**, 144–147.

Exposition. *See* Centennial, New Orleans, Vienna.

Expulsion, authority of committees and teachers, **49**, 84.

Eyes, hygiene of, **42**, 144.
    rules for the care of, **42**, 151.

Factories, employment of children in (*see also* Half-time schools), **1**, 67; **3**, 41, 46; **11**, 116, 123; **20**, 48.
    circular to manufacturers, **23**, 41.
        answers to, **23**, 41–53.
        deductions from, **23**, 53.
    discussion of laws relating to, **44**, 190.
    law respecting, **1**, 67; **3**, 41; **42**, 256, 258; **50**, 108.
        and comments, **20**, 48, 49; **30**, 67, 68; **31**, 47, 48; **38**, 186; **40**, 86.
        violation of, **26**, 51; **29**, 65.
    moral considerations, **23**, 54, 55.
    more stringent laws needed, **37**, 140.
    Oliver, H. K., appointed agent to secure obedience to laws regulating, **31**, 49.
    reference of Board to, **50**, 15.
    requirements of law, **45**, 67; **46**, 133–136; **48**, 71.
    their time of attendance at school should be increased, **20**, 50.

Factory school, **34**, 87.

Feeble-Minded, Massachusetts School for the, **40**, 357; **50**, 75.
    appropriations for, **24**, 171.
    opened, 1848, **12**, 30.

Fellenburg Academy, Greenfield, **40**, 343.

Felton, Cornelius C., president of Harvard College, death of, **26**, 16.

Female teachers, advantages of employing, **11**, 26.
    demand for, **11**, 28.
    high schools in charge of, **23**, 81.
    inadequate compensation of, **11**, 26–30; **27**, 42.
    increase in proportion of, from 1837 to 1848, **12**, 21.

Female teachers — *Concluded.*
> limit to, perhaps desirable, **36**, 14.
> number of, increased, **27**, 41.
> objections to, answered, **26**, 79–81.
> percentage of, increasing, **30**, 12; **32**, 7, 12.
> proportion increased, **10**, 69; **20**, 42; **36**, 14.
> successful, **25** (Abstracts), 171; **33**, 87.
> verdict of people in favor of, **30**, 12.

Finland, work schools in, translation of paper on, by Otto Salomon, **46**, 165, 166.
Framingham, plan for model school at, **18**, 12.
Framingham, State Normal School at, accommodations at West Newton insufficient
> and undesirable, **14**, 18.
> account of, **40** (Appendix), 135.
> advanced class at, **18**, 12; **20**, 24.
> Alumni Association, meeting of, **50**, 28.
> appropriations for school at West Newton, **16**, 15; **24**, 18.
> Bigelow, George N., appointed principal, 1855, **19**, 6.
>> resigned, 1866, **30**, 20.
> boarding-house, new, for, **50**, 31.
> Board of Education, vote of, to place a lady in charge of, **30**, 83.
> Bowditch, N. I., generosity of, to, **25**, 89.
> building at, completed, **17**, 6.
>> dedication of, address by George B. Emerson at, **17**, 29–53.
>> Esty, Alexander, architect of, **17**, 25.
>> report of building committee, **17**, 23–28.
> course of study at, **20**, 25.
> Encyclopædia Britannica presented to school at West Newton by Hon. J.
>> Phillips, **10**, 102.
> established at Lexington, April, 1839, **2**, 15; **3**, 5; **4**, 3, 4.
> Felton, C. C., president, death of, **26**, 16.
> generosity of friends to, **30**, 23.
> Hyde, Miss Ellen, appointed principal at, 1876, **40**, 15.
> Johnson, Miss Annie E., appointed principal at, 1866, **30**, 21.
>> resignation of, 1875, **39**, 27.
> May, Samuel J., appointed principal of school at Lexington, 1843, **6**, 6.
> Pierce, Cyrus, appointed first principal of school at Lexington, 1839, **3**, 5.
>> resignation of, **13**, 7, 16.
> practice school, important adjunct, **50**, 30.
> removed from Lexington to West Newton, 1844, **8**, 76.
>> from West Newton to Framingham, 1853, **16**, 5.
> report of visitors to, **50**, 27.
> sanitary regimen of, **39**, 50–52.
> Stearns, Eben, appointed principal, May 30, 1849, **13**, 8.
>> resigned, 1855, **19**, 6.

Framingham Academy, Framingham, **40**, 337.
Franklin Academy, North Andover, **40**, 339.
Franklin County, examination of schools in, **45**, 225.
Fraser, Rev. James, Commissioner of English schools, observations of, **41**, 92.
Free drawing classes. *See* Drawing.
Free Institute of Industrial Science, Worcester. *See* Worcester.
Free text-books (*see also* Books), advantages of, **48**, 10.
.... discussed, **49**, 77.

Free text-books — *Concluded.*
   general favor, **49**, 202.
   law respecting, **37**, 130; **48**, 10.
   plan for purchase, distribution and care of, **48**, 11.
   plan in Fall River, paper by Wm. Connell, **45**, 257; **49**, 241-258.
Friends' Academy, New Bedford, **40**, 270.
Fund, School, **2**, 17, 77; **28**, 59.
   account of, **31**, 61; **34**, 142.
   accumulation of, desirable, **14**, 60.
   act concerning management and distribution of, **30**, 63.
   act of Legislature of 1865 respecting maintenance of high schools, **29**, 18.
   act to change time of apportionment of income of, **31**, 40.
   amount and economical management of, **30**, 10; **32**, 44.
   amount and increase of, **11**, 38; **13**, 12; **14**, 12; **17**, 11-13; **20**, 7; **21**, 6; **22**, 45.
   amount and investments of, **23**, 69; **25**, 49.
   amount, income and appropriations, **29**, 15, 66-68; **35**, 9, 10.
   annual deficiency of, to be met, **35**, 10.
   annual statement of, **35**, 115, 116.
   apportionment of, **11**, 34-37.
      to towns and cities, 1880, **43**, 256.
   beneficiaries of, **10**, 228.
   benefits of, **14**, 12.
   change in disposition of, **20**, 70.
   conditions of receiving, **10**, 227; **27**, 57; **29**, 55.
   custody of, **24**, 74.
   distribution of income of, **23**, 70-74; **50**, 10.
      among districts, **8**, 77-101; **10**, 144; **16**, 35
      effect of, **23**, 70.
      inequalities in, **26**, 63; **50**, 10, 229.
      in towns sometimes illegal, **26**, 63.
      mode of, in each town, **8**, 79, 97.
      statutes providing for, **50**, 91.
   diverting funds, **34**, 137-139.
      repayment urged, **34**, 140.
   effect of, in securing returns, **22**, 46.
   ends accomplished by, **24**, 74-77.
   first loan, **39**, 8.
   forfeitures of, by towns, **28**, 60.
   "half-mill school fund." *See* Half-mill tax.
   history of, and management, **22**, 38-45; **39**, 6; **41**, 62; **46**, 104-108.
   how appropriated, **13**, 13; **14**, 13; **17**, 11-13.
   how divided, **23**, 70.
   importance of, **24**, 74; **29**, 16; **45**, 53.
   inadequate to the requirements at first contemplated, **20**, 72.
   income of, **42**, 63.
      and disposition of, **24**, 73-81; **27**, 54, 55.
   increase of, **10**, 103; **13**, 12.
      approved, **23**, 74; **27**, 56; **36**, 15; **42**, 11.
      in amount per scholar, **27**, 58; **28**, 61.
      need of, **35**, 115, 116.
   indebtedness to, **22**, 52.

Fund, School — *Concluded.*

inequalities of burden of taxation, **35,** 118–132.

Indians, fund for. *See* Indians.

investments of, **29,** 69.

laws respecting, **33,** 108; **34,** 125, 126; **42,** 258.

and comments, **24,** 78–81, **38,** 141; **43,** 255; **46,** 107.

legal provisions, **8,** 115.

lessened to meet exigencies of war, **29,** 16.

method of increasing, **24,** 23, 24.

methods of providing for free public instruction, **35,** 117.

our own method, **35,** 117.

misuse of, by towns, **36,** 74–179.

moiety of income insufficient, **39,** 9, 10.

.obedience to high school and truant laws should be conditions of receiving, **27,** 59.

origin and disposition of, **9,** 23; **10,** 226; **20,** 69; **24,** 74   **34,** 126.

payment to, from sale of lands in Back Bay, **25,** 49.

policy of, questioned, **19,** 49.

purpose of, **23,** 71.

report of commissioners on, **36,** 17.

resolve in relation to, **39,** 5.

should be devoted strictly to the aid and encouragement of public schools, **24,** 23.

statement of amount and forfeitures, **30,** 69.

statement of condition of, **36,** 14.

state tax discussed, **36,** 15–17; **39,** 10.

statistics, **9,** 22.

tax to increase, urged, **36,** 173; **42,** 12.

Todd, for normal students, **50,** 98.

towns obey laws, **48,** 67.

usefulness of, **22,** 42.

use of, by towns, **24,** 79.

what we owe to it, **26,** 42.

when established, **24,** 74; **45,** 65.

Furniture, what, needed, **50,** 212.

Geography, hints on teaching, **47,** 109.

in grammar schools, **15,** 65–68.

intermediate course in, **44,** 125.

how to teach, **44,** 125.

method of teaching, in foreign schools, **7,** 113.

Germany, account of schools in, by Victor Cousin, **37,** 7.

methods of teaching in, **49,** 259–283.

deaf-mutes in, **47,** 64.

reading in, **48,** 266.

science of education in, **49,** 279.

system of education in, **41,** 6.

Gladden, Washington, opinion of, concerning the present condition of schools, **44,** 230, 231.

Gladwin, George E., paper by, on industrial drawing, **34,** 180–182.

Government, errors of, **12,** 79–84.

oaths, multiplication of, an evil, **12,** 83.

Government — *Concluded.*
   .school. *See* Discipline.
   should attempt two things, **20**, 60.
Graded schools, argument in favor of, **14**, 30–47.
   basis of classification of, **50**, 216, 218.
   classification of towns in respect to, **14**, 46, 47.
   essential, **42**, 252.
   extract of report of school-committee of Amherst on evils in mixed schools, **26**, 58–60.
   gradually adopted. **18**, 56.
   inequalities in distribution of money, **26**, 63.
   plan for, **2**, 36, 39.
   .principle involved, **26**, 57–62.
Grammar, cramming in, **31**, 11, 12.
   method of teaching, in foreign schools, **7**, 105.
Grammar schools, Adams, Samuel, remarks of, on, **32**, 54.
   arithmetic in, **15**, 61.
   course of study for, **42**, 193–198.
   drawing in, course of study for, **49**, 214–221.
   English grammar in, **15**, 62.
   geography in, **15**, 65–68.
   how to teach topics, **44**, 127.
   object lessons, **44**, 128.
   reading in, **15**, 56, 61.
   studies of, **15**, 55.
Gray, F. C., answers of, to questions respecting religious instruction in the common schools, **18**, 95–96.
Greek and Latin required to be taught, **50**, 104.
Green, Samuel Swett, paper by, on libraries and schools, **48**, 235.
Greene, Samuel S., agent, appointed, 1850, **14**, 48.
Greylock Institute, South Williamstown, **40**, 346.
Guyot, Prof. Arnold, instruction of, **16**, 53; **17**, 70.
   lectures of, **15**, 18; **18**, 19; **20**, 23.
Gymnastics, **22**, 62.
   benefits of, **25**, 127.
   ends to be attained by, **47**, 111.
   successfully introduced into normal schools, **25**, 23.

Hagar, Daniel B., principal of State Normal School at Salem, appointed, 1865, **29**, 10.
Half-mill tax, argument for the proposed, **50**, 230–233.
   bill recommended to Legislature, **50**, 233.
   fundamental to the improvement and elevation of school system, **37**, 8.
   importance of, **35**, 117–132.
   question of more equitable division of, referred to Board, **50**, 229.
   recommended, **35**, 11, 117; **36**, 15, 173.
   special report on, **50**, 229.
Half-time schools, **31**, 8; **33**, 95.
   factory school at Fall River, **34**, 87.
   for children employed in factories, **34**, 87.
   in Woburn High School, **35**, 89.
Hammond, Charles, paper by, **40** (Appendix), 182.

Hampden County, examination of schools in, **45**, 225.

Hanover Academy, Hanover, **40**, 287.

Harvard College, **40, 48**.

    Divinity School, **55**.

    Law School, 56.

    Medical School, 57.

    Dental School, 58.

    Lawrence Scientific School, 59.

    Bussey Institution, 60.

    Astronomical Observatory, 61.

    Botanic Garden, 62.

    Museum of Comparative Zoölogy, 62.

    proposal from, to maintain scholarships in the Lawrence Scientific School, for the benefit of male graduates of normal schools, **44**, 11.

Haverhill Academy, Haverhill, **40**, 341.

Health. *See* Hygiene.

Heating apparatus, **42**, 129.

Higginson, T. W., opinion of, concerning the present condition of schools, **44**, 231, 232.

    remarks of, on hours of study, **31**, 8, 9.

High schools, argument for, **41**, 81–85; **43**, 86–98; **46**, 85, 86.

    branches to be taught in, **24**, 91.

    census of 1875 relating to, **39**, 128.

    classics in, **25**, 120.

    cost of, **27**, 53.

    course of studies in, **41**, 80; **47**, 106.

    defined by statute, **28**, 84.

    discussed, **47**, 81–86.

    established, 1826, **45**, 65.

    forfeiture of income of fund, **29**, 55.

        laws respecting, and comments, **29**, 55.

    good effects of, **18**, 58.

    history of, **43**, 86.

    importance of, **25**, 110.

    improvement of, **29**, 86.

    Latin in, benefits of study of, **28**, 12–15.

    laws respecting, **32**, 43; **41**, 84.

        and comments, **24**, 91; **45**, 72–76; **46**, 111.

        evaded, **19**, 72; **28**, 11, 17.

    maintenance of, act of Legislature of 1865 respecting, **29**, 18.

    names of delinquent towns, **27**, 52; **29**, 58, 62; **32**, 53.

    names of towns that maintain, **30**, 79.

    no social distinctions in, **28**, 83.

    number and success of, **35**, 88.

    number of, established, **20**, 85.

        increase in, **18**, 57; **28**, 53; **31**, 40.

        in 1855, **18** (Appendix), xcix.

    objections to, answered, **18**, 57; **41**, 85.

    obligation of towns to maintain, reimposed, **12**, 30.

    open to all, **28**, 16.

    origin and progress of, paper by A. J. Phipps, **40** (Appendix) 34–47

High schools — *Concluded.*

    penalty for failure to support, inadequate, **28, 95.**

        suggested, **28, 96.**

    reading in, **47, 107.**

    report of committee of education on, **28, 98.**

        of general agent on, **38, 90.**

        of Horace Mann on, **32, 54.**

        of Mr. Martin on, **48, 175.**

    requirements of law respecting, **27, 51.**

    should have fixed locality, **28, 85.**

    successful working of, **25, 127.**

    tables showing towns that support, **28,** 86–93.

    teachers of, difficulty in procuring, **14,** 59, 60.

    towns maintaining, principals and salaries, **38,** 103–107.

    towns where maintained and when required, **39,** 137, 141.

    training classes in, **32,** 62; **33,** 6. 91, 89.

    value of, **28,** 79–82.

Hillard, George S., answers of, to questions respecting religious instruction in the
    common schools, **18,** 96, 97.

Hinsdale Academy, Hinsdale, **40,** 344.

History, intermediate course in, **44,** 125.

    scientific course in, **44,** 136.

Hitchcock Free High School, Brimfield, **40,** 320.

Hollis Institute, South Braintree, **40,** 344.

Holy Cross, College of the, Worcester, **40,** 78.

Holyrood Academy, Lowell, **40,** 345.

Home influence, **13,** 34.

    training, **27** (Abstracts), 27.

Hopkins School, Cambridge, **40,** 280.

Hopkins School, Hadley, **40,** 271.

Hopkinton High School, Hopkinton, **40,** 344.

Horace Mann School for Deaf-mutes, Boston. *See* Deaf-mutes.

Hours of study, bearing of, on health, **31,** 10.

    eight hours to be required in normal schools, **31,** 10.

    half time, **31,** 8.

    inquiries in regard to, **31,** 9.

    length of, **31,** 6.

    letters of. Dr. S. B. Woodward, Dr. J. Jackson and Dr. Samuel G. Howe on
    the number of, **4,** 100–108.

    remarks of T. W. Higginson on, **31,** 8, 9.

    tendency to abridge, **13,** 32.

Howe, Dr. Samuel G., letter from, on the proper number of school hours, **4,** 104–
    108.

Howe's School, Billerica, **40,** 316.

Hubbard, E. A., agent, reports of (appended to the 39th–41st, 43d–46th reports of
    the Secretary).

    resigned, 1883, notice of, **47,** 98.

Hudson, Barzillai, death of, **35,** 61.

Human race divided into two classes, **18,** 25.

Humphrey, Heman, address by, at dedication of Westfield State Normal School,
    10, 7, 36.

Hyde, Alexander, opinion of, concerning the present condition of schools, **44,**
    233–235.

Hyde, Miss Ellen, appointed principal of State Normal School at Framingham, 1876, **40,** 15.

Hygiene, contagious disease, rules for preventing the spread of, **42,** 143.

    health dependent upon obedience to physical laws, **12,** 44.

    in connection with the public schools, **28,** 11.

    of public schools, paper by D. F. Lincoln, M.D., **42,** 123.

    of the eye, **42,** 144.

    study of, **6,** 56-83, 98-160.

Illiteracy, census statements relating to, **40,** 51.

    remedial legislation necessary, **48,** 20.

    responsibility for, **37,** 114, 116.

    tables of statistics of, **37,** 113, 115.

Indians, fund for the education of, **10,** 228.

    how applied, **24,** 81.

    laws respecting, **24,** 81; **46,** 108.

Industrial drawing (*see also* Drawing).

    annual exhibit of, **44,** 215.

    Centennial exhibit of, **40,** 5, 6, 42.

    commercial value of, **36,** 9.

    course in, **38,** 55.

    curriculum of studies in, **44,** 201-214.

    evening classes in, **37,** 63-68; **38,** 80; **44,** 216; **45,** 247.

        plan of instruction for, **48,** 113.

    exhibition of, report of committee on, **38,** 65-76.

        second, report of, **37,** 69-81.

    Free Institute of Industrial Science, Worcester. *See* Worcester County Free Institute, etc.

    law respecting, **36,** 38.

    list of State collection for, **36,** 38.

    need of instruction in, for skilled labor, **42,** 107.

    opening of classes in, admission, course of study and examination, **48,** 113.

    plan for first year's work in, in schools where drawing has not been taught, by C. M. Carter, **47,** 201-210.

    plan of instruction in, in Boston, **44,** 220.

    programme of, **48,** 114.

    reports of Walter Smith on. *See* Director of art education.

    scheme of instruction in, **36,** 54-56.

    special instructors of, **44,** 194-201.

    synopsis of thirteen years' course in, **37,** 63-65.

Industrial education (*see also* Technical instruction).

    argument of Secretary on, **50,** 117.

    at Gloucester, paper by L. H. Marvel on, **44,** 179-186.

    how to introduce it an unsolved problem, **42,** 109; **43,** 68.

    introduction of, into school system, discussed, **47,** 12.

    need of, **39,** 18; **45,** 12.

    no new light, **48,** 16.

    not accomplishing what the law contemplates, **47,** 48.

    progress in, **40,** 6.

    public demand for, **43,** 286.

    report of, for 1879, **43,** 279.

        of committee on, **46,** 155-159.

Industrial education — *Concluded.*

  report of director on. *See* Director of art education.

  value of, **40**, 38.

Industrial School Association, **41**, 219.

Industrial schools, act relating to, **36**, 181.

Institute of Industrial Science, Worcester County. *See* Worcester County.

Institute of Instruction. *See* American Institute of Instruction.

Institutes, account of, **31**, 63;-**43**, 251–257.

  aim of, **18**, 53.

  appropriations for additional sessions of short duration, **16**, 55; **22**, 7.

  at Amherst, largest and most enthusiastic yet held, **16**, 53.

  at Lawrence, report of school committee on, **27** (Abstracts), 21, 28.

  benefits of, **20**, 57, 58; **29**, 8; **32**, 31.

  circular letter of H. Mann on, **9**, 46.

  combined with inspection of schools, **48**, 147.

  conduct of, **21**, 56.

  day, suggested, **34**, 95.

  defensible in theory and in results, **20**, 66.

  detailed account of, **47**, 91–98.

  donation of Edmund Dwight for, **9**, 45.

  efficiency of, **17**, 68–72.

  elements should be taught at, **24**, 72.

  ends to be accomplished by, **47**, 88; **48**, 120.

  enthusiasm and hospitality of people at, **25**, 68; **31**, 64, 65.

  expenses of, **9**, 45.

  extemporized normal schools, **46**, 10.

  favors of railroad companies to, **26**, 85.

  first legal recognition of, **25**, 68.

  growing estimation of, **27**, 60.

  growth of twenty years, **20**, 65.

  held in cities, **16**, 55–57.

      in small towns, **47**, 14.

  high reputation of, **23**, 9.

  history of, **18**, 64; **25**, 66, 67.

  history, changes, **45**, 102.

  inference of, limited, **20**, 64.

  instructors at, **23**, 38; **26**, 44; **27**, 61; **28**, 61; **29**, 52; **30**, 70, 71; **45**, 103, 104.

      high character of, **17**, 69, 70.

  importance of, to teachers, **24**, 71; **43**, 252.

  interest in, **20**, 58; **41**, 116; **43**, 11.

  largest ever held, appreciation of, **25**, 69, 70.

  law respecting, **12**, 29; **46**, 101.

      and comments, **24**, 70–73; **37**, 142; **38**, 138.

  law suggested to secure attendance at, **32**, 46.

  lectures at, **22**, 86; **25**, 66; **26**, 44; **27**, 61; **28**, 62; **45**, 103, 104.

  length of sessions reduced, efficiency increased, **13**, 48.

  Mason, Lowell, instructor in, notice of, **17**, 70.

  method of conducting, first, **9**, 48–58.

  must be continued, **15**, 70.

  names of teachers and lecturers at, **9**, 60.

  names of teachers in 1851, **15**, 73; **21**, 58.

Institutes — *Concluded.*
    necessity and utility of, **15**, 70, 71.
    new inspiration of, **41**, 7.
    number of, and attendance at, **14**, 54–57; **24**, 54.
        and success of, **20**, 10; **21**, 56; **22**, 7; **23**, 38; **24**, 53; **26**, 8, 43;
            35, 98; **41**, 7; **42**, 70.
        desirable, **24**, 71.
        increased, success and value of, **9**, 10.
    obligation of teachers to attend, **37**, 7.
    of short duration recommended, **14**, 56.
    on the plan of school, **41**, 109.
    organized, **9**, 8.
    origin and results of, **42**, 72, 73.
    plans of work for, **40**, 60; **42**, 71.
    popular and useful, **21**, 13.
    preparatory efforts of agent, **25**, 125.
    principles of teaching taught at, **41**, 110.
    proposed, **8**, 69, 70.
    received with favor, **37**, 6.
    reference of Board to, **50**, 11, 12.
    regulations concerning, **10**, 223.
    report of E. A. Hubbard on, **44**, 168–176.
        of Secretary upon, **50**, 147.
        special, upon, **45**, 105–111.
    requirements for, **10**, 5.
    short sessions of, a success, **46**, 87.
    six held in 1848, **13**, 49.
    success of, **9**, 59; **10**, 98; **11**, 5–37; **12**, 27.
    teachers employed, **20**, 57.
    teachers in, **22**, 7, 36; **27**, 61.
        gratuitous services of, **9**, 60.
    time devoted to teaching methods, **48**, 16.
    usefulness of, **38**, 9, 10; **40**, 100.
        discussed, **25**, 69–72.
    value of, **44**, 12.
    where held, **20**, 57; **22**, 36; **25**, 65, 72; **28**, 61; **29**, 52; **30**, 70, 71;
        34, 114; **36**, 164–166; **37**, 125, 126; **39**, 141–143; **40**, 96; **46**,
        102, 103; **47**, 89.
        from 1845 to 1874, **38**, 140.
    wide influence of, **47**, 15.
    work and methods of, **41**, 94.
    yearly expenditures for, **25**, 74.
Intellect, cultivation of and effect, **9**, 70–76.
Intermediate course of studies, **44**, 121, 123, 130; **47**, 105.
Intoxicating drinks, error of licensing the sale of, **12**, 82.
Ipswich Female Seminary, Ipswich, **40**, 283.
Ipswich Grammar School, Ipswich, **40**, 238.

Jackson, Dr. James, letter from, on the proper number of school hours, **4**, 101–104.
Jackson, Dr. S. C., assistant secretary, **26**, 12; **27**, 10.
    appointed, 1848, **13**, 51.
    resignation of, 1876, **40**, 10.

Jacobs, John A. death of, **34,** 69.

Johnson, Miss Annie E., addresses at installation of, at Framingham Normal School, **30,** 37–50.

appointed principal, **30,** 21.

resignation of, 1875, **39,** 27.

Journal, School, **3,** 19.

appropriation for, **29,** 12.

character of, **1,** 14.

Massachusetts Teacher, furnished by state to each school committee, **24,** 6.

need of, **1,** 14.

of Education, notice of, **43,** 105.

valuable to teachers, **45,** 114.

success of, **8,** 13.

Jubilee Hill Academy, Pittsfield, **40,** 344.

Kindergarten, for the blind, **48,** 63; **50,** 73.

making its way, **46,** 12.

relation of, to primary school, **48,** 88–95.

should be philosophical, **45,** 100.

Kjennerud, H. K., paper by, on work-schools for boys in Sweden, **46,** 167–213.

Kneeland, John, agent, report of, **39,** 90–93.

Krusi, H., lectures of, **18,** 19.

Labor, skilled, demand for, **41,** 174.

Laborers, circular letter of Horace Mann on advantages of a common-school education for, **5,** 86.

answers to, from J. K. Mills, H. Bartlett, J. Clark, Jonathan Crane, **5,** 90–100.

value of education to, **5,** 100–120; **11,** 42–44, 117.

Ladd, William H., opinion of, concerning the present condition of schools, **44,** 235, 236.

Lancaster, normal institute established at, 1853, **17,** 11.

Lancaster Academy, Lancaster, **40,** 341.

Language, **2,** 40–44.

expression, **2,** 74.

how to be taught, **42,** 223; **44,** 103.

orthography. *See* Orthography.

plan of teaching, **48,** 98.

pronunciation, **2,** 46.

Lassell Female Seminary, Auburndale, **40,** 313.

Latin, benefits of study of, in high schools, **28,** 12–15.

required to be taught, **50,** 104.

Lawrence Academy, Falmouth, **40,** 296.

Lawrence Academy, Groton, **40,** 250.

Lawrence Scientific School, **40,** 59.

proposal from Harvard College to maintain scholarships in, for the benefit of male graduates of normal schools, **44,** 11.

Lawson Academy, Shelburne Falls, **40,** 343.

Lawson Classical and Scientific Institute, Shelburne Falls, **40,** 344.

Leach, Daniel, agent, appointed, 1851, **15,** 12; **18,** 69, 74.

report of, on ventilation, **17,** 74–79.

Lectures, **3,** 78–81; **21,** 43, 58; **25,** 23.

Agassiz, Louis, **18,** 19.

at Salem Normal School, **25,** 38.

Lectures — *Concluded.*
  circular letter concerning, **3,** 50.
  Guyot, A., **15,** 18; **18,** 19; **20,** 23.
  Krusi, H., **18,** 19.
  Northrop, B. G., subjects of, **25,** 113.
  Pope, Rev. A. R., **20,** 24, 57.
  Report of, and statistics, **3,** 74.
  Sharp, J. C., **18,** 19; **20,** 24; **25,** 30.
  to normal schools, **23,** 13.
Lee Academy, Lee, **40,** 344.
Lee prizes, **26,** 21.
  benefit of, **29,** 10, 37.
  conditions of receiving, **27,** 62, 65.
  generosity of Thomas Lee, **25,** 40.
Legislation, School, act of 1642, **38,** 127; **40,** 84.
        of 1647, **38,** 128.
  colonial laws, **45,** 64.
  effects of, **29,** 87.
  explanation of school laws, **45,** 70-76.
  frequent alterations a source of evil, **24,** 23.
  from 1875 to 1878, **42,** 255.
      1837 to 1886, **50,** 88.
  history of, and comments, **38,** 126; **46,** 91-95.
  history of, and prominent acts, **29,** 71, 68.
  laws the will of the people, **45,** 70.
  manual of, prepared by George S. Boutwell, **24,** 60-172.
  republication of school laws recommended, **43,** 13.
  revised statement of, with commentary, **38,** 126-200.
  state laws, **45,** 64.
      to be arranged and printed, **32,** 44.
Leicester Academy, Leicester, **40,** 234.
Lexington, State Normal School at. *See* Framingham.
Lexington Academy, Lexington, **40,** 340.
Librarian, assistant. Jackson, Dr. Samuel, C., appointed, 1848, **13,** 51.
        resigned, 1876, **40,** 10.
        salary of, **13,** 12, 51.
  Tillinghast, C. B., appointed, 1879, **43,** 12.
  Warner, Oliver, appointed, 1876, **40,** 11.
Libraries and schools, paper on, by S. S. Green, **48,** 235.
  of Massachusetts, paper by H. E. Scudder, **40** (Appendix), 3-33.
    Harvard College, 3.
    college, 4-6.
    academies and private schools, 6.
    public schools, 6.
    associations, 11.
    religious societies, 14.
    Boston Public, 21.
    numerical summary, 27.
    laws concerning, 30-33.
  Boston Public Library, laws respecting, **12,** 29.
  Bradford High School, paper by F. W. Anthony on, **48,** 257.
  character of books in, **3,** 58.

Libraries and schools — *Concluded.*
  circular of Horace Mann concerning, **3,** 50.
  district school, efforts to establish, **25,** 50.
  educational, **12,** 155.
  fiction in, **3,** 60–73.
  free, founding of, should be encouraged, **28,** 45.
  laws respecting, and comments, **24,** 149, 150; **38,** 197.
  provision for, repealed, **25,** 51.
  public, **3,** 56, 57, 82, 94.
    in state, **24,** 151.
    tables from returns of, **30,** 104, 108.
  report of Horace Mann on, and statistics, **3,** 74–77.
  reports of towns on, **24,** 152–163; **36,** 152–156.
  school. *See* School libraries.
  social, laws respecting, **24,** 163.
  state aid furnished, **25,** 51.
  State Library of Massachusetts, changes and additions in, **43,** 12.
  statistics of, **3,** 51–57.
  towns not availing themselves of the bounty of the state, **9,** 22.
Lincoln, D. F., M.D., paper by, on hygiene of public schools, **42,** 123.
  paper by, on school architecture, **48,** 263.
London Encyclopædia presented to State Normal School at Bridgewater by Hon. John Davis, **9,** 21.
Longfellow, Henry W., answers of, to questions respecting religious instruction in the common schools, **18,** 101.
Lotteries, licensing of, **12,** 80.
Lowell, plan of school-house at, **5,** 124–127.
Lynn Academy, Lynn, **40,** 339.

Maine, board of education in, established, 1846, **10,** 10.
Mann, Horace, appointed first Secretary of Board of Education, 1837, **1,** 5.
  circular letter of, concerning libraries, associations and lectures, **3,** 50.
    on advantages of a common-school education for laborers, **5,** 86.
    on proposed improvements in schools, and results to be expected, **11,** 49–58.
    on the study of physiology, **6,** 83.
    requesting information on the condition of schools, **1,** 73.
  elected to Congress, 1848, **12,** 3.
  reports as Secretary (appended to the first twelve reports of the Board).
  resigned from office, 1848, **12,** 15.
Manners. *See* Moral instruction.
Manual element in education, **41,** 100.
  paper by J. D. Runkle on, **45,** 131–200.
Manual labor (*see also* Industrial education, Technical education).
  hand-work instruction in Sweden, **46,** 163–213.
  province of common schools, argument of Secretary concerning, **50,** 117.
  school for juvenile offenders, **10,** 230.
  work schools for town and country, **46,** 167.
Manufacturing establishments, value of education in, **11,** 44, 117.
Manufacturing towns, influence of youth from, **19,** 43.
  relation of the Massachusetts school system to, **23,** 39–59.
Map, educational, **40,** 122.

Maplewood Institute, Maplewood, Pittsfield, **40**, 311.

Marble, A. P., paper by, on evening schools, **47**, 187.

on supervision, **49**, 225.

Marblehead Academy, Marblehead, **40**, 337.

Martin, G. H., agent, appointed, 1882, **46**, 9, 89.

report of, on high schools, **48**, 175.

reports of, as agent (appended to the 47th-50th reports of the Secretary).

Marvel, L. H., paper by, on industrial education at Gloucester, **44**, 179-186.

Mason, Dr. Lowell, instructor at teachers' institutes, **17**, 70.

notice of, **36**, 196-198.

Massachusetts Agricultural College, **40**, 80.

Massachusetts Asylum for the Blind. *See* Blind.

Massachusetts Historical Society, **40**, 85.

Massachusetts Institute of Technology, **40** (Appendix), 94.

grant of land for use of, **25**, 50.

Massachusetts School for Feeble-Minded. *See* Feeble-minded.

Massachusetts Teacher, furnished by state to each school committee, **24**, 6.

Mathematics, method of teaching, **49**, 127.

methods of teaching, in foreign schools, **7**, 100; **9**, 115.

May, Samuel J., appointed principal at Lexington, 1843, **6**, 6.

McLellan, Dr. J. A., paper by, on schools of Ontario, **45**, 271.

Memory, cultivation of, **19**, 55.

Mental application, **42**, 156.

Merrimac Academy, Groveland, **40**, 273.

Methods of teaching, **5**, 53-55; **15**, 33-43; **38**, 95.

attention to principles of, **43**, 66, 68.

books, aids only to, **18**, 31.

declamation and recitation, **48**, 108.

defective, **22**, 56-66; **42**, 68.

defects in elementary, **19**, 54.

discussion of, **41**, 105; **42**, 98; **43**, 77-86; **44**, 73-76; **48**, 172.

elementary knowledge, **15**, 37.

elementary and scientific knowledge, **43**, 63.

English, **48**, 133.

higher, state support of, **41**, 162.

improvement in, **10**, 72; **41**, 107.

how attained, **15**, 25.

needed, **15**, 25.

inductive, **9**, 150.

in German schools, paper by L. Dunton on, **49**, 259-283.

Latin and Greek, **48**, 123-127.

manner of teaching some topics, **47**, 107.

memory strengthened, **15**, 42.

proper means, **48**, 80.

question and answer, **47**, 161.

reading. *See* Reading.

results of, **44**, 83-91.

school committees have power to determine, **48**, 80.

science, **48**, 129.

should be analytical, **15**, 40.

superior in normal schools, **22**, 67.

things, not words, to be taught, **15**, 33, 34.

Methods of teaching — *Concluded.*

    two methods, **48,** 84.

    unphilosophical, **43, 59.**

Metric system, 98.

    practical value of, **42,** 111.

    teaching of, recommended, **41,** 99.

Milford Academy, Milford, **40,** 341.

Military Academy at West Point, report of agent concerning, **27,** 90–124.

Military drill, **27,** 9, 70.

    act authorizing, recommended, **27, 79.**

    arguments in favor of, **27,** 74–77.

    committee appointed to investigate the subject of, **27, 79.**

    in Brookline, letter of M. Williams, **27, 71.**

    report of committee on, **27,** 71–79.

    report of school committee of Brookline on, **26** (Abstracts), 232.

    resolve of Legislature on, **27,** 70.

Millbury Academy, Millbury, **40,** 343.

Milton Academy, Milton, **40,** 337.

Mineralogy, scientific course of study in, **44,** 137.

Model schools, **2,** 32; **3,** 6.

    agreement between the school committee of Framingham and the principal of normal school relating to, **18,** 13–16.

    at Westfield, **8,** 20; **10,** 9–58.

        plan for, **29,** 29.

    at West Newton, **12,** 7; **14,** 16.

    need of, **29,** 9.

    organization of, **18,** 13.

    plan for, at Framingham, **18,** 12.

    system extinct, **21,** 12.

Money, raising of, **2,** 77, 78; **3,** 37; **4,** 10–11; **5,** 32, 73–75; **46,** 68.

    decision of supreme court on right to raise, **10,** 135.

    power of towns to raise, not limited, **10,** 134.

Monroe, Louis B., notice of death of, **43,** 11.

Monson Academy, Monson, **40,** 264.

Moral instruction (*see also* Religious), **1,** 61; **2,** 78; **8,** 15–18; **11,** 89; **19,** 58–65; **21** (Abstracts), 3–134.

    book on, needed, **1,** 65.

    defined and discussed, **47,** 122–126; **48,** 148,

    effect of influences, **47,** 116.

    formation of character, **15,** 27.

    for prisoners, law respecting, **12,** 29.

    good behavior, **43,** 106–111.

        taught by example, **43,** 110.

    home training in, **21,** 54–59.

    how imparted, **43,** 68.

    lack of, **1,** 64.

    law respecting, **12,** 123; **24,** 95; **46,** 113.

    manners, **15,** 28.

    method of, in foreign schools, **7,** 170; **41,** 101.

    methods of correcting vices, **9,** 76–156.

    mistakes in, **19,** 59.

Moral instruction — *Concluded*.

    moral element in education, **22**, 11; **23**, 9; **41**, 100; **42**, 114; **46**, 113.

    morals and manners, **21**, 71; **25** (Abstracts), 140.

        how to be taught, **42**, 231.

    motives for study, **9**, 76.

    obstacles in way of, **44**, 9.

    plans of, discussed, **48**, 126.

    popular interest concerning, **45**, 13.

    relation of schools to morals and religion, **21**, 65–72.

    required by law, **43**, 13; **44**, 9.

    requirements of constitution concerning, **28**, 17, 19.

    suggestions relating to, **44**, 9.

    text books of, **44**, 10.

    use of keys, **9**, 112; **25**, 121.

    vigilant care needed, **43**, 13, 14.

    waste of the country's wealth on the care of criminals, **11**, 100–103.

    wisdom better than intellect, **28**, 17.

Morton, Nathaniel, extracts from report of, on heating and ventilation, **50**, 195–200.

Mt. Hollis Academy, Holliston, **40**, 344.

Mount Holyoke Female Seminary, South Hadley, **40**, 299.

Museum of Comparative Zoölogy, **40**, 62.

    act to incorporate, **24**, 140.

    articles of agreement between the trustees of, and the president and fellows of Harvard College, **24**, 143, 148.

    bequest of Francis Gray, and conditions, **40**, 141–143.

    donation to, of Agassiz collection, **24**, 148.

    increase of, report of Professor Agassiz, **24**, 148.

Museum of Fine Arts, **40**, 96.

Music in schools, **8**, 117–132; **34**, 6; **44**, 112.

Nantucket, improvement in schools of, **2**, 29.

Nantucket Academy, **40**, 337.

National Bureau of Education. *See* Bureau.

National education, convention in the interests of, at Louisville, **47**, 15.

    persons commissioned to attend, **47**, 16.

Nautical School, **24**, 164; **49**, 13–15.

Netherlands, supervision in, article on, by Victor Cousin, **41**, 67.

New Church Theological School, **40**, 104, 322.

New England Academy, Cohasset, **40**, 344.

New England Historic Genealogical Society, **40**, 90.

New Hampshire, school system of, **10**, 11.

Newman, S. P., first principal at Barre, died 1842, **6**, 6.

New Orleans, exposition at, **48**, 21.

New Salem Academy, New Salem, **40**, 258.

Newton Theological Institution, **40**, 103.

New York trade schools, paper on, by R. T. Auchmuty, **47**, 195–200.

New York, training schools in, plan of, **35**, 8.

Nichols Academy, Dudley, **40**, 272.

Norfolk County, report of examination of schools in, by G. A. Walton, **43**, 99, 123–248.

    significance of report of, **44**, 12, 162.

Normal Art School. *See* Art school.

Normal schools, **21** (Abstracts), 217–243.

   adaptation of, to needs of teachers, **10**, 48–53.

   additional school in Berkshire County, **16**, 7.

      in Essex County recommended; **16**, 7.

      in Worcester County recommended, **34**, 7.

   admission to, **35**, 84; **40** (Appendix), 124.

      uniform standard of, **27**, 65–66.

   advanced classes in, **14**, 59; **26**, 46.

   advantages of special training at, **18**, 8.

   Agassiz, Louis, made permanent instructor in, **16**, 53; **17**, 70

   aid from state to pupils in, **17**, 8; **18**, 7; **20**, 67; **23**, 68.

      number receiving, **21**, 11.

   approaching the ideal standard, **29**, 8.

   appropriation by Legislature for, **2**, 7, 9; **20**, 8.

      for reading in, **27**, 62.

      increase of, needed, **21**, 12; **33**, 7.

   assistants of, should be highly educated, **18**, 7.

   attention to elementary studies in, urged, **26**, 19.

   Barre. *See* Westfield.

   board, price of, advanced, **28**, 63.

   boarding arrangements in, **40** (Appendix), 13.

   boarding-houses, **33**, 8, 13, 25; **34**, 8, 14, 22 · **35**, 7.

      suggested, **32**, 59.

   books needed in, **20**, 36.

   Bridgewater. *See* Bridgewater.

   caution to committees regarding, **26**, 10.

   certificates and diplomas of, **40** (Appendix), 130.

   challenge scrutiny, **30**, 84.

   change of principals in, **50**, 88.

   classes for normal training in colleges, **34**, 97–100

   combining teachers' seminaries with academies, **10**, 29–31.

   committees to advise thorough preparation for, **26**, 10

   competition for permanent location of, **9**, 12.

   cost of, compared with that of reform schools, **15**, 10

   course of study in, **10**, 220; **21**, 11, 18; **29**, 88 89; **30**, 84; **40** (Appendix), 125.

      advanced course, **32**, 8; **34**, 100; **36**, 177.

         benefit of, **42**, 19.

      for one year, **18**, 21.

      length of, **40** (Appendix), 129.

      revised, **44**, 10.

   defective preparation for, **20**, 18.

   defensible in theory and in results, **20**, 66.

   demand for trained teachers in, **15**, 10.

   deserve the highest commendation, **29**, 54.

   different from all other institutions of learning, **18**, 28.

   discussed, **43**, 101; **46**, 82; **47**, 86–88.

   donations to cabinets and libraries of, **28**, 32, 35; **29**, 28, 32; **30**, 31.

      to cabinets of, **31**, 23, 26, 28; **32**, 22.

      to libraries of, **31**, 25, 28.

   drawing in, **34**, 158; **39**, 77, 78; **41**, 8; **45**, 246; **48**, 15.

Normal schools — *Continued.*

 Dwight, Edmund, efforts of, for the establishment of, **13**, 14.

 effective in cultivating moral character, **44**, 8.

 efficiency of, **24**, 7; **26**, 45.

 eight hours of study in, to be the limit, **31**, 10.

 ends to be accomplished by, **50**, 143.

 enthusiasm in study in, **25**, 24.

 equipments, **35**, 6.

 established and successful, **13**, 6.

 examinations of, **23**, 17.

 exclusively for teachers, **47**, 9.

 expenditures upon, **24**, 13.

  comparison with other expenditures, **24**, 13.

  economy in, **42**, 7; **43**, 8.

 expense to State of each pupil, fifty dollars, **30**, 8.

  to support each person in a reformatory institution, two hundred dollars, **30**, 9.

 expenses and pecuniary aid, **40** (Appendix), 131.

 first in importance in educational reform, **12**, 27.

 Framingham. *See* Framingham.

 generosity of Mr. Thomas Lee, Lee Prizes, **25**, 40; **27**, 62, 65.

 government of, **40** (Appendix), 121.

 graduates of, demand for, **23**, 6, 15; **30**, 85; **37**, 72–73.

  inquiries respecting, and answers to same, **30**, 92–103.

  must teach, **47**, 9.

  proportion of, in schools, **44**, 8.

  results of inquiries concerning, **22**, 67–160.

  success of, **33**, 89.

   circular to school committees on, with answers, **22**, 68–155.

  testimony in reference to, **44**, 34.

  towns employing, **39**, 126.

  work of, **40** (Appendix), 133.

 growth of twenty years of, **20**, 65.

 Guyot, Prof. Arnold, instruction of, in, **16**, 53; **17**, 70.

 gymnastics successfully introduced into, **25**, 23.

 Harvard College, proposal from, **44**, 11.

 high stand to be taken by, **37**, 6.

 higher education of teachers in, necessary, **32**, 59.

 history of, **10**, 31; **10**, 218; **50**, 96.

  and regulations of, **24**, 138–140.

  and teachers, **21**, 8.

  in foreign countries, and laws concerning, **41**, 85.

  in Massachusetts, and benefits of, **41**, 87.

  outline of, **50**, 98.

 importance of, emphasized, **43**, 7.

 increase of, in Europe, **41**, 87.

 increasing interest in, shown by statistics, **39**, 11–14.

 indirect benefits of, **15**, 19; **18**, 52.

 in fact as well as in theory, **29**, 8.

 influence of, **36**, 178; **40**, 8.

 in New York, **34**, 113.

 instruction in, **32**, 22.

Normal schools — *Continued.*

 lack of pecuniary support of, **19**, 72.
 lady principal, decided upon, **30**, 11.
  success of, **30**, 83; **31**, 16; **33**, 12.
 laws respecting, and comments, **34**, 122, 123; **38**, 190.
 lectures, **17**, 19, 24, 32; **23**, 13; **28**, 31; **29**, 23, 28, 31, 36; **30**, 23; **31**, 18, 22, 23, 25, 28; **35**, 16, 23.
 Lexington. *See* Framingham.
 lyceum, **19**, 20; **21**, 18.
 made their way to favor, **47**, 10.
 Massachusetts, history of, **40** (Appendix), 111.
 memorial of Charles Sumner and others for better accommodations, **9**, 11.
 methods of teaching in, **12**, 9; **19**, 16; **22**, 67; **27**, 24; **32**, 57; **50**, 144.
 moral instruction in, **11**, 6.
 must do the work of town schools, **20**, 8.
 names of instructors in, from their organization to 1861, **24**, 8–11.
 nature of work of, **48**, 142–144.
 necessity of, **1**, 10–12; **18**, 29; **27**, 7.
 need of elevating, **14**, 57.
 new regulations for, adopted, **13**, 8, 20.
 normal instruction·in academies and high schools, **32**, 63, 64; **34**, 98; **35**, 7, 8.
 number, location and character of, considered, **2**, 10, 16.
  of members and graduates of, **21**, 9, 10.
  receiving State aid, **21**, 4.
 object of, **3**, 8; **20**, 24; **25**, 24; **42**, 104; **50**, 10.
 obstacles to large attendance in, **32**, 58.
 offers of Plymouth and Northampton for establishment of schools within their limits, **9**, 13.
 opinions of merits and demerits of, **22**, 5, 68.
 origin of, **40** (Appendix), 109.
 paper on, by A. G. Boyden, **40** (Appendix), 108.
 plan for short course at, **35**, 7.
 practice schools, **50**, 145.
 private donation for, **2**, 7, 9.
 professional character of, **30**, 24.
 professional training in academies and high schools of, **28**, 83.
 prosperity of, **10**, 99–102; **20**, 66, 67; **21**, 48; **30**, 8; **40**, 7.
 Prussian system of, **41**, 85.
 regulations for study, exercise and recreation in each school, **31**, 7.
 regulations of the Board of Education concerning, **10**, 218–222.
 relations of, to state, **37**, 5
 remarks of Miss Johnson, Mr. Dickinson and Mr. Hagar on, **32**, 59, 61.
 requirements of all teachers in, **22**, 6.
 requisites for admission to and graduation from, **48**, 145.
 retrospect of several years, **41**, 3.
 rules and regulations, **40** (Appendix), 123.
 salaries of teachers in, increased, **15**, 11.
  too low, **20**, 68, 69; **30**, 22, 35.
 Salem. *See* Salem.
 satisfactory condition of, **38**, 5, 123.

Normal schools — *Concluded.*

scholarships in colleges provided by Legislature for the education of high-school
. teachers, **17,** 8, 61, 66; **18,** 5.

school in Worcester County advised, **33,** 8.

schools of observation needed, **36,** 12; **41,** 93.

settled policy of, **43,** 7.

should have teachers of highest ability, **30,** 31.

standard of, raised, **24,** 14; **48,** 14.

statistics of admission, attendance and graduation for year 1860, **24,** 15–17.

showing condition of, **30,** 11.

subjects taught, **25,** 24.

success of, **11,** 6–38; **12,** 5; **13,** 17, 19; **19,** 6, 7.

in 1847, **10,** 5.

of first schools, **3,** 5–11; **4,** 3–6; **5,** 4; **6,** 3–6; **7,** 4–6; **9,** 9, 10.

of teachers, **28,** 53.

under early difficulties, **46,** 10.

support of, **10,** 10; **13,** 7.

by income of fund, **30,** 10.

teaching of science in, **50,** 22.

term of study, **10,** 220.

change in, **18,** 20.

extended, **29,** 10; **34,** 109.

extended to two years, **27,** 8, 66, 67.

reasons, **27,** 8.

testimonials of success of pupils, **8,** 27–44.

theory of, **20,** 7.

time required at, **8,** 24.

to teach the art of teaching, **18,** 30.

training schools. *See* Training schools.

uniformity in studies in, desirable, **28,** 22.

value of diplomas and certificates, **26,** 10.

visit of joint standing committee to, **28,** 63.

well-assured position of, **39,** 125.

Westfield. *See* Westfield.

West Newton. *See* Framingham.

what the training implies, **45,** 112.

what they have done, **50,** 86.

where established, **45,** 67.

wisdom of establishing, **10,** 32.

wise investments, **34,** 113.

Worcester. *See* Worcester.

writing, importance of, **47,** 31; **48,** 9.

young men in the army, **26,** 9, 20.

Northampton, Clarke Institution for Deaf-Mutes at. *See* Deaf-mutes.

Northampton, offer of, for establishment of State Normal School at, **9,** 13.

Northampton Female Seminary, **40,** 343.

Northfield Academy, Northfield, **40,** 342.

Northrop, Birdsey G., appointed agent, 1857, **21,** 59; **22,** 9.

letter of, on the importance of employing superintendents of schools, **30,** 111–118.

reports of, as agent (appended to the 25th–28th reports of the Secretary).

resigned, 1867, **30,** 7, 23.

Northrop, Birdsey G. — *Concluded.*
    subjects of lectures of, **25**, 113.
    work of, **20**, 73; **29**, 51.

Oaths, error of government in relation to, **12**, 83.
Object lessons (*see also* Oral teaching), **15**, 44; **26**, 86; **44**, 128.
    absence of, **47**, 182.
    growing interest in, **40**, 59.
    in primary schools, **44**, 113.
    purpose of, **31**, 11.
Oliver, H. K., appointed agent to secure obedience to law regulating the employ
    ment of children in factories, **31**, 49.
Ontario, schools of, paper on, by J. A. McLellan, **45**, 271.
Oral teaching, successful, **42**, 68.
    use of, increasing, **43**, 12.
Ordway, Prof. J., paper by, on hand-work instruction in Sweden, **46**, 169.
Oread Institute, Worcester, **40**, 315.
Organization discussed by Secretary, **50**, 129.
    report of Mr. Prince on, **50**, 209.
Orthography, **2**, 46, 49, 50, 76; **22**, 63, 65; **25**, 94; **28**, 46.
    method of teaching, **47**, 107; **48**, 108.
        in primary schools, **44**, 102.
        intermediate, **44**, 123.
    spelling of colored children in Providence, **26**, 81.
    teaching of, **15**, 52.
Osgood, Rev. Joseph, opinion of, concerning the present condition of schools, **44**,
    236–238.
Oswego, schools of, **26**, 86.
Over-pressure discussed, **48**, 202.

Parents, duties and responsibilities of, **22**, 31; **27** (Abstracts), 31.
    co-operation of, **13**, 33; **20**, 52; **27** (Abstracts), 33.
    interest of, **4**, 82.
    more visitation of, needed, **25** (Abstracts), 17, 72.
    relation of, to schools, **47**, 17.
Partridge Academy, Duxbury, **40**, 287.
Peirce Academy, Middleborough, **40**, 297.
Penal institutions, circular to officers of, with answers, **23**, 60–63.
Pepperell Academy, Pepperell, **40**, 344.
Periodicals and books, **38**, 96.
Perkins Institution for the Blind. *See* Blind.
Peru, Mass., signs of progress in, **39**, 97.
Pestalozzi, J. H., **9**, 136, 150.
Philbrick, John D., appointed agent to prepare educational exhibit for the Centennial
    Exposition, 1875, **39**, 133.
    opinion of, concerning the present condition of schools, **44**, 240, 241.
    reference to report of, on truancy, **26**, 53.
Phillips Academy, Andover, **40**, 220.
Phipps, Abner J., agent, appointed, 1867, **31**, 66.
    paper by, on the origin and progress of high schools, **40** (Appendix), 34–47.
    report of, on school-houses, **36**, 87–148; **39**, 105–109.
    reports as agent (appended to the 31st–40th reports of the Secretary).

Physical education, **9**, 70; **12**, 43; **21** (Abstracts), 3-134; **25** (Abstracts), 51, 179; **27**, 28; **42**, 163.

Physiology, circular letter of Horace Mann on the study of, **6**, 83.

      answers to, from Drs. J. Jackson, S. B. Woodward, E. Jarvis, M. S. Perry, **6**, 85-98.

  effects of alcohol, **48**, 13.

  outline of topics, **48**, 118.

  hints on teaching, **47**, 111.

  law respecting, **48**, 81.

  laws of life and health, treatise on, **6**, 61-160.

  method of teaching, **48**, 81.

  reference of the Board to, **50**, 13.

  Secretary's reference to, **50**, 105.

  study of, **6**, 56-83, 98-160.

    introduced into schools, **45**, 67.

Pierce, Bradford K., letter from, on the State Reform School for Girls at Lancaster, **24**, 167.

Pierce, Cyrus, principal of the State Normal School at Lexington and West Newton, appointed, 1839, **3**, 5.

  notice of, **13**, 7, 16.

Pierce, Edward L., opinion of, concerning the present condition of schools, **44**, 239-240.

Pine Grove Seminary, Harwich, **40**, 344.

Plans of Bridgewater Normal School, **10**, 241-245, 253.

Plans of Westfield Normal School, **10**, 247-254.

Plymouth, offer of, for establishment of State Normal School at, **9**, 13.

Plymouth Colony, Legislature of, **29**, 73.

Political education, need of, **12**, 76.

Pope, Rev. A. R., agent, **19**, 6, 79.

  lectures of, **20**, 24, 57.

Poverty, not necessary, **12**, 54.

  what is it? **11**, 111-116.

Power's Institute, Bernardston, **40**, 323.

Pratt Free School, North Middleborough, **40**, 323.

Prescott, William H., answers of, to questions respecting religious instruction in the common schools, **18**, 97.

Primary schools (*see also* Elementary instruction), and elementary education, **21** (Abstracts), 135-216.

  composition in, **44**, 103.

  course of studies for, **42**, 193-195; **44**, 99-121.

  drawing in, **44**, 111; **48**, 214.

  improvement of, **31**, 5.

  lessons on color in, paper by Miss L. Crocker on, **46**, 247-258.

  music in, **44**, 112.

  natural tones to be used, **15**, 54.

  necessity of right early training, **45**, 98.

  neglect of elementary training, **21**, 57.

  object lessons in, **44**, 113.

  oral teaching in, **15**, 44.

  Philbrick, John D., plan of, **22**, 59.

  reading in, **15**, 51.

  relation of, to other schools, **27** (Abstracts), 35.

Primary schools — *Concluded.*
    state, act to establish, **30,** 65.
    studies, lessons, **47,** 103.
    teaching in, **22,** 58, 59.
        more attention to, **43,** 67.
    word method in, **22,** 61.
    work in, **48,** 185.
Prince, J. T., appointed, 1883, **47,** 101.
    report, **48,** 211; **49,** 193.
    report of, on school organization, **50,** 209.
Private schools, **1,** 48, 52, 53; **4,** 34, 39, 42, 43; **21** (Abstracts), 244–252.
    act relating to approval of, by school committees, **42,** 257.
    approval of, by school committees necessary, **50,** 162.
    argument on obligation to educate children, **10,** 111–128.
    breaking up of, **8,** 66; **9,** 39.
    causes of, **8,** 5, 8.
    deterioration of, **8,** 4.
    diminished in number, **20,** 43.
    duty of towns to maintain schools, law respecting, **10,** 132.
    effect of, on the common schools, **8,** 5, 6.
    effects of, **14,** 42.
    evils of, **1,** 56; **20,** 45.
    laws respecting, **50,** 105.
    monitorial, **7,** 60.
    number of, present and past, compared, **50,** 83.
    objections to, **1,** 54.
    should make returns, **41,** 7.
    state supervision needed, **41,** 7.
    theory of, **1,** 55.
    town indictable if it does not maintain a school, law respecting, **10,** 128.
Prizes, benefit of, **29,** 10, 37.
    for entering examinations at Salem, **27,** 28.
    Lee, **25,** 40; **27,** 62, 65; **28,** 36.
Prospect Hill School, Greenfield, **40,** 330.
Province of the public schools, Secretary's report, **50,** 117.
Prudential committee (*see also* Committees), **4,** 81; **20,** 82.
    action of, **19,** 76.
    are they needed? **13,** 36–46.
    choice of, **19,** 75.
    difficulties of, in acting with town, **18,** 54.
    duties of, and laws respecting, **10,** 148, 160, 161, 178; **24,** 115.
    first authorized, 1827, **29,** 85.
    lack of fitness of, **20,** 83.
    serious evil, **21,** 49.
Prussia, school system of, **2,** 28; **7,** 68.
    system of normal schools in, **41,** 85.
Public property, penalty for injuring, **46,** 141, 142.
Public schools. *See* Schools.
Punchard Free School, Andover, **40,** 312.
Punishment, Corporal (*see also* Discipline), **5,** 56–58; **10,** 81.
    discontinuance of, not advised, **31,** 13.
    discountenanced, **20,** 55; **31,** 12, 15.

Punishment; Corporal — *Concluded.*
    discussed, **48**, 82.
    in foreign schools, **7**, 161.
Putnam Free School, Newburyport, **40**, 306.

Quaboag Seminary, Warren, **40**, 344.

Rapet, M., extract from report of, on English art education, **38**, 8, 9.
Reading, **2**, 37–40, 55; **3**, 47–49; **22**, 63, 65; **25**, 94; **28**, 46.
    books used in foreign schools, **7**, 51–55.
    character of, **19**, 46.
    course of, for teachers, **48**, 136.
    elementary, method of, **44**, 99–101.
    Emerson, George B., circular of, on requisites of good, **27**, 62, 65.
        letter of, on acceptance of Lee prizes, **25**, 10.
    in high school, **47**, 107.
    method of, in Germany, **48**, 266.
        in intermediate schools, **44**, 123.
    neglect of, and causes, **25**, **95**.
    prizes offered by Thomas Lee for, **25**, 10.
    silent, **44**, 101.
    teaching of, **2**, 47–49; **15**, 56, 61; **25**, 115, 117; **48**, 112; **49**, 104.
    word method of, **2**, 47–49.
Redgrave, Richard, letter of, **38**, 48.
Rees' Encyclopædia, gift of, to Westfield State Normal School, **25**, 30.
Reform School, State, action respecting, **24**, 164.
    aid to pupils of, **24**, 109.
    established, 1848, **12**, 30.
    letter from B. K. Pierce on, **24**, 167.
    nautical, **24**, 164; **49**, 13–15.
    working of, **34**, 86.
Registers, School, **2**, 34; **5**, 35; **6**, 43–46; **9**, 37; **10**, 90.
    blank forms of inquiry and questions proposed, **10**, 200–207.
    form of, **2**, 35; **8**, 74.
        and explanation, **10**, 196–199.
    how to be kept, **50**, 164.
    indispensable, **8**, 74.
    laws respecting, **10**, 193; **38**, 177; **46**, 126, 129.
    required by law, **48**, 85.
Religious instruction (*see also* Moral), **3**, 14; **18**, 45, 102.
    argument for, **12**, 98.
    Bible in schools. *See* Bible.
    church and state, no union of, **42**, 9.
    common schools not religious institutions, **12**, 117.
    course of the Board of Education and Secretary relating to, misunderstood and
        censured, **12**, 114.
    effect of sectarianism, **12**, 135.
    honesty among pupils, how to secure, **9**, 102.
    in Massachusetts, extracts from paper on, by E. Twisleton, with answers from
        William Appleton, George Bancroft, Manton Eastburn, Edward Everett, F.
        C. Gray, George S. Hillard, H. W. Longfellow, W. H. Prescott, Jared
        Sparks, George Ticknor, Daniel Webster, William Winthrop, **18**, 79–102.

Religious instruction — *Concluded.*
    Massachusetts school system not anti-Christian, argument, direct proof, **12**, 121.
        second method of proof, **12**, 124.
    need of, **15**, 27.
    religious liberty, **10**, 187; **12**, 138.
    rigor of laws relaxed, **12**, 112.
    schools made unsectarian by law in 1827, **12**, 112.
    spirit inculcated, **9**, 64–70, 148.
    two systems of, **12**, 105.
    two views of, **18**, 45.
Reports of school committees. *See* Committees.
Returns, School, **3**, 18; **5**, 29; **7**, 12; **10**, 200, 206.
    abstracts of (appended to each report, from the 10th to the 50th), **1**, 37;
        4, 13; **10**, 63, 209.
        labor of preparing, **24**, 65.
    accuracy of, **16** (Appendix), iii.
        essential, **25**, 101; **42**, 10; **50**, 64.
    analysis of, **45**, 62; **47**, 78; **48**, 67; **49**, 51; **50**, 63.
    basis of, difficult to define, **50**, 65.
    bound each year, **16** (Appendix), iv.
    change in method of, **29**, 50.
    change of time of, **2**, 17.
    comparison of different years, **16** (Appendix), iv–vi.
    disparity in, **50**, 65.
    first required, 1827–28, **25**, 101.
    importance of, **29**, 5.
    laws respecting, and comments, **24**, 127; **38**, 177.
    loss of school fund made penalty of failure, 1836, **25**, 101.
    method of obtaining percentage of attendance, **25**, 99, 100.
    more exact scrutiny required, **13**, 33.
    neglect of, by towns, **22**, 46, 47.
        no penalty for, **25**, 101.
        penalty for, **22**, 50; **24**, 129, 130.
    particulars embraced in, **33**, 135.
    record should be kept for each half-day, **25**, 100.
    time when required, **1**, 5, 21, 71.
    value of, **13**, 10.
        statistics, **20**, 72, 73.
    vote of Board of Education respecting, and comments, **13** (Appendix), iii.
    what information they give, **24**, 64.
    wrong impressions received from, **13**, 32.
Rhode Island, school system of, **10**, 10.
Riverside Academy, Newton, **40**, 344.
Rogers, Miss H. B., report of her visit to European institutions for the deaf and
    dumb, **36**, 162, 163.
Rowe, David S., appointed principal of State Normal School at Westfield, 1846,
    10, 8.
    resigned, 1854, **18**, 6.
Roxbury Latin School, Boston Highlands, **40**, 210.
Runkle, J. D., paper on manual element in education, **45**, 131–200.
Russell, Prof. William, died, 1873, notice of, **37**, 148–150.

Salem, improvement in schools of, **2**, 30.

    plan of school-house at, **5**, 133–135.

Salem, State Normal School at, **40**, 156.

    appropriation for, **24**, 18.

    Bowditch, Nathaniel, bequest of, to, **25**, 11, 39.

    building at, dedication of, **18**, 10.

        defects of, and means of remedying, **33**, 19, 21.

        description of, **17**, 7, 8.

        plan of, **17**, 28; **23**, 26.

    buildings at, enlargement of, **35**, 24, 99.

    Crosby, Prof. Alpheus, appointed principal at, 1857, **21**, 7, 31.

        resigned, 1865, **29**, 10.

    dedication of, address of George S. Boutwell at, **18**, 10, 25–34.

    donors to library and museum at, **25**, 39; **26**, 26, 30; **27**, 26.

    Edwards, Richard, appointed principal at, 1854, **19**, 24.

        resignation of, 1857, **21**, 7, 31.

    established, 1853, **17**, 7.

    experimental class at, **29**, 36.

    Hagar, Daniel B., appointed principal at, 1865, **29**, 10.

    lectures at, **25**, 38.

    location of, fortunate, **18**, 28.

    prizes for entering examinations at, **27**, 28.

    visitors and teachers of, 1854–76, **40**, 156.

Sanderson Academy, Ashfield, **40**, 339.

Sandwich Academy, **40**, 339.

Saturday sessions, **28**, 48.

Sawin Academy, Sherborn, **40**, 332.

Scholarships, annual class, **25**, 11.

    applicants for, **18**, 6.

    candidates for, must not be inferior, **24**, 84.

        to be examined by Board of Education, **24**, 84.

    causes of failure, **30**, 13.

    classes entered colleges, **19**, 8.

    college, **18**, 59.

    defects in law relating to, **27**, 9.

    design of, **20**, 6, 10.

    examination for, not satisfactory, **26**, 48.

    free, to be established in Williams, Tufts and Amherst Colleges, **25**, 12.

    influence of state students in college, **24**, 86.

    law establishing, repealed, 1866, **30**, 12, 67; **38**, 144.

    laws respecting, and comments, **24**, 81–89.

        amendment of, **28**, 66.

        should be amended, **26**, 47, 50.

    method of selection open to objection, **26**, 47.

    mode of filling, suggested, **26**, 48.

    modification of legislative resolve needed, **21**, 12.

    names of students graduated, **24**, 86.

    object of law relating to, **26**, 49.

    other plans advised, **30**, 13.

    partially unsuccessful, **22**, 8.

    payments of, **29**, 39.

Scholarships, etc. — *Concluded.*

    provided by Legislature for the education of high-school teachers, **17,** 8, 61, 66; **18,** 5.

    provisions for, **18,** 6.

    purpose of, not accomplished, **26,** 47.

    standard elevated, **24,** 6.

    still an experiment, **22,** 8; **23,** 10.

    vacancies in, **21,** 12.

    wisdom of plan of, **24,** 88.

School age, **35,** 86; **36,** 111; **48,** 67.

School books. *See* Books.

School architecture. *See* School-houses.

School committees. *See* Committees.

School discipline. *See* Discipline.

School districts. *See* Districts.

School fund. *See* Fund.

School hours. *See* Hours of study.

School-houses, **3,** 37–40; **5,** 30, 121–135; **7,** 11, 47.

    amount expended for, in different years, **18,** 60.

        in 1837 and 1855, **20,** 38.

    architecture of, **24,** 53–69.

        paper on, by F. D. Lincoln, M.D., **48,** 263.

    bad condition of, **19,** 74.

    comparison of, **20,** 39.

    construction of, **1,** 8, 26; **42,** 124; **45,** 80–87; **48,** 79.

    defects of, **1,** 8; **17,** 75; **33,** 82–87.

    desks and seats, **42,** 154.

    district, laws respecting, **10,** 152.

    districts may raise money for, **24,** 119.

    duties of committees respecting, **46,** 71.

    estimated value of, **20,** 76.

    furniture for, what needed, **50,** 212.

    heating apparatus of, **42,** 129.

    improvements in, **1,** 9, 27; **2,** 31; **4,** 28–32; **8,** 14; **43,** 67.

    inferior when maintained by districts, and reasons, **20,** 79–81.

    land for, laws respecting, **12,** 30.

    large, undesirable, **30,** 16.

    law respecting ventilation of, **17,** 74.

    laws respecting, and comments, **10,** 146; **24,** 109; **46,** 123, 124.

    letter of C. S. Cartée on construction of, **17,** 76–78.

    liberal expenditures for, **34,** 83.

    location of, and laws respecting, **24,** 109, 110; **48,** 78.

    penalty for injuring, **46,** 141; **48,** 86; **50,** 114.

    plans of, **17,** 84–101; **36,** 91–147; **48,** 274.

        at Springfield, Lowell and Salem, **5,** 121–135.

        special study of, **17,** 73, 74.

    poor condition of, **32,** 30.

    proper distance of, apart, **21,** 53.

    report of Mr. Leach on, **17,** 74–79.

        of general agent, A. J. Phipps, on, **36,** 87–148; **39,** 105–109.

        of school committee of Andover on, **25** (Abstracts), 15.

    revolution in, **10,** 64–68.

School-houses — *Concluded.*

sewerage and water closets, **42,** 137.

statistics concerning, **7,** 11.

still defective, **20,** 76; **21, 55; 25,** 126.

towns and cities should support, **21,** 52–55.

value of, in state, in 1848, **12,** 28.

ventilation of. *See* Ventilation.

what they should be, **20,** 77.

School journal. *See* Journal.

School libraries, **4,** 63; **5,** 5; **6,** 46–50; **7,** 16–18; **50,** 106.

act of Legislature authorizing, **1,** 11.

benefits of, **3,** 97–100; **5,** 79.

books for, **1,** 13; **2,** 19–21; **3,** 12–18, 24–32; **6,** 7–12.

laws respecting, **10,** 216, 217.

resolve of Legislature concerning, **7,** 16.

success of, **8,** 66.

School of Art at South Boston, **36,** 85.

School of Observation at Westfield, **30,** 27, 28.

School registers. *See* Registers.

School returns. *See* Returns.

Schools (Common), **1,** 24; **3,** 20, 36; **7,** 46.

adult. *See* Evening schools.

advance of, during the war, **29,** 50.

advantages of town system of, **43,** 65.

age of entering, **21,** 54; **22,** 58.

agencies that have led to improvement, **15,** 69.

amount expended for, **28,** 59; **32,** 40.

annual increase of money raised by taxation for, **31,** 38.

apathy of people towards, **1,** 46; **13,** 84.

apparatus for. *See* Apparatus.

appropriations for. *See* Appropriations.

architecture of. *See* School-houses.

aspect of, cheerful, **22,** 9.

assistant teachers allowed, law respecting, and comments, **24,** 95.

attendance upon. *See* Attendance.

benefits of, needed in future, **28,** 7.

better preparation of teachers needed, **36,** 17.

Bible in. *See* Bible.

causes of want of entire success of, **19,** 38–49, 51, 52.

civil war a test of the efficiency of, **27,** 10, 11.

facts developed by the, **26,** 5.

classification of, **50,** 215.

colonial action concerning, **39,** 6.

committees, duties and laws relating to, **50,** 109–140.

comparison of, with England, **18,** 104.

with foreign schools, **7,** 19–26.

apparatus, **7,** 56-60.

arithmetic and mathematics, **7,** 100; **9,** 115.

articulation in deaf and dumb schools, **7,** 25–36.

attendance, **7,** 146.

Bible history and Bible knowledge, **7,** 125.

corporal punishment, **7,** 161.

Schools (Common) — *Continued.*

　　　emulation, **7,** 165.

　　　geography, **7,** 113.

　　　grammar and composition, **7,** 105.

　　　higher schools, **7,** 150.

　　　inequality of distribution of school funds in England, **7,** 39.

　　　moral and religious instruction, **7,** 170–198.

　　　music, **7,** 126.

　　　partial system of schools, effect of, **7,** 36–47.

　　　Prussian and Saxon, **7,** 68.

　　　reading-books, **7,** 51–55.

　　　school-houses, **7,** 47, 49.

　　　school inspectors, **7,** 145.

　　　seminaries for teachers, **7,** 128.

　　　"study plans," **7,** 117.

　　　writing and drawing, **7,** 107.

　　complaints of, **22,** 56.

　　concentration advised, **42,** 229.

　　condition of, in 1878, **42,** 64.

　　　in 1880, **44,** 67.

　　　inquiry into, **44,** 18.

　　　more definite information of, needed, **45,** 12.

　　　report of Mr. Kneeland, **41,** 118.

　　　　of Mr. Walton, **36,** 81–83.

　　connection with colleges, **18,** 59.

　　continued prosperity in "troublous times," **28,** 5.

　　conveyance of children to, **50,** 107.

　　"Daily Public School," criticism of the treatise, and answers to statements, **30,** 85–92.

　　decided measures opposed, **18,** 49.

　　defects of, **2,** 28; **18,** 71–73.

　　　not chargeable to system, **43,** 63.

　　delinquent towns, **30,** 76–78.

　　disturbing and injuring property, **50,** 114.

　　each town to have, six months in a year, **24,** 89.

　　early account of, **40,** 102–121.

　　economy of time, **48,** 18.

　　efficiency of, depends on the people, **13,** 34.

　　elements of most importance in, **30,** 17.

　　ends and plans of work, **47,** 102.

　　essentials, **42,** 79.

　　essential to state, **44,** 7.

　　established in 1647, **38,** 128.

　　evening. *See* Evening.

　　evidences of increased interest in, **45,** 68, 70.

　　　of progress in, **30,** 58–63; **36,** 12, 13; **45,** 8; **46,** 15.

　　evils and defects to be remedied, extracts from reports of committees, **19** (Supplement), 3–148.

　　examination into the state of, **13,** 30, 31.

　　expenditure of money, and number of schools increased, **32,** 5.

　　expulsion from, **25,** 118.

Schools (Common) — *Continued*.

failure of town to comply with law, and penalty; law respecting, and comments, **24,** 97.

failure to maintain the required time, **32,** 26, 29.

government of. *See* Discipline.

grading of. *See* Graded schools.

harmony of sentiment respecting, **5,** 65–69.

health in connection with. *See* Hygiene.

higher studies in, **25,** 119.

highest success dependent on the teachers of, **13,** 35.

hindrances to success of, **14,** 28; **39,** 110–118.

improvement in, general, **2,** 29–34; **4,** 12; **5,** 23–25; **6,** 50.

    in 1847, **10,** 3–64.

increased liberality, **18,** 59; **21,** 6.

inequality in different parts of the Commonwealth, **13,** 29; **31,** 61.

in Ontario, **45,** 271.

large numbers in one building not wise, **30,** 16.

law respecting, **1,** 51, 74; **31,** 40–48; **46,** 109–142.

    and comments, **24,** 89–111; **27,** 43; **38,** 144.

    explained, **45,** 70, 71; **46,** 113–122.

    not obeyed, **27, 44.**

legislation relating to. *See* Legislation.

length of, **46,** 68.

    average, **1,** 38; **5,** 36; **9,** 24; **19,** 73; **20,** 40; **27,** 7, 43; **29,** 13.

little improvement in agricultural towns, **33,** 8.

maintenance of, **1,** 49, 52; **4,** 39, 66–75.

management of, **48,** 76.

Mann, Horace, circular letter of, on proposed improvements in schools, and results to be expected, **11,** 49–58.

    answers to, from John Griscom, New Jersey, 58, 126.

        D. P. Page, Albany, 64, 126.

        Solomon Adams, 66, 127.

        Rev. Jacob Abbott, New York, 72, 127.

        F. A. Adams, New Jersey, 74, 128.

        E. A. Andrews, Connecticut, 78, 128.

        Roger S. Howard, Vermont, 81, 128.

        Miss Catherine Beecher, 83, 129.

    requesting information on the condition of, **1,** 73.

means of awakening public interest in, **18,** 50.

methods in, **41,** 105.

    unphilosophical, **43,** 63.

mistaken economy in, **27,** 6.

money, raising of, for. *See* Money.

moral instruction in. *See* Moral.

more liberal provision must be made, **41, 7.**

more visitation of parents needed, **25** (Abstracts), 17, 72.

must be made better than private, **20, 44.**

necessary equipments of, **40, 53.**

new era, a, **18,** 45, 50.

new ones constituted, **21, 6.**

no abatement of interest in, during the war, **26,** 38.

no special attention given to, till 1837, **24,** 61.

Schools (Common) — *Continued.*
 object of, **1, 24.**
 objections to, **21,** 70.
 one with one pupil, **21, 53.**
 one without a teacher, **21,** 44.
 opinions concerning present condition of, 1880, **44,** 229–241.
  papers by Miss L. Crocker, 229.
   Dr. C. O. Thompson, 238.
   Hon. J. H. Seelye, 238.
   Rev. J. Osgood, 236.,
   William H. Ladd, 235.
   Alexander Hyde, 233.
   T. W. Higginson, 231.
   Washington Gladden, 230.
   E. L. Pierce, 239.
   Hon. J. D. Philbrick, 240.
 origin of public, **40** (Appendix), 108.
 parents, relation of, to. *See* Parents.
 penalty for disturbing, law, **46,** 141; **48,** 86; **50,** 114.
 people, relation of, to, **47,** 17.
  to be reached by personal intercourse with, **13,** 31.
 physically injurious, **22,** 57, 63.
 prejudice against, disappearing, **18,** 59.
 pressure, **28,** 9.
  difficulty of finding the happy medium, **28,** 10.
 private. *See* Private.
 progress of, **40,** 52.
  during ten years, to 1851, **15, 5, 6.**
  in 1847, **11,** 3, 21–24.
  shown by table of comparison, **34,** 104.
 proper size of, **21,** 53.
 province of, **48,** 75.
  discussed by Secretary, **50,** 117.
 public interest greater than private zeal, **30,** 10.
 public opinion elevated, **26,** 57.
 reading in. *See* Reading.
 regulations of, **10,** 221.
 religious instruction in. *See* Religious.
 report of, **1,** 37.
 required number of, **48,** 68.
 required to be kept, **50,** 101.
 requisite of public safety, a, **43,** 61.
 results of, **44,** 76–83; **47,** 121.
  past work of, **18,** 45.
  possible, **11, 4.**
 retrospect of the year 1845, **9,** 60–62.
 Saturday sessions, **28,** 48.
 scholarships. *See* Scholarships.
 self-reporting system, effects of, **30,** 14.
 should be the care of the state, **41,** 156.
 signs of progress in Peru and West Springfield, **39,** 87.
 six months required, **28,** 72.

Schools (Common) — *Concluded.*

    spelling in. *See* Orthography.

    spirit of eager inquiry, **32,** 5.

    spirit of the people, **19,** 50.

    state tax for, recommended. *See* Taxation.

    statistics indicating progress, **22,** 10.

    statistics of information relating to, **36,** 12, 13.

    studies in, **8,** 103.

        too many, **29,** 24.

    studies to be promoted in, **50,** 104.

    summary of statistics relating to, condition of schools in 1850, **14,** 61–63.

        for 1862–63, **27,** 36.

    supervision of. *See* Supervision.

    temporary falling off, **27,** 6.

    text-books in. *See* Books, Free text-books.

    to be reached through local sentiment, **20,** 60 .

    too much attempted, **30,** 17.

    towns, power of, to raise money for schools, argument, **8,** 102–117.

        that fail to comply with law, tables, **28,** 73–76; **29,** 58, 62.

        where schools are kept less than six months, **27,** 45–48.

    truant, needed. *See* Truancy.

    uniform standard for, desirable, **42,** 13.

    vacations, **6,** 24–27.

    value of, discussed, **47,** 112.

    visitation of, **1,** 39; **25,** 117.

    waste in work, **41,** 98.

    what shall they attempt to secure? **42,** 87.

    what will insure good, **32,** 6.

    Worcester County, good record of, **30,** 9.

Schools, Model. *See* Model schools.

Schools, Private. *See* Private schools.

School system of Massachusetts, **2,** 27; **4,** 17; **10,** 104; **12,** 140; **19,** 5; **24,** 34; **41,** 5.

    advocated on grounds of political economy, **10,** 110.

    at the end of war, **29,** 12, 13.

    benefits derived from, **29,** 20.

    changes proposed in, **33,** 5, 6.

    civil war a test of, **26,** 18; **27,** 10, 11.

    college the foundation of, **41,** 5.

    colonial period of, act of 16½2, **29,** 71.

    compared with what it should be, **18,** 65.

    constitutional period of, **29,** 80.

    defects of, **19,** 71; **31,** 6; **44,** 144.

    deficiency in means, **15,** 6.

    discussed, **44,** 69.

    duty of each generation to carry forward the system of schools designed by founders of our government, **9,** 4–8.

    Dwight, Hon. Edmund, died April 5, 1849, **13,** 14.

    English *vs.* German, **41,** 6.

    established, **19,** 38.

    facts relating to, with statistics, paper by C. D. Wright, **47,** 139–156.

    first free system, **24,** 57, 60.

School system of Massachusetts — *Continued.*

four conditions necessary, **41**, 61.

four grades, account of, **48**, 71–75.

imperfect administration of, **19**, 51.

indebtedness to, **42**, 8.

inestimable advantages of, **30**, 17.

influence of, **20**, 86.

interest at stake, **26**, 14.

interest in, **25**, 111.

is it necessarily corrupting? **21**, 66.

its capacity to improve the pecuniary condition and to elevate the intellectual and moral character of our Commonwealth, report of H. Mann, **12**, 32.

leading features of, **29**, 70.

legal enactments for the organization of, **10**, 128–194.

limitation of power of teachers, **19**, 89.

means of extending and improving, **16**, 5; **29**, 14.

mistakes of, **19**, 38.

moral influence of, **21**, 67.

munificent aid to the cause of popular education, **13**, 14, 15.

need of, **10**, 104–107.

no longer an experiment, **20**, 85.

no social distinctions in, **22**, 11.

not anti-Christian, argument of H. Mann, **12**, 121–124.

of New Hampshire, **10**, 11.

of Rhode Island, **10**, 10.

of Vermont, **10**, 11.

origin of, **29**, 71, 75.

outline of history of, **39**, 5.

policy of, settled, **20**, 5.

principle at the foundation of, **9**, 3; **10**, 109.

principles of, **24**, 60.

priority of the parochial system of Scotland to that of New York, **24**, 58.

progress of, **34**, 5, 104.

provincial period of, **29**, 76.

public opinion sound on, **29**, 21.

public system, a, **18**, 33.

relation of, to manufacturing, **23**, 39–59.

    intelligent laborers more trustworthy, **23**, 57.

requires the unremitted attention of all its agencies, **27**, 6.

results of, paper on the, by C. D. Wright, **42**, 167–189.

retrospect of twenty years, **20**, 35.

security a source of danger, **27**, 5.

soundness and efficiency of, **44**, 13.

specific description of, by H. Mann, **10**, 107.

state system, **45**, 68.

state tax necessary for, **37**, 8.

success or failure of, dependent on the people, **26**, 13, 14.

support of, during the war, **29**, 47.

too much expected, **19**, 38.

tribute, a, to freedom of thought, **18**, 32.

two systems, **41**, 6.

utility of, doubled, **21**, 59.

School system of Massachusetts — *Concluded.*

    weak point in, **34,** 120.

    what it includes, **47,** 118.

    will be changed, **41,** 6.

Scientific course of study, **42,** 96; **44,** 130.

    botany and mineralogy, **44,** 137.

    history, **44,** 136.

    method of teaching, **44,** 134.

Scotland, priority of the parochial system of, to that of New York, **24,** 58.

    schools of, **7,** 60–68.

Scott, Joseph G., appointed principal of State Normal School at Westfield, **41,** 16.

Scudder, H. E., paper on the libraries of Massachusetts, **40** (Appendix), 3–33.

Sears, Barnas, circular letter of, on the district system, **16,** 37.

    elected Secretary of Board of Education, 1848, **12,** 4.

    reports as Secretary (appended to 13th–19th annual reports of the Board).

    resigned, 1855, **18,** 8.

Secretary of Board of Education, appointment of, and duties, **46,** 97, 98.

    appointment of first, 1837, **1,** 5.

    appointments for survey of educational work, **26,** 7.

    approval of work of, **12,** 3.

    assistant librarian to act as clerk of, **13,** 11, 50.

        as treasurer and agent, **29,** 7.

    Boutwell, George S., appointed, 1855, **19,** 8.

        resignation of, 1860, **24,** 19.

            resolutions of regret, **24,** 19.

    changes to be made when necessary, **13,** 29.

    commendation of, **50,** 16.

    Dickinson, John W., appointed, 1877, **41,** 8.

        notice of, **41,** 8–16.

    duties of, **14,** 11, 53, 54; **17,** 66.

        change in, **13,** 27.

        prescribed by statute, **1,** 5, 21, 71.

    expenses, suggestion that an appropriation for travelling expenses be added to salary, **12,** 5.

    first report of, **1,** 21.

    interruption of labors of, **47,** 16.

    Jackson, Rev. Samuel, appointed assistant librarian and clerk, 1848, **13,** 51.

    labors of, **17,** 66; **45,** 12; **45,** 8.

    list of, **50,** 88.

    made librarian of state library, 1848, **13,** 11.

    magnitude of work of, **12,** 150.

    Mann, Horace, appointed first Secretary, 1837, **1,** 5.

        elected to Congress, 1848, **12,** 3.

        resigned from office, 1848, **12,** 15.

    not possible to do all the work needed, **20,** 63.

    office provided for, **13,** 11, 50.

    operations during the year 1851, **15,** 68.

    opportunities for labor, **24,** 57.

    practice rather than theory required, **13,** 28.

    reports of, by Horace Mann, 1st–12th.

        by Dr. Barnas Sears, 13th–19th.

        by George S. Boutwell, 20th–24th.

Secretary of Board of Education — *Concluded.*
   report of, by Joseph White, 25th–40th.
      by John W. Dickinson, 41st–50th.
   resolutions of approval of work, **12,** 10.
   retrospect of twelve years of work, **12,** 15.
   salary of, **1,** 5; **12,** 154; **46,** 98.
   salary of assistant librarian, **13,** 12, 51.
   Sears, Barnas, elected, 1848, **12,** 4.
      resigned, 1855, **19,** 8.
   selection of, **50,** 16.
   time and opportunity needed by, for outside work, **12,** 151.
   two courses open; probable results of each, **12,** 17, 19.
   visit of, to Europe, **7,** 19.
   visiting towns, **24,** 67.
   what is expected of him, **20,** 10.
   White, Joseph, elected, 1860, **24,** 22.
      notice of, **41,** 8.
      resignation of, 1876, **40,** 10.
Sectarian schools, school money not to be applied for, **35,** 129.
Seelye, Hon. Julius H., opinion of, concerning the present condition of schools, **44,** 238.
Self-reporting system, effects of, **30,** 14.
Seminaries. *See* Academies.
Sewerage of school-houses, **42,** 137.
Sewing in schools, act relating to, and comments, **40,** 83.
   in Worcester, report of committee, **43,** 349–352.
Sharp, James C., lectures of, **18,** 19; **20,** 24; **25,** 30.
   lectures by, at Bridgewater State Normal School, **19,** 21.
Sheffield Academy, Sheffield, **40,** 344.
Sheldon Academy, Southampton, **40,** 342.
Sign language. *See* Deaf-mutes.
Simpson, M. H., generosity of, to schools in Saxonville, **28,** 52.
Smith, Walter, art director. *See* Director of art education.
Smith Academy, Hatfield, **40,** 331.
Smith College, **40,** 83.
South Berkshire Institute, New Marlborough, **40,** 322.
South Reading Academy, Wakefield, **40,** 340.
Sparks, Jared, answers of, to questions respecting religious instruction in the common schools, **18,** 98, 99.
Spelling. *See* Orthography.
Springfield, plan of school-house at, **5,** 121–123.
Springfield Female Seminary, Springfield, **40,** 342.
State, beneficence and home duty of the, **27** (Abstracts), 18.
   comparative insignificance in territory, political power and natural resources, **12,** 33–35.
      other standards of greatness, **12,** 36.
   constitution of, should be studied in school, **12,** 85.
   discussion, **47,** 118–122.
   education, origin of, **41,** 156.
      constitution of Massachusetts concerning, **41,** 159.
         of New Hampshire concerning, **41,** 159.

State — *Concluded.*

    education, support of higher, **41,** 162.

        three methods of providing for, **41,** 169.

    educational policy and system of, settled, **20,** 5; **43,** 14.

    education of youth belongs to the, **40,** 10.

    ends to accomplish, **47,** 118.

    equality the theory of, **12,** 55–57.

    leading idea of, **18,** 28.

    need of educated men, **18,** 34.

    our ambition, **12,** 56.

    position in education, **39,** 22.

    power of common schools to redeem it from social vices and crimes, **11,** 39.

        conditions necessary, **11,** 88.

        . practicability of these conditions, **11,** 88.

        universal education the sure means, **11,** 135.

    progress in wealth and population, **39,** 15, 16.

    proportion of population who cannot read or write, **17,** 5.

    prosperity of, **20,** 36.

    rights of, **47,** 118.

    scholarships in colleges provided, **17,** 8, 61, 66; **18,** 5.

    schools should be the care of, **41,** 156.

    survey of, **39,** 20.

    tendency towards extremes, **12,** 58.

State aid. *See* Blind, Normal schools.

State Library of Massachusetts, assistant librarian of, to act as clerk of the Board,
        13, 11, 50.

    Jackson, Rev. Samuel, appointed, 1848, **13, 51.**

    salary of, **13,** 12, 51.

    Tillinghast, C. B., appointed, 1879, **43,** 12.

    changes and additions in, **43,** 12.

    Secretary of the Board made librarian of, 1848, **3,** 11.

State Reform School. *See* Reform School.

Statistics, educational, act concerning, **31,** 46, 47.

Stearns, Eben, appointed principal at West Newton Normal School, May 30, 1849,
        13, 8.

    resigned, Framingham, 1855, **19,** 6.

St. Mark's School, Southborough, **40,** 326.

Stockbridge Academy, Stockbridge, **40,** 341.

Stone, Rev. Collins, death of, **35,** 60.

    resolutions on, **35,** 62.

Studies, Course of, adopted by the Hampshire East Association, **41,** 133.

    branches required to be taught, **50,** 104.

    certain studies required, order optional, **48,** 76.

    defined, **45,** 87.

    discussed, **44,** 99–137; **48,** 80.

    distribution of, in different grades, **15,** 43.

    elementary, **42,** 89.

    for county schools, report of national council, **46,** 77–82.

        grammar and primary schools, **42,** 193–198.

        intermediate schools, **44,** 121–130.

        normal schools, **29,** 88, 89.

        primary schools, **44,** 99–121.

Studies, Course of — *Concluded.*
    outline of, **45,** 89.
    physiology and hygiene, **6,** 56–83, 98–160.
    principles to be observed, **45,** 87.
    pursued, **6,** 51.
    report of committee appointed by Norfolk County convention of committees and
        teachers, **42,** 227–252.
    scientific, **42,** 96; **44,** 130–137.
    suggestions accompanying, **42,** 199–223.
    what is a good? **46,** 73, 74.
Sumner, Charles, and others, memorial to the Legislature, asking for appropriation
    for the benefit of normal schools, **9,** 11.
Superintendents, act relating to election of, **37,** 131.
    adapted to cities, **21,** 50.
    advised, **12,** 154.
    city superintendents and salaries, **38,** 101.
    duties of, **49,** 201; **50,** 139.
    first appointed in Springfield, 1840, **4,** 79.
    labors of Dr. H. Bigelow, **30,** 107–109; (Abstracts), 119.
    laws respecting, **24,** 10; **46,** 122.
    letter of Mr. Northrop on, **30,** 111–118.
    need of, **48,** 175.
    need of more general employment, **36,** 169.
    number of, increasing, **36,** 108.
    programme of studies adopted by, **36,** 201.
    requisites of a good superintendent, **30,** 110; **48,** 17.
    school for, **48,** 145.
    success of, **36.**
    town, and salaries, **38,** 101, 102.
    towns employing, in 1867, **32,** 49.
    views of Mr. Mann on, **32,** 48.
Supervision, additional, needed, **36,** 19–169.
    advantages of, **41,** 120.
    all defects in schools from imperfect supervision, **47,** 182.
    close and constant, needed, argument, **41,** 64.
    county, needed, **33,** 9, 92.
    Cousin on, in Netherlands, **41,** 67.
    defective, **41,** 114.
    discussion of question, **42,** 75–87; **43,** 69, 77; **48,** 92.
    district, **45,** 115.
    evils of a lack of, **48,** 189.
    excellence of schools proportioned to thoroughness of, **37,** 8.
    greater need in small towns, **36,** 5.
    history of, **30,** 108–110.
    indispensable, **43,** 64, 66; **46,** 75, 76.
    in Massachusetts, **38,** 89.
    in other states, **38,** 88; **43,** 74.
    in provincial periods, **30,** 108.
    in Quincy, Col. F. W. Parker, **41,** 120.
    lack of, a serious obstacle, **43,** 9.
    larger working force needed, **45,** 11.

Supervision — *Concluded.*

　　local, **46**, 13.

　　Massachusetts behind other states, **34**, 117.

　　need of, **18**, 66; **34**, 92; **39**, 98, 99; **48**, 12.

　　need of more, **42**, 9, 228; **50**, 13, 138.

　　paper on, by A. P. Marble, **49**, 225-237.

　　plan for more efficient, considered, **44**, 13; **45**, 10.

　　plan of, suggested, **37**, 9; **41**, 68.

　　report of general agent on, **38**, 87-100.

　　　　of Mr. Prince on, **48**, 221.

　　required as a business arrangement, **39**, 129.

　　schools in Ontario, paper by Dr. J. A. McLellan, **45**, 271.

　　superintendence, **30**, 108-120.

　　urged, with reasons, **47**, 10, 11.

　　what is required, **45**, 78.

　　why needed, **48**, 86.

Sweden, hand-work instruction in, **46**, 163-213.

Taxation, annual increase of money raised by, **31**, 38.

　　compensation to tax-payers who have no children, **9**, 4.

　　dog-tax law, **34**, 121; **46**, 142.

　　general, the only means by which universal education can be secured, **21**, 69.

　　half-mill, recommended. *See* Half-mill tax.

　　inequality of, **34**, 10; **35**, 118-132; **40**, 10.

　　laws respecting, and comments, **24**, 120-123.

　　rate of, **30**, 64.

　　recommended, **43**, 8.

Teachers, **4**, 43-60.

　　advance in quality of, **20**, 41.

　　associations. *See* Associations.

　　authority of, **10**, 188; **48**, 75.

　　　　limit in time and place, **48**, 76.

　　certificates, **1**, 29.

　　　　laws respecting, **10**, 167-171.

　　change of, **27** (Abstracts), 14; **39**, 123; **47**, 11.

　　college students not fitted for, **26**, 76, 79.

　　competency of, and laws respecting, **1**, 58, 59.

　　demand for, creates supply, **29**, 20.

　　demand for better qualified, **10**, 38; **16**, 14-17.

　　difficulty of procuring, for high schools, **14**, 59, 60.

　　dismissal of, law respecting and comments, **24**, 103.

　　education of, **1**, 10.

　　essentials, **42**, 81.

　　evils of existing modes of appointing, **13**, 40-46.

　　evils of frequent changes in, **34**, 105.

　　examination of, **1**, 29; **5**, 64; **18**, 68; **19**, 72; **21**, 51; **46**, 73.

　　　　by printed questions, **10**, 74-80.

　　female, **4**, 45-97; **8**, 60-62.

　　importance of permanency, **26**, 72.

　　improvement needed, **38**, 92; **42**, 67.

　　　　in county towns, **48**, 198.

Teachers — *Concluded.*

    incompetency of, **6,** 43; **13,** 36.

    inexperienced, **9,** 40–43; **48,** 170; **49,** 186.

    influence commanding, **47,** 11.

    influence of, report of school committee of Andover, **25** (Abstracts), 16.

    institutes. *See* Institutes.

    institutions for training. *See* Normal schools.

    laws respecting, **46,** 119.

        and comments, **10,** 161–177.

    office of, made respectable, **18,** 51.

    power of all towns to secure good, **13,** 36.

    professional spirit of, **20,** 42.

    proportion of male and female, **1,** 63.

    qualifications of, **6,** 43; **8,** 73; **50,** 203–206.

    relation of committees to, **45,** 77.

    requirements of, **10,** 44–48; **45,** 77; **48,** 74.

    requisites of good, **5,** 38–65; **9,** 83; **45,** 77, 93; **46,** 71, 72.

    salaries, **27** (Abstracts), 24.

    selection of, **13,** 11, 35; **14,** 93; **21,** 51; **48,** 84.

    tenure of office of, **44,** 96; **50,** 13.

        recent act relating to, **50,** 103.

    three things necessary to the good, **16,** 8.

    to receive certificates, laws respecting, and comments, **24,** 103.

    wages of, **1,** 61, 66; **4,** 11; **6,** 31–35; **9,** 30–37; **11,** 96; **29,** 19; **39,** 109.

        increased, **21,** 6.

        reduction in, **27,** 39, 40.

            unwise, **27,** 40.

    work of, **19,** 53.

Teaching, cheap, **27** (Abstracts), 15.

    cultivation of memory, **19,** 56.

    defective methods of, **42,** 68.

    defined, **42,** 98.

    demand for skilled labor, **41,** 174; **42,** 107.

    discussion of methods, **42,** 98.

    hints on, **47,** 110.

    improvement in, **34,** 5.

    Industrial School Association, **41,** 219.

    in primary schools, **22,** 58, 59.

    in relation to health, **22,** 57.

    methods of. *See* Methods.

    oral. *See* Oral.

    principles of, **50,** 133.

        not satisfactory, **41,** 74.

        three, explained, **41,** 77.

    securing attention, **19,** 56.

Technical instruction in schools (*see also* Industrial education, Manual labor).

    discussion of, **36,** 182–193.

    free schools suggested, **35,** 14.

    hand-work in Sweden, paper by Prof. J. Ordway, **46,** 163.

    in common schools, **50,** 105.

        discussed by Secretary, **50,** 117.

    in Dwight School, **46,** 217–223.

Technical instruction in schools — *Concluded.*

in foreign countries, **35,** 13.

Institute of Industrial Science, Worcester County. *See* Worcester County.

law respecting, **36,** 181.

law respecting schools a dead letter, **41,** 4, 6.

manual element in education, paper by J. Runkle, **41,** 185; **45,** 131-200.

Massachusetts Institute of Technology, **40** (Appendix), 94.

paper on, by C. O. Thompson, **43,** 261-275.

province of common schools, discussion by Secretary, **50,** 117.

resolve passed by general court, **35,** 11-14.

trade schools in New York, paper on, by R. T. Auchmuty, **47,** 195-200.

what are schools of technology? paper by Prof. Thompson, **41,** 173.

work schools for boys in town and country, in Sweden, paper by H. K. Kjennerud, School Superintendent, Christiana, **46,** 167-213.

work schools in Finland, translation of paper published by Otto Salomon, **46,** 165.

Temperance discussed, **50,** 150.

Tenure of office of teachers, **44,** 96.

provisions of law concerning, **50,** 13.

recent act relating to, **50,** 103.

Text-books. *See* Books, Free text-books.

Thayer Academy, Braintree, **40,** 345.

Thompson, Prof. Charles O., opinion of, concerning the present condition of schools, **44,** 238, 239.

paper by, on handicraft in schools, **43,** 261-275.

on industrial drawing, **34,** 170-180.

on the Worcester Free Institute, **41,** 173.

Ticknor, George, answers of, to questions respecting religious instruction in common schools, **18,** 99-101.

Tillinghast, C. B., assistant librarian, appointed, 1879, **43,** 12.

Time of confinement in school. *See* Hours of study.

Todd, Henry, deceased, 1848, bust of, presented by T. P. Cushing, **16,** 6.

legacy of, to be applied to normal schools, **13,** 13; **14,** 13, 14.

sketch of life of, **13,** 14; **16,** 14.

Todd Normal School Fund, **50,** 98.

amount in 1853, object of, **17,** 14.

history of, **24,** 63.

how appropriated, **15,** 11; **16,** 6; **20,** 10; **24,** 81; **29,** 41.

increase and distribution of, **21,** 13.

in trust of Board of Education, **46,** 96.

laws respecting, and comments, **38,** 143; **46,** 109.

Topsfield Academy, Topsfield, **40,** 340.

Town meetings, annual, **10,** 136-144.

Towns, distribution of income of school fund in, sometimes illegal, **26,** 63.

forfeiture of fund by, **28,** 60.

misuse of fund by, **36,** 74-179.

duties of, **33,** 121; **44,** 71.

educational advantages in, **41,** 7.

unit of our political system, **26,** 67.

Training classes in academies, **34,** 113.

in high schools, **32,** 62; **33,** 6, 89, 91.

plan of, in New York, **32,** 63, 64.

Training schools (*see also* Normal schools), **34**, 99; **35**, 8.

    Mr. Emerson's plan at Woburn, **32**, 50.

        advantages of, **32**, 51.

    plan of, in New York, **35**, 8.

    when established, **33**, 89.

" Travelling Museum," **36**, 22.

    list of examples in, **36**, 38-46.

    manner of procuring, and use, **36**, 22-24.

Truancy, **9**, 128.

    act concerning absentees, law of 1642, **31**, 42.

    action of Springfield, **30**, 76.

    and absence, **27** (Abstracts), 20.

    and truant laws, report of school committee of Lynn, **27** (Abstracts), 23.

    by-laws, **39**, 124.

    defined, **45**, 67.

    evils of, **20**, 53.

    extent of, **25**, 122.

    forms of legal procedure, **26**, 54–56.

    how to provide for, **37**, 133-136.

    increased attention given to, **27**, 67.

    increased danger of, **27**, 70.

    laws, by-laws, and forms of procedure concerning, **27**, 80-88.

    laws respecting, **24**, 131; **26**, 52, 53; **27**, 67, 80; **34**, 12; **37**, 131; **46**, 136-139.

        defect in, remedied, **27**, 67.

        discussion of, **44**, 142; **48**, 72; **50**, 168–179.

        obedience to, should be condition of receiving school funds, **27**, 59.

        operation of, **17**, 11.

        penalty for non-compliance with, **49**, 73.

        proposed, **34**, 120.

        requirements of, **45**, 75; **47**, 80.

        should be applied, **25**, 125.

    more stringent system needed, **36**, 19.

    officers of, **27**, 68; **48**, 74.

        appointed, **34**, 86.

        neglect to appoint, **42**, 10.

        report of, **27**, 69.

        towns that have, **29**, 63; **30**, 74.

    parents extend the evil, **25**, 123.

    provisions for instruction of truant children, **50**, 107.

    provisions for truants, **29**, 65.

    report of J. D. Philbrick on the operation of law, **26**, 53.

    report of school committee on, **27** (Abstracts), 23.

    schools for, **34**, 86.

        demand for, **48**, 69.

        needed, **27**, 67; **50**, 179.

        why needed, **46**, 65.

Tufts College, **40**, 72.

    divinity school, **40**, 107.

Twisleton, Hon. Edward, extracts from his " Evidence as to the religious working of the common schools of Massachusetts," **18**, 79-104.

Union schools, **4,** 24–28.

    act relating to the establishment of, **32,** 43.

Upham, C. W., agent, appointed, 1851, **15,** 12.

Vacations, **6,** 24–27.

Vaccination, law respecting, **24,** 134.

Ventilation, **7,** 49; **17,** 77, 100.

    and heating, **42,** 125.

    bad, of school-houses, **28,** 52.

    of British House of Parliament, **7,** 50–53.

    report of Daniel Leach, agent, on, **17,** 74.

        of Mr. Martin on, **50,** 195.

            extracts, **50,** 166, 199, 200.

        of Mr. Prince on, **49,** 195.

Vermont, school system of, **10,** 11.

Vienna, exposition at, law respecting, **37,** 147.

Visible speech. *See* Deaf-mutes.

Vocal culture, elocutionary training, **43,** 11.

    L. Monroe, death of, **43,** 11.

Walton, George A., appointed special agent for western counties, **35,** 6, 109.

    centennial report by, on academies, **40** (Appendix), 174–360.

    notice of, **47,** 101.

    paper by, **40** (Appendix), 174.

    report by, **37,** 85.

    report by, on schools in Bristol County, **45,** 203.

War (*see also* Civil war), cost of, **11,** 105.

Ware, William R., paper by, on industrial drawing, **34,** 182–186.

Warner, Oliver, appointed assistant librarian, 1876, **40,** 11.

    paper by, **40,** 174.

Warren Academy, Woburn, **40,** 288.

Washburn, Emory, address of, at the dedication of the Worcester Normal School building, **38,** 201.

Webster, Daniel, answers of, to questions respecting religious instruction in the common schools, **18,** 89.

Wellesley College, **40,** 85.

Wellesley Female Seminary, Wellesley, **40,** 345.

Wells, William H., appointed principal of State Normal School at Westfield, 1854, **18,** 6.

    resigned, 1856, **20,** 9, 19.

Wesleyan Academy, Wilbraham, **40,** 273.

West Brookfield Female Seminary, **40,** 340.

Westfield, model school at, **8,** 20; **10,** 9–58.

    plan for, **29,** 29.

    practice school needed at, **50,** 36.

    school of observation at, **30,** 27, 28.

Westfield, State Normal School at, **40** (Appendix), 139.

    Barre, State Normal School at, established Oct., 1839, **2,** 23; **3,** 6; **4,** 5.

        Newman, S. P., first principal at, died 1842, **6,** 6.

        removed to Westfield, 1843, **8,** 19.

        boarding-house at, **37,** 18.

            appropriation for, **36,** 11, 70.

Westfield, State Normal School — *Concluded.*
    building at, dedication of, **10,** 7, 9.
        address of Heman Humphrey at, **10,** 7, 36.
      plans of, **10,** 247–254.
    Davis, Rev. Emerson, resigned, **10,** 8.
    Dickinson, John W., appointed principal of, 1856, **20,** 9, 19.
      resigned, 1877, **41,** 16.
    donation to library at, **27,** 16.
      to the cabinet at, **27,** 16.
    donors to the cabinet at, **25,** 30.
    Encyclopædia Britannica presented to, **11,** 39.
    generosity of Lowell Mason to, **32,** 22.
    methods of teaching in, **26,** 22; **41,** 89.
    petition for longer course at, **16,** 7.
    Rees' Encyclopædia presented to, **25,** 30.
    Rowe, David S., appointed principal at, 1846, **10,** 8.
      resigned, 1854, **18,** 6.
    Scott, Joseph G., appointed principal at, **41,** 16.
    Wells, William H., appointed principal at, 1854, **18,** 6.
      resigned, 1856, **20,** 9, 19.
Westfield Academy, Westfield, **40,** 247.
Westford Academy, Westford, **40,** 242.
Westminster Academy, Westminster, **40,** 343.
West Newton, model school at, **12,** 7; **14,** 16.
West Newton, State Normal School at. *See* Framingham.
West Point, Military Academy at, report of agent concerning, **27,** 90–124.
West Springfield, signs of progress in, **39,** 97.
Weymouth and Braintree Academy, Weymouth, **40,** 341.
Wheaton Female Seminary, Norton, **40,** 303.
White, Joseph, elected Secretary of the Board of Education, 1860, **24,** 22.
    reports as Secretary (appended to 25th–40th annual reports of the Board).
    resignation of, 1876, **40,** 10.
Williams, Moses B., letter of, on military drill in Brookline, **27,** 71.
Williams College, **40,** 63.
Williamstown Academy, **40,** 340.
Williston Seminary, Easthampton, **40,** 306.
Winchendon Academy, Winchendon, **40,** 344.
Winthrop, Robert C., answers of, to questions respecting religious instruction in the
    common schools, **18,** 93.
Woburn High School, half-time schools in, **35,** 89.
Women (*see also* Female teachers).
    as members of school committees, **31,** 12; **35,** 107; **40,** 91; **45,** 111;
      48, 97.
      list of cities and towns having, **40,** 92, 93.
    higher education of, **21,** 54.
    reference to, on school boards, **50,** 206.
Women's Educational Association, formed 1872, **36,** 179.
Woodbridge School, Hadley, **40,** 342.
Woodman, John S., letter from, on industrial drawing, **34,** 199–203.
Woodward, Dr. Samuel B., letter from, on the proper number of school hours, **4,**
    100, 101.
Worcester, report on sewing in the schools of, **43,** 349–352.

Worcester, State Normal school at, building at, **36,** 177.

    dedication of, address of the Hon. Emory Washburn at the, **38,** 201.

    establishment of, **37,** 29.

    methods of teaching in, **41,** 30.

    opened, **38,** 6, 30, 124.

    resolves to establish, **35,** 7, 100.

Worcester Academy, Worcester, **40,** 292.

Worcester County, good record of schools in, **30,** 9.

Worcester County Free Institute of Industrial Science, **35,** 12; **37,** 122; **40,** 348.

    established, 1868, **41,** 173.

    founders, organization and object of, **37,** 123.

    law respecting, **38,** 197.

    paper on, by Prof. Thompson, **41,** 173–184.

    state aid to, **42,** 110.

    successful work of, **43,** 103.

Wright, Carroll D., paper by, on the public-school system of Massachusetts, with statistics, **47,** 139–156.

    on the results of the Massachusetts school system, **42,** 167–189.

www.ingramcontent.com/pod-product-compliance
Lightning Source LLC
Chambersburg PA
CBHW071356050326
40689CB00010B/1668